To

Henry Wakefield

4/25/96

With thanks for your
support + interest in
maintaing family structure
for all of us!

Ralph Underwood

Hollida Wakefield

Return of the
Furies

Return of the Furies

An Investigation into Recovered Memory Therapy

Hollida Wakefield
and
Ralph Underwager

OPEN ✸ COURT

Chicago and La Salle, Illinois

OPEN COURT and the above logo are registered in
the U.S. Patent and Trademark Office.

© 1994 by Open Court Publishing Company

First printing 1994

Printed and bound in the United States of America.

Library of Congress Cataloging-in-Publication Data

Wakefield, Hollida.
   Return of the furies : an investigation into
recovered memory therapy / Hollida Wakefield
and Ralph Underwager.
      p.   cm.
   Includes bibliographical references and index.
   ISBN 0–8126–9271–3.—ISBN 0–8126–9272–1
(pbk.)
   1. Adult child sexual abuse victims.   2. False
memory syndrome.
I. Underwager, Ralph C. II. Title.
RC569.5.A28W35 1994
616.85′83690651—dc20   94-27555
                                   CIP

To
Pamela Freyd
and
Peter Freyd

*whose courage to live in the face of betrayal
has been a fount of hope for many who had
surrendered to despair*

Contents

Prologue: How We Came To Write This Book

When David Ramsay Steele of Open Court first suggested we write a book dealing with the claims of recovered memory of childhood abuse, we accepted eagerly. It felt like a natural progression of our professional work. We are deeply pleased with the opportunity to assemble our understanding, experience, and interests in this volume. As clinicians who have spent years sharing the struggles, the pain, and the fears of persons courageously trying to put their lives together, we are honored to have the chance to share the lives of those who may read this book. In part, this book also represents our pain, particularly the experience of touching persons at the end of their lives trying to handle the rage, terror, guilt, and fear when betrayed by an adult child accusing them of actions they had never imagined even in their worst nightmares. This is how we got to the place where this book seems the most reasonable thing for us to do now.

We became actively involved in defending victims of child abuse long before it had become fashionable or lucrative. Since 1953, we have been trying to respond to the fact that children are abused, physically and sexually. That is 41 years of standing face-to-face with the darkest underside of our human nature, the incredible fact that some of us savage our children. As a young Lutheran pastor, R.U. started a Lutheran parochial school in the Los Angeles area in the fall of 1952. He noticed a seven-year-old girl, quiet and shy, a slim, tall child with light brown hair. Some days she was not too clean and looked a bit shabby. R.U. took care of the playground to give a break to the teacher and, gradually, Denise began to spend time interacting with him. During morning recess on a day early in January, she said, "My daddy screws me." At that time there was no child protection system. The police were not interested.

That afternoon he took Denise to her home, pointed his finger at the father and said, "You are the man!", Nathan's words to King David confronting him with his adultery with

Bathsheba. He arranged for Denise and her younger brother to stay with a family in the parish and for elders and other members of the parish to visit the mother and father daily. The father was confronted by the elders in meetings and R.U. spent time advising the mother and father on their life, marriage, sexuality, and parenting. Within two months the children returned home. Close contact with and supervision of the father were maintained until R.U. left the parish a year later.

When R.U. returned ten years later to preach an anniversary sermon for the school, Denise was there. She had continued both in the parochial school and in the parish. She was graduating from high school with honors and going to college on a scholarship. The mother had died a year after R.U. left and Denise continued to live with the father who never remarried. She said there was never any further sexual abuse by her father and that he was very happy she was doing so well.

R.U. dealt with several other cases of incest during the years he was an active parish pastor. In 1962 he was chosen to receive the Wheatridge Fellowship in Mental Health. This fellowship sent him to the Ph.D. program in clinical psychology at the University of Minnesota. At the University of Minnesota Hospital, during clerkships and internships, because of this experience, he was given the sexual abuse victims to assess and as patients. This was also the case during his internship at the Nicollet Clinic, a large multispecialty private medical clinic.

We evaluated and treated both abuse victims and perpetrators after beginning the Institute for Psychological Therapies (I.P.T.) in 1972. We were among the first to use behavioral treatment methods for sex offenders in the Twin Cities. We had both out-patient and residential programs and provided treatment programs for half-way houses when prisoners were released to them. This was before there was a treatment program available through the Minnesota Corrections System.

As public attitudes shifted towards greater attention to the reality of child abuse, wildly exaggerated claims about its prevalence began to be made. Then we had our introduction to the reality of false accusations. In 1976 we were asked to assist in the defense of a father accused of incest with his nine-year-old daughter. In the course of the trial, the psychologist who headed the newly established Ramsey County Child Protection Team testified that the father was a sex abuser because he had produced two pure 'C' responses on the Rorschach Ink Blot Test. But after R.U. had insisted on looking at the test, he was able to see that it couldn't possibly bear that interpretation. The psychologist admitted under cross-examination that she had fabricated that statement because she believed the man was guilty. Later in the trial the daughter recanted and said the mother had forced her to lie about the father. At the end of the trial the father was acquitted. Judge Marsden issued a scathing indictment of the Ramsey County Child Protection team.

In the fall of 1983 we were contacted by an attorney from Sioux Falls, South Dakota. She had come to the Twin Cities to find an expert to assist her in defending a woman charged with committing incest with her three sons. The mother denied it. Two were mentally retarded teenagers and the youngest, a ten-year-old, was normal. She started calling psychologists beginning with the As in the Yellow Pages. She got to U before she found anybody willing to be involved. We reviewed the documents and, for the first time anywhere so far as we know, in Winner, South Dakota, we offered the testimony that the coercive behavior of the sheriff and the social worker likely produced the statements from the children. The jury was hung but the woman was never reprosecuted.

This led to our involvement in the Bentz trial in August and September, 1984. Barry Voss and Earl Gray asked us to assist in the defense of Robert and Lois Bentz, the first couple to be tried in the Jordan, Minnesota, sexual abuse morass. Kathleen Morris, Scott County attorney, had charged 25 adults in Jordan, a small rural suburb of Minneapolis, with abusing 40 children. Earlier Ms. Morris had successfully prosecuted the Cermak family in Lonsdale, Minnesota, on charges of sexual abuse. In that summer we also got involved as experts and therapists with the parents in four other Jordan families that had been accused. In the Bentz trial we gave testimony related to suggestibility of children, human memory, and the coercive and leading techniques of questioning the children we had observed in videotapes of interrogations. The jury acquitted the Bentzes.

While the Bentz jury was out deliberating, on September 17th, 1984, R.U. was sitting in the hall of the Scott County Courthouse waiting to testify in a family court hearing for Don and Cindy Buchan, who had also been accused in Jordan. Their criminal trial was to begin in October but their defense attorney had pursued the family court hearings as well. When R.U. got there at noon, the attorney said that Judge Young had told him that he was not going to rule in the family case but would wait for the criminal trial and regard that as dispositive. But they wanted to make their record and so R.U. would testify later in the afternoon.

While R.U. was waiting to testify, Ms. Morris came down the hall, stopped, and said, "I am going to get you for your testimony. I'll destroy you!" There was nobody else about, but R.U. told the defense attorneys immediately when there was a recess, and it was reported to the Minnesota Lawyers' Board of Professional Responsibility. The incident was also investigated by the Governor's Special Commission later while investigating Ms. Morris's conduct in the Jordan cases, but she denied it.

R.U. testified that afternoon in the family court case. Again he testified about suggestibility of children, memory, and the coercive and leading nature of the interrogations by the mental health professionals. To everybody's surprise, three days later Judge Young issued a ruling, heavily citing R.U.'s testimony, and concluding that the state had failed to meet its burden: there was no reasonable proof of abuse. When the criminal trial for the Buchans started, their attorney fought to admit Judge Young's ruling and to get the evidence from ongoing investigations which Morris was refusing to give. After the jury was impanelled but before the trial began, Judge Fitzgerald ruled that the defense should get both. The next morning at 9:00 AM Ms. Morris dropped all the abuse charges against the Buchans and everybody else. Ms. Morris said that the order to turn over her evidence would jeopardize her investigation into murders, satanic and ritualistic abuse, and other bizarre events allegedly recounted by the children and this was why she had dropped the charges.

Minnesota's Attorney General, H. H. Humphrey III, took over and with the F.B.I. and Minnesota's B.C.A. conducted a five-month investigation. The final report concluded in essence that there had been so much leading, coercion, and pressure placed on the children that nobody could ever know what had actually happened. The attorney general's investigation found absolutely no evidence to corroborate the stories of murders and satanic ritual abuse.

In the meantime, the Jordan acquittal had hit national news and was covered throughout the U.S. We began to get calls and inquiries from all over the country. We responded and our practice gradually shifted to more and more forensic involvement in cases where we felt there was a false allegation. We do not know specifically what influence Ms. Morris's enmity and her promise to destroy R.U. had on subsequent events, but we do know that prosecutors in cases where he was listed as an expert began to get anonymous phone calls accusing him of a variety of heinous acts, including sexual abuse and having sex with clients and students. Some prosecutors tried to pursue these accusations but found nothing. We know that the Hennepin County attorney's office took over investigating us in 1985 and began to distribute material about us including false information about our finances and our clinic affairs. We know that investigative reporters tried to find dirt on us and failed to find anything.

We also know that in November, 1986, the National Center for Prosecution of Child Abuse, a program of the American Prosecutors' Research Institute, publicly identified us as their Number One enemy experts at a training meeting for prosecutors in New Orleans. Since that time they have systematically tried to discredit us personally and professionally. At another training meeting at the Chesapeake Institute in 1990 they identified the top five experts on their 'Hit List.' We have a copy of the Hit List and it has over 50 names of experts who have testified for a defense case. We quickly learned that being willing to assist a person falsely accused of sexual abuse meant lots of instant enemies wherever we went. We learned that few mental health professionals were willing to pay that price.

We learned that there are thousands of persons who have been falsely accused. We learned that it is very difficult to defend yourself against an accusation of sexual abuse. We learned that the presumption of innocence does not apply when you are accused of sexual abuse of children. You are guilty unless you can prove your innocence. We learned that an accusation of sexual abuse can elicit from each person involved a primitive, atavistic level of emotion which is little understood. We learned that many judges treat a person accused of sexual abuse more harshly than they do convicted murderers.

We know that sexual abuse of children is a reality. We have continued to provide treatment for child victims and for perpetrators of sexual abuse and physical abuse. We downsized our office and moved to Northfield five years ago and reduced our patient load but we still treat sex offenders and victims.

We learned that the involvement of a small group of mental health professionals has helped create a system of unfounded dogmas, false claims, advocacy numbers, pseudoscience, and procedures with no demonstrated validity or efficacy, and with no accountability. We learned that we had to work harder and longer and that our only hope was to know as clearly as possible what was scientifically sound. So we began to do research. We wrote articles. We wrote books. We began to publish a journal. We made presentations at professional societies. We gave workshops and seminars around the world. We have aimed at being as responsible professionals as we can be.

In 1990, we began to receive calls about cases in which adults were claiming to have recovered repressed memories of having been abused in childhood. The frequency of these calls soon increased dramatically. Several of our colleagues said that they, too, were getting inquiries and calls about such claims of recovered memories. We put some of the people who called us in touch with each other and supported the beginning of the FMS Foundation. In March of 1992 we organized the first seminar and workshop critical of recovered memory claims in Dallas. In June we organized and presented a symposium at the

American Psychological Society challenging the recovered memory claims. The presenters were Robyn Dawes, Elizabeth Loftus, Martha Rogers, Joseph Wakefield, and ourselves.

From then until now we have been called and consulted by hundreds of persons, families, and relatives who have experienced the impact of claims of recovered memories. Patients who doubt the therapy procedures they are subjected to and the memories elicited have also contacted us. We have become more firmly convinced that the science of psychology must be asserted to redress the wrong done in the child abuse system. At times we have felt ashamed to be called psychologists. This happens when we face up to the appalling injustices done to people by false accusations and the role of some mental health professionals in causing them. At other times, when we consider the nature of institutional science and scientific knowledge and the courage of those researchers who have produced the illuminating recent studies that provide more solid factual understanding, we feel hopeful and proud to be psychologists.

It is our intention in this book to be what we want to be—responsible psychologists.

Chapter One
The Furies Return

> *And of course the easiest way to escape the Furies, we think, is to deny that they exist. . . . The conspiracy to forget them, or to deny that they exist, thus turns out to be only one more contrivance in that vast and organized effort by modern society to flee from the self.*
> William Barrett (1958)

The demand in the attorney's letter was for $1,500,000 to compensate the daughter for sexual abuse by her father, 50 years before. While she was in therapy with a feminist therapist, the daughter claimed to have recovered long-lost memories of childhood sexual abuse. Against our advice, the father, 88 years old, agreed to pay the money. He vehemently denied ever abusing his daughter but ill health and his desire to keep his daughter's accusations private and avoid public speculation led him to pay the blackmail. His wife, 87 years old and also in poor health, angrily denied any abuse, but tried to understand it as the daughter simply getting her inheritance earlier than the other children. Within two months, both parents were dead. The two other children believed that they had died of broken hearts and that their sister's accusations were totally false.

When the sexual abuse charges against him were dropped, Cardinal Joseph Bernadin of Chicago said he felt himself "totally vindicated" but also knew that the damage to his reputation was done, never to be erased, and the psychological hurt and anguish were permanent. The man, Steven Cook, who had accused the cardinal of sodomizing him when he was a seminarian, now thought his memories may have been flawed. They had been prompted under hypnosis by his therapist, who was not a psychologist but was in the graphic arts business (Carlson 1994). The cardinal had many, many resources available to him, personal, psychological, social, and financial, to fight the accusation and maintain his emotional strength. Most of those falsely accused of child sexual abuse don't have anywhere near the resources of Cardinal Bernadin (Greeley 1994). Even when shown to be false, such accusations are devastating and destructive for everyone.

In testimony before the Senate Finance Committee in October 1993, Miller and Cohen reported their study on the costs of violent crime in America for 1991–92. The cost of mental health care for recent violent crimes was $3,500,000,000. The cost of mental health care for adults physically or sexually abused as children was $4,000,000,000. This may be one of the reasons Americans spend more on health care than any other country in the world. The Victims Compensation Fund in the state of Washington reported for 1991 that average claims for recovered memory cases cost $9,127—more than any other type of claim allowed. By comparison, nonfamily sexual assault was $1,552, family sexual assault was $1,997, and all other types were $1,742 (*FMS Foundation Newsletter*, February 1994). While actual victims of abuse must be assisted, the potential costs of false allegations of child abuse to our entire economy are staggering.

The McMartin case in Manhattan Beach cost California over $15,000,000 and the Kelly Michaels case in New Jersey cost over $7,000,000 to prosecute. There were no convictions in the McMartin case and the conviction of Kelly Michaels was overturned by the New Jersey Appellate Court. The costs of insurance for day-care centers has skyrocketed because of damages awarded in sexual abuse cases which in turn increases the costs of child care. The availability of suits based on allegations of child sexual abuse that must be covered by home-owners' insurance raises the rates of insurance for the entire nation.

In less than two years over 12,000 families contacted the False Memory Syndrome (FMS) Foundation reporting false accusations of childhood sexual abuse. These accusations, mostly against parents by their now adult offspring, were all based on memories supposedly recovered in therapy. Highly publicized examples include Roseanne Barr, Marilyn Van Derbur Atler, and Latoya Jackson, all of whom say that they can now remember being abused by their parents. A widow wrote this after her adult daughter had accused her husband of sexually abusing her in childhood and refused to accept his last letter:

> There is no doubt in my mind that the stress he had suffered from her false accusations was at least partially responsible for his untimely death. He was a vigorous, healthy, 66-year-old man. Now I am trying to cope with the loss of my dear, loving husband of almost 46 years while, at the same time, struggling to overcome the bitterness I feel toward my daughter and her therapist. The tragedy of this almost overwhelms me. In my opinion, the therapists who are promoting these false memories are guilty of murder. (*FMS Foundation Newsletter,* November 1993, p. 8)

Reader's Digest, hardly an avant-garde magazine, published an article on false allegations of sexual abuse in April 1993 (Armbrister 1993). It describes a system that is out of control and creating havoc for families, children, and parents. The author emphasizes these points:

> Yet when the charge is child abuse, social workers call the shots, and the system doesn't hold them accountable. What's worse, once parents are accused, the burden is on them to prove their innocence, unlike in a criminal trial where the burden of proof is on the accusers. Children are often taken away without the

> parents even having a chance to state their case. . . . and when
> social workers make mistakes, the people the system is designed
> to protect—innocent children—often wind up its victims. . . .
> Some will be far more seriously harmed—whether physically or
> psychologically—than if state officials had never heard of them.
> (p. 104–06)

After the article appeared, the author reported (personal communication, July 1993) that he had received the largest volume of mail ever in response to one article. The mail was overwhelmingly favorable, saying in one way or another that the article was right, that it accurately described what happened in the correspondents' family, neighborhood, community, to their friends, or to them. This response led to a second *Reader's Digest* article on false allegations which appeared in January 1994 (Armbrister 1994).

A seven-year-old boy was brought to us for therapy. He had trouble sleeping and was deathly frightened of two older boys who lived up the block. He didn't want to leave his mother or leave his home so he was school phobic. He had an acute anxiety attack every time he heard a siren or saw a police car. When he was four-and-one-half years old, during the bitter divorce of his parents, a day-care worker thought he was too aggressive in his play. He was playing by having cars crash together and TV characters fighting with swords. She had read lists of behavioral indicators of sexual abuse and thought the boy was showing signs of abuse, so she reported it. Two social workers came to the day-care center, interrogated the child using anatomical dolls, concluded he was abused, and took him into protective custody. When his mother came to pick him up that afternoon, she was told he had been taken away but nobody would tell her where. It took nine months before the child was returned, nine months during which he was repeatedly interrogated by social workers and police. He was physically examined three times, including, for example, having the physician stick two fingers up his anus while asking him if Mommy did this. He was in one children's hospital, two foster holding homes, and three treatment foster homes. When he was first returned to his mother, he didn't leave her side for three days. This child was the victim of sexual, emotional, and physical abuse and neglect perpetrated by the state.

If adults make a mistake and treat nonabused children as if they had been abused, this is not innocuous or benign. It can amount to child abuse. Smith, a psychologist, tells about a letter brought to him on the fourth visit by Stephanie, a 17-year-old client:

> I am so miserable, Dr. Smith, I need your help now. As you know, I have told you how my mother and I just don't like each other. We fight and argue all the time. But I have never told you why. When I was little, six I think, I dearly loved my dad. I think he and I were very close and did many things together. I knew my mom and dad didn't get along but somehow things were all right between me and my parents.
>
> Then one day, my mother told me my father was very sick and needed to go to a doctor to get well. She told me I would have to say that my dad had hurt me by touching me (in) places that were nasty. She said if I would say this Dad would have treatment and get better and be a nicer Dad to me and bring me more presents.
>
> My mother rehearsed with me what I was to say and then took me to a doctor in another city and practiced with me again what I was to say and I said what she told me to say.
>
> Later my mom said that Dad had to go to a hospital to get the help he needed, but when I was 12 I found out he was in prison because he had molested me.
>
> Once I got to go see Dad in prison. He told me he had written me many times, but Dr. Smith, I never received any of those letters. I think Mom burned them. Later Mom told me that Dad was living in another state.
>
> Just last night my mom and I got in a big fight and she told me Dad had committed suicide. I feel so bad. I'm to blame because I lied for my mom. I hate her and I hate myself. I can't stand myself! I can't wait to leave home when I get older.
>
> Please help me Dr. Smith. (Smith 1991, p. 203)

The next night Stephanie died from an overdose of her mother's sleeping medication.

The Child Abuse System

The system set up to deal with allegations of childhood sexual abuse has expanded in scope and approach to include claims of recovered 'repressed' memories. The sudden spate of people remembering being abused years before when they had no memories in between is the most recent extension of the system. It reveals the weaknesses, errors, and folly of the entire system as nothing before it had done. The illogic of the initial assumptions in developing the system lead inexorably to recovered memory claims which in turn expose what has been wrong all along about the entire venture, though obscured by good intentions and passion for social reform. Our observations in this book about the recovered memory craze also have implications for the entire system dealing with allegations of child sexual abuse.

The National Center for Prosecution of Child Abuse (NCPCA) first funded by the Office of Juvenile Justice and Delinquency in 1985, had an article in their newsletter, *Update* (NCPCA, July 1992), dealing with the FMS Foundation's skepticism and opposition to claims of repressed memory. The NCPCA identifies the FMSF as the real danger, allies itself with the incest survivors' network and Bass and Davis, co-authors of *The Courage to Heal* (1988), and says: "Professionals who intervene in child sex abuse cases can expect to be subjected to the 'backlash' suggesting that children and now adults have been brainwashed into claiming abuse by parents and caretakers."

Following the trial and conviction of Raymond and Shirley Souza for sexually abusing their grand-daughters, the prosecutors once again allied themselves with claims of recovered memories in *Update* (NCPCA, April/May 1993). When national news coverage depicted this trial as part of a witch hunt and suggested the Souzas were innocent, *Update* denied there was any witch hunt, saying, "it is the classic Big Lie," and asserted that defendants have been getting away with presenting their defense outside the courtroom through the media. This, it was claimed, is done by a "pack of lawyers, publicists, and 'specialists' who earn money by smearing sex abuse victims to get their clients off the hook."

In an earlier *Update* (NCPCA, January/February 1991) the prosecutors disparage the report on the Kelly Michaels case by Rabinowitz (1990) in *Harper's* along with a *Time* magazine article on child witnesses as part of the "backlash." They say that the articles "infuriated both practitioners . . . and professionals" and claim that these articles are biased, ignorant, factually and legally false, and lacking any research. The backlash is attributed to "media coverage of other cases and aggressively promoted by defense lawyers, members of VOCAL (Victims of Child Abuse Laws), fathers' rights organizations, and a growing number of 'experts' who appear on behalf of defendants." *Update* then recommends as factual, accurate, and excellent sources of information *Nap Time* (Manshel 1990) and *Unspeakable Acts* (Hollingsworth 1986). Both of these books are crassly biased toward the prosecution and are immediately recognizable by any sentient organism as unreliable, one-sided hatchet jobs.

This prosecutors' organization, funded by federal tax revenues, thus officially accepts and endorses the concepts of repressed memory and the recovered memory accounts of childhood abuse. So far, approximately half of the states have succumbed to pressure and passed legislation accepting the concept of repressed memories and extending statutes of limitations to permit civil actions and in some states criminal prosecutions many years after the alleged acts.

What began as an admirable effort to protect children has evolved into a system of laws, justice and law enforcement authorities, social workers, and allied professionals that intrudes into American families with almost despotic power. It is based on pseudoscientific balderdash supplied by unscientific mental health professionals, unfounded and unsupported dogmas propounded by radical feminist propagandists, and the gullibility of politicians eager to build an image of probity at no apparent cost to themselves. The system is out of control and has no accountability.

The prosecutor is the single most powerful figure in the entire justice system, with absolute authority to determine who gets charged with what. Nobody, including judges, holds prosecutors accountable for their behavior; rather, they are immune from any attempt at redress or correction. It is a system with all the incentives awarded for making accusations and little interest in the accuracy of the decisions made. It pursues neither truth nor justice, but winning, as an American Bar Association task force (1984) concluded about prosecutors.

The U.S. has exported the system and its ill-founded ideology around the world. First, the English-speaking countries emulated our actions and policies on child abuse. Just recently it has begun to be evident in the Scandinavian countries. We have had people around the world describe the impact of the system on them. Invariably they compare it to Nazi storm troopers and the Communist KGB. We have heard this bitter and frightening conclusion in England, Canada, Australia, New Zealand, Holland, Sweden, Ireland, and Norway.

More Harm than Good

Any decision-making procedure built on false assumptions is going to produce error at an indeterminate, unrecognized, but significant level that causes harm (Gambrill 1990). Among attempts made to codify the principles of rational judgment, one of the most popular is Bayesian inference. Its proponents admit that it is not the way the human mind naturally works, because our minds are not very good at processing large amounts of information (Meehl 1993).

Although Bayesianism, as a full-blown analysis of scientific method and rational behavior, is highly controversial (see Horwich 1982; Howson and Urbach 1993; Miller 1994), it rests upon Bayes's Theorem, which has a narrower field of application and which is now an undisputed part of statistical method. Bayes's Theorem can produce results which are startling to the comonsense outlook. Tests which seem as if they ought to be dependable will yield a large number of 'false positivies.' Thus, a test for AIDS may be '95 percent accurate,' which sounds very reliable, but this may still allow that more than 50 percent of the positive results are false.

A number of scientists have applied Bayesian inference to child sexual abuse, endeavoring to assess the level and types of error produced by the system.[1]

Every Bayesian analysis of the decisions made by the child abuse system that we have found concludes that the most probable and most frequent type of error is an unacceptable level of false positives, that is, identifying an individual as abused or an abuser when it is not true.

This is true even when a 95 percent accuracy level for the decision making is assumed as Gambrill (1990) does. Starr (1979) assumes a procedure that is 83 percent accurate in correctly identifying abusive situations. Still he reports a ratio of 20 false positives to one true positive. More realistic and probable lower estimates of the accuracy of the decision-making process but higher base rates produce unconscionable and unacceptable levels of false positives ranging up to a ratio of over 200 false positives to one true positive (Gambrill 1990). Our analysis (Wakefield and Underwager 1988) suggests a ratio of nine to one. No democratic society can prosper for long when its legal system is producing such massive injustice.

Much has been made of the harm to children if there is a false negative decision, that is, failing to identify a child as abused when it is true. To a large degree the system has been built on the assumptions (aphorisms) that less damage is done by misidentifying a few innocent people as guilty or a few nonabused children as abused and that all children must be preserved from abuse at all costs. At this point what reliable data are available suggest that this is not true, and that greater damage may be done to nonabused children and innocent people than is done by missing some children who have been abused. It may also be that the severity of damage is greater when a nonabused child is treated as if abused than when an abused child is not correctly identified.

---

[1] See these references: Abel et al. 1994; Altemeier et al. 1984; Caldwell 1988; Gambrill 1990; Horner 1992; Horner and Guyer 1991a, 1991b; Kotelchuck 1982; Lindsay and Read, in press; Melton 1993; Milner 1984; Paradise 1989; Realmuto et al. 1990; Starr 1979; Wakefield and Underwager 1988; Zeitlin 1987.

Politicians, law enforcement, social welfare, mental health, and the citizenry should agree that the least harm is done if the decisions made are the most accurate possible. Few problems pose a greater threat to free, democratic societies than that of wrongful convictions by the justice system. A study of cases of innocent people being convicted found a systemic regular phenomenon in our legal system: ratification of error— meaning that errors made at lower levels are ratified, not corrected, at the higher levels (Huff, Rattner, and Sagarin 1986). This study also reports that most of those who have investigated the problem of wrongful convictions conclude "it is not a rare phenomenon" (p. 520). We suggest that the proportion of wrongful convictions may be larger when there is an allegation of child sexual abuse than for any other crime.

Anybody who claims the system is working well and is worthy of continued financial and governmental support must be forced to produce evidence, not just vacuous repetition of slogans. At this point the credible scientific data suggest that the system, and the billions of dollars spent on it, is producing harm and damage to the whole country. Although efforts toward child protection appear to have brought about a decrease in physical violence to children, thousands of children and families are needlessly damaged, particularly when there are sexual abuse allegations. This is especially evident in claims of recovered memory. The loyalty of citizens and their confidence in the government is being grievously undermined. If the finding concerning false positives by competent scientists across at least 15 years is right, then the system is unlikely to respond to tinkering. It must be dismantled, and a fresh start made.

What It Does to Our Nation

The effect of this child sexual abuse system on the nation is more than simple injustice writ large. It is more than state-sanctioned child abuse. It is an attack on the very foundations of our culture and civilization. It assaults personal freedom and the exercise of reason. It is the leading edge of tyranny and oppression covered by the ostensible aim of protecting children, a noble goal that cannot be ignored or abandoned.

The recent progression to involvement in notions of recovered memory, with the acting out of anger by confrontations, legal actions, and total alienation that is supposed to heal the damage of childhood sexual abuse, makes it clear that the entire venture is based on irrationality and rage. The system and the persons in it dealing with child abuse have pushed it too far and committed intellectual suicide for there is no credible scientific support for either the basic concepts of recovered 'repressed' or 'dissociated' memories or the claims of satanic, ritualistic abuse.

The Beginning of Freedom and Reason

Over 2,500 years ago, at the Acropolis in Athens, a civilization emerged based on personal freedom and the exercise of human reason. The old matriarchal Greek tribal deities were superseded by the patriarchal gods of Olympus and the process of western culture and civilization began. Today, all over the world, persons are showing by their behavior that they are willing to die for that vision of life. The United States stands at the head of a world united by the concepts of freedom and reason that have prevailed after millennia of struggle. There is a limited, finite set of issues that our humanity must cope with. The same fundamental concerns the ancient Greeks had are our concerns. We live today and our humanity is defined by the beliefs and values of the Athenians. But here, in the nation that is the model for what the rest of the world only hopes for, the return of the Furies, the ancient matriarchal Greek goddesses of vengeance and vitriol, rage and bitterness, threatens to overturn our freedom with tyranny and our reason with irrationality.

Today in the United States freedom is abandoned and individual rights surrendered for fear of crime and rage at drugs. Violence is met with greater violence and harsher and more draconian punitiveness. Gender warfare breaks out in wild and bizarre attacks and convoluted reasoning produces wholesale blaming of entire categories of persons, for example:

all men are rapists; all women are emotional and hysterical. Whining and complaining replace courage, self-reliance, and personal responsibility. Random acts of violence shatter the veneer of order. Victimization supersedes virtue and political correctness covers rudeness and ill-mannered behaviors unthinkable 20 years ago. These actions and attitudes are those of the ancient Furies for whom justice is vengeance, reason is intuition, and healing is rage. Cassandra describes the house of Agamemnon during the time he was away leading the Greek forces besieging Troy:

> I shall not speak in riddles any more.
> Be witness that I smell out swiftly
> the tracks of evils that have long been done.
> There is a choir that never leaves this roof,
> unmusical, in concert, unholy.
> And it has grown drunken and overbold
> on human blood, it riots through the house,
> unriddable, blood-cousins, the Furies. (Boardman, Griffin, and Murray 1986, p. 161)

A life of freedom and reason is not the natural state of humanity. History demonstrates the dominance of slavery and emotion (Patterson 1991). When Athens, in the seventh to fifth century B.C., changed from a matriarchal tribal society to patriarchy and constructed the first free capitalist democracy, the linear development from that time to this has produced Western civilization. It is fact that this Western civilization is better than many others and may, indeed, be the best.

There are serious concerns about our civilization. At its worst, it has elicited alienation, selfishness, unchecked greed, and dehumanizing neglect of those who can't make it. But in terms of the quality gradation of goods in the old Sears and Ward's mail order catalogs from good, to better, to best, there is no other civilization that has produced a comparable quality of life for as many people. Though Mussolini made the trains run on time and Plato acknowledges the efficiency of tyranny, the collapse of communism makes it plain that personal freedom with all of its warts and roughness is best. Nothing else has so fully captured the aspirations of humanity. The Athenian playwright, Euripides, in his last and greatest play, *The Bacchae*, during the ferment of building democracy, has the chorus joyfully celebrating their right to worship as they please:

> whose simple wisdom shuns the thought
> of proud uncommon men and all
> their god-encroaching dreams.
> But what the common people do,
> the things that simple men believe,
> I too believe and do. (Euripides, *The Bacchae*, 424–433)

When Christianity later brings the concepts of grace and mercy and an individualized relationship to God who knows clearly and loves totally each person and commands that we love one another, personal freedom cannot degenerate into licentiousness. Loving our fellow human beings means confronting their equality with us. Personal freedom for me then means personal freedom for all people but that is not some abstract, bloodless collective. Loving my neighbor means I cannot avoid the flesh and blood person next to me. In this manner personal freedom entails personal responsibility.

In Western civilization the advance of science suggests the answer to Socrates's perennial question whether virtue is really knowledge and therefore all perversities of the will are merely forms of ignorance. Yes! The great mass of human anguish and pain is not caused by some mysterious cosmic force, as Luke Skywalker encounters in Darth Vader, but rather by plain, simple, garden variety human stupidity. It is ignorance that causes governments of whatever form to pursue folly, that is, policies and actions that are known to be destructive (Tuchman 1984). It is ignorance that causes your contractor to set your basement a foot too low or your mechanic to overlook a clogged filter in your fuel line or your child's day-care center to believe that punishment is the best way to change behavior. It is ignorance that leads politicians to view war as an acceptable implementation of policy. It is ignorance that clogs systems of production and distribution with the tragedy of the commons so that an apparent self-advantage obscures the disadvantage to all.

It is also fact, lamentable though it may be, that the human mind is not very good at handling information (Meehl 1993). Even in very simple situations with a small number of variables requiring thoughtful choices, the human mind is not adept at making wise or effective decisions, summarizing data, weighing evidence rationally, or assessing probabilities (Arkes 1989; Crocker 1981; Dawes 1988; Einhorn and Hogarth 1978; Kahneman and Tversky 1979; Turk and Salovey 1985). The use of rationality is required to overcome the innate deficits of the human mind. Though we may find it difficult to admit, we do far better with a $3.95 calculator in making choices than with the brilliant and clever insights of our subjective creativity and intuitive certainties (Dawes, Faust, and Meehl 1989; Cronbach 1992; Gambrill 1990).

Personal freedom and commitment to reason, once elected and achieved, are not automatically maintained. Adequate comfort and sufficient security can be obtained by less arduous and less demanding goals. The onerous responsibilities of freedom and reason may lead most persons to abandon them for the promise of greater ease. Once free from Pharaoh and on their own in the Sinai, the People of Israel longed for a return to the fleshpots of Egypt even though they had been slaves there. The regularities and dependability of life in prison can be attractive. John Dewey described the need to maintain the devotion to freedom and reason:

> Is the struggle for liberty so arduous that most men are easily distracted from the endeavor to achieve and maintain it? Does freedom in itself and in the things it brings with it seem as important as security of livelihood; as food, shelter, clothing, or even as having a good time? . . . Is love of liberty ever anything more than a desire to be liberated from some special restriction? And when it is got rid of does the desire for liberty die down until something else feels intolerable? Again, how does the desire for freedom compare in intensity with the desire to feel equal with others, especially with those who have previously

been called superiors? How do the fruits of liberty compare with the enjoyments that spring from a feeling of union, of solidarity with others? Will men surrender their liberties if they believe that in doing so they will obtain the satisfaction that comes from a sense of fusion with others and that respect by others which is the product of strength furnished by solidarity? (Dewey 1939, p. 3)

There can be no serious effort to maintain personal freedom and commitment to reason apart from an understanding of human nature. Is there such a thing at all? What can we say about it? Is psychology as a science of human behavior also a science of human nature? Who is Man/Woman? The patriarchal Greek answer is the oracular command, 'Know thyself!' The dignity, freedom, and rationality of humanity are functions of self-knowledge. Who am I? It is the unexamined life that is not worth living. But there is a dark side to honest self-knowledge, which may tap forces that in the end destroy us and those we love the most. So Euripides, Athenian dramatist, has Agave unwittingly butchering her own son, then exiled and enslaved, as a consequence of her instinctive and nonrational worship of Dionysus. It is this dark side of ourselves, the subjective, irrational, intuitive that is embodied in the Furies.

Greek Tragedy

The tragedies of Greek drama in fifth-century B.C. Athens were the vehicle for the examination, development, and solidification of the most profound cultural and social values that shaped the emergence of the free democratic society of reason. It is the nature of Greek tragedy to see not just that bad things happen to good people but rather that the most tragic of all possibilities occurs when good people set out, with good intentions, to accomplish good ends, yet the outcomes are evil.

The institution of Greek tragedy flourished precisely when the democratic city was coming into being, at the dawn of western civilization. The tensions of a changing society, tensions between public and private life, tensions between the old ways and the new ways of the emerging order are captured and examined in the dramas the Athenians produced, watched, discussed, and lived. While a great deal has changed and daily life today is far removed from fifth-century Athens, the questions posed then remain alive and well and the answers are still taking shape. Relationships between male and female, humans and gods, the individual and the state, parent and child, good and evil are as much a part of our time as theirs. Hence the dramas of ancient Greece are remarkable as descriptors and prophecies of our contemporary experience 2,500 years later.

The great *Oresteia* trilogy of Aeschylus is a prophecy of our own conflicts and may still offer the only reasonable proposal for the solutions. The story is that when Agamemnon comes home victorious from the 20 years of the Trojan war, Clytemnestra, his wife, who has ruled the kingdom in his absence, murders him. Their son, Orestes, is commanded by Apollo, a pro-masculine diety, to avenge his father's death. Orestes kills his mother and the man she took for a husband, Aegisthus. Immediately, the Furies, infernal goddesses of night and earth, seek to wreak vengeance on Orestes and punish the son who murders his mother, as the perpetrator of the most heinous crime imaginable. Their names are Tisiphone, Megara, and Alecto. The male force, Orestes, that was a necessary agent of revenge must now pay his debt to the female spirits of vengeance (Patterson 1991).

The final play of the trilogy, *Eumenides,* is the trial of Orestes before a jury of Athenian citizens on the hill of the Acropolis. Now it is the gods who are involved and front stage. Apollo, the new god of the emerging patriarchy, defends Orestes against the wrath of the Furies, the old matriarchal deities who are being replaced throughout Greece, and who seek the destruction of Orestes. The question of the play is what kind of price the new order of enlightenment, freedom, and reason will have to pay the old matriarchy of darkness, mysticism, and dominance (Barrett 1958).

The vote of the jurors, all citizens of free, democratic Athens, is a tie. The tying vote was cast by Athena, an ambiguous female goddess, halfway between man and woman.

As the rules stipulated, Orestes is set free. The Furies are enraged and threaten all manner of destruction on the state. However, Athena placates them by telling them they are to be given a sanctuary and every child born of woman shall be under their protection. The very first child protection agency is the Furies who must reconcile the goals of protection and justice.

The key step in building the new order is the agreement for co-operation and respect with the old order. We must find a way to accomplish the goals of each—freedom and reason and the protection of children. This is the same conflict we have today. In 1994, one of the leading authorities on child protection and child abuse, Murray Levine, presented an analysis of the American child protection system showing a constant tension between protecting children and enforcing justice (Levine 1994).

The centuries-long development of personal freedom and human reason that started in Athens is the greatest triumph of humanity but it is still in process. It is still incomplete, still to be brought fully into being. The forces of vengeance, rage, and passionate emotion must still be controlled and placated. Children must still be protected from the dark side of human nature.

We wish to preserve and extend what goes under the name of liberalism, humanism, intelligence, decency, and a rational understanding of life but, in the face of the events of the twentieth century and the current confusion, we cannot escape the reality. A decent life of freedom and reason is always balanced on the sharp edge of the subterranean darkness of the return of the Furies and the recrudescence of irrationality, vengeance, and vitriol. We must find that balance again and restore and renew the pact with the Furies struck so long ago in the days and nights of drama and discourse on the Athenian Acropolis. We must find a way to satisfy the Furies' goals and still control irrationality and rage. Otherwise we may lose our freedom and not know our reason.

It would be the final act of ignorance for human reason to give way to pride and unreason by denying that the Furies exist. Nothing is accomplished by hiding from the fact that we are essentially troubled human beings. That can only generate more trouble. If the pact with the Furies decays or is abandoned, the dark side of our humanity will once again emerge, most likely through our intelligence for it is only our own cleverness that can conceal the truth about ourselves from us. We are most dense about our own blind spots as attribution research demonstrates (Edwards and Potter 1993; Funder 1987). The solution is to give the Furies their place, acknowledge them as part of ourselves, not aliens. At the very heart of our enlightenment, there is a darkness that requires respect, recognition, reasoned compromise, and shared control.

The prophetic insight that the touchstone of the duality of our existence is in the caring for children foreshadows the rational choice of our nation to decrease the brutal savaging of children that, more than any other behavior, is the hallmark of our darkness and capacity for evil. Adults have abused children since the beginning of history (Bakan 1971). This is a grim and frightening manifestation of our potential for wrong-doing. For the first time in history, our society has chosen to stop the brutality of adults against children, but, in doing so, we have not listened to reason but rather have unleashed the Furies. The system we have established to decrease child abuse is the leading edge of tyranny and the exaltation of irrationality. Justice has gone crazy (Armbrister 1994).

For the first time in the history of our country we have identified a specific group of people, child molesters, and officially and legally determined to treat them differently from anybody else. So laws have been passed and Supreme Court decisions have been handed down that remove constitutional guarantees and individual rights from those accused of child molestation. The individual rights of confrontation, due process, and freedom from self-incrimination do not apply to a person charged with child sexual abuse. A person convicted of child molestation gets much harsher sentences than for any other crime (Champion 1988; 1991; Manross 1992).

The selection of child molesters as the group to be treated differently becomes most clear in the sudden emergence of dramatic charges and horrific stories centering around claims of recovered repressed memories of childhood abuse. The swift response of legislators to pass special laws singling out child molesters is amazing (McMullin 1992; Salten 1984; Slovenko 1993). The claims of recovered memories have produced a firestorm of state laws that remove the protections of statutes of limitations and permit civil or criminal actions against those accused of abuse many years ago.

Conspiracy Theories

The child sexual abuse system includes conspiracy theories held by its proponents. Several will be described in the chapters ahead. Now we want to lay the foundation for understanding both the presence and the prevalence of the conspiracy theories found in the system. When Orestes kills his mother and her husband, he must flee the wrath and vengeance of the Furies. Elektra and the women of the household have successfully conspired to seek vengeance for the murder of Agamemnon. All of the violent acts in the trilogy are the outcome of conspiracies. The Furies, either two or three in number, are beautiful women, but their hair is striped and straggled with snakes. They live in the frightening region just before the entrance to Hades. From here they conspire together to pursue their charge. The chorus expresses the nature of the wrath of the furies:

> The female force, the desperate
> love crams its resisted way
> on marriage and the dark embrace
> of brute beasts, of mortal men. (Aeschylus 1953, 599–602)

Real conspiracies abound in the real world. They go on all the time. They include plots to shoot deer out of season, play practical jokes on fellow employees, destroy reputations, smuggle drugs, acquire properties, commit adultery, overthrow nations, or win Olympic gold medals. The earliest recorded conspiracy may be that between Eve and the serpent who plotted to lure Adam into a fateful choice. In addition to actual conspiracies, however, the history of the world and human experience is filled with innumerable conspiracy *theories*, that is, strange, unprovable plots that may involve wildly bizarre and improbable claims of dark, demonic confederations engaged in wholesale mischief and mayhem of all sorts.

If we want to explain any complex past event, we are most likely going to come up with some form of a conspiracy theory. Remember, the human mind is not very good at processing large amounts of information. But what separates a conspiracy theory from the real world is the amazing and satisfying simplicity that a conspiracy theory provides to explain terribly complex and multidimensional events. As the movie about the assassination of President Kennedy, *JFK*, has a character say, "never mind the what and the how. That is window dressing. Concentrate on the why and you have the answer" (Wernick 1994). Then you already know the answer and you can see how everything fits together. You can find your way through the blooming, buzzing mass of confusion created by the facts because you already know where you are going. Once you know the villains, you can always see a pattern of behavior that supports your identification of the source of the trouble.

There are conspiracy theories to explain the beginning of World War I (the munitions makers and bankers), World War II (the Jews and President Roosevelt), the depression, the assassinations of presidents and rulers, the transfer of technology such as the atomic bomb, increased smoking among teenagers, welfare recipients, the failure of politicians and their policies, and disasters of various types. The alleged conspirators include Jesuits, Jews, Freemasons, the Mafia, the Comintern, the CIA, the U.S. Chamber of Commerce, the K.G.B., Blacks, Muslims, Irish Roman Catholics, Teutonic Knights, business leaders and bankers, satanists, demons, spies, and mountebanks of every sort.

Conspirators can be anywhere, in your own neighborhood, or world wide. They are indistinguishable from normal, non-conspirators. There are always large numbers of people involved, with great power, and they are sworn to secrecy, so no one ever talks. They are awesomely efficient and so highly organized that they leave no evidence, but because there is no evidence, that proves they really exist. Yet, for the most part, they accomplish almost nothing that is visible or evident.

At any time when the social contract of a given society decays and the unwritten common understandings of how we act toward each other have eroded, individuals who have insufficient personal identity to live with ambiguity experience great stress. One of the easiest ways to alleviate that personal stress is to formulate a conspiracy theory that lays responsibility on some external entity. This permits the insecure and anxiety-ridden individual to develop an identity based on an enemy. It is the Flip Wilson defense: "Don't blame me! The devil made me do it." I know who I am because I know whom I am against. The more evil and powerful the conspiracy I fight, the greater the virtue and identity I confer on my fragmented and indeterminate self. We all become victims together.

Victimization and Magic

In addition to conspiracy theories, there are several other concepts crucial to understanding the child sexual abuse system. The only heroes and heroines we have now are victims. Labor is victimized by management and management by unions. Racial minorities are victims of white majorities in the suburbs but it turns around in the inner cities. Teachers are victims of insensitive administrators and uninvolved parents. Taxpayers are victims of unfair tax laws which always favor the rich, unless you are rich. Women are victimized by the patriarchy and the elderly by the young. In media, political maneuverings, and social perceptions the competition is to establish who has been victimized most grievously.

Victimization is an effective strategy for special interest groups, but paradoxically the effect on individuals is devastating. The victim role requires being both helpless and innocent at the same time, while the adversary is both powerful and malevolent. Playing a social role has a powerful effect on the individual. It brings about the conditions of the role. For the individual, becoming a victim means being ever vigilant in a frightening world to ward off the powerful enemy. But also, the only source of self-esteem is an illusion of self-righteousness that is empty and unrealistic. Seldom is anyone as innocent as the mythology requires. Healing from victimization is the new virtue that justifies all extremism (Mould 1984).

We are all victims of our parents for, after all, we are told repeatedly on PBS TV by John Bradshaw that 96 percent of American families are dysfunctional. Our parents did not love us or they loved us too much. They did not give us good role models. They beat us and emotionally abused us by not accepting bad report cards or insisting we do our chores and brush our teeth. Dads didn't play catch and Moms didn't cook. They divorced each other. They drank too much and made us develop eating disorders. Dads raped and savaged their children regularly and repeatedly.

If we don't think that really happened to us, it is only because we have repressed the memory and are in denial. Talk show hosts and columnists compete to find the latest victim with the greatest number of personalities and claiming the highest number of ritual murders. From Latoya Jackson, Marilyn Van Derber Atler, and Roseanne Barr we learn how to denounce parents, a procedure that used to be reserved for those in the Hitler Youth or Young Communist Pioneers. The Inner Child in each one of us teaches that personal grievance has priority over principles, politeness, and productivity. Ellen Bass, co-author of *The Courage to Heal,* leads workshops of professionals in mind visualization trips to find the Inner Child and recover memories of abuse (McGovern 1994). Pop psychology and the therapeutic model provide the jargon, the mirrors, and the smoke to fashion a self-deluding magic show of responsible irresponsibility, free slavery, and rational nonsense.

The triumph of the therapeutic model means everyone is sick. Everyone has a disease caused by some alien entity so there is no personal responsibility and hence no freedom. Healing from the disease is paramount and so any behavior which can be labelled as a healing process is admirable and acceptable. In *The Courage to Heal,* Bass and Davis (1988) title one of their chapters 'Anger—The Backbone of Healing.' Thus rage and anger, vengeance and vitriol—the actions of the Furies—become acts of healing (Roiphe 1993), whereas in our view, it is better to see the history of Western Civilization as in large part the effort to control rage and vengeance.

At official symposia of the American Psychological Association some psychologists claim that therapeutic values overcome considerations of truth, scientific fact, and objective reality. What counts is therapeutic truth and sensitivity to the pain of the victims. Herein, it is claimed, lies the true nobility of the clinician, not in inconvenient, disconfirming research (Briere 1993). Many therapists continue to regard research as irrelevant and unhelpful to their practice (Campbell 1994; Weisz and Weiss 1993). Therapy, however, then shifts from science to magic. When the clinician ignores the research and refuses to use it in a way that affects actual practice, this is irresponsible and unethical. This can only result in bad practice and harm to the patient (Stricker 1992).

Magic is the art or group of arts that claims to have power to control the order of natural events and compel the world to conform to individual desires or expectations (Clark 1958). The deeds of the magician are essentially persuasive behaviors, persuading either some cosmic force or other people that, indeed, the arcane knowledge possessed by the operator compels conformity. The power to persuade is the same in the technologically sophisticated twentieth century as what is commonly labelled magic in prior ages.

Magic has three components—the spell, the rite, and the character of the person performing the act of magic (Oates 1973). The spell is cast by uttering a set of words in a set order according to a formula that is known only to the initiated. However, a parent who says repeatedly, 'You will never amount to anything!' or 'You are destined to be a great writer' can, in effect, be casting a spell on a child. The therapist says, 'You are sick, but you can get well. Relax! breathe deeply! Let your mind go back, back . . .' It is often claimed that the similarity among stories dredged up in this way shows they are true. But when the same kind of story appears many times, another explanation is that there is a common set of ideas, words, and acts being employed to generate the stories.

The rite is the set of acts and the environment conveying the spell that elicits the desired effect. The rites may be appointments, offices, couch or recliner, procedures or techniques that become repeated, habitual, traditional, and expected. All behaviors that are understood to be part of the unique relationship with the operator may constitute the rite.

Sympathetic magic works by the principle of 'like affects like.' Persons imitate those they like. Divination is the magic means of gaining knowledge. Dreams, omens, hunches, intuitions, feelings are presented to the magician who divines their hidden or obscured meaning. Role plays in which a person addresses an empty chair imagining that an absent or dead person is sitting in the chair are akin to the magic of necromancy. Incantation blends suggestion and hypnosis in the repetition of formulas of words, acts, or music.

The magical personage is the central component of magic. He or she believes faithfully in the efficacy, the sanctions, and taboos of the system of spells and rites. The magician cannot be an ordinary person but must maintain some claim to special knowledge and ability. The acts and attitudes required by the nonrational codes shared only by the truly knowledgeable maintain the mythological world of assumptions, beliefs, feelings, and intuition. The personal prestige of the magician is the most important aspect of the working of magic. It must be nourished and supported by the group in a mutual system of dependency between magician and subject (Bakan 1966). So the therapist-magician becomes a highly credentialled soothsayer who reads MMPIs instead of goat guts.

The triumph of the therapeutic/victimization model has produced a therapeutic state (Szasz 1984) where the central government function becomes healing all manner of ills. When social problems, political problems, and economic problems are all redefined as ills, as diseases, a patina of nobility of beneficent purpose is cast over all governmental policies. Remember the three greatest lies: 1. One size fits all; 2. The check's in the mail; 3. I'm from the government and I am here to help you. Any government is most dangerous when it appears most benevolent.

The Therapeutic State in Action

On April 19th 1993, America watched as American battle tanks, made by American workers in Lima, Ohio, the heartland of America, killed 86 American citizens in the fires at Waco, Texas. That night Americans watched Ms. Janet Reno, newly confirmed Attorney-General of the United States, explain her decision to invade the Branch Davidean compound that morning. She said her decision was based primarily on the reports she had been given alleging child sexual abuse by David Koresh. These reports came from Dr. Bruce Perry, a Baylor College of Medicine psychiatrist, responsible for the treatment of 19 children who had come out of the compound in February (Carroll et al. 1993). The social, political, ideological, emotional, and legal system we have built up around the fact of child sexual abuse led to the senseless, mindless slaughter of American citizens, including 17 children, by the government whose sworn duty it is to protect citizens and guard their rights, their liberties, and their life.

The reports from Dr. Perry disclose that the 19 children who left the compound in February all denied any abuse, either physical or sexual. They presented a positive picture of their life in the compound. But for two months they were kept at the in-patient psychiatric unit and subjected to daily sessions of interviews and other procedures, called therapy but really the coercive imposition of persuasive influence and far-fetched interpretation of innocent behaviors or statements as child abuse.

A hospital in-patient psychiatric unit is a total environment in which everything impacting upon the lives of the people inside the environment is under the control of a single, unitary authority. The Soviet Union controlled many of its dissidents and 'enemies of the state' by putting them in psychiatric care.

From the initial denial and positive depiction of life in the compound, 17 children (the other two were too young) ages four to eleven, two months later were producing accounts of physical and sexual abuse which were then relayed to Ms. Reno who promptly ordered the deadly assault.

When there is a progression in the development of an account from an initial denial to a later account of abuse, and there is evidence of powerful persuasive influence during the development of the abuse account, one likely explanation is that the statements about abuse were caused by conformity to the intrusive adult influence and do not reflect a memory of an actual event. Research continues to accumulate demonstrating the ease with which memories of events that never happened can be implanted in children by suggestive and coercive interviews. This fact is now generally accepted in the scientific community (Ceci and Bruck 1993; Goleman 1993; Lepore 1991; Loftus 1993), and has, of course, been perfectly familiar to those experienced in raising children, for thousands of years. In addition, children often come to believe subjectively what they have learned from the adult interviewers. At the same time, research indicates there is a very weak correlation between subjective confidence and accuracy (Brigham 1988; Loftus and Ketcham 1991; Smith, Kassin, and Ellsworth 1989).

Putting these facts together makes it likely that the slaughter of American citizens by their own government was caused by a false allegation of child sexual abuse, believed by Attorney-General Janet Reno. The official Justice Department report on the event flatly concludes that the reports of child abuse are false. Whatever other errors of judgment may have been made throughout the sad and tragic interaction of the federal government and the Branch Davidians, the proximal cause for the assault on the morning of April 19th 1993 was the false report of child sexual abuse.

Janet Reno is no stranger to false reports of child sexual abuse. She was responsible for the prosecution of many sexual abuse cases during her tenure as Dade County District Attorney. Her readiness to believe the most incredible claptrap is shown in her prosecution of the Fijnje case (Armbrister 1994).

Here there were outlandish claims of satanic, ritualistic abuse supposedly committed by Bobby Fijnje, a 14-year-old volunteer in a church nursery, during services when parents left their children in the nursery. One of the things that is supposed to have happened was that horses were brought into the nursery and killed by Bobby Fijnje. Once this was seen to be impossible, the prosecutors shifted the claim and said he used toy horses, told the children they were real, and cut off their heads to frighten the children.

Such mental gymnastics accommodate the impossible nature of childish claims by inventing even the most feeble explanations for assertions that would otherwise be dismissed. Ms. Reno proceeded to bring the case to trial knowing that the prosecution had to perform such contortions. The jury heard evidence about suggestibility and interviewing effects, and found the lad not guilty. This case alone should have resulted in Ms. Reno knowing that claims produced after significant pressure ought to be dealt with cautiously. Nevertheless, having apparently learned nothing, she proceeded to invade the Waco compound.

The system responding to claims of child abuse is set to respond to minimal information with maximum credulity. Detectives in Memphis spent a month looking for the garage in which Frances Ballard, an elderly black grandmother who had never learned how to drive, kept the helicopter in which she flew children from Georgian Hills Baptist day-care center into the mountains where she gave them rifles with which they shot bears, tigers, and lions. Denise Perrigo spent a night in jail and her two-year-old daughter spent eight months in foster care before the grandparents were given custody. Finally, after a year, her child was returned to her. This happened because she called to ask for the phone number of the La Leche League to ask a question about normal feelings during breast feeding (Ryckman 1992). Because of an anonymous phone call claiming they picked up a black-eyed infant by the neck and confined it in the bathroom, James and Mary Seay were on the Florida Central Registry of child abusers for 30 days. They were informed that they had to go to sex abuse counselling, and when they explained to the H.R.S. worker they had no children but only a pet raccoon, they were told they were in denial (Whalen 1991).

Juries convict innocent people because they believe that children must be telling the truth even though what the children say is impossible. Something had to have happened. Where there's smoke, there's fire. Prosecutors take advantage of this tendency by piling up counts. Judges leap to early conclusions that the person charged is guilty and then slant, distort, and sometimes twist the legal process to convict innocent people. This was one of the conclusions of the New Jersey Appellate Court about Judge Harth in overturning the conviction of Kelly Michaels.

The result of the credulity granted to outlandish, impossible, and patently foolish allegations is a child protection system with tremendous power to destroy children, families, and individuals and with no accountability and no checks (Brannigan 1989). This child protection system is allied with a law enforcement system that commits illegal acts such as murder and fabrication of evidence; officials do whatever they think they need to do to get convictions (Roberts 1993). Police may resort to trickery, deception, and perjury when they believe they have found a guilty person (Underwager and Wakefield 1992).

Concern for saving children is the current ploy of politicians of every persuasion, bureaucrats at all levels, and all manner of demagogues. Not only did Janet Reno use the concern for children to justify Waco, but Anita Bryant's right-wing crusade against homosexuals was carried out by her organization called Save Our Children. Ross Perot's latest book against NAFTA is subtitled "How we can save America for our children." President Clinton fought for his economic package by accusing the Republicans of holding children "the hostages of the Senate filibuster. . . . When I go out there on the lawn and I think about those kids picking up Easter eggs, I want to be able to think about them all being immunized" (Futrelle 1993, p. 14). The caricature of the sleazy politician kissing babies at every photo-op is all too accurate. The reason is relatively simple.

Portraying innocent, helpless, and dependent children in need of protection elicits very powerful emotion. The emotional appeal of children to juries has been known and exploited at least from the days of Aristophanes in ancient Greece (Underwager and Wakefield 1989).

> There isn't a form of flattery they don't pour into a jury's ear. And some try pleading poverty and giving me hard luck stories. . . . Some crack jokes to get me to laugh and forget I have it in for them. And, if I prove immune to all these, they'll right away drag up their babes by the hand. (Casson 1987, p. 123)

An Australian judge, in overturning a conviction of child sexual abuse on the basis of prosecutorial misconduct in arousing such emotions, observed "In cases of this type, prosecuting Counsel are required to be particularly vigilant not to do anything which appeals to the prejudice or sympathy of the jury where such emotions are so easily aroused" (O'Gorman 1991, p. 203).

The picture of the child used to manipulate opinion changes across time from the rebellious child to the deprived child to the sick or starving child and now to the victim child (Mosher 1991). There are still pictures of children on milk cartons after the spurious claims of 50,000 American children abducted every year by strangers were reduced to 67 in the year 1984 by FBI crime statistics (Best 1988; 1989). The use of exaggeration and false claims of huge numbers is termed 'advocacy numbers'; their purpose is to inflame emotion rather than inform accurately (Gilbert 1991). So invoking the specter of troubled, abused, abandoned, and assaulted children brings together both the extreme left and the extreme right (Wakefield and Underwager 1988). The political agenda of the child advocates is presented by Helfer (1991) who describes a monolithic empire of ostensible child services that would operate without any control and with no funding limitations.

The contemporary system for dealing with allegations of child abuse began with the passage of the Child Abuse Prevention and Treatment Act of 1974 (Nelson 1984). The Children's Bureau, which had been established in the 1930s during the progressive social reforms of the New Deal Era, had come into disfavor, and in 1968 had been reorganized almost out of existence. It was reduced to about 20 employees and had no programs assigned to it. Child abuse, however, was getting more and more media attention and moving ahead in public consciousness.

The Impact of Radical Feminism

Heightened public awareness of child sexual abuse began with a conference in April 1971, sponsored by New York radical feminists. Here we see the beginning of the currently fashionable view of men as socialized to be violent toward women and children. The conference led to public recommendations and statements about rape and sexual abuse. Florence Rush gave a new feminist view of the sexual abuse of children:

> Sexual abuse of children is permitted because it is an unspoken but prominent factor in socializing and preparing the female to accept a subordinate role: to feel guilty, ashamed, and to tolerate through fear, the power exercised over her by men. . . . The female's early sexual experiences prepare her to submit in later life to the adult forms of sexual abuse heaped on her by her boyfriend, her lover, her husband. In short, the sexual abuse of female children is a process of education that prepares them to become the wives and mothers of America. (Armstrong 1978, p. 133)

Roberts (1988) describes how left-wing radical feminism is also a large causal factor in the similar development of the system to deal with child sexual abuse in England. The legal revolution and focus on the absolute credibility of the child victim is a consequence of the radical feminist anti-rape campaigns of the 1970s (Jenkins 1993). The radical feminist perspective maintaining that sexual abuse is inherent in a patriarchal society where males connect sexuality and violence was first articulated then (Butler 1986; Conte 1982). Feminist analysis continues to blame the patriarchal context for abuse of children, both physical and sexual (Clark 1986; James and MacKinnon 1990). Radical feminism can be distinguished from cultural, liberal, and socialist feminism along a number of variables and approaches. One of the most crucial and significant distinctions is the epistemological assumption of radical feminism that women have a unique, non-male way to know the truth—intuition—so that truth is not objective but subjective. Truth is not rational but experiential and emotional. Truth is not real events but relational and invented in social constructions (Enns 1992). The Task Force of the American Psychological Association Division 35 (Psychology of Women) reported that feminist research is ". . . co-operative, participative, . . . interdisciplinary, [and] non-hierarchical . . . [beginning] with personal experience" and recognizes that ". . . truth is not separate from the person who speaks it" (cited in Wilkinson 1989, p. 261–62). Feminist research is not objective, neutral, or value-free but rather pursues an advocacy of women and a commitment to social and political change to benefit women and their causes (Wilkinson 1989). In an earlier age of romanticism, James Wilson, founder of the *Economist,* responded to this same stance: "There is no inconsiderable school of talkers and writers now-a-days who seem to forget that reason is given us to sit in judgment over the dictates of our feelings, and that it is not her part to play the advocate in support of every impulse which laudable affections may arouse in us" (Edwards 1993, p. 23).

Radical feminism, emphasizing the unique relational and contextual experience of women and claiming special knowledge of truth for women, abhors distinctions, principles, universals, or consistency. The editor of a textbook on feminist jurisprudence, observes that "the feminist intellectual movement, like many postmodern movements, regards the truth of all propositions relating to society and certainly to law as depending on context, perspective, and situation" (P. Smith 1993, p. 212).

Feminist attorneys and judges who advance these feminist concepts seek to purge the law of 'male' concepts such as objectivity, reason, respect for rules, individual rights, autonomy, which are only instruments of male dominance and oppression (P. Smith 1993). This school of feminism wants the law to focus on individual needs, hurt, pain, the victim's interest and individual cases rather than universal principles (Letwin 1991). What this feminist legal scholarship has produced is a situation in American jurisprudence where, if a man is alleged to have raped a woman, his belief that she had consented to the intercourse must not be considered by the court, however much it may be warranted by the facts, while if a woman is alleged to have murdered a man, her belief that she was threatened by him must be accepted by the court, no matter how contrary to the facts.

Another example of contextual consideration is the *Washington Post*'s report of President Clinton, responding to Vice-President Gore's question, asking Mrs. Clinton if the operation to re-attach the penis of the man whose wife had severed it would be covered by the health care plan. In the oval office:

> Clinton held the phone up so that others in the room could hear the laughter at the other end from Hillary Rodham Clinton. After a moment's deliberation with the First Lady, the preliminary determination was that one could argue that having a penis was a pre-existing condition and therefore covered by the plan as corrective—rather than cosmetic—surgery. (*Star Tribune*, October 2nd, 1993)

When the President, the President's wife, and the Vice-President can publicly laugh and make a joke out of a serious, savage assault of cutting off a man's penis, feminist anti-male rhetoric has reached into high places, indeed. Compare this with the likely response if the question of coverage by the health plan were about a female rape victim.

The next day Americans were saddened, outraged, and distressed by pictures of the mutilated and desecrated body of a dead American soldier dragged through the streets of Mogadishu in a savage, carnival atmosphere. The return of the Furies' spirit of vengeance, vitriol, and irrationality can hardly be more forcefully and sharply demonstrated.

A Paranoid Style of Living and Thinking

When there is an ever-widening rift between what a society and culture believes and what the members actually do, and duplicity becomes accepted, the result is a paranoid style of living and thinking (Hofstadter 1967). When reason is abandoned and there are no overarching principles any more, we settle for consensual validation. If most people, or even most people I know, share feelings and certain ideas, then they must be right. Then error and deviance are no longer discernible and the error becomes a normal way to live. Uncommonly angry minds flourish.

The paranoid style is a style of mind characterized by heated exaggeration and over-reactions, suspiciousness, and conspiratorial fantasies. It is characteristic of a paranoid mentality never to accept personal responsibility for personal failures or errors. The blame is always located on some outside entity. If anybody should be so bold as to challenge this shifting of responsibility, then that person becomes the enemy against whom all manner of vengeance and destruction can be directed. This paranoid style is not necessarily limited to profoundly disturbed minds. It is the adoption of the paranoid style by more or less normal people that gives it power and significance.

A feeling of persecution is central along with some concept of special standing for oneself. The hostile and conspiratorial world out there is not so much directed against oneself but rather against some positive idea or a virtuous cause. This permits a self-concept of unselfish righteousness and moral indignation. Whatever the paranoid style is against, that hated entity is always flourishing in epidemic proportions. It is vast, insidious, and able to perpetrate acts of fiendish character.

What is at stake is always a conflict between absolute good and absolute evil. This justifies all manner of personal attacks, invective, and efforts to destroy anyone who gets in the way. The enemy has some special strengths that must be combatted. It may be control of the press, wealth, positions of power, social status or influence. There is an elaborate concern with demonstrating the accuracy of the paranoid mentation so there will be heavy reliance upon evidence of some sort or another. It may begin with some relatively simple, straightforward facts that are not in dispute but then moves to accumulate supporting speculations that may appear valid on their face. At some point there will be a curious, subtle leap of imagination that may not be at all evident but puts the whole structure on what looks like solid ground when, in fact, it has lost all touch with reality.

Consider this brief description: The world has ignored the terror and horrific acts of sexual abuse and denies it in order to keep on doing it, but a small band of insightful and courageous heroes who love children are exposing the secret. There is an epidemic of sexual abuse and millions of children are abused. At least three out of five girls and almost as many boys are violated. Perpetrators can be anybody, even the most respected and probative citizens. Child molesters can be anywhere. The effects of abuse are always horrible and cause all manner of terrible consequences.

Now add these ingredients: Children cannot lie about sexual abuse, except when they deny that it has occurred. They cannot talk about things they have not experienced. They cannot be 'coached' to describe personally significant acts that have not happened to them. Therefore anybody accused by a child is guilty. Children must always be believed at all costs, except when they deny that abuse has happened. All errors in judgment must be 'on the side of the child.' Child molesters must be prosecuted to the extent of the law and imprisoned, preferably for life. Abusers will deny the abuse, since denial is characteristic of molesters. People who don't believe the child must be protecting molesters, and are probably molesters themselves.

Spence (1993), in his presidential address to the American Psychological Association Division 24, described the paranoid qualities of the responses of the recovered memory advocates to the challenging article by social psychologist Carol Tavris entitled 'Beware the Incest Survivor Machine' (Tavris 1993). Tavris had simply advised caution in evaluating claims of recovered memory. In over 100 responses from 'survivors,' Spence observes an extreme emotional outrage, along with a depiction of Tavris's cautionary suggestion as the assertion that child abuse doesn't exist; therefore Tavris is the enemy. Not a single one of these letters referred to any research but all instead relied upon the claim to authority based on personal experience of being an incest survivor. Spence comments:

> The abuse-believers take the position that only they have access to the truth. . . . it often takes on a paranoid cast; the Enemy is motivated by other reasons than what they claim and only those speaking for children's rights have a reason to be heard. (p. 7)

Finally add: belief in a world-wide conspiracy of satanists and pedophiles, and belief in recovered memories. Because anybody can be an abuser, these conspirators can be found in any neighborhood, any occupation, but especially any involving contact with children, in any town.

The world has been transformed into a very scary place. This is the paranoid style of living and thinking that re-appears in American life about every 40 years (Hofstadter 1967).

Conclusions

The recent emergence of claims by adult children of re-pressed memories of childhood abuse, uncovered in the course of therapy, illuminates the serious threat to our society produced by the system set up to deal with sexual abuse of children. The emotions and concepts at the bottom of these social phenomena are the antithesis of the foundational ideas of Western Civilization. The therapeutic state has triumphed and is eroding both freedom and reason. Radical feminism feeds these concepts and introduces the behaviors that represent a modern return of the ancient Furies of Greek drama and religion. The concepts and convictions of those who believe the unfounded dogmas and unsupported claims of the system that has developed around child sexual abuse suggest that this is another experience of conspiracy theory, victimization, and a paranoid style of thinking that has entrapped many, many citizens.

Chapter Two
Sexuality, Freedom, and Reason

Set me as a seal upon thine heart, as a seal upon thine arm: for love is strong as death.
Song of Solomon, 7:6

Keeping freedom and reason at the center of our civilization requires knowing ourselves. Our sexuality is the touchstone to our human nature and how I think and act sexually is the most intimately revealing level of myself. Sexuality is the aspect of myself that is most closely related to my very existence. This arises from the fact that human existence is the consequence of sexuality.

Sexuality is also the closest we can come to personal wholeness and individual selfhood because it is here that the unity of mind and body is most clearly experienced. While there are many, many psychological events which seem to have no relationship to my body and many physical events which do not feel as if they belong to the mind, sexual interest, arousal, and congress confront us with the essential linkage of the physical and the psychological. Only humans make love face to face, looking at each other, personally involved with each other. This shift from animal to human marks the emergence of humans as psychological creatures (Underwager 1984). Finally, among all creatures, human sexuality is the least bound to reproductive capacity and the most free for intimacy, joy, and pleasure.

For these reasons, and there may well be others, human sexuality is at its best when it is a choice freely made and behavior reasonably able to be understood as love. The best sex is discovered and experienced when two whole persons choose freely across enduring time to open body and mind (some would add soul) to each other and to the potential reality of being joined in a new, single entity. The communion which our humanity opens up for us in our sexuality is what both enables and builds family, community, and society (Bakan 1966).

The mutuality which is known and illuminated in good sexuality is the building material for all other mutual endeavors. This is what makes the family the indispensable building block of all nation states and tribes. Therefore, a society's values and attitudes toward sexuality are fundamental to the ability of that society to maintain itself and provide sufficient benefits to its populace to produce loyalty and commitment. A full-orbed and fulfilled sexuality is both a consequence of and a preservative for freedom and reason.

Even as sexuality is a touchstone for knowledge of self, it is a powerful index to the strength and well-being of a society. In the countless experiments in alternative communal utopian living styles of the 19th and 20th centuries, only those groups with a clearly defined and strongly held view of sex lasted beyond a few years. The Shakers eschewed sex, while the Oneida Community greatly emphasized it, but there had to be a specific understanding of sexuality shared by the group.

At a somewhat broader level, the relationship between women and men is crucial for determining the quality of life for a given culture. No society can do any better than what it values and pursues in the behavior between male and female. The

Athenian choice, demonstrated in the acceptance of the Furies and their responsibility, is a mutuality, a co-operation. The Christian concept of man and woman relating is that of carrying a burden together (I Peter 3:1), the meaning of the original Greek verb, *hypotage*. Both of the major streams of western civilization, though it may have taken many centuries to strive after it, have as their concept of desirable gender relationships co-operation and mutuality.

Antisexuality and the Child Abuse System

The network of laws, policies, practices, and persons who implement the child sexual abuse system embodies a pervasive and pernicious antisexuality. This has consequences not only in actions and decisions made about child sexual abuse allegations but also for the broader well-being of the society. Governmental intrusions into the privacy and liberties of citizens may well begin with what appear to be worthwhile and necessary steps but which then have unintended consequences. Benevolent paternalism has a long history of errors (Besharov 1992). Policies are shaped by prevailing political fads in the absence of factual knowledge and too often have failure built in (Shore 1993). Some examples:

- A man had befriended a woman who was a single parent with a ten-year-old son. After several months of friendship with the woman, he asked the boy to spend Good Friday with him. They had a good time making Easter eggs and taking them to an old people's home. After dinner the boy asked if he could stay overnight with the man. The man called the mother who said it was fine. When they were ready for bed, the man kissed the boy on the cheek and patted him on the buttocks. The man slept downstairs on a couch and the boy used the bed upstairs. The next day the boy went home.

  A week later the man was arrested for sexual abuse of the boy. In the trial the only discrepancy from the above account was that the boy said the man kissed him on the neck. The prosecutor's closing argument included this statement: "No man should ever be allowed to get away with anything that makes a child uncomfortable by claiming he was just being affectionate." She went on to claim that because the child felt uncomfortable when he was kissed this was an act of sexual abuse; the man was more powerful than the boy who could not resist being kissed. The man was convicted and sentenced to two years in prison.

• A 73-year-old man was charged with indecent liberties for allegedly putting his hand down the blouse of a 93-year-old woman at an East Wenatchee retirement home and ordered to undergo a 15-day observation at Eastern State Hospital. (*Wenatchee World*, 1991, p. 13)

• A college professor and his wife sold Mary Kay cosmetics as a sideline business. When the man was charged with sexual abuse of two neighborhood children, he was acquitted of all charges but one. He denied all other charges but admitted rubbing Mary Kay suntan lotion on the shoulders of a nine-year-old neighbor girl while demonstrating the cosmetics to the family. He was convicted of child sexual abuse and spent two years in prison.

• In Minneapolis a man was accused of child sexual abuse because he sat nude in a spa hot tub with his four-year-old daughter. He was in the tub by himself when the child came running in and jumped in the tub. There was no allegation of any touching or actual physical contact by either father or daughter. The water was filled with foam so the nudity was not visible. We provided testimony that research evidence showed 50 percent of American families bathe with their children and many experience genital touching (Rosenfeld et al. 1986; Rosenfeld et al. 1987). The judge ruled, however, that it was sexually abusive for the man to be in the hot tub nude with his daughter.

• The Arizona Supreme Court upheld the revocation of probation for a 16-year-old juvenile found guilty of shoplifting because, while on probation, he was said to have sexually abused a child. The juvenile had touched the breasts of his 14-year-old girlfriend in a consensual petting session. The Arizona Supreme Court ruled it was a criminal act. (Thompson 1992)

• In Minnesota, a 15-year-old girl became pregnant and later married her 20-year-old boyfriend. The man worked nights as a truck loader to support his wife and daughter and the young couple, although struggling financially, were happy and self-supporting. Despite this, the man was criminally charged and convicted of child sexual abuse for the act that had conceived his daughter. (Duchschere 1992)

Shifting the meaning of behaviors that once, while possibly questionable, were regarded as relatively innocuous into the realm of abusive and molesting behavior can only come from a stance which sees as abusive anything even remotely approaching a sexual behavior or that can be forced into some sexual context. This extends a negative perception of human sexuality into borderline behaviors that may well have nothing to do with sexuality at all.

In 1970 in the United States 86,324 persons were arrested for sexual offenses. In 1986, 168,579 persons were arrested for sexual offenses. By 1991 the number had increased to 247,520, nearly a tripling of the number of persons arrested. From 1970 to 1979 the rate of increase for sexual offenses other than forcible rape and prostitution was 5 percent. From 1979 to 1988 the rate of increase for sexual offenses other than forcible rape and prostitution was 44.5 percent. From 1982 to 1991 the rate of increase was 56.2 percent (U.S. Department of Justice, 1981, 1989, 1992). It appears that the single largest group in our prison population may well be those convicted of sexual offenses. If not, it is second only to the broad category of convictions for drug offenses. In one Ohio correctional institution the Senior Law Clerk wrote that "child sexual abuse cases . . . probably comprise more than half of the offenders incarcerated. In this camp alone, I believe their numbers exceed 70 percent. The Parole Board generally deals with them harshly with three and four continuances being the rule rather than the exception" (Jeffrey Myers, April 5th 1994, personal communication).

In a trial in December 1986 in Anchorage, Alaska, we first testified about the antisexuality inherent in some aspects of the endeavor to deal with sexual abuse of children. At that time, we described the criminalization of behaviors which had formerly been viewed as foolish or deplorable but not as criminal acts.

We also wrote about the antisexuality of the system responding to child sexual abuse in our 1988 book, *Accusations of Child Sexual Abuse* (Wakefield and Underwager 1988). Nothing that has occurred since then has caused us to change that view (Underwager and Wakefield 1993a).

The manner in which our society attempts to reduce sexual abuse of children represents the most virulent and violent antisexuality the world has known since the days of Tertullian in the second century. Tertullian was an early Christian theologian who maintained that the only proper way to be a Christian was to emasculate yourself. (Fortunately the church officially labelled Tertullian a heretic and his view never became dominant.)

The view that there has been a movement towards antisexuality and over-reaction to childhood sexuality is supported by a poll of mental health and legal professionals reported by Haugaard and Reppucci (Okami 1992). The poll indicated that 20 percent of these professionals believed frequent hugging of a ten-year-old child by parents required intervention, between 44 and 67 percent believed intervention was required if parents kissed the child briefly on the lips (as when leaving for work), and 75 percent believed intervention was required for parents who appeared nude in front of their five-year-old child.

Antisexuality and Farrall Instruments

Another example of the effect of a spreading antisexuality is the destruction of slides and stimuli that Farrall Instruments had developed for use with the penile plethysmograph. The penile plethysmograph is a device used in the assessment and treatment of sex offenders. It measures penile circumference in response to different sexual stimuli and therefore provides information about the sex offender's arousal pattern.

For several years Dr. William Farrall of Grand Island, Nebraska, who also manufactured the machines, co-ordinated efforts under the encouragement and direction of the Antisocial and Violent Behavior Branch of the National Institute of Mental

Health to produce a standard set of stimuli. This is an important scientific step which would allow for much more valid and reliable research to be done. It was a goal determined by experts in penile plethysmography to be necessary to advance the factual basis for treatment procedures.

Dr. Farrall had obtained an opinion from the local county attorney that it was legal for him to do this. The State Attorney General's office had been advised for many years of Dr. Farrall's efforts regarding developing standard stimulus materials and the information was in their files.

One of the sets of pictures was intended to assess erotic arousal in response to visual stimuli of naked children. All the pictures of children were of single children alone in the photo. To minimize any potential harm to the children posing for the photographs, all of the models came from nudist families. Parental consent was obtained and at least one parent was present during the photo sessions. There was no sexual behavior depicted in any of the pictures, these were simply slides and photographs of nude children. This was a purely scientific procedure using standard methodologies to produce a standardized administration of an assessment procedure. From thousands of photos produced by Dr. Farrall, a standard set was selected, pretested, and then developed and sold to be used with the plethysmograph.

Four of Farrall's plethysmographs were used in Vermont in treatment programs for juvenile offenders, and there an offender complained about the procedure. Vermont began an investigation which resulted in great pressure on Nebraska to enforce its laws against child pornography. The slides were then declared to be child pornography by Nebraska officials and Dr. Farrall entered into an agreement to destroy all the slides and photographs of children to avoid criminal prosecution. This was done on January 17th 1994. The end result of this, along with harassment about the plethysmograph from the FDA, has been a severe blow to scientific efforts to improve treatment of sex offenders, the end of Farrall Instruments, and the destruction of Dr. Farrall's career. This happened, despite the fact that these stimulus materials have never been found in a court of law to be either pornographic or illegal, and despite the agreement by researchers that standard stimuli are essential to reliable research and to effective treatment.

What happened to Dr. Farrall reflects the radical feminist position on child pornography. This radical feminist position is described by the National Council Against Censorship: "a very traditional theory of gender difference (which argues that) pornography is not speech, because men are beasts . . . It is not simply that pornography is bad. It is the combination of pornography and men that's bad, because men are bad" (NCAC 1993, p. 6). Okami (1990) observes that the link between the work of the crusaders against child sexual abuse and the crusaders against pornography is so strong that the two movements are virtually synonymous.

The Fate of a Book

Okami (1992) gives, as another example of the massive shift in national mood towards antisexuality, the history of the book *Show Me!* (Fleischhauer-Hardt and McBride 1975). *Show Me!* was originally published by a Lutheran-sponsored educational group in Germany and released in the United States the following year. The book, which was written by a Swiss psychologist and illustrated with photographs depicting child and adult nudity as well as graphic depictions of sex play, masturbation, intercourse, childbirth and breast-feeding, was subtitled *A Picture Book of Sex for Children and Their Parents*.

Although the book was somewhat controversial, it sold over 100,000 copies in the United States and was enthusiastically endorsed by 'progressive' sex educators, obstetricians and child psychologists and received essentially favorable reviews in the mainstream press, including *Time* magazine. Liberal parents bought it and read it to their children. But by 1982, all copies of *Show Me!* had been withdrawn from distribution out of fear of prosecution under child pornography and obscenity laws. Okami notes that today mere possession of the book could result in prosecution on felony or misdemeanor charges in half of the United States.

Children's Sexuality

Antisexuality is also evident in the need to deny and ignore the sexuality of children. The oft-repeated but unfounded assertions that children cannot talk about anything they have not experienced and that age-inappropriate sexual behavior means the child has been sexually abused are contradicted by research concerning children's sexuality. What children normally do sexually is more involved than most people believe (Best 1983; Friedrich et al. 1991; Gundersen et al. 1981; Langfeldt 1981; Martinson 1981; Okami 1992; Rutter 1971). Haugaard and Tilly (1988) found that approximately 28 percent of male and female undergraduates reported having engaged in sexual play with another child when they were children.

Before assuming that any sexual behavior by a child reflects sexual abuse, it must be demonstrated that normal, nonabused children rarely show that behavior. In the absence of knowing the scientific facts, adults may see children as much less sexual beings than they are.

In one trial, a pediatrician testified that a four-year-old boy had been abused because he got an erection when she was inspecting his penis. In another case, a Canadian judge ruled that five-year-old girls could not have fantasies about sexuality, therefore the child's accounts were true.

When mental health professionals deny the reality of children's sexuality, any sexual behavior by children may be labelled age-inappropriate and therefore indicative of abuse. Children who French kiss, masturbate, like being tickled, use sexual language, laugh about feces or urine, joke with other children about genitalia, or engage in sex play with peers may be labelled as abused because such behaviors are said to be beyond normal expectations. That simply is not true. For example, in societies where baby food comes out of Gerber's cans, even professionals may forget that in some parts of the world, mothers still masticate food and put it in their babies' mouths with their tongues. A child who may kiss and stick their tongue in an adult's mouth is instinctively looking for food, not sex.

The only behaviors that appear to be more closely related to a history of sexual abuse are those that imitate adult sexual behaviors, such as oral sex. And even then, alternative explanations may have to be ruled out (such as seeing an X-rated video, or learning from older children) before concluding that the behavior signifies abuse by an adult. The evidence now shows that such linkages between behavior and an inference of abuse are almost always wrong and sexual abuse should never be identified on the basis of behavioral indicators alone (Berliner and Conte 1993)

A New Category of Sexual Abuse Perpetrator

The antisexuality is also evident in the development of the new category of sexual abuse perpetrator. Young children are being labelled sexual abusers. A nine-year-old California boy was charged with rape, sodomy, unlawful sexual intercourse, and child molestation of a seven- and an eight-year-old girl, allegedly occurring at a birthday party (Lachnit 1991). A nine-year-old boy was convicted of rape of a seven-year-old boy (Logg 1990) in Washington. The charge, which the older boy denied, was that the older boy attacked the younger one in the school restroom handicapped stall. The police detective said: "We see many cases of offenders that are three, four, seven, eight years old, offending against younger children, usually" (p. A1). A ten-year-old San Francisco boy was charged with rape and sodomy of four younger playmates in 1989 (Thompson 1989).

Okami (1992) notes that the criminalization of childhood sexual behavior has resulted in a new category of criminal deviant—a 'child perpetrator' or very young 'sexual offender.' Johnson (1988, 1989) exemplifies this view in her description of a child perpetrators' treatment program at Children's Institute International (the organization that interviewed the children in the McMartin Preschool case). Johnson applies the label of 'child perpetrator' to children as young as four and, in some cases, when the 'perpetrator' is younger than the 'victim.' Others seriously offering this theory include Cantwell (1988), who gives case examples of child perpetrators, including a six-year-old and a seven-year-old, and Hartman and Burgess (1988), who label a four-year-old boy an offender and abuser, when a three-year-old girl's play was interpreted to suggest that the boy had been sexually aggressive towards her at the day-care center. Virtually any sexual behavior by a child can be labelled abusive.

> A woman from Iowa called us in distress. They had sent off several roles of film to be developed. A week later the police came to their home and arrested them. One of the rolls of film had a picture of the genitals of their four-year-old daughter. It turned out their eight-year-old daughter had taken the picture, using their automatic camera without the knowledge of the parents. It took several months but charges of sexual abuse were finally dropped against the parents but they had to respond to a criminal charge of neglect and the eight-year-old daughter was labeled a sexual abuse perpetrator and required to be in treatment.

A Negative View of Adult Sexuality

The antisexuality of the child sexual abuse system is also evident in a critical or even hostile view of adult sexuality. Prosecutors and mental health professionals portray an adult who is accused of child sexual abuse as some sort of perverse monster. Former wives, girlfriends, neighbors, relatives may be quizzed about their knowledge of the accused person's sexual behavior. Any departure from the narrow pattern of straight missionary position with the wife or steady girlfriend is used as evidence to show how deviant the accused is.

Adult sexual behaviors such as fellatio, mutual masturbation, cunnilingus, anal intercourse or unusual positions, massage, use of massage oils, lubricants, dildos, sexual aids, pornography, including *Playboy* and lingerie ads, *ménage à trois* or *à quatre,* adultery, and unusual fantasies may be used to portray an accused person as being sexually deviant and thus a child molester. An interest in fantasies of bondage or fantasies of rape or fantasies of orgies or multiple partners is used to present the accused as a sexual sadist. Even homosexual experiences may be used to prove the person accused is a child sexual molester. The prosecutor in the Kelly Michaels trial in New Jersey spent two entire days belaboring the fact that Ms. Michaels had a single homosexual experience during her freshman year in college. This was used together with the fact that she was a drama major as evidence that she was a molester.

Where Does the Antisexuality Come From?

Okami (1992) notes that the increasing concern with negative aspects of human sexuality is reflected in the *Psychological Abstracts*. In 1969 there were no index categories for *sexual abuse, sex offenses, sexual harassment, rape, incest, sexual sadism* or *pedophilia*—these were all included under the category of *sexual deviations* which listed 65 journal articles. Of the 65, most were concerned with topics such as homosexuality and transvestism rather than sexual crime and incest.

But by 1989, these categories were added and 400 articles were listed that were expressively concerned with sexual aggression, crime, or intergenerational sex, an approximate 20-fold increase (2,000 percent) over listings in these categories for 1965. In terms of the category, *child abuse*, not only has there been a 34-fold increase in the number of articles listed between 1969 and 1989, but in 1989 between 75 and 85 percent were concerned with sexual rather than physical abuse of children, a reversal from 1979 (when 85 percent were concerned with physical rather than sexual abuse). Okami comments that this supports the observation that the term *child abuse* has come to mean *child sexual abuse*.

Money (1991a) sees the antisexuality of the child sexual abuse system as a reaction to the sexual revolution of the 1960s and a response to the fear generated by AIDS. Okami (1992) also believes there is a "covert moral crusade" against the "sex positive" changes occurring in this era. Victor (1993b) also sees a moral crusade as underlying the belief in a satanic cult conspiracy. One symbolic meaning of the satanic cult scare is that sexuality is dangerous and evil and readily perverted by the satanists in their bizarre and sadistic abuse of pure and innocent children.

Okami (1990) adds the component of historical social political feminism and observes, "Thus, it appears that many moral crusaders against pornography and sexual abuse view violence, aggression, degradation, and exploitation to be the logical consequences of sexual freedom or even of intrinsic sexuality (or heterosexuality)" (1992, p. 124). He quotes feminist social critic Ellen Willis who characterizes many feminist writings as demonstrating a clear revulsion against heterosexuality which serves as "the thinnest of covers for disgust with sex itself" (Okami 1992, p. 123).

Darwin (1936) sees the beginning of civilization as associated with child abuse both as reproductive control and creation of life at will. Infanticide and child abuse have instrumental functions and serve to advance the process of evolution. Bakan (1971) believes child abuse is the ultimate expression of agency (self-protection, self-assertion, self-expansion, isolation, and aloneness) and therefore is the fundamental nature of sin. For Bakan, agency requires the repression of thought, feeling, and impulse. Antisexuality flows from both of these views.

Money (1991a) discusses the antisexuality evident in the prevention programs and the sexual terror induced by good touch/bad touch presentations (1991b). The sexual abuse prevention programs which have proliferated throughout the country are based on empowerment theory. The orientation of empowerment theory is political ideology which has at its core antisexuality (Krivacska 1991). This antisexuality may be seen in the language of sexual abuse that has its own peculiar, idiosyncratic usage of terms such as 'hurt,' 'touch,' 'feel funny,' 'body parts,' 'yucky,' and 'uncomfortable.' The system does not use direct language about sexuality but instead uses circumlocutions such as 'parts covered by a bathing suit.' This communicates to children that sex is viewed negatively and cannot be talked about freely and openly. When a young child is questioned repeatedly about deviant sexuality, that child has been taught a negative view of sexuality. This focus on parts of our body and genitals teaches a genitalized and partial view of sex that will hinder the development of concepts of intimacy and sexuality (Krivacska 1990; 1992; 1993; Nelson 1978).

Power and Sex

The concept of power is at the root of the antisexuality of the sexual abuse system. Sexual abuse is defined as "any form of coerced sexual interaction between an individual and a person in a position of power over that individual" (Dolan 1991, p.1). Logg (1990) reports that therapists distinguish between children's exploratory sexual play and sexual abuse by children primarily on the dimension of power. It is the disparity in power that is believed to be the cause of the harm that is done to children by sexual abuse (Bass and Davis 1988; Solomon 1992). It is because older and bigger people are more powerful than smaller and younger people that any sexual contact is judged always harmful.

The concept of the power disparity first emerged in the feminist literature regarding sexuality between men and women. Andrea Dworkin maintains sex between men and women is always rape. In intercourse the woman is always "a space invaded" and occupied even if there is no resistance. Susan Estrich, Harvard Law School professor, claims that when a woman says 'yes,' it is not true consent, because everything is rape until proven otherwise (Hughes 1993).

Herman (1981) puts it this way: "Any sexual relationship between the two (an adult and a child or an adolescent) must necessarily take on some of the coercive characteristics of rape" (p. 27). Brownmiller (1975), early on in the development of feminism, asserted that when there is an actual rape, the rapist rapes for all men. She asserts that rape is "nothing more or less than a conscious process of intimidation by which *all men* keep *all women* in a state of fear" (p. 15).

Because such aggressive power is so terrible, when the individual understands how it harmed the victim, the best and most desired response is anger and rage (Dolan 1991; Bass and Davis 1988). In the records of therapy sessions with 405 young children we found in almost every case some effort to teach the child to be angry at the perpetrator (Wakefield and Underwager 1988). This has included weekly sessions practicing assassinating father with toy pistols, throwing a father doll in a cardboard box labelled jail, role playing hitting and kicking the perpetrator, and sending angry and accusing letters to the alleged perpetrator. The Freudian assumption of a positive value in catharsis, expression of emotion, means that therapists who accept it encourage the ventilation of feelings when, in fact, this is harmful and negative (Campbell 1992; 1994; Smith 1992; Weisz and Weiss 1993).

Even if the abusive behavior is gentle, tender fondling by an older and bigger person within a context of a caring and loving interaction and is experienced by a younger and smaller person as pleasant genital stimulation, it is defined as abusive, traumatic, and a stressor experience that may lead to dissociation, numbing, hopelessness, and all the possible negative effects of sexual abuse. Even if an event of sexual contact is a single nonintrusive and nonviolent occurrence, if it is between a child and an adult, it is defined as abusive, destructive, and likely to generate long-term damage. There is an assumed dichotomy between the child who is powerless, asexual, and innocent and the adult who is powerful, sexual, experienced in lust, and therefore reprehensible.

The frequent use of the circumlocution of 'hurt' when adults question children about possible sexual abuse demonstrates the assumption that the power imbalance is harmful. When an adult asks a child if Daddy 'hurt' her and both the adult and the child understand that what is being asked is a question about sexual contact, the child has already learned the language game of antisexuality. The message is that sex and violence are inseparable. In and of itself 'hurt' does not imply sexual contact and most child sexual abuse does not physically hurt. When it is understood that sexual contact is included, the power imbalance has been broadened to be the cause of the 'hurt.'

Sex Is Genitalized

The genitalization of human sexuality in the child sexual abuse system is evident in the circumlocutions for genitals: 'private parts,' 'parts covered by your bathing suit,' 'parts that nobody else should touch,' 'parts that make you feel uncomfortable when they are touched.' The body is viewed as a fortress that must be defended against all incursions from the outside. Anybody who tries to penetrate the body's boundaries is dangerous. Here, too, the connection with aggression and violence becomes evident in the names elicited from children for genitals. The words used for penis tend to be tool names and poking, penetrating words are used for intercourse. Younger children tend to use more direct expressions while older children use somewhat more indirect expressions (Sutton-Smith and Abrams 1978).

The consequences of genitalizing human sexuality are often overlooked. It is a return to dualism and the idea of the body as bad, evil, wicked, and a prison for the soul. This dualism is linked to the oft-reviled perception of sex as evil and wicked. When the body is alienated from the self and viewed as a thing, an object, the consequence is the objectification both of sex and the sexual actions, as well as any sexual partners. Tertullian, in a reference to female genitalia, called women the "gate to hell." Augustine saw every act of sex as an act of lust because of what he understood as concupiscence. The genitals were no longer under voluntary control but rather drove the person.

It is the genitalization of sex that leads to the various forms of performance anxiety. In turn, almost all sexual dysfunctions can be traced to performance anxiety. The genitalization of human sexuality by the child sexual abuse system can only result in an increase in sexual dysfunction in the years to come (Masters and Johnson 1970a; 1970b; Nelson 1978).

Another consequence of the genitalization of human sexuality is that men once again are driven back to seeing themselves as tough, hard, cold, unemotional, and aggressive. After 20 years of trying to persuade men that they can be soft and gentle, that they can have feelings and cry, that they can be tender and intimate, now when they believe it and love and affectionately touch children, they may go to prison.

All over this country men have told us they are afraid of children. They see an attractive, cute child in the supermarket and they don't go down that aisle. They don't make reinforcing comments to children in elevators. They worry about coming home and kissing their children. They cannot watch their child nursing or bathe their children for fear of being misunderstood. They cannot go into hot tubs or showers with their children. Teachers who were taught that children need to be touched and that they need to know their teacher cares for them get accused of sexual abuse, lose their jobs and careers, and may go to prison. Crichton has the main character in his recent novel, *Disclosure* (1994), advise men never to approach an unknown child or lift up a little girl but to be extremely cautious with children. Even in a marriage, it is good to be careful with your own children because, if a marriage collapses, a wife can destroy a man completely with a charge of sexual abuse.

Children who have been taught to see themselves as distinct from their bodies and to abhor any sexual pleasure as 'hurt' cannot experience the wholeness and unity of their own selfhood nor that created by the union of persons who abjure power and embrace mutuality. The mingling of violence and sex is dangerous as is shown in Kincaid (1992):

> Take the following two scenes enacted in a shopping mall, say, or on the street or in the park: in the first an adult is striking a screaming child repeatedly on the buttocks; in the second an adult is sitting with a child on a bench and they are hugging. Which scene is more common? Which makes us uneasy? Which do we judge to be normal? Which is more likely to run afoul of the law? A society, I believe, which honors hitting and suspects

hugging is immoral; one which sees hitting as health and hugging as illness is mad; one which is aroused by hitting alone is psychotic and should be locked up. (p. 362)

The Scientific Data on the Effects of Sexual Abuse

Linking sex, aggression, and anger is not a minor event. It has major and long-lasting impact upon individuals and the society. But this linkage is also a necessary prior condition for the concept of repressed or dissociated memories. The assumption that someone who has had no memories of sexual abuse can suddenly recover memories in adult life requires that the sexual acts be viewed as traumatic—so traumatic that the person 'represses' the abuse, or 'dissociates' during the abuse, or develops 'traumatic amnesia' for the abuse. Fredrickson (1992) typifies this stance: "Dissociation always occurs during abuse, because abuse is always traumatic (p. 59). . . . The damage from the abuse is so profound that your life and physical well-being are in grave danger" (pp. 25–26).

The event must be horrible, repulsive, intrusive, or violent to trigger these internal processes, whatever they may be said to be, into action so that there is no conscious awareness of the sexual event. The abuse cannot be simply unpleasant or discomfiting. Otherwise, all manner of difficult, embarrassing, and distressing events that are part of everyone's childhood would be banished from consciousness. Only pleasant events would be remembered, and learning from experience would become impossible. According to the theory of recovered memories, the banishment from consciousness is not simply forgetting, which is a passive and ordinary process. It is instead an active, robust process which protects the person by removing the memories of terrible and unbearable trauma from conscious awareness.

Evidence that sexual abuse may be something other than traumatic will falsify the major premise of the theoretical scheme for recovered memories. If being abused can be an experience other than traumatic, there is no need to set in motion whatever active, internal process is offered to account for the lack of memory. If sexual abuse is only unpleasant, simple forgetting may explain things. Hence, no memories have been actively buried, hidden, or removed from conscious awareness. If there is no trauma, then the claim that some sort of special trauma memory process is switched on cannot be invoked.

The literature on the effects of sexual abuse falsifies these assumptions. There are numerous reports indicating that many people perceive their childhood sexual experiences with adults as neutral and even that some people report that they were positive.[1] The proportions of the samples reporting a perception of abuse experiences as positive ranges from about one-quarter to more than two-thirds.

The most recent review article on the effects of sexual abuse reports a consistent finding that a substantial proportion of abuse victims show no symptoms. This can be interpreted to mean that the experience was more neutral (Kendall-Tackett et al. 1993). These findings constitute powerful scientific replication and it must be understood that significant proportions of persons actually abused later report their subjective experience to be neutral or positive rather than traumatic. These data disprove the radical feminist concepts of sex as aggression and of the power imbalance meaning that all sexual acts are traumatic. The linkage of sex and aggression can no longer be advanced as an explanatory theory.

Why Sexual Abuse Is Harmful

Even though the data seem to suggest otherwise, we maintain that sexual abuse is always harmful, though it may not be recognized as such by the individual and though there may be no obvious psychological effects. To say that it is always harmful

---

[1] Bernard 1981; Bunge 1993; Celano 1992; Coulborn-Faller 1991; Daugherty 1986; Kilpatrick 1992; Li 1993; Metcalfe et al. 1990; Nelson 1982; Okami 1989, 1990; Powell and Chalkley 1981; Rush 1980; Sandfort 1982; 1987; 1993; Tsai 1979; Vander Mey 1988; Yorokuglu and Kemph 1966.

is not the same thing as saying that it is necessarily traumatic. But we do not believe sexual contact between an adult and a child can be acceptable or positive. We wrote in our 1988 book, *Accusations of Child Sexual Abuse:* "We do not agree that the effects of childhood sexual experiences with older partners are ever likely to be positive, as is sometimes claimed. Rather, the effects are apt to range from neutral to seriously damaging" (p. 352). We have regularly dealt with sexual abuse and have never approved a sexual offender's behaviors or said that sexual contact between an adult and a child can be beneficial.

We have advanced a theory to explain why sexual contact between adults and children can never be positive. We believe that all of human life is aimed at intimacy, closeness, and love, and that sex is within that larger whole. Sex can serve the expression of intimacy, wholeness, and unity (Wakefield and Underwager 1979; Wakefield 1984; Underwager 1984). Intimacy between persons is not created by taking your clothes off or feeling vulnerable or taking trust falls in sensitivity training groups. Rather, intimacy is behaving closely and co-operatively with another to reach a shared goal. We feel intimate and close when we play a duet, write a book together, finish a game or sport competition, get through an obstacle course, or fight a war. Intimacy is learned behavior and we can all learn how to be intimate with another.

Intimacy may be missing in our lives but, if so, it has nothing to do with being lovable or beautiful or having a good or poor self-image. Having an alcoholic father, or a crazy mother, or a smarter, prettier sister, or being teased at school does not incapacitate us for intimacy. We do not need years of therapy to learn to share intimacy. Just look at people who are acting together and feeling intimate. See what they do. They co-operate, expend effort, and finish the behavior, whatever it is. This is the reason for co-workers so frequently falling in love. But intimacy is not a sexual experience as any prostitute or John can tell you. It is the experience of being in emotional, psychological, and behavioral contact with another person.

But sex is also the first way that people try to avoid the possible unity, intimacy, and wholeness. They do this by limiting sexuality to genitals and genital sensations. One of the first learning experiences humans have is the discovery that genital stimulation is pleasant. When we do not learn anything beyond that, we have a limited grasp of our sexuality that inevitably produces sexual problems and dysfunctions. Also, when the focus is on genitals, children may experience abuse as relatively pleasant. This is what makes it possible to later report that the experience was positive, especially when the child cares about the adult. From our theoretical position, this is predicted but is an error because the focus on genitals misses the wholeness and is only a partial experience. Each and every time a person experiences only the partial and incomplete genitalized sexuality is a learning experience. Each time the focus on genitals alone is reinforced and rewarded. Each time makes it less likely the person can learn to relate to another person in love, wholeness, and unity.

Sex between a child and an adult is always a penultimate, partial experience of genitalization and can never be an experience of wholeness. We can accommodate the fact that some individuals judge their childhood sexual experiences with adults to have been positive, since the genital stimulation may have been pleasant, but still maintain that adult-child sexual contact is never beneficial. When sexuality is genitalized, the consequences are negative. Genitalization of sex is the basic cause of all nonorganic sexual dysfunction, as Masters and Johnson (1970a; 1970b) have demonstrated. Bakan (1966), possibly the only original American personality theorist, maintains that sex as sex alone is an expression of the agentic will of people, not the communion nor unity that is possible. The aim of agency is the reduction of tension whereas the aim of communion is union.

Unity, wholeness, and the full intimacy of love that includes the expression of human sexuality requires an equality across all facets of humanity. This includes all intellectual, abstract, cognitive, emotional, moral, and spiritual capacities. Achievements and abilities to symbolize and manipulate the world and navigate one's way through life must be at comparable levels. The greater the discrepancy in maturity and equality, the greater the emphasis will be on sex as sex alone if it is brought into the relationship. If one party can only talk about imaginary tea parties and the other can discourse on the metaphysics of particle physics, any sexuality between them must be genitalized, agentic, and only penultimate. When the learning experience of genitalized sexuality leads to the development of this limited and partial comprehension, the impact upon the capacity for wholeness, unity, and love is limiting and negative. For this reason, we maintain that sexual contact between an adult and a child is always harmful in its impact on both parties.

The History of Recovered Memory Claims

The current system for dealing with child sexual abuse began in 1974 when President Nixon signed the Child Abuse Prevention and Treatment Act (CAPTA). Senator Mondale had begun hearings on such legislation in 1973 (Nelson 1984). Federal money was first available in 1976 for the establishment of county child abuse teams.

Claims of adults recovering memories of repressed childhood abuse in the course of therapy did not occur at the beginning of this process. The first books and professional literature about child sexual abuse do not mention repression or the phenomenon of recovered memories. Meiselman, in her landmark study of incest (1978), describes her sample of 58 incest cases collected across three years. Forty-seven of the cases reported range from one to 40 years after the incest, with an average of 15 years. She thinks it is probably the largest 'years after' sample in the literature. She also refers to four other studies that include an indeterminate number of 'years after' cases. There is no mention of any case of repressed recovered memories. Later, Meiselman (1990) speaks of theoretical effects of sexual abuse based on clinical observations that need to be carefully established by empirical research and includes the possibility of repression but it is not presented as anything more than a hypothesis.

Herman describes how she began her professional involvement in cases of incest in 1975. As a new psychiatrist, she began a five-year program of clinical observation that resulted in the 1981 book. She describes her review of all the literature available, a clinical sample of 40 incest victims and 20 women whose fathers were seductive but not overtly incestuous, and visiting 10 centers for victims of sexual assault around the nation. In a lengthy chapter on disclosure of incest, which includes an awareness that victims may not tell immediately and a description of keeping a secret, there is not a single mention of repression, dissociation, or recovered memories.

Finkelhor (1986) offers a model for the impact and effects of child sexual abuse. It is a model of four factors often referred to today. The four factors in the dynamics of child sexual abuse are traumatic sexualization, stigmatization, betrayal, and powerlessness. The psychological impact of each factor is carefully described. There is no mention of repression, dissociation, amnesia, or any special kind of traumatic memories. Neither is there any mention of repression or recovered memories in his earlier book (Finkelhor 1984) which purports to be a description of all the new theory and research in child sexual abuse.

It is not that the concept of repression and dissociation as suggested consequences of child sexual abuse was unknown. Fairbairn (1943), an English psychoanalytic theorist, wrote about his understanding of the impact of sexual abuse on children. He maintained that children who are sexually abused dissociate bad aspects of both the object or perpetrator and the self and then repress the awareness of these now split-off aspects of the self. Miller (1981, 1983, 1984) expands on Fairbairn's concepts even though later she abandoned psychoanalysis altogether and stressed that analysts hear what they want to hear, focus on intrapsychic fantasies and patterns, and ignore any disconfirming information.

It was not until 1985, in a widely circulated unpublished manuscript (later published in 1987), that Herman and Schatzow claimed that from a sample of 53 adult women reporting to have been abused as children, 14 had severe memory deficits. The women were put in this category if they could recall very little from childhood, or if they reported recent eruption into consciousness of memories that had been entirely repressed, or if this kind of recall occurred during the course of group treatment. No breakdown of the 14 in terms of this three-part definition is given. It could be that all but one had some memory of the abuse.

All the women studied were in both concurrent individual therapy with someone and in group therapy with Herman and Schatzow. The average age of the 14 severe memory deficit women at the time they claimed the abuse began was 4.9 years with a standard deviation of 2.4 years. This means that half, or seven of the 14, were in the age period of birth to 4 or 5 where the fact of infant amnesia (see Chapter 6 for a discussion of infant amnesia) meant they would likely have no independent memories. Of the remaining seven, there is no indication as to whether one or more had no recall, or whether one or more had some suggestive influence either in the individual therapy or the group therapy. Certainly the research evidence on group therapy shows a high probability of group pressure causing conformity in the members.

If a group of people spend twelve weeks with a majority of the group talking about memories of abuse they have always had, those few in the group with no memories will be under great pressure to produce them, especially since those without memories "strongly suspected" they had been abused. Herman and Schatzow (1987) state, in all seriousness, that the group was a "powerful stimulus for recovery of previously repressed traumatic memories" (p. 1).

In her 1992 book Herman describes the groups she ran with Schatzow for this sample:

> The cohesion that develops in a trauma-focused group enables participants to embark upon the tasks of remembrance and mourning. The group provides a powerful stimulus for the recovery of traumatic memories. As each group member reconstructs her own narrative, the details of her story almost inevitably evoke new recollections in each of the listeners. In the incest survivor groups, virtually every member who defined a goal of

recovering memories has been able to do so. Women who feel stymied by amnesia are encouraged to tell as much of their story as they do remember. Invariably the group offers a fresh emotional perspective that provides a bridge to new memories. In fact, the new memories often come too fast. At times it is necessary to slow the process down in order to keep it within the limits of the individuals and the group's tolerance. (1992, p. 224)

Anyone familiar or experienced with groups immediately recognizes this as a description of a powerful, coercive group experience intended to enforce conformity to group norms. If the group norm includes having memories of childhood sexual abuse, group members who do not have such memories will produce them. It is the price paid for full membership in the group.

Furthermore, there are at least two earlier published reports, before 1985, by Herman, based on similar samples of women incest victims in her group therapy program. All were identified as incest victims who were in individual therapy for the incest. While the women in these earlier reports were said to repress memories, and recover them in therapy, there was no mention of people with severe memory deficits in those earlier articles. Why not?

The 1985 report was not published in a professional journal until 1987. In the meantime it was circulated in the feminist network and was cited by Russell (1986) as proof of "massive repression," so that she claims her study findings underrepresent actual incest.

Further, Herman and Schatzow nowhere describe what kind of records or documentation they kept on the group in order to produce the numbers they claim. How many years after the groups ended did they develop the material on memory? Did they audiotape the groups? Did they write notes on each group member after each session? Did they produce their own recollections of what individuals said weeks or months after the groups were over? What kind of data did the raters have to produce ratings of the level of memory?

These are very thin data upon which to base a claim that

"massive repression" occurs. There are so many questions, and so many potential sources of error, and so much over-interpretation of minimal data that this report is worthless for anything other than the most careful, cautious, and qualified hypothesis which must be checked out by more rigorous methods. Yet it is what is referred to as the first indication of anybody finding recovered repressed memories of childhood sexual abuse.

This temporal sequence of Herman's reports suggests that the need to account for women who joined incest survivor groups, even though they had no memory of abuse, and then, under the impact of powerful group influence, developed uncorroborated and probably fabricated memories, led to the extension of repression to these women also. In order to claim that the memories were true, some way of explaining the absence of such memories for years past had to be conjured up.

In a similar amazing feat of intellectual legerdemain Herman (1992) now cites Russell (1986) and her claim of under-reporting because of repressed memories based on Herman's 1985 unpublished paper as proof of Herman's belief in repressed memories. This is ping-ponging your way to a tautological reality that has no connection to the real world (see Chapter 8 for further discussion of the Herman and Schatzow report).

Bootstrapping up to Blarney

By the mid to late 1980s we have a child sexual abuse system established, which began with radical feminist concerns, drew from radical feminist perceptions and practices regarding adult rape victims, attracted support and funding from the federal government by manipulating the image of the abused child, and structured a powerful legal capacity for control and sanctions. It has a widespread and entrenched bureaucracy in every state and county in the country with few real limits on funding since County commissioners are unlikely either to cut or control the costs of child welfare and child protective services. To do that would be to doom any political ambitions. There are allied networks of women's shelters, rape victims support groups, victims advocates, and battered women's groups.

Ideologically, for all of these groups, the concepts used are primarily a bastardized Freudianism that angrily rejects anything in Freud judged to be sexist while enthusiastically using the concepts of psychodynamics. The basic assumption of Freudianism is that the past controls the present. One of the fundamental psychodynamic assumptions most important to this system is the erroneous notion that understanding and insight into past events produces cures. Another is the equally erroneous notion that expression of feelings, especially anger, is curative.

Added to this is the unrealistic radical feminist notion that all sexual behavior is characterized by the power discrepancy between men and women. Of course, all relationships between adults and children are also affected by the greater power of adults. Therefore the mistaken notion is that all sexual molestation victims are severely damaged. Therefore the negative effects of sexual abuse are wide-ranging, ubiquitous, and pernicious. Lists of so-called indicators of sexual abuse include almost every symptom or behavior known to mental health professions. On top of this are added the exaggerated and unfounded claims about prevalence and incidence so that it is believed that sexual abuse is a raging epidemic. Now consider the factor Briere (1989) describes:

> Most clinicians who specialize in abuse, however, have clients who they are relatively convinced were sexual abuse survivors, despite their clients' claims to the contrary. (p. 118)

The stage is set. By pulling on its own bootstraps the system has climbed up to the Blarney Stone.

Suddenly, all around the country, professionals dealing with sex abuse see the next step, recovery of repressed memories of childhood sexual abuse! Data from 267 surveys of families where such accusations emerged show that while a few accusations emerged prior to 1988, there was a sudden spurt in 1989 (15 percent) and growing numbers since then with over half of those reporting the beginning of the accusation in 1990 (25 percent) and 1991 (28 percent) (*FMS Foundation Newsletter*, March 1994).

Conclusions

This is how it works. If a person has vague complaints about anything, or real emotional problems, it may be caused by sexual abuse. The antisexuality and the abandonment of personal responsibility and reason have opened the door to interpret anything with any superficially valid idea. Gaining insight and understanding and then explaining the current malaise, whatever it is, with past events is curative and healing. If you don't recall having been abused, it may be because you have repressed it. But repressed memories of abuse can be recovered. The cure is to create recovered memories of childhood abuse and become enraged at the abuser.

By conferences, newsletters, incest survivors' networks, and literature, the final step of recovering repressed memories of childhood abuse is added to the system and the story spreads like wildfire. There is no exercise of critical acumen to challenge any of these notions. Rather, in the manner pioneered long ago by Freud himself, the mantle of science is wrapped around a pile of nonsense by the simple expedient of declaring it to be science and repeating it over and over. Before anybody fully realizes it, thousands upon thousands of American families are destroyed by bogus claims of recovered memories of childhood sexual abuse. Billions of dollars are expended. The confidence of the citizenry in our justice system is shaken, if not shattered. The paranoid style of thought takes over the system and the life and vitality of our civilization is endangered. The Furies have indeed returned. They're here.

Chapter Three
Who Gets Hurt?

Honor thy father and thy mother that thy days may be long upon the land which the Lord thy God giveth thee.
Exodus 20:12

I get so depressed. I have lost over 30 pounds, my hair has turned quite gray, I have developed high blood pressure for the first time in my life, I can't sleep, I am up pacing much of every night. I have no appetite. I have almost become a hermit because I find it hard to be with people recently. Even though everyone in my family thinks my daughter needs serious help we are still caught in this nightmare which is compounded by a lawsuit. It is as though her therapist has turned what, at one time, not too long ago, was love, into hate. In a letter she wrote, "If Dad died, I wouldn't even go to his funeral, except to spit on his ugly, old, wrinkled corpse." It is hard to live with statements like that, when they come from someone that you have raised, nurtured, did everything that you could for. Sometimes I get up in the morning and wonder why I should even bother. What can be good in the day ahead that can over-ride the hell that I am going through in my mind during every conscious moment? (*FMS Foundation Newsletter*, December 1993)

Accused parents are devastated when their adult child confronts them with recently recovered 'memories' of abuse. They are embarrassed and distraught and, especially at first, find it impossible to tell even very close friends about what has happened. How can they explain this to anyone? They push for specifics about what it was they are supposed to have done, but often nothing is forthcoming. When fathers are accused, mothers are pressured to believe the story and support the accuser, which puts the mother in an intolerable position. Siblings are forced to take sides and families are split apart.

The closest parallel is having a child die. Many parents say that their child's death would be far easier to handle. When a child has died, there is closure. The life is ended. When a child accuses a parent of abuse and then cuts off all contact, the parent knows the child they love is alive, but cannot know anything else. There is no end to the questioning about how the child is doing. There is no end to the wondering about what is happening. There is no end to the pain of rejection because every day that goes by without a call or letter is a day of new rejection. Each day begins with the hope, "Maybe I'll hear something today" and ends with the conclusion, "My child still hates me!"

Sometimes, accused fathers or mothers wonder if they themselves could have 'repressed' their own memories of abusing their child—that even though they have no memories, perhaps they did something. Eventually they realize this is impossible—if they had done such terrible things, they certainly would remember. They are left puzzling over how their child could have developed such untrue memories. When the accusing adult child is successful and outwardly adjusted and the parents recall a close and happy family, their bewilderment is all the more profound.

Parents who have been most concerned about their children's life and happiness are very likely to feel guilty. They at least partly believe the new American dogma that if the children have trouble, it's the parent's fault. They know they didn't abuse their child, but they still believe the accusation is caused by some failure on their part. So they ransack their memories for anything they could have done that might explain what is happening. They may come up with innocuous events that could be misinterpreted and so they feel more guilt and self-doubt.

Goldstein and Farmer (1993), who have spoken to hundreds of people involved in these situations, describe the impact on the entire family:

> When a parent is accused of child abuse, his or her life is changed forever. No matter how he or she has lived life—with dignity, honesty, and esteem—it is all gone in a flash. Family members are pitted against one another and forced to take sides. The seeds of suspicion are sown; divorce sometimes occurs; grandparents are forced to choose one side or the other; siblings, as we have seen, are distraught. Aunts, uncles, cousins, friends are often brought into the fray. When they believe the accuser and don't believe the accused, the hurt is multiplied for the parent. (p. 483)

Until recently, accused parents felt completely isolated. They had never heard of this happening to anyone else. We received several phone calls from people who had read our books or heard about us. They were looking desperately for any kind of guidance. At the American Psychological Association meeting in San Francisco, 1991, a psychologist contacted us, told us of accusations by her daughter of childhood sexual abuse, and asked for any assistance we could give. With permission, we gave her Pamela Freyd's name and suggested she contact Dr. Freyd. She did, and then, in the fall of 1991, several parents whose adult children had accused them of childhood sexual abuse based on recently recovered memories, and professionals who had had experience with these allegations, began contacting one another. For the accused parents, it was wonderfully helpful to realize, finally, that they were not alone.

In January 1992, we agreed to assist these parents in

organizing. We worked together to develop the initial questionnaire and got an 800 number. We began to answer the phone and parents around the country began to get the number out. We talked to callers, sent out the questionnaire, and gave the names to Dr. Freyd. In February, 1992, Dr. Freyd, along with several other parents and professionals, formed the False Memory Syndrome (FMS) Foundation,[1] organized as a tax-exempt research and educational institution. The FMS Foundation acquired an office and on May 1st took over the 800 number and began to send out the questionnaires.

Early in 1992, local newspaper columnists in Philadelphia, San Diego, Toronto, and Provo, Utah, described the phenomenon and the formation of the FMS Foundation, and published the 800 number. In its first six months of existence, the Foundation received calls from approximately 600 families and by spring 1994 had heard from over 12,000 afflicted families, representing every state in the union as well as several foreign countries. In the three days following the single article in the Provo weekly paper, over 150 families in that single geographical area called to report their experience. The FMS Foundation receives dozens of telephone calls each day and hundreds of letters each week.

The goal of the FMSF, which has a professional advisory board with well-known scientists from throughout the country, is to understand and work towards the prevention of these cases. Its focus is on collecting and disseminating relevant scientific information and on promoting and sponsoring research. It held a scientific conference in April 1993.

Without exception, the parents who contact the Foundation tell stories of pain, shock, and distress. The following are excerpts from some of these letters (*FMS Foundation Newsletter*, 1992–94):

- Our daughter confronted her father in November 1991, the day after Thanksgiving. I think it literally broke his heart. He

---

[1] The False Memory Syndrome Foundation is located at 3401 Market Street, Suite 130, Philadelphia, PA 19104 (214-387-1865).

was diagnosed with liver cancer in early December 1992, and died less than a year later. Just one week before he died, she wrote to him saying that her stories may be metaphors for her anger and that she loved him. She is a part of the family circle again, but has never really recanted. It remains a deep sorrow for me to know of the suffering that she and her therapist brought to our family. (February 1994)

• On April 4th our daughter wrote to her father (70 years old) and me (67 years old). She accused her father of molesting her over and over again and abusing her from ages three to eight. She accused her older brother of knowing about the abuse because, she said his room was under the attic where it was supposed to have gone on. There was no attic in that house. I asked her to go with me to that house to see if there was an attic but she refused. On April 30th, my husband of 46 years died of a ruptured aneurysm. I know he died of a broken heart. (June 1993)

• The meeting with my daughter and the therapist was the most devastating and numbing experience I remember ever having experienced. My daughter was supported by the therapist in a very emotional and angry tirade directed at me. The therapist insisted that I had had an abused childhood, that I was either deliberately or unwittingly withholding painful episodes of abuse involving myself, relatives or family friends. The more the therapist made these statements, suggesting things that I was 'denying,' the angrier and more unreasonable became my daughter's tirade. It broke my heart to sit and watch and hear my daughter, whom I love with all of my being, hurting so very deeply. And I was unable to hug her or say anything, except to very feebly express my total bewilderment. The therapist in my presence, as though I were not there, pointed out to my daughter that not only was I a person who needed to control everything and everyone, I was also a 'great denier.' (May 1993)

• (Message left on the FMS Foundation answering machine) I confronted my mother. She told me that she had nothing more to live for, and she drove her car off a bridge. She is dead. Now I'm not sure about the memories. (July 1993)

Data From The Recovered Memory Survey Project

The False Memory Syndrome Foundation is engaged in an ongoing research project in which questionnaires are sent to people whose adult children have accused them of childhood sexual abuse based on their recently recovered memories (Freyd et al. 1993). The first 26-page questionnaires were sent in February 1992 and are continuing to be sent. This analysis is based on the first 493 questionnaires. A total of 282 were returned at the time of this analysis; this is a return rate of 57 percent.

The subjects were people who responded to newspaper articles or other media presentations about this phenomenon. The newspaper articles contained an 800 number to call for information. Questionnaires were sent to the callers who reported that their adult child had recently recovered a memory of repressed sexual abuse which the caller denied. These respondents therefore are not a random sample and there has been no effort to make an independent determination as to the truthfulness of the denial. In addition, the information comes from the accused parents and not the accusing child. Therefore the issue of the generalizability of the data must be borne in mind. These, however, are the first data available regarding families, parents, and adult children where there are allegations of recovered repressed memories of sexual abuse. In a new research area, this is the way to begin—with as much descriptive data as possible.

The questionnaires gathered a wide range of information, including family socio-economic status, educational level of the family and adult child, psychiatric history, personality characteristics of the adult child now and as a child (as reported by the parents), current stresses or problems in the life of the adult child predating the allegations, presence or absence of civil lawsuits, nature of the abuse allegations, the number of people accused, the age of the child when the alleged abuse began, the progression of the allegations across time, the nature of the disclosure, the years the memory was repressed, whether the allegations arose in therapy, and the nature of the therapy provided, the effects of the allegations on the families, and so forth. There have been refinements of the questionnaires between mailings but the basic information requested has remained the same.

Although we had anticipated that most of the families would be dysfunctional and that the adult child reporting a repressed memory of childhood sexual abuse would have a history of significant psychological disturbance, the questionnaire results do not support this hypothesis. Instead, the data suggest that these are functional, intact, successful and affluent families. The parents are well educated—three-fourths of the fathers and almost two-thirds of the mothers have gone to college and 30 percent of the fathers and 17 percent of the mothers have a graduate degree. The annual median family income is $60,000 to $69,000.

Three-fourths of the parents are still married and three-fourths report being active in their church or synagogue. The majority report routinely eating dinner together as a family, going on family vacations, and being actively involved with their children when the child was growing up. It appears these families did what you are supposed to do to have a good family.

The accusing adult children, 92 percent of whom are females, are also highly educated—only 23 percent have only a high school degree. Almost one-third (31 percent) have a graduate degree and the rest have a B.A. or some college. Almost half were married. Although we had believed the accusing child would have a long history of serious psychological problems, in only 29 percent of the cases did the individual have psychological or psychiatric treatment prior to adulthood.

In almost two-thirds of the cases, only the father was accused. In almost one-third of the families, mothers were accused, most often along with the father, but occasionally alone. In one-third, a variety of other persons were accused, most often along with the parents. The abuse typically was alleged to have started at a very young age and the years the memory was 'repressed' ranged from eight to 51 with a median of 25 years.

The parents often had great difficulty getting specific information as to exactly what it was that they were supposed to have done. When they asked for clarification they were told things such as, 'You know!' 'You are an abuser,' or 'You incested me.' The allegations that were specified were often of extremely deviant and intrusive behaviors, including violence, forced anal or vaginal penetration, or satanic ritual abuse (see Chapter 10 for a more complete discussion of the abusive behaviors of which parents are accused).

The parents seldom had any warning that anything was wrong prior to the accusation. Most were told suddenly by a phone call or letter, or by an announcement at a family reunion or holiday, when they reacted to the accusation with surprise and shock. All report being completely devastated. Two-thirds now not only have no contact with their children, but also have no contact with their grandchildren. For many of the parents, civil lawsuits are a serious concern.

Siblings were put in the middle of the conflict but only a minority (18 percent) believed the allegations. Many (40 percent) are no longer in contact with their accusing brother or sister.

The feature common to the sample appears to be the therapy received by the adult children. Although many of the parents know little about the therapist or type of therapy, those who do report similar information. The memories were recovered in therapy in almost all of the cases. The book, *The Courage to Heal* (Bass and Davis 1988), was frequently used along with other survivor or self-help books. Hypnotherapy, dream interpretation, and rape counselling were reported along with incest survivor groups, eating disorder groups, and 12-step programs such as Adult Children of Alcoholics. The therapists, 70 percent of whom are females, included social workers (17 percent), psychologists (25 percent), psychiatrists (9 percent), and "counselors" (25 percent).

Who Else Is Hurt?

There are thousands of accounts similar to those in this chapter. We and other professionals have talked to countless people and the FMS Foundation receives dozens of letters and telephone calls every day. Since the formation of the FMSF, newspapers and magazines throughout the country have featured articles describing cases of allegations of recovered memories and the effects on the accused parents and families.

Other family members besides the parents are hurt. The next chapter talks about the damage done to the accuser. The questionnaire project indicates that although only a minority of the brothers and sisters (18 percent) believe the allegations, the family is often destroyed. The accusers think anyone who does not completely believe them is against them, so skeptical siblings often lose contact with their accusing brothers and sisters. Siblings who take the accuser's side may become alienated from the parents. Sometimes a sibling will visit the accusing child's therapist or read *The Courage to Heal* and also recover memories of abuse.

Goldstein and Farmer (1993) provide examples of the devastation to the entire family in several accounts by brothers and sisters:

- Alice's recovered memories of abuse involve her father and grandfather, both now deceased, and a family friend. She "knows for a fact" that not only she, but all six of her sisters as well as the six children of the family friend, were sexually abused. Her memories go back to the age of three months. . . . We have been living with this for a few years now, but the pain is still so deep. . . . We can now see that our pain is no match for the pain Alice is living with. She is living her life believing that our father viciously and sadistically molested her, our mother did nothing to protect her, and her own sisters are so deep in denial that they abandon her to heal alone. (pp. 13–22)

- My sister's stories would eventually culminate into three-and-a-half years of agony and anger. Amazing stories emerged of satanic ritual sexual abuse which grew to include "all the members of my father's family." Eventually my father had to pay a lawyer $30,000 in order to defend his innocence. . . . I have lost my shadow, a part of my strength. I have re-entered therapy to help me decide just what it is I should do about her. . . . Do I want her back? Not if she continues to reside in her stories. Do I miss her? Enough to stop my breath. . . . I might not ever be able to forgive her, but I know I can't ever forget her. (pp. 23–27)

• Well, I can't say that this 'adventure' has been easy on our family. My parents were devastated at first, and so very hurt. Now they are mad. I'm angry at her too, but also feel somewhat sorry for her because she is such a mess. . . . I no longer have an older sister, at least not the one I knew for 35 years. . . . My sister decided to 'settle' out of court for $15,000. Compared to what it would have cost to go to trial it doesn't seem like a lot of money, but when you are retired, it's a hell of a lot. My parents felt like they bought her off, just to get rid of her. But we will never be free of her, although it is unlikely any of us will ever see her again. You just can't exorcise a family member. We'll always think about her, wonder what she's doing, what she looks like, if she's happy or miserable—sometimes hoping she's miserable after what she's done to us. (pp. 29–32)

• (My dad), my mother, my grandfather and a neighbor have all been accused of the most horrifying thing imaginable, sexual abuse of a child. . . . I remember the dream I had as a child, of my sister helping me put on my wedding dress, getting ready for the big day. My childhood dream has now been shattered. . . . I can't even tell her if someone in our family is sick, because I don't know where she lives, or what her phone number is. She changes her phone number all the time because she is afraid that someone will contact her. . . . My only hope for my sister is that if she ever does come out of this cult she will be able to live with the consequences of what she has caused for the past two-and-a-half years. (pp. 33–45)

• For months, I had tried my best to maintain a neutral position, but that night I was lured into choosing a side. She threatened to take legal action against our father. It was then apparent I had to let my feelings be known. I challenged her allegations, much to her dismay, because I couldn't support them. . . . Because I chose to defend my father, Catherine let me know that I would be considered dead to her. . . . My father was not only accused of beating his daughter but charged with emotional neglect and sexual abuse. My sister's therapist warned the authorities that minors were living in my father's home and therefore he was a threat to his grandchildren. . . . This has driven a stake through the heart of the whole family. (pp. 87–92)

Grandchildren lose contact with grandparents and elderly relatives are brought into the fray. The whole family becomes entangled in the battle. We spoke to one accused mother about a newspaper that was in her house from a small town in another state. She told us it was from her daughter's hometown—she subscribed to it in the hopes of receiving news or perhaps seeing a photograph of her grandchildren whom she had not seen in three years. She said her daughter had refused to give a picture of the children to her mother, the daughter's grandmother. This dignified and gracious woman had been very close to her grand-daughter as the girl was growing up but now was not allowed a picture of her only great-grandchildren. The reason given was that the accuser was afraid her mother might see the picture. The daughter was determined to completely sever all contact between her children and her parents.

A case in the *FMS Foundation Newsletter* demonstrates how an entire family may be profoundly affected by a recovered memory:

> A woman, following an allegation by her older sister, became afraid that her father had also abused her five-year-old daughter. She questioned the child and took her to a child therapist who told the woman that, yes, the child had been abused by her grandfather. Although the child never said anything concrete and later changed her story, the woman was told the abuse was real and retractions are common in abused children.
>
> Now not only was the daughter with the recovered memories alienated from her parents, the younger sister and her family were also and the five-year-old was deprived of her grandparents. In addition, after the allegations concerning the five-year-old, a brother, who had initially disbelieved the older sister's accusations, now believed them and said such hurtful things to the father that they weren't speaking. Prior to these events, this had been a close family who saw each other regularly.
>
> Eventually the woman saw a videotape of the therapy session with her five-year-old daughter and recognized the pressure placed on the child to talk about abuse. Following more research,

she realized that her grandfather had not abused her child and that her sister's recovered memories were false. (*FMS Foundation Newsletter*, April 1993)

In another case in the *FMS Foundation Newsletter* (October 1993), the daughter accused both parents and the paternal grandparents of satanic ritual abuse. The father describes the effect on his 87-year-old father:

> My father is 87 years old. He has health problems. He should be enjoying the company of his adult grand-daughter, having fun with his great-grandson, and looking forward to his 60th wedding anniversary. Instead, he is involved in a horrendous nightmare.
>
> Briefly, our 32-year-old daughter has falsely accused first me, then my wife, then my mother, and now my father of sexual and satanic ritual abuse. She has also filed a civil lawsuit against my wife and me. As difficult as it was to tell my mother of the allegations against her, it was even harder to later tell my father that he too was accused of horrible acts. He was always so loving and giving, both as a parent and a grandparent. I was a perfect son in his eyes. Of course, they made mistakes as parents, and so did we. But abuse—never.
>
> This past summer our attorney requested that I bring my father to his office so that the accusations against him could be discussed. Prior to that visit, I can't think of the last time my father spoke to an attorney. He was understandably anxious about the meeting, and wondering about the questions he would be asked. I spent some time trying to reassure him that our attorney was a very nice man and that the atmosphere would be nonthreatening. I don't think I appeased his qualms very much. More than anything, he wanted to feel that he was doing something to help us. Considering the circumstances, it was pleasant spending this time together with my father, just the two of us.
>
> The meeting went well, as I had hoped it would. My father told his story, and managed to put in a plug about what wonderful parents my wife and I were to our daughter.
>
> Now he has the trial to look forward to, another source of worry for him. This is not how I envisioned him spending his last years. Life is not fair, but this is ridiculous.

In a family we know, allegations against a brother by a sister destroyed an entire family, including the 90-year-old mother and 98-year-old father, both in a nursing home:

> This had been a close family of three daughters and three sons. The father was a clergyman and the mother a nurse, although she did not work after the children were born. The family was not wealthy, but the children respected and loved their parents and they had many good times together. Despite tight finances, all six children were sent to college. As the children grew up, family and friends gathered for holidays and the children's friends have fond memories of playing touch football and board games on crisp fall days. After the children married, there were yearly reunions where the cousins played while the adults talked. The parents eventually retired in a small town and, as the grown children, now in their late fifties and sixties, began retiring, several also moved to the area so the family could stay in close contact with each other. The parents were active until recently, but eventually both entered a nursing home. Their minds remained sharp and the contacts with their grown children, grandchildren, and great-grandchildren provided them with much joy. In many ways, this family exemplified the American dream.
>
> But one of the daughters had long been dissatisfied with her life. She thought that the success her brothers and sisters had achieved had eluded her. She became more unhappy when an older brother retired and moved to their town and bought a nicer house than she had. She began ruminating over vague childhood resentments and decided that her siblings had been favored by her parents. One of her sisters read *The Courage to Heal* and suggested she read it. The theory that a repressed childhood trauma could account for her perceived failures and dissatisfactions made sense to her and she tried to remember what happened. She and her sympathetic sister spent hours talking about it. Finally, she 'remembered' that her older brother had anally raped her in a strawberry patch one late spring day when she was 12 and he was 16.
>
> She confronted her brother, who completely denied the accusation, saying that not only had he never done anything remotely resembling this, but in his rather protected childhood in the 1940s, he had never even *heard* of anal rape. The

distressed and bewildered elderly parents and the two other brothers supported the accused brother, the sister who provided *The Courage to Heal* supported the accusing sister, and the remaining sister attempted not to take sides. The grandchildren, now grown with children of their own, didn't know what to do. The two sisters became angry at the rest of the family and refused to have contact with the parents because they did not believe the accusations.

The mother's 90th birthday celebration was a tense and stressful affair in which the believing sister appeared but the accusing sister did not and no one knew what to say to one another. The father, now aged 98, does not fully understand what has happened to his family. The mother is devastated. She recently wrote a letter to one grandson describing her sorrow over the fact that her accusing daughter's children will not visit her, although they live nearby, and she has not been allowed to see her new great-grandchild. A family has been destroyed and the end of a long, productive life for these two old people has become a tragedy.

In addition to the harm done to individuals and families, the society itself is damaged by false accusations of sexual abuse. In addition to the staggering and frightening economic costs, including costs of criminal justice programs, welfare, victims' assistance, and indirect costs such as higher insurance rates and higher costs for day care, voluntary associations like the Boy Scouts, the YMCA, and other youth-oriented associations may find it difficult, if not impossible, to recruit suitable adults as leaders. Any man who volunteers to go for a weekend retreat with a youth group is risking an accusation of sexual abuse.

What is the cost to the society of having men become frightened of touching children? What is the cost to the society of having more and more people view their political and governmental institutions with fear and a conviction that they are unfair? Tyler (1990) has shown that Americans are far more interested in fairness than in specific outcomes. We obey laws when we believe they are fairly applied and disobey when the perception is that they are not fairly and equitably enforced. When government policies and actions turn out to be as destructive to the family as an institution as are the child abuse laws, at some point, as happened already once in our history, the population will choose the family first and do what needs to be done to keep their family intact.

How Can This Happen?

How can it happen that outwardly normal adults suddenly 'remember' their parents sexually abusing them as children? Even if we assume that therapy played a major part, this doesn't answer the question of why some people are vulnerable to the therapists. It also doesn't explain situations where memories are recovered in the absence of therapy.

There have been a number of explanations for how this can happen. Although some are more plausible than others, they are all only initial attempts to make sense of this extraordinary phenomenon.

Pathological Patients and Dysfunctional Families

Our original hypothesis was that people who recovered false memories were not normal. We believed that they had significant psychological problems, such as borderline, paranoid, or histrionic personality disorders, and probably a long history of serious maladjustment. We expected many might be psychotic. We thought many of the families would be dysfunctional. We argued that normal people don't develop false memories of abuse by their parents, even with a charismatic and persuasive therapist.

We were wrong.

The results from the questionnaire project falsify our original hypothesis. Although some of the accusers and families may fit this theory, the majority do not. The data from the questionnaire project suggest that most of the accusers come from functional, intact, and successful families where the parents were actively involved with their children. Most of the accusers are educated and successful and only a minority had a history of psychological treatment prior to adulthood.

These findings are consistent with a study by Spanos et al.

(1993), who examined whether people claiming alien encounters were psychologically disturbed. They recruited 49 UFO reporters and compared them to two control groups—53 community volunteers and 74 university students—and gave all of them a series of standard psychological tests and questionnaires. Although the UFO subjects had significantly more exotic beliefs than did the control subjects, there was no support for the hypothesis that they were psychologically disturbed. In fact, subjects reporting UFO experiences scored higher on five of the psychological health variables than did the control subjects. What distinguished the UFO reporters from the controls were the prior beliefs and assumptions of the UFO subjects. They believed in UFOs before having the experience.

Spanos, Burgess, and Burgess (in press) also report on a series of hypnotically-induced age regression experiments. Subjects who reported detailed past-life experiences scored no higher on measures of psychopathology than those who did not report a past life.

Anomie

Originally, *anomie* simply meant lawlessness. The word was given a modern meaning by Émile Durkheim, the early French sociologist. He needed a word which would express what he saw as reaction to bewildering economic change. He described a state of society in which there are no common values and no agreed-upon morals which effectively control conduct. In his famous work on suicide he observed that suicide increases when the economy is extremely depressed *and* when it is extremely prosperous. Oscar Wilde remarked that there are two tragedies in life: not getting what we want and getting what we want. Each can produce *anomie*, a normless, rootless, standardless state of society (Marty 1964).

Based on a survey of a national sample of 5,444 people, Strommen et al. (1972) describe the second most powerful factor that emerged from second-order factor analysis as *anomie*. When people grow up learning a set of values and morals that are supposed to produce a good life, their expectation is that if they just keep the rules and follow the prescriptions it should work and they should be happy. So that's the way they do it. They work hard. They achieve at a high level. They do what they are expected to do. Go to college. Get married. Have a family. Get a good job. Then they find out it doesn't work. They're not happy. They're not settled. They keep working hard, maybe even harder, but nothing makes it get better.

A law professor came for therapy because he was depressed, drinking too much, missing his classes, and in danger of losing his tenure. He said he had been a good student, at the top of his class. He edited the law review at a prestigious law school. He was a good litigator and a good teacher. Recently he had gotten a divorce. His wife and children were gone. His Jaguar automobile had broken down and he couldn't get it fixed right. Some investments had gone sour. His expensive stereo system wasn't working. He regarded his students as little twits. He saw teaching as babysitting. Then he screamed, "They lied! They told me if I did it right, I'd be happy! They lied!"

The same feckless stance toward life can come about when everything that is supposed to be satisfying has been obtained and it, too, doesn't work. Happiness is not guaranteed by success, fame, money, achievement, marriage, suburban homes and barbecues in the back yard, cars, romance, children, good food, and great wine. It is all there but the emptiness still echoes through each day.

Anger, rage, disappointment, surge beneath the surface. In desperation, various answers, panaceas, cures, and alternatives are tried. If one clicks, makes sense out of the morass of confusion, and puts the responsibility out there on someone or something else, it can be very attractive. If it also lets the person believe he or she is vindicated and justified in focussing the anger, this becomes an additional incentive for adopting the approach. It permits the expression of vengeance and vitriol.

The second dimension on the factor of *anomie* is prejudice and hostility. Then comes a self-orientation and a privativism so that everything is interpreted in terms of the impact on the self. Reliance upon external structures and authorities is part of the picture also. The person does not have sufficient ego to manage living so there is a need for external support.

The therapist can provide the external structure, authority, and support. The therapist can give the explanation, the answer that makes everything fit into place. The therapist can legitimize the rage. For people who have tried to be everything they have been taught they should be and find that it does not deliver a good life, that can be very rewarding. Claims of recovered memories of childhood sexual abuse can do this

The High-Achieving Therapy Client

This hypothesis was suggested in the August/September issue of the *FMS Foundation Newsletter* and comes out of the questionnaire data. The parents contacting the FMSF ask, 'How could my child who was highly educated and trained to look for evidence fall for this?' The hypothesis is that perhaps it is *because* the people who recover memories were such good students.

The data suggest that the majority of the accusing children were very high achievers. They made good grades and did well in music lessons and extracurricular school activities. They could go into a classroom, figure out quickly what was expected, and then deliver what was needed to earn an A.

When they went into therapy, they continued this pattern and became compliant and good therapy clients. They quickly picked up on the expectations of the therapist so if the therapist believed that sexual abuse is rampant and is the cause of multitudinous problems, these adult therapy clients recovered memories of abuse. "They are the best students the therapist has and so recover not only the most memories but also the most bizarre memories. They are great students."

This theory is supported by some of the anecdotal accounts of the therapy experiences of women who have now retracted their allegations. For example:

I was not the only MPD patient. My therapist had a group of five women participating in this dysfunctional, cult-like treatment. Our therapist was using mind games to control us and convince us he was the only person who could help us. In 'private,' he would drop comments about the other MPD 'girls.' As patients, we became very competitive and jealous of each other.

I was especially jealous of one woman who was very pretty. He had made sexual advances toward one of her sexiest alters, and I was convinced he was infatuated with her. He would play his guitar and sing for her, but never me. He compared the two of us and said we were very much alike. He often confused our names which made me feel hurt. I wanted him to like me in the way he liked her.

I clearly understood the sickest patient received the most attention. So, I devised behavior that would get his attention: act like a five-year-old, come intoxicated to my session, threaten him with a knife, or even attempt suicide. Every one of us in the support group was in some way in love with our psychologist.

I wanted to be the best. I became a model MPD patient and exhibited all the right traits. I learned MPD and let it in, but soon it took control of my mind and body.

The doctor decided I needed five to seven years of therapy. He explained to me and my husband, "Because Lauri now has MPD behavior, it follows that she had MPD. Thus, some terrible abuse in her childhood must have caused it. So terrible that she's repressed those memories deep in her mind. With my help, the alters will reveal the abuse, then she'll remember her own experiences. Finally, she will work through those old feelings and get better."

This was about the time he raised his rates to $120 per hour.

We bought it, and I worked hard to recall repressed memories. Of course, there were no real memories, but the mind is an amazing thing. Let me explain, in lay terms, how repressed memories were created on one occasion. The therapist called up Beth, a five-year-old alter, and hypnotized her. He suggested sexual abuse had occurred at the hands of her daddy. He explained she needed to see a "big movie screen" in her mind and tell him what she saw. Then, he asked leading questions about touching, etc. Beth performed just as the therapist predicted she would. Beth and I were rewarded with much attention and sympathy.

In reality, I didn't have those memories, but the doctor

considered them true and wanted more. For months, I allowed other alters to write anything they could remember. The memories grew worse and worse and I became horrified. I thought it was all true, and I felt worthless and betrayed.

I recalled various fragments of movies, books, talk shows, and nightly news, and soon I had plenty of child abuse memories. But, it didn't stop there. Eventually, I said I had taken part in satanic rituals, been buried alive, drunk blood, and helped to kill a baby. With every new memory my therapist was intrigued and building a case to prove he was right about me all along. I was rewarded with his attention to me and was his 'best' patient. But I started to have feelings of death and became suicidal.

I truly exhibited all of the MPD symptoms even though I had learned them. Control of my mind, emotions, and will was given to the personalities the therapist had empowered. (*FMS Foundation Newsletter*, January 1994)

Adolescent Rebellion

George Ganaway (1993; and see Wylie 1993) hypothesizes that the accusers aren't playing an exaggerated good-child/good-student role in therapy, but are finally getting around to a long-delayed adolescent rebellion against their parents. In this view, the accuser, usually a woman, may never have separated emotionally from her family. Although she deeply desires to break away, she is also guilty about doing so, is afraid of standing alone, and is angry at her parents, whom she unconsciously blames for keeping her tied to them. This conflict, dating to early childhood, has left her with a feeling of hostile dependency on her parents, hostility she can't tolerate, and a love-hate relationship she can't acknowledge.

The woman, despite being a high achiever, lacks self-confidence and displaces her dependency onto the therapist. The therapist becomes the ideal substitute mother figure—all-accepting, all-believing, all-approving—who offers the woman a way to finally separate from her parents.

But to do this, she must develop a new symptom—the belief that her parents committed such terrible crimes that her previously unacceptable anger toward them is now explained and is totally justifiable. She now has an excuse to cut the umbilical cord and make the separation she was unable to do otherwise.

The problem is that not only does this prevent her from working through the transference issues with her therapist, the new symptom is hardly benign if the abuse never happened. The patient is also now enmeshed in a dependent and unhealthy relationship with her supportive therapist.

According to Wylie (1993), the accused parents like this explanation because it makes sense to them and fits with their experiences.

The Folie-à-deux

Richard Gardner (1992a, 1992b) believes that some accusers are angry women who use men as targets for their resentments and hostility. Such women have paranoid traits and have selected the currently in-vogue scapegoat as the target for their paranoid rage. Since the paranoid solution to problems is likely to be greatly oversimplified, the accuser readily accepts that her father's sexual abuse of her is the cause of all her difficulties. Once this is accepted, the accuser is impervious to logic and arguments from her father, mother, siblings, and extended family. Once convinced of the reality of the abuse, she divides family and friends into two categories—those who support her belief and those who don't.

Gardner believes such women carefully select a therapist to help them delve into their past and uncover possible evidence of sexual abuse. Not just any therapist will do; the woman wants one who is an expert in recovering repressed memories. He notes that, although some of these therapists may be pandering to individuals who are involved in the latest fad of psychiatric disorder, currently sexual abuse, many really believe that most of their patients have been sexually abused. They hold similar resentments and anger toward those who mistreated them, especially men. Gardner believes that some of these therapists are overtly paranoid and such paranoid therapists are particularly attractive to adult women suspicious that their fathers may have abused them.

When such therapists begin work with these angry, suspicious women, they may develop a *folie-à-deux* relationship. A *folie-à-deux* is a disorder where a more assertive and aggressive person inculcates her psychopathology into a weaker and more passive person. The bonding between therapist and client becomes unbreakable and attempts by family members to convince the woman that her therapist is making her worse are futile.

As noted by Gardner, although this explanation fits some of the accusers, it cannot be used for all therapists and clients.

Social Consensus and Suggestibility

Another explanation is that people are vulnerable to developing false memories of sexual abuse when they accept the basic assumptions of recovered memory therapy. These assumptions are that up to half of all women have been sexually abused but many can't remember the abuse, that it is possible to completely repress traumatic memories but later recall the traumas, and that repressed abuse is behind many of the emotional difficulties a person may commonly have.

It can be very reinforcing to finally have an explanation for all of one's problems:

> Guided by my therapist—and I believe she meant well—I began to enjoy my status as a victim; she rewarded me with outpourings of sympathy and commiserations as well as an entree into a select group of her patients, all incest survivors. I now had an answer to all my questions about myself. I no longer had to think or struggle. Problems at work? With friends? With me? Well, what could I expect? I had been sexually abused. It was almost like joining a cult, with my therapist as guru and me a faithful disciple, the pitiful casualty of a horrendous crime. (By Elizabeth Godley, reprinted in *FMS Foundation Newsletter*, February 1994)

If the recovered memory beliefs are accepted, an unhappy and distressed person may develop false abuse memories when she encounters a therapist (an authority) who also has these beliefs. This can happen whether or not the client has discernible psychopathology, was a good or poor student, or is a low or high achiever. The possibility increases when the therapist is unaware of the dangers of influencing a vulnerable and suggestible client, places the person in a survivors' group, and uses techniques such as hypnosis and survivors' books.

The importance of the persons's beliefs is supported by the the research of Spanos and his colleagues described above. In the UFO study, Spanos et al. (1993) note that what most clearly discriminates the subjects who reported having a UFO experience from the two control groups was the belief in the existence of UFOs and in the reality of alien life-forms. In fact, many of the UFO subjects reported having these beliefs long before having an UFO experience.

In their age regression studies, Spanos and his colleagues report that following the age regression procedure, the major factor influencing whether subjects believed their experiences were memories of actual, reincarnated personalities rather than imaginary creations was the degree to which the subjects believed in reincarnation before the experiment and the extent to which they expected to experience a real past life. In addition, the content of the past-life identities was strongly influenced by the beliefs and expectations conveyed by the experimenter (Spanos et al. in press; Spanos, Menary et al. 1991).

The specific memories recovered in therapy will reflect the views of the therapist. If the therapist believes in widespread satanic cults, clients are likely to produce memories of satanic cult abuse. Although few therapists believe in reincarnation, these therapists are likely to use age regression techniques and their clients are apt to uncover memories of past lives.

Recovered Memories in the Absence of Therapy

Although therapy with a believing therapist is a common feature in many, if not most cases, false memories of abuse can occur without therapy. In the example given above of the sister accusing her brother, there was no therapy that we know of until after the sister produced her memories. People who accept the central assumptions of recovered memory therapy can be influenced after reading *The Courage to Heal*, watching talk shows that feature survivors, or talking to friends who report sexual abuse, But therapy appears to be the main factor in most cases we have seen and in those that have been reported to the FMS Foundation.

Is There a False Memory Syndrome?

'Syndrome' is defined in Appendix C of the DSM-III-R (American Psychiatric Association 1987) as follows:

> *Syndrome:* A group of symptoms that occur together and that constitute a recognizable condition. 'Syndrome' is less specific than 'disorder' or 'disease.' The term 'disease' generally implies a specific etiology or pathophysiologic process. In DSM-III-R most of the disorders are, in fact, syndromes. (p. 405)

The name 'False Memory Syndrome Foundation' was selected by the parents and professionals who met with each other in Philadelphia and decided to form a nonprofit research and educational organization. The term 'false memory syndrome' (FMS), was chosen after much discussion as to what would best describe the set of behaviors the FMS Foundation was seeing in the families who contacted them. They first considered 'confabulations' but some of the families didn't know what this word meant. They tried to avoid alarming and threatening terms such as 'hysterical' and 'induced delusions.' They eliminated 'pseudo-memories' because of the resulting abbreviation. Their goal was to find a term that would permit those affected to abandon their 'memories' with some grace and face-saving.

'False memory syndrome' is intended to describe the following:

> An adult reports to have been sexually abused in childhood, typically by a parent or relative, and claims to have recovered the memory of this abuse after a period of several years of complete amnesia. These memories did not appear until the person was exposed to a suggestive influence. Most often, the suggestive

influence comes from therapy where the person was told that he or she shows the symptoms of someone who has been abused. Some sort of childhood trauma is seen as the cause for the problem that brought the person into therapy, even when the person denies memories for abuse. Therapy techniques designed to help retrieve these memories are recommended and the patient typically is told that these techniques will uncover historical truth. Many patients are put into survivors' groups. Sometimes, suggestive influences other than therapy, such as reading *The Courage to Heal*, result in the development of abuse memories.

There is no external corroboration for the alleged abuse, the accused denies the allegations, and there is evidence that the abuse did not occur. Examples of evidence that the abuse did not occur comes through such things as reports of other family members who were present during the period of the alleged abuse, the fact that there were no memories until after the person was exposed to the suggestive influences, and/or extremely implausible and improbable 'memories' such as abuse at age three months or participation in ritualistic satanic cults. When the person is removed from the suggestive influences, the belief in the accuracy of the memories may waver.

There have been continuing criticisms by the recovered memory proponents over use of the term 'false memory syndrome' (for instance APS Observer 1993; Barstow 1993; Cote 1993; Harvey 1993; Pezdek 1992). The crux of these criticisms is that there is no evidence that the above behaviors fulfill the criteria for a syndrome since the false memory syndrome has no signs and symptoms. In response, the FMS Foundation notes that the term 'syndrome' is appropriate since syndrome means a collection of reproducible features which derives from some common cause. Therefore false memory syndrome is a syndrome since this definition fits the above description.

Myers (1993) provides an excellent discussion of the issue of syndromes. He notes that both diseases and syndromes share the medically and forensically important feature of diagnostic value. Both point with varying degrees of certainty to particular causes. But whereas with many diseases the relationship between symptoms and etiology is clear, with syndromes, this relationship is often unclear or unknown. The certainty with which a syndrome points to a particular cause varies with the syndrome.

Myers discusses the difference between two syndromes often offered in expert testimony in cases of alleged child abuse. The battered child syndrome has high certainty since a child with the symptoms is very likely to have suffered non-accidental injury. Therefore, this syndrome has high probative value and, in fact, has been approved by every appellate court to consider it. This can be contrasted with the child sexual abuse accommodation syndrome (CSAAS) which does not point with any certainty to sexual abuse. The fact that a child shows behaviors of the CSAAS does not help determine whether the child was sexually abused. Therefore the CSAAS has little probative value.

Myers gives as examples of other syndromes with little certainty and thus low probative value the false memory syndrome, the parental alienation syndrome, and the rape trauma syndrome. He cautions that the use of the word 'syndrome' may inflate the probative value of these weaker syndromes. Myers is referring to the legal arena and we agree with him that great caution should be used in court when referring to syndromes with low certainty.

But we believe the recovered memory advocates are applying a double standard. They frequently refer to syndromes with little empirical support and low certainty that have not been accepted in the DSM-III-R or the DSM-IV. These include, in addition to the ones mentioned by Myers above, the battered woman's syndrome and the sexually abused child's syndrome. Given this, we suspect that the 'syndrome' objection is a red herring to divert attention away from the lack of empirical support for their claims and assumptions.

In fact, the empirical data the FMS Foundation has from 12,000 families suggest good support and high certainty for the concept of a false memory syndrome. The FMSF does not need to apologize for using this term. When 'memories' of abuse are uncovered only in therapy or as a result of other suggestive influences, when there had been total amnesia for the alleged traumatic abuse prior to this, when the abuse is highly improbable and implausible, and when there is no external corroboration, this points with high certainty towards a false memory syndrome that meets the requirements for a syndrome contained in the DSM-III-R and the DSM-IV. The thousands of instances that contain those common elements are likely to be more support for this syndrome than for any other that has been accepted as a legitimate classification category.

The history of currently accepted syndromes is that there is often a long period after they are first described before they are generally accepted and appear in diagnostic manuals. Posttraumatic stress disorder first appeared under the name 'survivor syndrome' in 1952 to describe people who had been imprisoned in German concentration camps (*FMS Foundation Newsletter*, February 1994). It was later used to describe the Vietnam war veteran's symptoms and was only included in the DSM-III in 1980.

We believe it is quite likely, as information accumulates on the behavior patterns described by the false memory syndrome, that it will eventually find its way into one of the Diagnostic and Statistical Manual revisions, assuming that the recovered memory phenomenon continues. Until then, it cannot be said to have less support than many other 'syndromes' commonly used today.

Conclusions

It is likely that none of the hypotheses about how false memories develop are completely right or completely wrong. There are different paths to the uncovering of a false memory of sexual abuse and individual differences as to the factors that contribute to this. But it is unlikely that without the acceptance of the basic assumptions by the therapists and their clients—1. childhood abuse is widespread and is responsible for a wide variety of problems; 2. many people have amnesia for their abuse; 3. memories which have been completely repressed or dissociated can be accurately retrieved—that individuals will develop a false memory of childhood sexual abuse. The belief in these assumptions appears to be a much more important factor in making an individual susceptible to the development of pseudomemories than does personal pathology or family difficulties. Whatever the reasons behind the development of a false memory, the results are devastating to the accused and their families. Serious damage is also done to the accuser and to the society as a whole.

Chapter Four
The Manufacture of Victims: The 'Retractors'

First you shall meet with the Sirens who capture the minds Of all whom they can acquaint with their attractions.
Whoever shall approach them unforewarned And heed their song will never again turn His affection home, and will despise His wife and children, as they gather to greet him— The sirens will so enchant him with their song, Shrill, and yet powerfully sensual.
Homer, *Odyssey*, Book 12, lines 39–44

Since the beginning of the FMS Foundation, there have been calls from 'survivors' questioning the accuracy of their memories. By Spring 1994 there were over 200 'retractors' who now believed their recovered memories were false. The FMSF is gathering information from these people and several of their accounts have appeared in the *FMS Foundation Newsletter.* In their 1993 book, *True Stories of False Memories,* Goldstein and Farmer present nine stories by retractors. We published two accounts in the special issue of our journal, *Issues in Child Abuse Accusations,* devoted to recovered memories (1992, Volume 4, Issue 4). There is a newsletter called *The Retractor* which is published "for survivors of recovered memory therapy" that contains descriptions of the retractors' experiences.

These first-person stories from 'retractors' give invaluable information about recovered memory therapy, its effects, and how the person later realizes that the 'recovered memories' were false. These descriptions cannot be generalized to all recovered memory therapists and clients, nor to all people who have retracted their memories. It is a small and select group and probably atypical in some ways. For example, one of the most difficult things for most people to do is to openly admit error, as the retractors courageously do, and this strength sets the group apart.

The retractors' accounts have not been independently verified, except in cases where retractors have sued their therapists and medical and therapy records are available as part of the discovery. Despite these limitations, these stories allow us to examine the subjective experiences of people who have gone through recovered memory therapy and observe the damage that such therapy can cause. Their accounts do show that the techniques and approaches described in the books on surviving incest are actually used in the real world. These accounts also give some minimal information about the number of therapists who use the techniques of recovering memories.

Accounts from Retractors

Melody Gavigan

It all began back in November of 1989. I was hospitalized for depression in Long Beach, California when I started getting my first false memories of child sexual abuse.

While hospitalized for the depression, I was asked by several hospital workers if I had ever been touched sexually in my childhood. Although I could not remember anything, I felt pressured to come up with some 'answers' for my condition that would be acceptable. I also felt that if I could come up with a single reason for my troubles, I would be able to get well and get out of the hospital sooner.

My psychologist kept asking about my childhood and he seemed insistent that I had been sexually abused as a child. I tried to be very co-operative because I wanted out of that hospital. I didn't understand why my therapist was not interested in hearing about the recent causes of my depression—a painful divorce, sexual harassment on the job, unemployment, stress from a new marriage, and a recent drastic change in lifestyle. I trusted him, however, and if he believed that all of my problems were due to some traumatic incident in my childhood I apparently had forgotten, I assumed he must be right because he was the psychology expert, not I.

I continued to wrack my brain to try to remember being sexually abused, and I had a severe mental breakdown. After the breakdown, I told him that I thought I had been raped by my father. I was not sure of the age in which it happened. (I started with the age of four and then changed it to six and then seven.) I was encouraged by my psychologist to talk about the abuse in groups and in therapy sessions. My psychologist and I confronted my mother about it. I wrote a letter to my father and with the help of the hospital social worker, reported him to a child abuse hot line and continued to accuse him.

I was on four or five different medications and I became dependent upon Halcion and Xanax in order to function at a minimal level. Over the next few years, my doctors placed me on several more medications including lithium, Tegretol, Ativan, desipramine, Stelazine, Triavil, and nortriptyline.

For the next three years, this problem ruled my life. I was obsessed at how unresolved it all felt. I was tormented constantly. I became too sick to work regularly and went on disability as I could not work without having 'flashbacks.' I did little besides reading *The Courage to Heal* and crying and feeling depressed and angry. It didn't seem as though I was 'healing' at all, but instead was just getting worse. I felt a desperate need to remember more of what happened to me so that I could get well and get on with my life. I was always thinking and trying, trying hard to remember. I tried all the 'tricks' in *The Courage in Heal* and the *Workbook,* but still I could not remember anything concrete, although I was convinced that it had happened. Hoping to get away from my pain, I moved to another state.

At the same time, I was constantly beset by doubts about my experience. It felt that I was 'making it up,' but it said in *The Courage to Heal* that the memories often feel that way.

At the recommendation of friends, therapists, and a person I knew who had started an organization called Sexual Abuse Victims Enlightenment, I started litigation against my father for the imagined childhood rape. I was told that I would be 'validated' by doing this and that it would help my 'healing' along by much.

Also, in hopes of my memories being triggered, I founded the only Survivors of Incest Anonymous (S.I.A.) group in my city. I was the leader of the group and supplied everyone with literature on 'remembering' and the 20 questions of S.I.A. [See the end of this chapter for this checklist.] In the questions, it says that if you have answered yes to three or more of these questions, "Survivors of Incest Anonymous can help." Upon close inspection of the questions, however, many of them can be applied to just about anybody.

After starting the group, my internal pressure to remember the sexual abuse increased greatly and that is when I entered regular therapy. I went to both a hypnotherapist and a clinical psychologist at the same time. I told them that I believed I had been raped at a young age and that it was causing all my present emotional and mental problems.

Both of the therapists encouraged and pushed me to 'remember' more and more, even though I was starting to show signs of psychosis during the treatment sessions. I was rapidly losing the ability to differentiate between my imagination and my real memory. I also started, at that time, to have 'memories' of satanic ritual abuse that were always accepted by my therapists and that I was never asked to question. As a result, I came up with many more visualizations, and some graphic and detailed sexual abuse stories which started to involve murder. The 'memories' became increasingly more shocking and violent, and I became more ill with each therapy session.

In the fall of 1991, with the enthusiastic encouragement of my hypnotherapist, I began showing signs of MPD (multiple personality disorder). In the hypnosis sessions, the therapist would have me 'relive' the rape but all the while it never felt real, never like a real experience. He would ask me if there were any other 'people' there with me, and then he would have me identify and name the other 'parts' of me. Afterwards, when I went home I would draw them for him. Meanwhile, I read books such as *The Courage to Heal* and books on MPD. My symptoms grew much worse with therapy until I finally suffered a mental breakdown and was hospitalized.

During this recent hospitalization, I finished sorting out what I had already started—that the detailed and graphic memories had not been real, but were some kind of hallucination or figment of my imagination that had been accept as historical fact and encouraged by my therapists.

The realization that the memories were not real came on gradually, over a period of a few days to a few weeks. I had been taking a course in college psychology and was studying the brain and memory when the scientific research that I was reading was not in agreement with what the therapists seem to believe. I learned in textbooks about memory that our brain 'loses' much of what we experience and that our entire childhood was not somehow recorded and is not buried, waiting to be brought up like a video movie in the way the therapists would have me believe.

I have since stopped the litigation against my father and apologized to him and my family. I still remain perplexed and disturbed as to how this all could have happened to me, but I know that the *Courage to Heal* book had a lot to do with it, along with the three different therapists who coached me over a period of three years. During that time, I also saw two different psychiatrists, but the psychiatrists did not encourage the false memories as the other therapists did—in fact they expressed doubt that my memories were real.

I now feel very well emotionally since quitting 'therapy.' However, my life has been ravaged though all of this. I lost a good job, my husband divorced me, and worst of all, I lost my family. The pain and destruction that have been wrought upon my life and that of my family can never be reversed.

Reprinted with permission from *Issues in Child Abuse Accusations* 4 (4) (1992), 246–47.

Mary Elizabeth

I was hurt so terribly by my doctor and have worked awfully hard to get over it that a lot of things have been put aside. I'm just now starting to feel like it wasn't my fault and I have done nothing wrong, but the shame hangs over me like a cloud. I feel so betrayed, so foolish.

I started therapy five years ago with a young psychiatrist who suggested that I needed therapy. Right off he said that something had been missed, something hidden. I agreed. I knew I had come from an abusive household. My father regularly beat us; my stepbrother was sexually abusive, but these things I never forgot. But the doctor said, "No, obviously there is something else there," and he said I would never get better without help. He seemed so compassionate, so caring. I soon came under his spell and agreed to hypnosis to "unlock the secrets of my past."

I started having false memories about six months into therapy. When I would come out of a trance, he would tell me the things I had said. Unbelievable things. That was the first time in my life I felt like killing myself. He said I had PTSD (Post-traumatic Stress Disorder) and suggested MPD (Multiple Personality Disorder). I told him he was nuts. He told me I was "in denial and severely depressed." He begged me to stick with it and I'd feel better. I believed him. He started 'regression hypnosis' and it really went downhill in a hurry after that. He encouraged me to call him every day and to write in a journal my thoughts, feelings, fantasy life.

Soon, I needed an anti-depressant. Then a sleeping pill because the nightmares were keeping me awake. Then a tranquilizer, than an anti-psychotic. He told me I was definitely MPD, then down the pike came satanic ritual abuse. Then the day came when he said he couldn't handle things; told me he was leaving me because he was scared that the cult would hurt him and his family. Then he decided to keep seeing me. I managed to convince him the cult didn't want to hurt him.

He made me sever all ties with my family and most of my friends. By that time I was on 13 different medications and had lost my job. I spent months and months in the hospital due to suicide attempts; several serious ones. I never could quite deal with the fact that I had killed and eaten several hundred infants and children in rituals.

My husband stood by me and was at first caught up in it, as was everyone in my family. Then, as time went on and I got worse and worse, he stopped and said, "Hey, this is nuts. Something is wrong here." It was then that my husband stopped believing everything that came out of my mouth and he saw through the doctor's smoke screen.

Since last September I have managed to crawl out of the hell hole my doctor dug for me. I try every day to make up for those five long years that I was away from my husband and kids—I never can. I can never say I am sorry enough. But every day I am discovering new things about what it's like to be a human being again. What a trip—reality.

Reprinted with permission from *The Retractor*, Fall 1993.

Lynn Gondolf

I was in therapy with two therapists after I sought treatment for an eating disorder in 1986. I was taught that my family was really a bunch of satanic cult people who kill and eat babies and human flesh. Such an experience was devastating. It put me in a very serious medical place where I hadn't been before. I'd never tried to kill myself until I started therapy. And by that time I didn't have my parents.

The therapists told me that I needed to make this group of sick, dependent women my new family. I loved those women and still today I love every one of them. I hope they all get better. But we were not a group that needed to depend on each other. You've got a bunch of women trying to kill themselves. Who's trustworthy, who's dependable?

By this time I was seriously depressed so I missed work. I didn't communicate with people on the outside because what would I say to them? All the people in the group talked about was incest and cutting and eating and depression and medicine and what's their latest flashback. Normal people on the outside don't have flashbacks.

Therefore there was this group of sick women. We went to therapy, worked enough to pay for therapy, and called each other to talk about our flashbacks. That's how my life went for a while. I became real sick.

You lose a lot of years doing this and I was fortunate in that I was able to come out of it and go on to build the life I have today. One of the women in my group always wanted to have a family. She's been in the group now for six years and she's getting past childbearing years and she can never have a normal relationship while she's in this group because all you've got is this sick bunch of dependent women.

Everything was interpreted as supporting the abuse. When my parents sent a birthday card, it was interpreted as a suicidal message. Part of the treatment was something called trance writing. The therapists claimed that trance writing was different from hypnosis but I've yet to understand the difference except probably trance writing is just even more dangerous because the garbage I wrote was sure nowhere near truth. I can't remember what it was. It was just real gory.

Another thing they used was called 'body memories.' They believed that certain physical sensations reflected abuse that couldn't be remembered. That is, although there were no conscious memories, the body remembered. They told me that because I had some numbness in my hand, that this was from holding my father's penis. The reason I had numbness in my hand is the day before I wasn't taking anything, all of a sudden I'm taking 900 milligrams lithium, I'm also taking a bunch of Xanax and a bunch of Mellaril. This made my fingers numb.

We believed we were being treated by one of the greatest therapists alive. He could heal eating disorders and by that time I'd had mine for 18 years and I didn't have a whole lot longer to have this eating disorder. I believed that he could heal me and that if trance writing would enable me to get to that one thing that's down there in my gut, that magical one experience, I'm going to be well.

They convinced me that if they found this mystical, magical thing then I would be okay and be a healthy, normal functioning person. But that wasn't what happened.

Day in and day out I listened to screaming and shouting and to graphic details about abuse and I then had to draw them since that's what the staff wanted to see and that's the only way I could stay out of seclusion, I finally started to say what they wanted to hear. The sad thing is I started to believe it, almost.

After a while I said what my therapist wanted to hear if I wanted any attention from him. And at that point I wanted attention from this man. He was about the only person I had left in my life. I began to believe the abuse by my parents was true.

After Lynn ran out of insurance she was discharged from the hospital. Away from this program, she gradually recovered

I was released with a couple of black trash sacks that had been mine when I was in the hospital, which had all my belongings from the hospital. I had no friends because they had told the other group members for their own good not to talk to me or I would harm them. I don't really remember how I got an apartment that day but somehow I did and I began to try to put my life back together.

I didn't do a real good job of it for a while. I didn't have my medication. I called the psychiatrist who had given me all that and he said, "Well, I'm sorry to hear that." I said well, you've got me on all this. I need to get off of this or something, because I'm beginning to shake, I couldn't talk hardly, different things such as that.

I called Jerry, a therapist I had known before. He didn't get into all this recovered memories of abuse stuff. He was a behavioral cognitive therapist. I told him the awful shape I was in and he was angry because he hadn't seen me in a year and when he had last seen me I was a normal functioning human being. He knew about the incest with my uncle. He told me that he had a friend who was a doctor and they'd get me the medication I needed immediately and then work on getting me off of it.

Jerry also encouraged me to believe that I could recover from what had happened. At that time it felt like I had destroyed my family. I'd said all these things about them and if they weren't true, then I was really sicko. I was some kind of sexually perverted person for even thinking these things about my father. If they were true and I was as mentally ill as the doctor said, then I'm some mentally ill pervert. Either way, I didn't believe I had a lot of hope.

I didn't have my therapy friends and by that time I had cut off my normal friends. How am I going to go back to them a year later and say, hi, guys, here I am. I didn't have my job at E.D.S. which I obtained after I had gotten a four-year degree in two years. I felt like I had just blown my life.

But I've found out that I'm a survivor. I got the apartment that day and I talked to Jerry who helped me get some medication and who assured me that insurance or not he'd stand by me. He'd see me and we'd get through this.

I saw him probably three days a week for that first week or two. I cried about this other therapist and all that went on. And Jerry would just sit there and listen. He was angry over what had been done but he didn't get real involved with it but let me express my feelings and worked with me on getting on with my life.

Finally, after two years, it was time to get off all this medication. For one thing it was eating me up financially. Several people had said I was addicted to it and by this time it's almost chic to be an alcoholic addict. So, I went to a drug rehab program.

At first I didn't like the plan they had for me. They didn't want to hear much about the abuse and I didn't really understand that. That was all we had talked about in the other environment. But they weren't interested. Instead, they stressed, "What are you going to do about now? You can't drink today, you can't take pills. You have to do the normal things you used to do. So what, you're depressed today. Everybody has days they feel lousy. You still must go to work, you must eat, you still must take a bath, you still must comb your hair, you still must do these things."

I'd not had therapy like that before. In my incest

victimization therapy, I'd been taught that I didn't have to do any of that. If I felt bad, I'd stay home. I'd stay in bed all day. I'd read a yucky book. I'd bawl, I'd take an extra Xanax. I didn't have to be responsible. If I'd had kids I wouldn't have to take care of them because I'm an incest victim. Because all of these awful things happened to me I didn't have to live by the same rules the rest of you all do.

But this place didn't go along with that. They thought I was just like anybody else. It was good for me. I had to relearn how to live. This was difficult to do since I'd got real used to that sick way of life that I was taught. I'd become used to whatever you say can be turned into whatever they want. I'd become used to flashbacks and gory details of sexual abuse, to people saying oh, you're an incest victim. We feel so sorry for you. It must have been horrible.

I got better. It took a while, though. I'm in a 12-step recovery program today. I believe that it probably has truly saved my life. It definitely taught me how to live again. Just because I'm an alcoholic or just because I'm an incest victim, I don't have any less responsibility than anyone else. By the time I got to where I was back to the type of emotional health, really emotional health, was probably by mid-1989. About a year later I began dating the man I'm now married to. He understands what went on and sometimes gets extremely angry when he hears what happened to me.

I reconciled with my parents at a family gathering. I told my sister I'd come and she told me that my parents would also be there. My dad has never asked me for an apology. He's never told me that we've got to talk about it. He's never said, 'How could you accuse me of something like that?' My mom's never said anything to me about it and I'm very grateful for that. I'm very grateful they didn't say, 'Well, after accusing us of something so horrible, how dare you set foot in our place?' Today, I can tell you I have a better relationship with my parents, probably, than I've ever had.

What allowed me to realize that the 'memories' of abuse by my parents were not true was time away from that therapy group. I do not believe that this could have happened if I had remained in the group. I did believe the group and the therapists were going too far when they decided that I was a multiple personality disorder, but I wouldn't have been ready to just leave on my own. I know that I never would have realized those things were false while I was still in the group.

The truth did not come to me immediately after leaving the group. It happened gradually as I was putting my life back together. As I was restored to some health and emotional well-being, I was able to get a sense of what memories were based on actual experiences and which were not. It became obvious to me after a while that my dad never did it.

But although I lost four years of my life I'm grateful. I'm a lot more fortunate than some. I got a chance to go on with my life.

In Dallas, there's five of us from that same group who have since recanted all of the accusations we made. You heard about one woman who confronted her mother and was able to retract those remarks before her mother died. Most have been able to heal their family relationships. One left because the therapist thought he had healed her but she later told her mother she knew her mother did not do all she said. One woman's husband took charge and removed her from the therapy program. After that time she began to get better than she's been in years. Another woman had been in group for seven or eight years and finally just realized that it was getting sick and crazy. By this time the group was talking about people hanging on meat hooks in trees and stuff during the cult activities. She was able to break away for a while and could then see that this was nuts. But such realizations occur only after getting away.

Abstracted, with permission, from *Issues in Child Abuse Accusations* 4(4) (1992), 239–245.

A Retractor's Story

I entered therapy in the late fall of 1985 because I was unhappy at the way I was dealing with my son, age nine. I thought he might need some counselling because he had seemed very angry for a young child. I wanted a therapist who could work with both of us. At the same time that I began therapy, I also became aware that I was an Adult Child of an Alcoholic. My therapist was a real leader of this movement attending national conferences and beginning meetings in this area.

Soon the therapy began to focus only on my adult child issues and we did no work with my son. As I described my childhood, my therapist would say things like 'being an adult child is like growing up in a concentration camp.'

I will agree that my home was quite dysfunctional because, in fact, my dad was an active alcoholic. I did indeed have some real memories of some pretty chaotic and scary times. As this 'therapy' proceeded to dredge up everything negative about my childhood I began to get very depressed. Clinical depression unfortunately runs in my family and I had previously been treated for it. I began treating my depression with alcohol until I realized that I was drinking every night. I entered a rehab and got sober and have never had a drink since.

My therapist, however, kept me involved in digging up my past. He kept looking for more, more, more! He kept asking me if I had any memories of being sexually abused and I kept saying no. He then begin telling me that I had all the symptoms of an incest victim and that the only way out for me was to "recover a memory, relive it and heal from it." I was so depressed and I desperately wanted to feel better. I began to have a series of hospitalizations as I grew more depressed and suicidal. I asked a psychiatrist at one hospital if my psychological testing showed any indication of sexual abuse and he said no. He thought my main issue was my marriage. My outside therapist disagreed and kept pushing.

I was finally hospitalized in a women's program whose main focus was on sexual abuse issues. I still continued not to have memories. I felt like I was flunking therapy. At the hospital, I watched real victims really struggle with their issues. As I look back now I am convinced that there was another woman whose memories were false. I didn't believe her even then. I began to have periods of severe anxiety and I was told these were probably 'body memories' and 'flashbacks.' I thought this is what I had to do to get better. By now I was diagnosed with PTSD and MPD. The hospital was trying to teach me how to 'manage the flashbacks.'

When I left the hospital in March of 1989, I still had no memories and I was obsessed with finding one. All my energy was focussed on journals, therapy, etc. I had to get help taking care of my children and my house. My therapy was my life. When I was not in the therapist's office, I was thinking about all the time of talking to him. I spoke with him on the phone every night for about 20 minutes.

Finally, I recalled having been given an enema as a child. The therapy became focussed on regressing me to an early age around five and reliving the enema over and over again. He tried to convince me that my mother took great pleasure in inflicting this kind of pain on me. He called her a sex addict and sexual pervert. He said my parents were toxic for me and that I should screen all my phone calls and not see them.

This was so painful for me because I really did love my parents. I was incredibly torn between my loyalties to my family and the clutches of this therapist. He had created such a sick dependency that I thought I had to let him know my every move. He was also trying to convince me that an uncle and my older brother had molested me.

Twice a week I would go to therapy and be told the only way to feel better was to relive these memories. He would sit next to me on his couch covering me with a blanket while I, in a regressed, hypnotic state would start to have these 'body memories.' This therapy continued and I had to be hospitalized six or seven weeks at a time. I'm now convinced that my depression and suicidal ideas were mainly caused by the incredible conflict between wanting to be with my parents and pleasing my therapist.

He had never done this kind of therapy before and he kept telling me how much he was learning from me. By now I knew that I was very special to him especially when he told my 'inner child' that she could be his little girl. I would do anything that he wanted me to do to please him and to keep this 'nurturing' relationship going.

Everyone around me saw me going down the tubes and was really concerned. My brothers actually found out the home address of the therapist and were very tempted to hurt him physically. They were tired of watching me destroy the family. I couldn't listen to anyone. I was totally owned by the therapist.

In the meantime, my mother's health was deteriorating mainly due to stress. She had idolized me, her only daughter, and the pain she was in over this was incredible. I saw my mother in September of 1990 and was shocked at her appearance. I then became acutely aware that I wanted again to be close to her. I started to ask my therapist to help me heal the relationship. It never happened because his own issues got in the way. My mother died in January 1992 and I never had a chance to tell her how sorry I was. I now have to make my apologies at her grave. You cannot imagine how painful this is.

After her death, I stopped working on my earlier issues and began dealing with my loss and my marriage which was falling apart. I began to slowly wean myself from the therapist. My husband and I had started marriage counselling with another therapist whom I began slowly to trust. In the meantime I had been reading the case of Dr. Bean-Bayog and Paul Lozano and heard about FMS. It took me eight more months to finally get clear. I went to see the marriage counsellor and sobbed my way through an hour session telling her what I believed now to be the truth.

I then typed my therapist a four-page letter stating what I thought had really happened in our relationship. I also told him I was not going to pay him any more money, although he was claiming that I owed him $3,800. As it was, I had paid him out of pocket around $10,000 and I am not a rich woman.

In the meantime I contacted a lawyer who sent him a request for my records. He didn't reply to either of us for about two months when he sent me a brief note congratulating me for making so much progress in therapy with him and asking for payment.

This past year has been very painful to me as I've really begun to acknowledge what I lost as a result of this therapy. I went from being a very productive woman who was raising three children and was serving on a school committee (I had formed a parent-teacher organization and was quite known and respected in my community) to a dependent, depressed, repressed, and suicidal woman.

I've lost six-and-one-half years of my life, the opportunity to have an intimate relationship with my mother, time with my three young children, and my marriage of 21 years. I also was forced to drop out of a graduate program which had only accepted 49 students out of 750 applicants. I have lost so much in terms of self-esteem and confidence. It is amazing to me that this situation could have occurred and wreaked such havoc in my life. I will forever carry the burden of probably hastening my mother's death and for the grief that I had caused my family.

I hope so much that telling my story will save at least one child-parent relationship. I strongly believe that these stories must be told because I suspect that similar situations have occurred all across the country.

Reprinted with permission from *FMS Foundation Newsletter*, November 1993.

Effects on the Accusers

In all the cases in which we have been involved and in the stories from the retractors, the effects of recovered memory therapy are iatrogenic.[1] As therapy progresses, the person becomes sicker. The diagnoses become more serious. The person often becomes unable to function. We have reviewed many thick stacks of medical documents that demonstrate this. The retractors quoted above also give vivid descriptions of their psychological deterioration. Some other examples:

- (From a sister.) She's a mess. She sounds terrible. She has nothing left, friends or money or job. Her insurance ran out and then she cashed in all her retirement money for therapy and then that ran out and she has not been in therapy. She owes money to

---

[1] *Iatrogenic:* (of a medical disorder) caused by the diagnosis, manner, or treatment of a physician. In other words, the illness is caused by the doctor's intervention.

the Internal Revenue Service. She wants to see Mom and Dad. She said that she loves them and that she doesn't believe in the horrible memories that she had. What a waste! (*FMS Foundation Newsletter*, October 1993)

- (From a mother.) She showed up after three years when her Dad had a triple bypass. I was worried that she planned a "death bed" scene out of *Courage to Heal* but she let me hug her. She acted like everything was perfectly normal but her eyes looked so funny. They were glassy and had black circles and her hair was stringy. After the operation she talked with her father and she said she wanted to be a part of the family and wanted to have joint counselling with a new therapist. (*FMS Foundation Newsletter*, October 1993)

- (From a retractor who ended up with 58 personalities and who accused her father, aunt, minister, two family friends, and the town doctor of abuse.) My daughter thought she was losing me because I was never there for her. I tore my family apart piece by piece; I hated them all . . . I nearly destroyed my husband's life, my son's life, and my family and I really don't know where to turn or how to put my life back together. . . . I wish with all my heart that I could erase the past two years but I can't. (*The Retractor*, Fall 1993)

- (From Laura Pasley, a retractor who successfully sued her therapist.) These therapists are doing something as evil as evil can be. It wasn't just my life they took. I had a six-year-old daughter when I began treatment. When I woke up she was 12. (Gross 1994)

The parents worry about what it will do to the accusing child if and when she realizes her memories were false. What happens when the accused parent dies without resolution? Suicide of the accusing child is a real concern for many of the parents.

- Our daughter, who was estranged from us, came home after her father had a massive heart attack. He never regained consciousness. She was by his bedside for the 10 days before his death. No one will ever know if he knew she was there. Not one word about the false accusations has been mentioned. I am sure that the stress of the last two years led up to the heart attack. It was something he could not understand, but he had forgiven her. (*FMS Foundation Newsletter*, October 1992)

● My husband died about three months after our daughter's confrontation which was, of course, absolutely devastating. I'm afraid now that the truth will be even more painful to our daughter, if or when she finally realizes that her memories are false. It's so sad and there is no way I can help her. (*FMS Foundation Newsletter*, October 1992)

● My husband and I were in attendance at the Memory and Reality conference last April. The conference meant so much to him. It was a real help. He died June 10th—just couldn't hold on any longer for the heart transplant. The hardest thing about his death for me is that he died without this terrible accusation being resolved. (*FMS Foundation Newsletter*, October 1992)

What happens when the families cannot forgive the accusing child? Although most of the parents want their child back and are prepared to forgive and work towards reconciliation, this is not universal. The rift created by such a horrible accusation may be impossible to heal.

● (From an retractor) I realized I had made a mistake. I was brainwashed by a thought and a terrible book. I began therapy with a new doctor and began piecing my life back together again. It was then I decided to write my parents a letter of explanation, apology, and love. The woman I talked with also wrote a letter to my mother relating her situation to mine. It was then that I took both of these letters to my mom and just left afterwards. Three days later, I received a court summons saying my mom filed charges on me for criminal trespass. All I did was give her what she asked for in an effort to rebuild my family's name and bring my father together again. My new doctor asked them to come in and they still refused saying I wasn't in enough pain yet. My mother today says she wants no relations with me whatsoever. (*FMS Foundation Newsletter*, October 1993)

The recovered memory proponents are suspicious of the retractors. Kristiansen (1994), for example, claims that some women might retract their allegation because of "family pressure" or "to receive positive regard from their family and the

FMS Foundation" as well as to avoid confrontation with a "horrific reality" (p. 13). There is universal resentment toward the FMS Foundation for making 'survivors' doubt the validity of their newly recovered memories of abuse and the recovered memory skeptics are seen as 'revictimizing' the survivors by not accepting their claims as true. Some assert that members of FMS Foundation are real abusers and the denial of the claims of abuse is actually a continuation of the childhood abuse.

Harm to the Accuser

The accuser is grievously damaged by the consequences of recovered memories. Damage comes from the erroneous belief that rage can be healing and positive and from the resulting alienation from the family. Anger is a destructive emotion and the expression of anger can be damaging (Brody 1993). There is an effect on physical health—the greater the anger the less healthy the person is likely to be. Next, comes the impact on social relationships. Anger separates people. The angry and abrasive person simply does not get along well with others and is more isolated, alienated, and alone. When therapists encourage dwelling on resentments and impulsively expressing anger, they teach clients a maladaptive, immature, and counterproductive way of handling problems and frustrations.

The theory behind 'ventilation' and 'getting your feelings out' is that there is a reservoir which holds anger somewhere in our bodies and if it becomes too full the anger will cause problems and distress. The solution, according to this model, is to 'empty' the reservoir by yelling, pounding pillows, or telling someone off. Then, the theory goes, the anger will be reduced and the person will be better. Healing will be accomplished. Clients are therefore encouraged to throw darts at pictures of their perpetrators, pound pillows, role play by screaming and cursing, and plan and carry out punitive confrontations.

But this model is wrong. There is no anger reservoir in our bodies. Instead, anger is *created* by the expression of anger. The more a person behaves in an angry way, the more anger the person will feel. This does not mean it is healthy or desirable to passively do nothing when people treat us badly. But the solution is to assertively communicate what is bothering us and engage in productive problem solving. These skills can and should be taught in therapy.

Campbell (1994) comments on the effects of therapeutic techniques that encourage blaming parents and graphically expressing anger:

> This therapy is determined to subject the parents of clients to the most vicious kind of character assassination. One can only shudder at the long-term future consequences for clients who are treated in this manner. Once a therapist engages in these cruel, irresponsible indictments of a client's parents, how will that client relate to his family in the future? What is the likelihood of such a client ever enjoying mutually supportive relationships with his family? (p. 83)

Recovered memory therapists encourage hostile family confrontations and breaking off relationships with family members who don't support the allegations. They may recommend symbolic funerals or divorce ceremonies. But, as the accounts of retractors show, the group or the therapist cannot substitute for the lost family and the accuser eventually winds up alone. The future will likely have a large number of 70- to 80-year-old women whose families have nothing to do with them because of the allegations. The therapy groups and therapists are gone when the insurance money runs out. Their own children have no model of close-knit families but rather the model of blaming one's parents for all problems. The accuser, if she eventually retracts her 'memories,' will be riddled with guilt over what she has done to her parents and family under the guise of treatment. This is not an attractive picture.

On a recent Sunday night when one of the networks was showing a made-for-TV movie about claims of recovered memories, we got two anonymous, obscene, threatening phone calls from women who claimed to be survivors of incest. While watching this movie, having heard of our skepticism and work in this area from the survivors network, they called simply to let us know what absolute scum we were. Their language was incredibly vile and foul. One threatened to do a Bobbitt job on Dr. Underwager. The other insisted that we were all getting filthy rich from the FMS Foundation. Neither would give a name. To resort to anonymous, obscene, and threatening phone calls reflects a level of disturbance that certainly cuts across all of life and reveals a bitter, unhappy, and vengeful person. But this is the type of anger often learned in recovered memory therapy.

Conclusions

As one reads stories from people who have undergone recovered memory therapy, several themes emerge. The person generally seeks therapy for a problem other than sexual abuse. Once in therapy, the therapist suggests that repressed or dissociated sexual abuse is responsible for whatever problems brought the person to therapy. The person may be questioned repeatedly about abuse. Suggestive and intrusive techniques, such as survivors' groups, Amytal interviews, or hypnosis, are often used in the attempt to retrieve these hypothesized memories. Although the reason for these procedures is the belief that recovering memories is necessary for healing, as therapy progresses, the person becomes sicker.

The focus of therapy becomes abuse rather than the problems for which treatment was originally sought. Some people become so dysfunctional that they are hospitalized where they are given a variety of medications. Diagnoses such as post-traumatic stress disorder (PTSD) and multiple personality disorder (MPD) may be given.

People are encouraged to terminate relationships with family members who don't believe their new memories and who don't support them. They may be told to make the members of their survivors' group their new 'family.' They are encouraged to express anger and rage in the erroneous belief that 'getting your feelings out' is therapeutic. Confrontations with the 'perpetrators' may be role-played and supported.

Accused parents try desperately to discover what is going on, push for specifics concerning the allegations, and attempt to meet with their child's therapist. These attempts are seldom successful. Most often, the accuser refuses to meet with her parents or discuss the situation 'until you admit what you did.' Brothers, sisters, nonaccused parents, and extended families members are caught in the middle. Often, all contact is severed. Families are destroyed.

When the accusing child eventually retracts the allegations, a major factor appears to be getting away from the therapy. Sometimes insurance runs out and the person is discharged from the program. A sibling or husband or wife may finally become skeptical (although most spouses support their husband's or wife's accusation) and encourage them to leave a therapy program that is not helping them. Persistent brothers and sisters appear to play a key role in persuading their accusing sibling to re-examine their newly discovered memories and the therapy that produced them. Occasionally, an individual simply begins to doubt her memories. This sometimes happens as a result of encountering the media attention to the FMS Foundation and false memories. Sometimes, a significant event such as a death, serious illness, or birth is a factor. But leaving the therapist appears to be necessary.

Even with a retraction, the destruction to the parent-child relationship and to the family is unlikely to be readily healed: "An apology and a retraction does not end the family disruption caused by unvalidated accusations, the cruel confronting, the obsessive anger and the unilateral cutting off. It's probably impossible to undo the countless divorces between parents when one is accused and the other not and between people with memories and their questioning spouses" (FMS *Foundation Newsletter*, May 3rd, 1993, p. 11).

The 20 Questions of the Survivors of Incest Anonymous (from Gavigan, 1992)

1. Do you have problems with self-confidence and self-esteem?
2. Do you feel you are either passive or aggressive? Do you have problems acting assertively?
3. Do you feel you have to 'control' your emotions?
4. Do you feel easily intimidated by authority figures?
5. Do you sabotage current relationships, especially sexual relationships?
6. Do you fear that people are interested in you primarily for sex? Does the importance of sex seem exaggerated? Do you feel that you have to be careful how you act and dress because you might sexually arouse others?
7. Are you afraid to love—always questioning 'what will they want from me now?'
8. Do you act 'different' or passive around your family of origin?
9. Currently, do you over-react or misdirect your anger in situations that frustrate you? Are you afraid of anger?
10. Do you avoid taking control of your life today? Do you have trouble making decisions?
11. Are you a perfectionist, over-achiever, or generally a compulsive person?
12. Do you get upset when you hear a rape, incest or child abuse victim tell their story?
13. Do you have trouble trusting others or trusting your own perceptions?
14. Do you have unrealistic, unreachable expectations of yourself as a parent? Do you feel you have to compensate for something? Do you try to be a superior parent or have you deliberately avoided becoming a parent altogether?
15. Do you have blocks of your childhood you can't remember? Do you have a sense that 'something happened'? Do you have memories of abuse with no emotions associated with those memories?
16. Have you ever been promiscuous? When you have sex, are you really seeking love, affection, and acceptance?
17. Do you feel sex is 'dirty'? Do you avoid mirrors? Do you feel you're unattractive?
18. Do you feel you are different, a freak? Do you fear someone will discover your secrets?

19. Do you have a problem with alcohol, drugs, food, migraines, or back pain?
20. Have you ever considered suicide? Have you ever suffered from depression or felt there was a 'black cloud' hanging over you?

If you have answered 'YES' to three (3) or more of these questions, Survivors of Incest Anonymous can help.

Chapter Five
Who Are The Therapists Who Uncover the Memories?

> *We find that whole communities suddenly fix their minds upon one object, and go mad in its pursuit; that millions of people become simultaneously impressed with one delusion, and run after it, till their attention is caught by some new folly more captivating than the first.*
> Charles Mackay (1852)

Therapists who claim to uncover 'repressed' memories are part of a network of professionals who believe that as many as half of all women have suffered childhood sexual abuse but that many have repressed their memories. Summit (1990) refers to the victims "we don't know about, those who don't disclose" and asserts that the memory of abuse is often buried within a conscious memory of a happy childhood. He says that half of all women were sexually abused in childhood but many do not remember the abuse and recommends using therapy methods that are "invasive and intrusive" in order to uncover the abuse (Roan 1990).

Maltz (1990), who claims that half of all incest survivors have some form of memory loss, lists a variety of physical and psychological problems she believes are caused by sexual abuse.

Paxton (1991) says that half of all incest survivors do not remember the abuse, that many will have only vague bits and pieces of memories and/or awareness, and that some will never remember the abuse. Fredrickson (1992) claims that "Millions of people have blocked out frightening episodes of abuse, years of their life, or their entire childhood" (p. 15). Courtois (1992) thinks a therapist can suspect childhood sexual abuse through "disguised presentation" of symptoms and lists presenting problems that are likely to indicate sexual abuse, even when the patient provides no history of abuse.

Blume (1990) believes half of all survivors do not remember the abuse and gives a long list of symptoms she claims suggest the person is an incest victim. Blume's symptoms are so varied that anyone reading the list will find several that apply to them. They include fear of being alone in the dark, headaches, arthritis, eating disorders, spontaneous vaginal infections, an aversion to being touched in vaginal exams, wearing a lot of clothing, problems with intimacy, phobias, obsessive/compulsive behaviors, depression, extreme solemnity, aversion to making noise, avoidance of mirrors, feeling different, low self-esteem, high appreciation of small favors by others, the inability to express anger or constant anger, high risk taking or the inability to take risks, a need to be perfect or perfectly bad, the inability to trust or trusting indiscriminately, and the desire to change one's name. On the jacket of her book is an endorsement from Gloria Steinem: "This book, like the truth it helps to uncover, can set millions free."

Dolan (1991) recommends helping a client recall repressed abuse when the client and therapist suspect abuse or when the client is exhibiting symptoms indicative of abuse, and when these symptoms have not responded to other forms of treatment. The symptoms she describes include a wide range of problems, including dreams of being pursued, sleep disturbances, eating disorders, substance abuse, compulsive sexuality, sexual dysfunction, chronic anxiety attacks, depression, difficulties with relationships, distrust of others, guilt, impaired self-esteem, self-destructive behaviors, and personality disorders. These symptoms are similar to those suggested by Blume.

These therapists maintain that memory deficits, amnesia and dissociation are characteristic of trauma and that abuse survivors must be helped to retrieve their memories so that they can process the trauma (Bass and Davis 1988; Blume 1990; Courtois 1992; Dolan 1991; Fredrickson 1992). Retrieval of these alleged autobiographical memories of abuse is deemed necessary for healing and recovery.

The therapists support these assumptions by referring to one or more of several psychological concepts. Adult survivors are said to have 'repressed' the memory because it was too painful, or to have 'dissociated' during the abuse as an automatic protective mechanism. They may have defended themselves against the devastating memories by developing 'traumatic amnesia' for the abuse. If the abuse was frequent and prolonged, 'alter personalities' will form to protect the child during the abuse and the adult survivors will therefore have 'multiple personality disorder.' Although the abuse is 're-pressed' or 'dissociated' and not available to conscious memory, the trauma exerts itself through a variety of emotional and behavior problems and will later show itself indirectly through 'body memories,' 'flashbacks,' or 'nightmares' (we look at these concepts in Chapters 8 and 9).

Therapy For Uncovering Memories

The questionnaires in the FMS Foundation survey project described in Chapter 3 indicate that the adult 'memory' of childhood sexual abuse most often first surfaces in therapy. What takes place in such therapy? Descriptions of the type of treatment offered are found in anecdotal reports from women, such as those in Chapter 4, who have undergone such treatment as well as in the writings and workshop presentations of many therapists. However, we found no outcome data in the descriptions of these programs. There is no information given on validity or reliability of the techniques used in the books and articles by the recovered memory therapists.

Treatment programs use many different techniques to help

patients recover 'memories' of sexual abuse. These include direct questioning, hypnosis, reading books, attending survivors' groups, age regression, and dream analysis. In the FMS Foundation questionnaire, respondents were also aware of a variety of other unconventional techniques, including prayer, meditation, age regression, neurolinguistic programming, reflexology, channelling, psychodrama, casting out demons, yoga, trance writing, and primal scream therapy.

A typical example of recovered memory treatment is Lundberg-Love's program at the University of Texas at Tyler (1989, undated). The first goal is to work on memory retrieval. After the woman can develop memories of the abuse and talk about what happened, she is encouraged to express her rage by throwing darts at pictures of the perpetrator and writing him angry letters. Her feelings of shame are dealt with through art and music, and by taking bubble baths to eliminate dirty feelings.

Courtois (1992) assumes that events can be perceived and stored by a preverbal child, that visual or imaginal and other sensory cues can stimulate the retrieval of these memories, and that since abuse memories were stored during experiences that produced arousal and helplessness, the client may have to re-experience painful emotion in order to remember. Triggers for recall include developmental events or crises; events that symbolize the original trauma; crises associated with recollection, disclosure, confrontation, reporting, and criminal justice; issues in therapy; and life states or events. Survivors' groups and self-help groups can help stimulate memories.

Recommended techniques include hypnosis, guided imagery, drawing, guided movement, body work, psychodrama, writing an autobiography, making a family genogram, constructing a lifeline, drawing the floor plan of the family house, and bringing in family pictures, toys, report cards, and so forth. The memories may return either overtly or in symbolic form such as flashbacks, body memories, and nightmares or other dreams. Courtois also believes that memory can return physiologically through body memories (see our Chapter 9 for a discussion of the 'body memory' concept).

Courtois (1992) maintains that a strong alliance between therapist and survivor is necessary for memory work. The therapist should be calm, accepting, reassuring, encouraging, and validating of the disclosures. Although she cautions against the therapist *conclusively* informing the patient that the abuse happened, Courtois says that it may be necessary for the therapist to *speculate* about it to the client.

Fredrickson (1992) believes that repressed memories of abuse stalk the individual's life but have been held in storage until the person is strong enough to face them. She differentiates between five types of memories: ordinary memories, or 'recall' memories; 'imagistic' memories (memories that break though the conscious mind with images like a slide show); 'feeling' memories (memories that are the feelings that something abusive has happened without the actual memory); 'body' memories, the physical manifestation of abuse—"Our physical bodies always remember sexual abuse" (p. 93); and 'acting-out' memories (unconscious memories in which a repressed incident is spontaneously acted out through some physical action).

Fredrickson (1992) maintains that the "journey" towards retrieving these memories is necessary for recovery, serenity, and even survival. Since few survivors experience spontaneous recall, various memory retrieval techniques are necessary. She recommends dream interpretation, free association writing, massage therapy, body manipulation, hypnosis, feelings work, art therapy, and expanding on imagistic memories. She recommends that the survivors experience deeply buried rage towards the perpetrator by yelling and hitting a footstool or pillow with a bataca bat and express grief by curling up, relaxing, and moaning, crying and sobbing whenever a sense of sadness is felt. She cautions against not believing the memories:

- Sometimes the things you remember seem like they could not possibly have happened. (p. 163)

- The existence of profound disbelief is an indication that memories are real. (p. 171)

- If your memories are unusually grisly or bizarre, you may be a survivor of ritual abuse. (p. 164)

- If you have memories that could not possibly have happened, first consider trickery designed to instill doubt. Ritual abusers combine sadism with intelligence. (p. 165)

- Most therapists who work with abuse and repressed memories agree that the overwhelming majority of survivors' memories are true. (p. 166)

- Ritual abuse is estimated to account for "7 to 10 percent of all sexual abuse survivors." (p. 165)

Dolan (1991) recommends hypnosis, ideomotor signalling with the unconscious, age regression, and automatic writing as aids to memory retrieval. She also describes a variety of techniques for "facilitating integration of recently retrieved memories . . . [to] strengthen the client's ability to connect consistently to her inner resources . . . and rituals to facilitate feelings of completion and letting go" (p. 129). These include making and carrying around an Indian "medicine bundle" composed of symbolic articles and written words evocative of the client's healing resources, holding an imaginary funeral for the family of origin, burying pictures of the family, having a divorce ceremony from the family member(s), doing "bodywork," producing art projects such as face masks, collages, and Amish quilts, taking herb-scented bubble baths and buying flowers, writing down feelings and then burning the paper, tape recording expressions of anger, making a tape to the inner child and then burying the tape in the childhood yard, and nurturing the inner child by buying a cuddly teddy bear or rag doll, eating ice cream, and getting a puppy.

Several presenters at a symposium at the 99th Annual Convention of the American Psychological Association (Grand et al. 1991) described how to help a patient uncover memories of sexual abuse. They see the role of the therapist as helping the patient become convinced of the historical reality of the abuse, even when there is no external corroboration and even when the patient herself doubts that the memory is real. The therapist, therefore, should never show doubts to the patient, but should stress that the abuse really happened and was terrible. Body memories, dream analysis, and analysis of transference are used both to retrieve the memories and to provide "validation" of the historical reality. The therapist should not be limited by the fact that the historical truth cannot be verified.

An illustration of a network actively engaged in recovering memories is Three in One Concepts, an organization begun and headed by one Gordon Stokes who claims a clinical background in behavioral genetics, psychodrama, and role play training (David 1992). Stokes claims to have taken specialized kinesiology into new avenues of self-discovery. There are said to be at least 1,500 facilitators of this new specialized kinesiology and seminars in this approach are offered all over the world. The technique is to have the individuals extend their arms, then ask them questions and press on their arms. The body, through the unconscious, answers the questions. If the arms stay rigid, that means yes. If the arms fall back, that is a no answer (David 1992). When the calls came in from Provo, Utah, several of the persons described their experience in therapy that led to the development of putative memories as precisely this procedure.

Therapy Techniques from the FMS Foundation Survey

A survey of 282 families where there have been allegations of recovered memory of childhood sexual abuse included data about the types of therapy provided (Freyd et al. 1993; see the table overleaf).

The most recent, most thorough and most exhaustive search of all meta-analytic studies dealing with the effects of psychotherapeutic approaches (Lipsey and Wilson 1993) does not report any study providing scientific data bearing on the validity, reliability, or efficacy of any of these techniques.

Yapko's Survey

Michael Yapko (1994a, 1994b) gathered data from over 860 psychotherapists from all over the United States about their ideas and practices concerning clients who do and do not report a background of sexual abuse. His respondents completed two questionnaires about the roles of suggestion and memory in

	Yes	No	Don't Know
Courage to Heal	150	5	122
Hypnosis	88	30	161
Dream interpretation	76	7	195
Rape counselling	44	34	195
Survivors' groups	131	14	92
Women's center	45	31	195
Eating disorder clinic	27	27	209
AA type program	53	74	147
Drugs	48	41	194

OTHER TECHNIQUES

Satanism expert brought in	Prayer therapy
Primal scream therapy	Sodium Amytal
Psychodrama	Meditation
Trance writing	Regression therapy
Neurolinguistic programming	Yoga
Fasting	Massage therapy
Astrology	Channeling
Crystals	Reflexology
Casting out demons	Laying hands on patient,
Amytal interviews	has a 'gift' or 'divination'

therapy, particularly as these related to the issue of recovering repressed memories of sexual abuse. Respondents were primarily psychotherapists who had attended conventions or workshops dealing with therapy or hypnosis. Almost two-thirds (64.4 percent) of the respondents held masters' degrees, 23.9 percent Ph.D.s, 3.9 percent M.D.s, 4.7 percent B.A.s and 3 percent other or no answer. His results are summarized below.

The results of the survey indicate an alarming tendency for Yapko's sample to believe in past lives, the retrievablilty and accuracy of infantile memories, and the infallibility of hypnosis as a tool for recovering accurate memories. Although there was a tendency for the respondents with advanced degrees to be more skeptical and better informed, this was only slight.

Item	Proportion of Respondents Agreeing
1. Hypnosis is a worthwhile psychotherapy tool.	97%
2. People cannot lie when in hypnosis.	18%
3. Psychotherapists can have greater faith in details of a traumatic event when obtained hypnotically than otherwise.	47%
4. When someone has a memory of a trauma while in hypnosis, it objectively must actually have occurred.	31%
5. Hypnosis can be used to recover memories of actual events as far back as birth.	54%
6. Hypnosis can be used to recover accurate memories of past lives.	28%
7. It is possible to suggest false memories to someone who then incorporates them as true memories.	79%
8. Do you know of any cases where it seemed highly likely that a trauma victim's trauma was somehow suggested by a psychotherapist rather than a genuine experience?	19%

Yapko concludes that too many therapists treat their patients on the basis of their personal beliefs and philosophies, and not according to an objective consideration of the facts. His survey indicates that many practitioners are misinformed about basic scientific issues and that having an advanced degree does not prevent the therapist from erroneous assumptions about memory, suggestibility, and hypnosis.

The Courage to Heal

Ellen Bass and Laura Davis's book, *The Courage to Heal* (1988), is sometimes referred to as the Bible of the recovered memory movement. This book came up most often of all techniques mentioned by the parents who completed the False Memory Syndrome Foundation questionnaire. By 1992, 750,000 copies were reported to have been sold (NCPCA July 1992).

The Courage to Heal is used by many therapists. The assumption is that any vague feelings about abuse mean that the reader has been abused but cannot remember it. Demands for details or corroboration are seen as unreasonable and the veracity of the recovered memories is never questioned—one section uncritically presents an account of ritual abuse by a satanic cult of town leaders and church officials that included sexual abuse, murder, pornography, drugs, electric shock, and forcible impregnation of 'breeders' to produce babies for sacrifice.

The authors do not have degrees or formal training. Ellen Bass describes herself as not academically educated as a psychologist, but as acquiring counselling skills through practice, and as a partner of an abuse survivor. Her collaborator Laura Davis reports having recovered memories of abuse by her grandfather. Here are some quotations from their book:

- If you are unable to remember any specific instances like the ones mentioned above but still have a feeling that something abusive happened to you, it probably did. (p. 21)

- If you think you were abused and your life shows the symptoms, then you were. (p. 2)

- If you don't remember your abuse you are not alone. Many women don't have memories, and some never get memories. This doesn't mean they weren't abused. (p. 81)

- You are not responsible for proving that you were abused. (p. 137)

- If you're willing to get angry and the anger just doesn't seem to come, there are many ways to get in touch with it. A little like priming the pump, you can do things that will get your anger started. (p. 124)

- You may dream of murder or castration. It can be pleasurable to fantasize such scenes in vivid detail. (p. 128)

- Example given: [A woman], abused by her grandfather, went to his deathbed and, in front of all the other relatives, angrily confronted him right there in the hospital. (pp. 128–29)

The authors say this book is based on the "premise that everyone wants to become whole, to fulfill their potential. All of us, like seedlings or tadpoles, intend to become our full selves and will do so if we are not thwarted" (p. 14). This assumption is the Rogerian perfectionist concept that we all have a genetic blueprint which we will follow to self-realization. But to do so we need the co-operation of others to provide unconditional positive regard. Bass and Davis put it this way: "People don't need to be forced to grow. All we need is favorable circumstances: respect, love, honesty, and the space to explore" (p. 14). The difficulty is that anybody who gets in the way, who thwarts the natural growth to perfection, is by definition an obstacle, a block, and can be removed by any means, fair or foul. That is what this book is about. Healing is getting rid of those persons who thwart your growth to perfection. That is what takes the courage.

This is where the most telling criticism of Rogers's personality theory has focussed. Is it, in fact, the case that all of us are capable of constructive self-direction and are all aspects of our being capable of full awareness? Are schizophrenics really capable of self-direction? Remember, schizophrenia has a large genetic component. Are persons with an IQ under 50 capable of self-actualization? Is the stainless-steel psychopath, also largely a genetic condition, capable of being trusted for self-actualization? What determines whether the rapist, serial murderer, drug addict, or incest perpetrator is engaging in self-actualizing behavior and is simply growing into his full potential? The normative question cannot be evaded. The same criticism must be made of this book.

Bass and Davis answer with a claim that sets the entire basis for western civilization on its ear. Their answer is simple— feelings. They repeatedly offer only subjective, personal feelings as the basis for knowing what we know. This epistemological assumption that truth is known through subjective feelings destroys the possibility of any co-operative development of civilization. If followed, the outcome of knowledge determined by feelings is that we live in caves with assault rifles at every opening.

This is clear also in the positive value Bass and Davis place on rage and anger. Healing is said to occur through rage. But the history of humankind is the history of painful, slow, often fruitless efforts to control and reduce human rage and anger so that we can live together with at least some semblance of peace and harmony. If Bass and Davis's prescription for growth to fulfill potential is followed, the world would once again fit the description of Cyprian in the third century: "The whole world is wet with mutual blood; and murder, which in the case of an individual is admitted to be a crime, is called a virtue when it is committed wholesale. Immunity is claimed for the wicked deeds, not on the plea that they are guiltless, but because the cruelty is perpetrated on a grand scale" (Coxe 1957, p. 277).

The Courage to Heal is an exercise in irrationality. The authors are honest in saying that everything in the book comes "from the experiences of survivors" (p. 14). Experience is not a trustworthy guide to anything (Dawes 1989b, 1994). The entire field of decision theory research shows that the human mind is not a good instrument for handling data. There are so many ways in which subjective bias distorts and twists information. Because decisions are flawed and basically irrational it is only through the assiduous exercise of human reason that positive outcomes can be produced.

The bibliography of the book has 180 references. Only two of them are anywhere near what could be termed reasoned approaches. These are Finkelhor's 1979 book and Russell's 1986 book. The other references appear to be anecdotal, personal experience, and subjective opinion. Often a reference is described as "feminist." Even if this book is not a radical feminist tract, it is a caricature of what has frequently been described as a feminine characteristic—reliance upon emotion and a limited concern with reason.

This book is dangerous. It has a surface appeal and uses language that is familiar because of the pop psych jargon that has spread throughout the culture. This increases the likelihood that it may be read with some credulity and given a status it does not deserve. Like Hitler's *Mein Kampf*, it may have a large impact on the society and the world, but the nature of the impact may contribute to a horrendous, unanticipated disaster.

Other popular books include Renée Fredrickson's (1992) *Repressed Memories: A Journal to Recovery from Sexual Abuse,* E. Sue Blume's (1990) *Secret Survivors: Uncovering Incest and Its Aftereffects in Women,* and Yvonne Dolan's (1991) *Resolving Sexual Abuse.* All of them are similar to *The Courage to Heal,* emphasizing emotion as the guide to truth and encouraging the destructive emotions of anger and rage. Reading them in a block is like walking inside the worst nightmare of junior high school cliques, jealousies, and rages. For whatever reason, somebody is on the outs and the response is to ostracize them and hold them out as the worst and most miserable of all creatures.

Hypnosis and Amytal Interviews

In the FMS Foundation questionnaire project (Freyd et al. 1993) most of the respondents who knew something of the type of therapy reported that hypnosis was used. The use of hypnosis for memory retrieval raises serious questions about the accuracy of the memories. There is agreement and empirical verification about several aspects of hypnosis (Cardena and Spiegel 1991; Orne et al. 1985; Putnam 1991a; Spanos, Quigley et al. 1991). Under hypnosis, people are more suggestible and therefore more likely to agree with a persuasive communication. However, there are serious problems with the accuracy and validity of memories elicited in hypnosis. The person is apt to experience these memories, which can be quite vivid and detailed, as subjectively real, which increases their confidence in the memories. Therefore the person appears confident and certain about the memories, and can be persuasive and convincing when talking about them. This problem is exacerbated in the case of people diagnosed with multiple personality disorder since such persons are likely to be easily hypnotized.

The fact that hypnosis can result in 'memories' for events that never happened is well documented. Spanos et al. (in press) describe how people under hypnosis can fantasize entire scenarios and later believe these are memories for actual events.

They describe research demonstrating how some people come to believe that they can recall complex past life identities under age regression. Ofshe (1992) describes the case of Paul Ingram who was given relaxation techniques that produced dissociation, pseudomemories, and confessions of raping his daughters and participating in a baby-murdering satanic cult.

Although most people are skeptical of age regression to past lives, many believe hypnosis can help capture memories of actual experiences in their childhoods. But this belief is not supported by research. Nash (1992), reporting on a review of over 60 empirical studies on hypnotic age regression, observes that hypnotic age regression to childhood is not a literal reliving of a childhood event. He notes that the hypnotist can obtain equally dramatic, compelling, and subjectively real portrayals from hypnotized subjects who are told to *progress* to an age of 70 or 80:

> Hypnotic age regression may be of the same ilk as hypnotic age progression or past life regression: It elicits a profoundly believed-in experience that undoubtedly has important diagnostic and therapeutic properties, but its relationship to actual events must be regarded with great care. (p. 9)

To illustrate his point, Nash (1992) describes a man who, with the help of hypnosis, developed vivid and detailed memories of abduction by space aliens. The man had for some time had a vague memory involving a camping trip in which he and a friend encountered a kind of brightly glowing caterpillar on the path, a bright flash of light, and the loss of two hours of time. Many years later he read a popular book on UFO abductions. He and his childhood friend contacted that book's author and were hypnotized. Although the friend's memories remained vague, the man uncovered extraordinary memories involving vivid details of the aliens, their spacecraft, their voices, and a peculiar machine that they attached to his penis to obtain samples of sperm. The UFO expert concluded that while the man's friend had not really been abducted, the man had.

The man came to Nash for therapy three months later with turmoil, anxiety, nightmares, flashbacks, withdrawal, and, in general, symptoms of post-traumatic stress disorder. Although the therapy was successful in treating his presenting symptoms, the man left therapy completely convinced that his memories were of an actual abduction. This was despite Nash's efforts to present the abduction material as immensely important but symbolic as opposed to being literally true.

Nash's client's persistent belief in the reality of his abduction memories is consistent with the effects of hypnotically-developed memories—they are subjectively real to the patient. Nash observes that there was no difference between this man's clinical presentation concerning the trauma and that of many of his sexually abused patients.

Lynn and Nash (1994) describe a case where a client provided a strongly believed in but false memory under hypnosis:

> One of our (SJL) clients missed a therapy session. Because she had a history of suicide attempts and was depressed at the time, she was contacted the next day, after several unsuccessful attempts to contact her the night of the session. She was puzzled by the concern expressed and stated, "Are you kidding me? I was there." Although she had no clear memories of what we discussed during the session, it was difficult to convince her that she had missed her appointment. At the next session, she requested hypnosis to relax her and to explore her memory lapse. During hypnosis, she stated that she had been angry with her seven-year-old son, had left her house crying, and had driven to a nearby cemetery. With much emotion, she related how she went to an open grave, got in the grave, and became terrified when she could not get out. After several frantic attempts, she finally succeeded in extricating herself from the grave, She reported that she then drove home and went to sleep. After hypnosis, she was extremely upset by the thought that she would engage in such 'bizarre' behavior. (p. 194)

SJL had his doubts regarding the accuracy of this recollection. He visited the cemetery with the client the next night and found no grave that matched the client's description. Her son told him that his mother had slept through the psychotherapy session. The client expressed much relief that she had not actually engaged in such bizarre and 'crazy' behavior and decided that the uncovered memory was actually a dream. Lynn and Nash use this example to emphasize the importance of not uncritically accepting clients' memories as historical fact, especially those obtained under hypnosis.

Ganaway (1991) notes that memories retrieved in a hypnotic trance are likely to contain a combination of both fact and fantasy in a mixture that cannot be accurately determined without external corroboration. Since hypnosis increases confidence in the veracity of both correct and incorrect recalled material, the therapist should be very cautious about reinforcing the truthfulness of any memories which are elicited through hypnosis unless there is outside corroboration.

Weissberg (1993) points out that the hypnotist's expectations and the person's prior beliefs will affect what is recalled under hypnosis. He states that suspicions may be transformed into vivid pseudomemories with hypnosis and the person will have difficulty discriminating between accurate and inaccurate recollections.

There are similar difficulties with Amytal interviews. Amytal is often believed to be a type of 'truth serum' that can reveal memories of real events which are somehow hidden in the brain. Piper (1994) reviewed all of the literature on Amytal interviews from 1930 through 1993. Twelve studies examined patients' abilities to tell the truth while under the influence of the drug. None of these research reports endorsed using Amytal as a truth serum. Instead, Piper reports that the authors noted major deficiencies of the procedure that destroy the ability to accurately relate past events.

As in hypnosis, people interviewed under Amytal are more suggestible than they are in their normal waking states. This is not surprising since during Amytal interviews, people demonstrate numerous phenomena characteristic of hypnotic states. They are therefore vulnerable to the influence of the interviewer. Also, the procedure may lend an aura of authenticity to any information elicited so that the Amytal interview will falsely confirm the person's beliefs about abuse.

Most of the research reviewed by Piper indicated that,

under Amytal, people often distort reality and may produce
grossly distorted or even psychotic material. In addition, people
can tell lies while under Amytal. Therefore, reports obtained
under the influence of the drug cannot be assumed to accurately reflect past events.

Putnam (Chu 1992) concludes about memories recovered
by hypnosis or Amytal:

> Research has shown that pseudomemories can be suggested
> under these conditions and that these false memories may be
> experienced by the subject as genuine recollections of past
> experiences. Confabulation can occur. Individuals in such al-
> tered states of consciousness are more susceptible to suggestion
> and may unconsciously produce material that they perceive as
> expected of them. . . . In short there is no acid test for determin-
> ing the veracity of memories recovered by hypnosis or Amytal.
> (p. 7)

Ideomotor Questioning and Guided Imagery

Ideomotor questioning, a variant of hypnotherapy, is purported to be a way of getting information from the unconscious.
Dolan (1991) defines it as "[A]n unconscious response that
often feels effortless to the client, as if it were occurring 'all by
itself'" (p. 144). The client, who is hypnotized, is told to relax
and let her mind drift "while her unconscious does the work"
(p. 145). While in a trance, she is asked questions which are
answered by finger signals which indicate 'yes,' 'no,' or 'I'm not
ready to know consciously.'

Dolan says that through this technique, the therapist and
client can retrieve information about dissociated abuse. She
maintains that material uncovered in this fashion can validate
and confirm the reality of the abuse. Obviously, there is no
research supporting this claim. All the criticisms of hypnosis
and Amytal interviews apply here. Ganaway (Chu 1992) observes that the theory behind ideomotor questioning—that
everything that happens to a person is stored somewhere in
memory in complete detail—is unsupported by research and is
not accepted by scientists. He states that ideomotor questioning
"has become a major nemesis in the dissociated disorders field

when used in the diagnosis of MPD or for exploration of unconscious trauma memories" (p. 8).

A related technique is guided imagery. The client is asked to close her eyes, relax, take deep breaths, and then imagine a scene. When a scene is pictured, the person is encouraged to relate as many details as possible. The therapist asks questions to guide the images. The theory is that these images represent fragments of actual repressed traumatic events that are hidden in the unconscious. Guided imagery or imagistic memory work, as it is also called, is a form of hypnosis.

Flashbacks

Flashbacks are used to confirm the reality of abuse and are important in recovered memory therapy. Blume (1990) defines a flashback as "the reliving of a traumatic experience, or an aspect of a trauma, as if it were happening now" (p. 100) and asserts that "flashbacks and memories may represent an unwanted truth, but a truth nevertheless. Believe them" (p. 60). Blume also believes that since the incest survivor has dissociated the original experience, when she has a flashback, "it is as if she is experiencing the trauma for the first time" (p. 102).

But as McHugh (undated) points out, flashbacks cannot be assumed to represent a memory of an actual life event. He notes that flashbacks are common in people who have been frightened or traumatized and are universal everywhere. However, as studies of flashbacks following war experiences indicate, flashbacks are *not* replications of an actual event, but are the development from the experience of a 'worst fear' scenario. For example, the soldier's flashback may include an image of a hand grenade falling at his feet or of enemy soldiers appearing and overwhelming his comrades. Intense fear accompanies this experience. "Thus, it was not that memory was jogged but rather that fear ran riot" (p. 10).

We cannot assume that a flashback is a reproduction of an actual past experience. Instead, it is likely to be an expression of the patient's worst fears generated out of the focus in therapy on abuse. This is especially probable when the person is in a survivors' group where others are describing their own horrible flashbacks of terrifying abuse. Flashbacks are simply not relivings of actual events and flashbacks cannot confirm abuse.

Survivors' Groups

Individuals are frequently referred to survivors' therapy groups or self-help groups such as those for adult children of alcoholics. Although such groups may be beneficial for some actual abuse victims, they are dangerous for people without memories who want to explore the possibility that they were abused. Such groups are apt to give continual encouragement for uncovering memories of increasingly intrusive and deviant abuse.

But many therapists and survivors' books recommend such groups for people without abuse memories. *The Courage to Heal* states, "If you're still fuzzy about what happened to you, hearing other women's stories can stimulate your memories" (p. 462). Herman and Schatzow (1987) report that their survivor therapy group "proved to be a powerful stimulus for recovery of previously repressed traumatic memories" (p. 1). Courtois (1992) sees group therapy as "useful" and says, "Groups are very powerful in eliciting memories since survivors associate or 'chain' to each others' recollections and feelings" (p. 29).

Laura Pasley (Goldstein and Farmer 1993) notes that the women in her group all systematically had similar flashbacks, uncovered similar repressed memories, and reported similar types of severe and bizarre abuse. Lynn Gondolf (1992) describes the suggestibility and group influence where, after one woman would suddenly recall a new abusive event, others would soon recall similar events:

> Group therapy doesn't work for a person who is suggestible or is early in therapy. Such a person may not have any sexual abuse issues. But if she is placed in an incest-oriented group, it is contagious. If that's all they hear every day of the week, if that's what they're paying their hundred dollars an hour for, if they're given a book like *Courage to Heal* or *The Monster Within*, they will come to believe that they are incest victims also. . . . If one woman had a flashback of snakes and cannibalism in the woods, a few days later, someone else had a similar flashback.

A retractor gives a lengthy description of the techniques used in group therapy to help the members recover abuse memories (Goldstein and Farmer 1993). These include 'make-up-a-story' in which a woman would describe unpleasant emotions she had recently experienced and then tell about when she had similar feelings in childhood. If the woman couldn't remember an actual experience, she was to make up a story. The group members also did 'chair work' in which they pretended the perpetrator was sitting in an empty chair and then talked to him about their anger at the abuse. If the woman couldn't think of what to say, the group leader would supply the sentences. The theory behind such techniques was that when one group member would talk, this would remind the others of similar experiences and emotions. Thus, the group experience would help the members to recovered their repressed memories.

Since the norm is that group members were abused whether or not they remember it, and the task of therapy is to uncover the hidden memories, group members are given attention, encouragement, and reinforcement as they uncover and report their repressed memories. Campbell (1992) observes that given the process of conformity and compliance that will characterize any group, clients in such a group who deny a history of sexual abuse run the risk of being ostracized as denying deviants.

When they are also encouraged to break off contact with family and friends who don't believe in their accounts of abuse, the group becomes the new 'family.' They can become increasingly isolated from anyone who could give them skeptical feedback. Lynn Gondolf (1992) describes how her therapists told her she had to make her survivors group her new family. She cut off contact with her parents and all of her interactions were with her therapist and the women in her group. They talked about incest, depression, medications, eating, and their latest flashbacks. Eventually, most of the women developed memories of bizarre, ritual abuse. Laura Pasley (Goldstein and Farmer 1993) also describes the progression in her therapy group: "We began as Eating Disorder, then Sexual Abuse

Victims, then Incest Victims, then Satanic Ritual Abuse Victims, then Multiple Personality Disorders" (p. 354).

Other Commonly Used Therapy Techniques

Dream interpretation is often used in retrieving memories. The client brings in the dream which is discussed and interpreted by the therapist. Dreams may also be presented in survivors' groups. The assumptions regarding dreams are expressed by Fredrickson (1992):

> During sleep, you have a direct link to your unconscious. Because the channel is open, memory fragments or symbols from repressed sexual abuse memories often intrude into the dream state. Even though the memory is embedded in the symbolism of the dream world, it is possible to use the dream to retrieve the memory. (p. 125)

But there is no evidence that material from dreams accurately depicts actual past events, particularly those that are not consciously remembered. The best documented source of dreams is 'daily residue,' that is, the concerns, events, and thoughts of everyday life (Lindsay and Read, in press). Dreams can therefore come from what is read, heard, or talked or thought about and hence can result from therapy itself. If the client is in therapy where the focus is on sexual abuse as the most important thing in her life, she is very likely to have dreams about sexual abuse. It is particularly mistaken to attempt to interpret dreams symbolically.

'Body memories' are used to gain information about hypothesized abuse that is not remembered. The assumption is that, although there are no conscious memories, the body remembers and the client has physical symptoms that correspond to the childhood abuse. Proponents are particularly apt to use this concept for events that occur before the age of two or so, when the child can begin to process verbal information. There is no evidence supporting this theory. We describe the body memory concept in more detail in Chapter 9.

People are often asked to spend time writing in a journal or diary in the attempt to recover memories. Obviously, forgotten memories may gradually be remembered by thinking and writing about them, and this information may be accurate. At the same time, totally false memories can be created and then embroidered and embellished by thinking and writing about them, especially when the client is told that her current problems reflect repressed sexual abuse and that journal writing will produce accurate memories.

Sometimes people are asked to return to the place where the abuse supposedly occurred or to look at childhood diaries and photographs. This is a valid technique for memory retrieval (Geiselman and Fisher 1989). We routinely show young children photographs when questioning them about their families. Such techniques can aid in recalling forgotten material. But if the memory search begins without any memories for the event and is combined with strong suggestions or preconceived ideas concerning what is supposed to be remembered, there is no way to know whether the retrieved memories are accurate.

Encouragement to File Lawsuits

Survivors' groups and books often recommend filing a civil lawsuit as part of the healing process (Bass and Davis 1988; Crnich and Crnich 1992; Nohlgren 1991). As a result, many 'survivors' have filed civil lawsuits against their alleged abusers. The FMS Foundation reports that one out of 16 accused parents have had lawsuits filed against them. Many others have been threatened.

Several states have extended the statutory period of limitations in civil cases so that the statute of limitations begins two or three years after the alleged abuse is *remembered* and/or after the claimant understands that the abuse caused injury (Bulkley and Horwitz 1994; Colaneri and Johnson 1992; Loftus 1993; Loftus and Rosenwald 1993; Slovenko 1993). By 1993, courts and legislatures in more than 23 states had created legal mechanisms for both criminal and civil actions based on recovered memories (Loftus and Rosenwald 1993).

Many recovered memory therapists and some attorneys believe that civil litigation is an important and sometimes essential part of the healing process. Williams, writing in *The Courage to Heal*, states: "In my experience, nearly every client who has undertaken this kind of suit has experienced growth, therapeutic strengthening, and an increased sense of personal power and self-esteem as a result of the litigation" (Bass and Davis, p. 310). Mallia (1993) believes civil litigation can ensure that the abuser will be held accountable for the abuse and can therefore bring a therapeutic sense of closure to the victim. He says that winning the lawsuit "can cleanse the victim's tortured psyche" (p. 129). Although Clute (1993) acknowledges the risks in suing and losing, she describes the effect on a survivor she represented who won $3 million: "[I]t was clearly a victory of the human soul, a liberation from a bondage that had changed him for a long time. . . . I knew I had participated in a significant healing experience" (p. 122). (Clute also recommends making surreptitious tape recordings in conversations with the accused in order to gather evidence.)

But others are more pessimistic about the psychological benefits of suing the alleged perpetrator. Particularly if the recovered memory is false and the abuse never occurred, a civil lawsuit can be extremely damaging, not only to the falsely accused, but to the 'survivor' who is initiating the lawsuit. It makes any hope of reconciliation with the family extremely difficult, if not impossible.

'Penelope' (1992) describes her lawsuit against her parents. Her stated purposes in suing were to empower herself, to stop her father from molesting other children, and to stop him from getting away with his crime. The result of the lawsuit was that she lost contact with both parents and three siblings, although one sibling supported her. She describes the lawsuit process as emotionally devastating: "I feel violated all over again" (p. 121). She reports decompensating, having difficulty dealing with her (male) attorneys, and finding her deposition intensely humiliating and traumatizing to her 'inner child.' Her trial is yet to come.

In commenting on the Penelope case, Walker (1992) observes that the costs of a civil lawsuit are often higher than expected but she still believes the use of the civil courts to redress injuries by financial compensation is a "new and exciting tool in the war against child sex offenders" (p. 125). But Ewing (1992), commenting on the same case, notes that Penelope's complaints are like "sticking one's head in a lion's mouth and complaining when it's bitten off" (p. 129). Ewing discourages such lawsuits since they are likely to be painful and costly and to fail to accomplish the goals of personal vindication. The plaintiff is likely to be worn down and the case may never make it to court. If she does persist to trial, the defense's goal will be to destroy her credibility and they will bring in witnesses to portray her as vindictive and/or mentally ill. There is a good chance that she will lose unless there is strong corroboration. Even if she wins, it is quite likely she will never see a penny of the award. Ewing stresses that survivors considering lawsuits should confront this reality and understand that the probability is that they will "come away from their lawsuits empty-handed and broken-hearted" (p. 132). He believes that such litigation is countertherapeutic.

Thompson (1993) presents a similar view. He notes that litigation is inherently stressful and is not necessary or beneficial in the majority of cases. It is likely to cause estrangement among other family relationships and victimize other family members. The only goals likely to be achieved are that of inflicting pain and exacting revenge, goals which are unlikely to produce any significant therapeutic benefit.

Examples of Therapy Experiences

The information from women who underwent recovered memory therapy described in Chapter 4 as well as other anecdotal accounts illustrate the treatment techniques described above (*FMS Foundation Newsletter*; Gavigan 1992; Goldstein and Farmer 1993; Gondolf 1992; Salter 1993; Sifford 1992). These accounts give vivid details, not only of the techniques and procedures used, but of the harmfulness of such 'treatment.'

The cases show a common pattern. Treatment was entered for problems other than sexual abuse—for example: depression, eating disorders, marital distress, or PMS. However, the women were questioned extensively from the beginning about abuse. Their therapists assumed that repressed abuse was at the root of their problems and therapy sessions consisted of pressure to recover the memories. Several were hypnotized. They were given a variety of medications, encouraged to confront their parents, told to read survivors' books, and they participated in group therapy where the group norm was talking about the abuse.

As therapy progressed, they were encouraged to remember more and more about the alleged abuse and eventually several developed graphic, detailed stories involving violent, sadistic ritual abuse. If they questioned the validity of their emerging memories, they were told to accept them as real. Several began to show symptoms of multiple personality disorder and they all became worse as a result of therapy. They were encouraged to cut off relationships with family and friends and they became isolated from the stable and healthy things in their lives. None were able to recover from the experience until they discontinued the therapy.

In another example, the FMS Foundation received a letter from a woman who had never forgotten the incest, neglect, and emotional abuse in her childhood. Following successful therapy as a young woman, she became interested in mental health and now works as a counsellor. Upon hearing of a therapist who was diagnosing satanic ritual abuse, she made an appointment with this therapist. Although she did not succumb to the therapist's suggestions, she could see how this could happen to someone unsophisticated and unprepared:

> I didn't tell him I worked in mental health, but that I was a survivor of incest and brutality. I decided to focus on a real nightmare I had as a child and see where he would go with it.
>
> What an amazing experience! After one-and-one-half hours he told me I had MPD. Even one of my alternate personalities came out while he was talking to me and told me my parents

were Satan worshipers and I had been gang raped by the cult. When I refuted this he told me I was in denial and would not be whole again until I remembered all these things and worked through them. He also said that was the reason I was so overweight. He told me that inside me there was a lovely four-and-one-half-year-old girl waiting to grow up and become the very best person she could be!

Had I not had my education and training, I could have bought into nonsense. It bothers me to think what these people are doing to their clients and their families.

He didn't hypnotize me. But he 'walked' me through my dream, pushing and prodding, until I actually saw weird pictures in my mind. I realize what he did was coach my imagination and then label the fantasy a memory. (*FMS Foundation Newsletter*, November 1993)

In a participant observer study, a journalist, Debbie Nathan (1992), immersed herself in the incest survivors' movement, including attending a marathon retreat for survivors of incest. There were six therapists for three dozen women survivors, who clutched stuffed animals and began the retreat in a room furnished only with mattresses. They were told to have their 'inner children' express rage at the perpetrators by beating telephone books with rubber hoses while squatting over the mattresses and screaming obscenities.

They were all encouraged to give detailed descriptions about their abuse in the group setting because hearing stories might help others trigger memories. When one woman, recalling memories of cult abuse by her mother, sobbed and said she didn't know if the memories were really true, the therapist told her she had to face the memories and ordered her to do mattress work, "Now!" She told another woman that, "When your kids inside are ready, more memories will come." Eleven of the women had no abuse memories but nevertheless were told to join in the activities.

Nathan observes that a competition began over the satanic abuse reported by several of the women in which each produced more and more detailed and bizarre accounts. The only kind of victims with status among the women and therapists were the women who had suffered rape, torture, and black robes. Others who only reported emotional abuse or battering or couldn't remember the abuse had no status in the "swimsuit competition atmosphere" of the retreat.

Diagnosis as a Club

A particularly effective technique for coercing conformity is to use diagnosis as a club to both punish and shape the patient into expected behavior patterns. This totally destructive use of diagnosis becomes evident only when patients who have been in the treatment programs talk about their experience. First, they are told their behaviors are 'typical of' or the 'classic' behaviors of a person sexually abused. They are then given a diagnosis, told what it is, and then told that the typical set of behaviors of that diagnosis is what they can expect. They are told that the diagnosis and the behaviors 'consistent with' it are the consequences of having been sexually abused. Some may be told that they will need therapy for the alleged abuse or for MPD or PTSD for the rest of their lives. They are told they may come in and out of hospitals for years. They may be on medication for the rest of their lives. They will never be fully functional sexually or able to get along with a man. Whatever the description of the behavior, it is labelled 'typical' or 'classical' for survivors, and the switches are set for the expectations. This in turn produces the very behaviors labelled 'typical' which in turn reinforces both the authority and power of the therapist and the patient's acceptance of the diagnosis as real.

Why do These Therapists Believe?

Perhaps no issue has so polarized psychology as the debate over recovered memories of childhood sexual abuse. Some persons are believers and others are skeptics. Some try to take a middle position but this is difficult to accomplish when such strong emotions are involved. The commitment shows through whichever direction it is in. We, as skeptics, have tried to understand how mental health professionals can hold beliefs we consider to be nonsense.

Lack of Training

Some observers have seen the proliferation of uncredentialled therapists and a weakening in the scientific training and standards at graduate programs as a major factor in the recovered memory movement (Dawes 1992; Gravitz 1994). But a Ph.D. or M.D. is no guarantee that the therapist will be a skeptic. In the FMS Foundation survey (Freyd et al. 1993) the therapists reported by the parents included all disciplines, including psychiatrists, psychologists, and social workers as well as less credentialled therapists. Bottoms, Shaver, and Goodman (1991) surveyed doctoral-level clinical psychologists and report that of those who had encountered cases of ritual or religious abuse, the great majority, 93 percent, accepted the clients' claims as true. Many of these cases involved adult survivors who reported amnesiac periods. In Yapko's (1994a, 1994b) survey, described earlier in this chapter, the academic degree held by the respondent made little difference. Yapko found that 22 percent of the therapists who believed in age regression and past lives held Ph.D.s and 28.1 percent held M.D.s.

It may well be that training has become less rigorous in all disciplines. Feld (1994) examined 48 M.S.W. programs and reports that most students are not exposed to material on memory or memory retrieval and of those who are introduced to these concepts, the exposure is minimal. Dawes (1992) observes that fewer and fewer (between 13 and 18 percent) clinical psychologists are being trained at the top 200 graduate institutions while more and more (almost 40 percent) are graduating from professional schools. He notes that in 1970 the former figure was close to 40 percent and the latter was zero. His conclusion is that the scientific training of clinical psychologists has "gone to hell" (p. 217). Even when properly trained, few practitioners keep current with the relevant scientific literature and use it in their practices (Campbell 1994; Dawes 1994).

Attitudes

We believe that the therapists who help uncover memories are absolutely persuaded that they are right and are doing a good and noble thing. We expect there are very few who are deliberately engaging in recovered memory therapy solely for financial payoff or for any other nefarious reason. Rather, their stance is characterized by Renée Fredrickson (1993b) who says she knows she is right because she keeps her feet firmly planted in the "river of truth," by Sue Grand who believes the therapist is the one person in the patient's life who "really sees the truth" (Grand et al. 1991), and by Marilyn Mason (1993) who compares the believing therapists to those who rescued victims from the Holocaust and who proudly asserts, "we are the ones who can be the truth tellers."

These therapists give great weight to the importance of feelings as opposed to empirical evidence. Bass and Davis in *The Courage to Heal* (1988) state that everything in the book comes "from the experiences of survivors" (p. 14). They are offering subjective personal feelings and intuition as the basis for knowing what they know. McHugh (1994) terms this the "romanticist tendency" and observes, "The romanticist tendency in psychotherapy is to rely upon feelings for evidence, on metaphors for reality, on inspiration and myth for guidance" (p. 17). But McHugh optimistically believes that the empiricists will prevail over the romantics because:

> [T]he romantics have become infatuated by their own thought. They claim to know things they never try to prove. They are charmed by novelty and ignore, even disdain, drab facts. More recently, in their thinking they have taken a nightmarish turn towards chaos that has caused patients and their families much suffering. (p. 18)

Consensus and Authorities

Robyn Dawes (1992) explains the belief in recovered memory in terms of social consensus and reliance on authorities. Dawes notes that all of us depend upon authorities when we hear about subjects such as global warming since we are seldom in a position to check out the data ourselves. This tendency to accept the authorities is strengthened when there is a great deal of social consensus.

Until approximately 1992, the believers in recovered memory were seldom challenged. They all went to the same conferences, talked to each another, reinforced one another, and were rarely confronted with disconfirming evidence. They were told that half of all women were sexually abused in childhood and that many of these did not remember the abuse. They were told of ritualistic satanic cults. They were given long lists of symptoms and signs that indicated repressed abuse. They were told that they must help their clients retrieve their memories and then validate the reality of the abuse if their clients were to recover. When scientific criticisms started to appear and the False Memory Syndrome Foundation began, the recovered memory therapists had been operating unchallenged for several years.

Mulhern (1992), as a participant observer, provides insight into the training offered for ritual satanic abuse that illustrates the networking and dissemination of information in recovered memory therapy. She systematically analyzed 14 satanic cult/ritual abuse training seminars. All were professionally accredited and offered to mental health professionals. All were held between 1987 and 1990 and all offered training in the identification and treatment of satanic ritual abuse victims. In addition, 23 other presentations and papers on satanic ritual abuse presented at other conferences were included.

The analysis showed that all followed a two-stage procedure. The first stage is to construct a belief filter with listeners exhorted and admonished to believe. In the majority of conferences, a parallel was drawn between the disbelief which surrounded the reality of child sexual abuse during the 1970s and the skepticism which surrounds ritual abuse patients' recovered memories today. The participants were told that it is essential to believe in the reality of recovered memories and satanic cults and that the vast majority of satanic ritual abuse victims enter therapy amnesic for their extraordinary abuses. They were assured that unless these memories are retrieved, there is little hope for recovery.

The second stage is built on the first and assumes that all claims are real. Therapists are given suggestions for treatment using techniques with unknown validity and reliability. Mulhern observes that none of the seminars cautioned clinicians about risks of confabulation, suggestibility, source amnesia, even when intrusive techniques such as hypnosis are used. She concludes:

> Conversion to belief provides individuals with the intimate conviction that they can suddenly see and understand realities which they have never seen before. However, when uncritical belief becomes the linchipin of all understanding, anything which would cause the believer to doubt must be systematically eliminated. To put it succinctly, the ear educated exclusively by belief is also a deaf ear. (1992, p. 232)

Carol Tavris (1993) notes how the believers refer to the same studies and quote the same experts. She describes how recovered memory therapists write a book, are given expert status, and then conduct workshops and train other psychotherapists:

> [T]he authors of these books all rely on one another's evidence for their own; they all endorse and recommend one another's books to their readers. If one of them comes up with a concocted statistic—such as 'more than half of all women are survivors of childhood sexual trauma'—the numbers are traded like baseball cards, reprinted in every book and eventually enshrined as fact. (p. 17)

It appears that therapists who are not tightly committed to recovered memory therapy are now becoming more cautious. But we expect those who have been strongly committed for years to remain entrenched. As Goldstein and Farmer (1993) observe:

> Once started on a course of regression therapy it becomes a closed system. In twenty years, the ideas formulated by a few therapists have permeated the entire culture and regressed memory therapy is well entrenched. . . . Anyone who questions retrieved memories gained in therapy is considered to be 'in

denial'—a euphemism for lying, guilt, evil, or stupidity. (p. 168)

Political Commitments

The controversy over recovered memories is to a large extent a political issue rather than a scientific one. As was discussed in Chapter 2, incest has been interpreted by some feminists in terms of sexual assault by powerful males against powerless women and children. Incest is seen as common and as a way of subjugating and socializing women.

We conjecture that the motivating factor for some of the recovered memory therapists is a strong commitment to a type of feminist ideology. Chris Barden (1994) observes: "The real basis of 'memory retrieval' therapy and the 'incest survivor movement' is not the science of psychology but rather a confused and confusing combination of the pain of genuine victims and the political ideology of ultra-radical ideologues" (p. 6). Barden, a psychologist and attorney who has been involved in large numbers of these cases, notes that political indoctrination is a standard component of the therapy in many of the cases he has seen. This political indoctrination takes the form of diatribes against the patriarchal society, the Catholic church, and the male-dominated scientific community.

The FMS Foundation is frequently depicted as a white patriarchal organization of sexual abusers who are using considerable money, power, and influence to continue the status quo, continue their abuse and revictimize their victims by making them doubt their recovered memories. The FMS Foundation is also falsely believed to be financing lawsuits against recovered memory therapists. Rational discourse becomes more difficult when an issue becomes so politicized.

Paranoia

In 1991 we hypothesized that one difference between those who believe in the satanic cult conspiracy and those who are skeptical is in the personality characteristics of the believers (Underwager and Wakefield 1991). We speculated that at least some of the believing therapists showed characteristics of paranoia. This does not mean that such people are psychotic, since paranoid thinking can occur in people in the absence of other psychopathology.

Paranoid thinking is expressed in a tendency to falsely interpret the actions of others as threatening. Paranoid persons expect to be harmed or exploited and may read hidden meanings into benign remarks or events. They are hypervigilant and fear that information about them may be used against them. When in a new situation, they intensely and narrowly search for confirmation of their expectations and beliefs, with no appreciation of the total context. Paranoids may be convinced that they possess some special talent or insight into the truth. Paranoia leads to deep resentments, especially toward others who have attained a position of acceptance, power, or eminence. Paranoids believe that they are slighted and overlooked and that their rightness and righteousness is not properly acknowledged (Millon 1981).

Gardner (1992b) believes that therapists who readily 'find' sexual abuse may be paranoid and that the paranoid patients find paranoid therapists. He notes:

> Paranoids are hypervigilant, are obsessed with any detail that might support their delusional system(s), and view as evil and/or corrupt those who would question their beliefs. . . . What more noble cause can there be than to rid the world of sex perverts, people who perpetuate terrible abominations on innocent children? Paranoids tend to band together with others of similar persuasion and ignore or remove themselves entirely from those who would shake their delusional systems. (p. 332)

Obviously, there has been no empirical study of the personality characteristics of therapists who recover memories of sexual abuse, but there are observable data that suggest paranoid thinking. The examples that follow involve professionals, several well-known, who have spoken, written, and/or given workshops on the subject of recovered memories and satanic ritual abuse.

- Roland Summit, M.D, in a debate with Dr. Underwager over the Canadian Broadcasting Corporation radio program, *Ideas,* in

1986 described those who believe that sexual abuse of children is epidemic: "We've never really wanted to understand it [child sexual abuse]. We as adults in western history at least, have always put it away when it comes up. The people who have done best at putting it away are the ones who emerge with power and respectability. The people who say this is real and we have to do something about it have traditionally been trivialized into positions of being not credible or falsely motivated or even maliciously motivated. Certainly not scientific and not authoritative. . . ."

• Roland Summit, M.D., in a conference in Huntsville, Alabama, in Spring, 1993, claimed that the tunnels under the school where the McMartin children were allegedly ritually abused had been found, but that the press conspired to kill the story and cover it up (Summit 1993). Summit's presentations (for example Summit 1990) indicate that he and his followers see themselves as having the special power to discern abuse and reach into children and adults who deny being abused, to discover the truth.

• Catherine Gould, Ph.D. and Louis Cozolino, Ph.D. (1992) maintain that satanic cults program 'alter personalities' to disrupt therapy. Neither the therapist nor the patient have any awareness of this, so therapists should presume that their patients are active in a satanic cult but are unconscious of their involvement.

• James Friesen, Ph.D. (1992) claims that some people diagnosed with multiple personality disorder are actually possessed by evil spirits. This is part of the spiritual warfare in which Satan's forces are trying to overcome the true believers. He recommends exorcism for such cases and proposes a new diagnostic category, Oppressive Supernatural States Disorder.

• The Ritual Abuse Task Force in Los Angeles, an official county group, insists that the satanists are attempting to poison them along with the therapists who treat satanic cult survivors, by pumping toxic pesticides into their offices and homes through air-conditioning vents. (Curtiss 1992)

• Daniel Ryder, L.S.W. (1992), in his book on satanic ritual abuse, recommends 12-step groups for satanic cult survivors. But he believes that cult members will try to infiltrate the groups. He also claims that the cult holds "mock therapy sessions" and uses "highly sophisticated psychological techniques" in order to make the survivors distrust therapists.

• In June 1992, we chaired a symposium, involving six professionals, on recovered memories at the annual meeting of the American Psychological Society. The day before the presentation, each participant received a certified letter from the attorney for Jennifer Freyd, Ph.D., threatening a lawsuit if Jennifer Freyd were mentioned in the symposium. (Jennifer Freyd is the daughter of Pamela Freyd, the executive director of the FMS Foundation.) Jennifer Freyd was somehow convinced that the topic of this symposium was going to be her. Contrary to Dr. Freyd's completely irrational belief, none of the participants had any intention of mentioning Dr. Freyd, or any other alleged 'survivor,' in their scientific presentations and two of the participants had no idea who she was until they received her threatening letter.

• Hollida Wakefield attended a continuing education conference on recovered memories in Minneapolis in 1993 and attempted to tape record the presentations in order to have an accurate record of what was said. Her tape recorder was openly placed on the table. When this was observed, she was confronted and accused of being unethical, and the tapes were confiscated. She was told that no taping was allowed because the presenters would not feel 'safe' if what they said was recorded.

• At a conference at Clark University in 1993, the speakers who supported the recovered memory concept also refused to let their presentations be taped. This was also represented as a scholarly, scientific conference.

• At the above Clark University Conference, Ralph Underwager was first invited to give a presentation but was later disinvited when three of the recovered memory advocates refused to appear if he were there. The reason given was that they were "afraid" of him.

• During the 1993 MPA (Minnesota Psychological Association) annual meeting at which we, along with three others, gave a presentation on recovered memories, we attended a presentation by Renée Fredrickson, Ph.D., whom we had never met, spoken to, nor communicated with. Her presentation had been specifically organized to counter ours. We sat quietly towards the rear of the room and said nothing during her presentation. Afterwards Dr. Underwager spoke to the president of the MPA for a few minutes, and then we left. Several weeks later Dr. Fredrickson (Fredrickson 1993a) stated that she was afraid of retaliation and reprisals from Dr. Underwager if she "disagreed with his theories," that he had "raised his cane (and) waved it around in a threatening manner while I was speaking," and that, because of Dr. Underwager's threatening and intimidating behavior, she had to be escorted out of the building to safety. But none of the people with us during this entire period, including the president of the MPA, observed any such behaviors or had any idea what she was talking about. We surmise that Dr. Fredrickson's skewed and inaccurate perceptions of Dr. Underwager resulted from her own paranoia.

• At the recovered memory conference in Minneapolis in 1993, the False Memory Syndrome Foundation was described as an organization of patriarchal offenders who are attempting to revictimize their victims by making them doubt their recovering memories. Renée Fredrickson said the FMS Foundation is a "well-funded media campaign" that has very large amounts of money and the ability to "capture the white-collar press." The FMSF was depicted similarly at the 1993 Fifth Annual Eastern Regional Conference on Abuse and Multiple Personality (Wylie 1993) where possible C.I.A. connections were also mentioned.

• Colin Ross, M.D. head of the International Society for the Study of Multiple Personality and Dissociation and Director of the Dissociative Disorders Unit at the Charter Hospital of Dallas, Texas, maintains that multiple personalities have been implanted in people by the C.I.A. so that they could spy while in one personality but if captured, switch to another and convincingly insist on their innocence. As these unwilling C.I.A. spies began to uncover memories of what the C.I.A. had done to them, the C.I.A., in an effort to keep its tactics from being known, orchestrated the campaign against the recovered memory movement. (Aguilera-Hellweg 1994)

• Kenneth Lanning, from the Behavioral Science Unit at the F.B.I. Academy in Quantico, Virginia, has investigated hundreds of cases of alleged satanic cult abuse, and reports that he has found no corroboration for the existence of a conspiracy of organized satanic cults. The result is that he himself has been accused of being a 'satanist' who has infiltrated the F.B.I. to facilitate a cover-up (Lanning 1992). This is a common response of the satanic cult believers—we and other skeptics have also been accused of belonging to a satanic cult.

• Susan Smith (1993), in the process of interviewing recovered memory therapists, reports that one therapist became very agitated toward the end of the interview and became concerned that Smith was a cult member. The therapist explained that "the establishment," including the academic community, is supposedly involved in satanic cult activity on a large scale.

• A recovered memory advocate, reporting on a skeptical presentation by Dr. Harold Lief which several members of the FMS Foundation also attended, stated: "[M]any audience members, especially FMS Foundation members, tried to stare us down with eyes of ice. These stares were too long and too intense to be anything other than scare and intimidation tactics. And slowly, more and more of these people sat closer to us" (Kristiansen 1994, p. 15). The recovered memory supporters heckled and disrupted the meeting so violently that Dr. Lief never spoke. Later, one of them boasted that she had put a 'leaf' on the bull's-eye of the lab bulletin board as a metaphor to allow for a more socially acceptable expression of their feelings about Dr. Lief.

We have provided several examples because these behaviors and beliefs are so strange and irrational. Paranoia appears to supply the most satisfactory explanation.

Other Possible Explanations

There are other well-established areas of psychological research that may help understand how some therapists come to believe so fiercely and absolutely in the truth of recovered repressed memories. Cognitive dissonance reduction research shows that when people who hold a belief are presented with contrary information a state of dissonance is created. Most then try to reduce that unpleasant state by demeaning or ignoring the disconfirming information and attending only to what confirms their belief (Aronson 1988). This may also mean that they become much more aggressive in trying to convert others to agree with their belief (Festinger et al. 1956).

The scapegoat research shows that when frustration or anger is caused by a person or force too powerful or too vague to be directly confronted, a substitute is targeted as a scapegoat. The more vile and evil the scapegoat, the more justified the anger (Underwager and Wakefield 1991).

A well-replicated body of research on the authoritarian personality shows there are some people who simply need to hate others (Adorno et al. 1950). The beliefs and attitudes are held rigidly and are highly resistant to change. These people are suspicious, highly punitive, and take extreme negative positions toward those who differ from them. The authoritarian personality has high levels of anger, fear, and insecurity, but maintains an outward respect for authority (Aronson 1988).

Another personality variable that may be applicable is intolerance of ambiguity. When a person has trouble dealing with an ambiguous situation, premature closure on the basis of inadequate information takes place. Rumors and speculation are immediately seized upon and believed. There may be errors in perception linked to the person's habitual defenses. The world of such a person must be black-and-white, all good or all evil with nothing in between (Berelson and Steiner 1964; Vernon 1970). Rokeach's (1960) closed-mindedness research demonstrates how people can have their beliefs highly compartmentalized. The more closed-minded a person is, the more they depend on irrelevant personal needs to form cognitions.

Conclusions

As disconfirming evidence accumulates, the recovered memory therapists will find themselves in increasingly difficult and awkward positions. They are making wrong assumptions, using invalid techniques, and harming many people. Already, some former patients who have retracted the memories acquired in therapy are filing malpractice suits and making complaints to licensing boards. These numbers are likely to grow.

Although the believers in past-life regression and satanic cults may appear to be fringe groups who can easily be discounted, Steele (1994) points out that the basic assumptions of these therapists are the same as for recovered memory therapists in general. He predicts:

> Soon the recovered memory therapists will begin to be called to account for the misery that they and their infinitely gullible clients have unleashed upon this society. They will undoubtedly jettison memories of previous lives pretty quickly, and will denounce these stories as the work of a tiny minority of incompetents. Then, more hesitantly, they will dissociate themselves from the Satanic cult fables. It is therefore helpful to understand right now that the quality of all evidence for recovered memories of childhood sexual molestation is *precisely the same in every respect* as the quality of the evidence for recovered memories of past lives or Satanic rituals. (p. 40)

This evidence will be discussed in Chapters 8 and 9.

Chapter Six
The Nature of Human Memory and Forgetting

> *Thus our representation of the past takes on a living, shifting reality; it is not fixed and immutable, not a place way back there that is preserved in stone, but a living thing that changes shape, expands, shrinks, and expands again, an amoebalike creature with powers to make us laugh, and cry, and clench our fists. Enormous powers— powers even to make us believe in something that never happened.*
> Elizabeth Loftus and
> Katherine Ketcham (1991)

Remembering past events is a universally familiar experience. It is also a uniquely human one. As far as we know, members of no other species possess quite the same ability to experience again now, in a different situation and perhaps in a different form, happenings from the past, and know that the experience refers to an event that occurred in another time and in another place. Other members of the animal kingdom . . . cannot travel back into the past in their own minds. (Tulving 1983, p. 1)

The nature of memory itself is central to the issue of recovered repressed memories of childhood sexual abuse. The current popular view of memory is that it operates like a videotape or a computer. According to this view, everything that happens to us is precisely recorded and stored somewhere in our brain. Memory consists of pushing the play-back button and retrieving the event. Although events may be forgotten, if the correct button can just be found, the memory can be retrieved.

This assumption, which is basic to the belief in recovered memories, is widely accepted by both lay persons and professionals. Loftus (Loftus and Ketcham 1991) reports on a survey where 169 people were asked about how they thought memory works. Of the sample, 75 had graduate training in psychology and the remaining 94 represented occupations such as attorneys, physicians, secretaries, taxicab drivers, fire investigators, and philosophers. The subjects were all asked this question:

> Which of these statements best reflects your view on how human memory works?
>
> 1. Everything we learn is permanently stored in the mind, although sometimes particular details are not accessible. With hypnosis, or other special techniques, these inaccessible details could eventually be recovered.
> 2. Some details that we learn may be permanently lost from memory. Such details would never be able to be recovered by hypnosis, or any other special technique, because these details are simply no longer there.

Despite the fact that the second view is scientifically accurate, 84 percent of the psychologists and 69 percent of the nonpsychologists chose the first response. The most common reason given was the personal experience of having remembered an idea that the subject had not thought about for a long time.

Memories are personal and subjective. We don't doubt our memories. We may know we have forgotten some things but what we remember feels certain and clear. The memories may be accompanied by appropriate feelings as if we were reliving an actual event. That is a powerful support for subjective certainty. Unfortunately, the memory may be totally mistaken (Loftus et al. 1994).

The Reconstructive Nature of Memory

Although people often suppose, on the basis of hasty introspection, that their memories are a process of dredging up what actually happened, in reality our memories are largely determined by our current beliefs and feelings. This conclusion is solidly established in psychology and is supported by laboratory studies and surveys (Dawes 1988; Goodman and Hahn 1987; Loftus et al. 1989; Loftus and Ketcham 1991). What we remember is much more than the original encoding of an event. It is also affected by everything that has happened to us since the event occurred. Even if we accurately perceive and encode an experience, the original memory will be subjected to contamination over time.

Through the influences of other information given to us, our motivations and current state of mind, and the passage of time, our memories are distorted and changed. We can even develop detailed and subjectively 'real' memories of events that never happened:

> Truth and reality, when seen through the filter of our memories, are not objective facts but subjective, interpretative realities. We interpret the past, correcting ourselves, adding bits and pieces, deleting uncomplimentary or disturbing recollections, sweeping, dusting, tidying things up. Thus our representation of the past takes on a living, shifting reality; it is not fixed and immutable, not a place way back there that is preserved in stone, but a living thing that changes shape, expands, shrinks, and expands again, an amoebalike creature with powers to make us laugh, and cry, and clench our fists. Enormous powers—powers even to make us believe in something that never happened. (Loftus and Ketcham 1991, p. 20)

There are many anecdotes about errors in memory for personal events from childhood. The most famous example of the creation of a false memory is by Piaget:

> ● [O]ne of my first memories would date, if it were true, from my second year. I can still see, most clearly, the following scene, in which I believed until I was about fifteen. I was sitting in my pram, which my nurse was pushing in the Champs Elysées, when

a man tried to kidnap me. I was held in by the strap fastened around me while my nurse bravely tried to stand between me and the thief. She received various scratches, and I can still see vaguely those on her face. Then a crowd gathered, a policeman with a short cloak and a white baton came up, and the man took to his heels. I can still see the whole scene, and can even place it near the tube station. When I was about fifteen, my parents received a letter from my former nurse saying that she had been converted to the Salvation Army. She wanted to confess her past faults, and in particular to return the watch she had been given as a reward on this occasion. She had made up the whole story, faking the scratches. I, therefore, must have heard, as a child, the account of this story, which my parents believed, and projected it into the past in the form of a visual memory. (Loftus and Ketcham 1991, pp. 17–18)

Lindsay and Read (in press) provide another example:

In an angry confrontation, 30-year-old Laurel accused her mother of having said a hurtful thing to her many years earlier when she was a child. Laurel had been carrying the hurt and anger about this offense for years. Her sister, Penny, who was present when Laurel unburdened herself of this painful memory, immediately said, "Laurel, that wasn't you! That was me!" Evidently, Laurel had witnessed or heard about the remark years ago, identified with her sister, and eventually came to believe that she was the victim of the hurtful remark.

Such reconstructed memories are not limited to distortions concerning minor details of actual events. Researchers now understand that entire pseudomemories may be implanted. Ofshe proposes that there are two fundamental paths through which pseudomemories can be created. One path, demonstrated through the literature on hypnosis, involves creating experiences (hypnotic fantasies) that the individual misclassifies as memories. The second path, demonstrated through the social-psychological literature on conformity and belief change, depends upon first eliciting conformity to the expert's conclusions ('I must have been sexually abused') and then by using suggestion and leading questions, to shape answers into a scenario of the event that is told and retold. These two pathways may interact with one another in creating the pseudomemory (Lynn and Nash 1994).

The most painstaking study of ordinary, normal autobiographical memory is by Marigold Linton at the University of Utah who studied her own memory for 12 years. She used a variety of techniques but relied most heavily on daily diary cards. Events from the most recent year were easier to recall but as time passed the memories became less detailed, harder to recall, less responsive to memory jogs, and were less accurate. For events recorded two to six years previously, each year added a 6 percent loss to her ability to recall events described in her cards. Many of the earlier events were also re-interpreted. She recorded meeting a new person tersely and matter of factly. When that person, years later became her husband, the memory for that event changed. Linton's careful work shows that autobiographical memory is changed by the perception of later events, details are lost with time, distinct events merge, and new categories of memory evolve (Linton 1979).

People remember things that are consistent with the concept they have of themselves (Huyghe 1985). Rubin (1985) describes a study in which graduate students were asked to record three events daily for four months. Five times during the next two-and-one-half years they were tested by presenting them with descriptions of events and asking them if they were their own. Some were their own but others were changed and some were another person's descriptions. The thesis was that people don't reproduce the past but reconstruct it in accord with their self-theories, that our personalities and beliefs about ourselves shape our memories. This is exactly what happened. After five months, false descriptions that were congruent with the self-theories were just as likely to be accepted as rejected.

These findings show why our autobiographical memories seem accurate even though we may know other parts of memory are not so certain.

> Our recall is often organized in ways that 'make sense' of the present—thus reinforcing our belief in the conclusions we have

reached about how the past has determined the present. We quite literally 'make up stories' about our lives, the world, and reality in general. The fit between our memories and the stories enhances our belief in them. Often, however, it is the story that creates the memory, rather than vice versa. (Dawes 1988, p. 107)

Source Monitoring Errors

A useful concept for explaining how memories may be reconstructed is *source monitoring* (see Johnson et al. 1993). People sometimes mistake their memories of events they have only imagined for memories of real events that have happened.

All of us have experienced not remembering where we received a piece of information. We may wonder whether we actually locked the door before leaving on a trip or only imagined that we did or whether some event took place or we only dreamed about it. Although such memory difficulties usually are only disconcerting and inconvenient, they can be very serious, as in the case of delusions. Accurate source monitoring allows us to differentiate between reliable and unreliable sources of information, between fact and fantasy in remembering, and between intentions and actions.

An example of source monitoring errors is described by Ketchum (1991). Ketchum, a historian doing research for a book about the battle for Bunker Hill, located three volumes containing the depositions of 40 Revolutionary army veterans taken in 1825, 50 years after the battle. These 40 veterans all claimed to have been present on June 17th 1775, the day the British stormed the rebel redoubt.

Seventeen years after the depositions were taken, they were examined by a committee whose task was to report on the nature and historical value of the depositions. The committee's findings were so discouraging that the depositions were ordered sealed and stored as 'curiosities.' The committee report states that the contents of the depositions were:

most extraordinary; many of the testimonies extravagant, boastful, inconsistent, and utterly untrue; mixtures of old men's broken memories and fond imaginings with the love of the marvelous. Some of those who gave in affidavits about the battle could not have been in it, nor even in its neighborhood. They had got so used to telling the story for the wonderment of village listeners as grandfathers' tales, and as petted representatives of 'the spirit of '76,' that they did not distinguish between what they had seen and done and what they had read, heard, or dreamed. (Ketchum 1991, pp. 142–43)

Gleitman (1993) describes an incident about himself that demonstrates how wishful thinking became a real memory:

I happen to recall an incident in my own life. I am not terribly proud of it. I am not terribly ashamed of it. And I told it over and over again. I remembered that roughly at the age of 15 or 16, in order to impress some young women on the other side of a river, I climbed on the underside of the bridge together with some other kids. (It was one of those bridges over the Harlem River from upper Manhattan to the Bronx.) And I remember how scared I was and how proud I was when I got to the other side.

But unfortunately for the veracity of this memory, I met much, much later, some of the boys now in late middle age or later yet who were there and they said that, "Hey, look Henry, you were scared of heights. You stayed behind."

It is so sad—I would have loved to have gone. It was such a magnificent story to tell myself about myself, such a magnificent story to construct about myself. I mean—Henry the young, dashing and ever so chivalrous little hero. He was not. He was scared of heights.

Can a memory of a real event be distinguished from one that was imagined after reading *The Courage to Heal*, hearing abuse discussed in a survivors' group, or being given suggestions by a therapist? We suspect that many, if not all, of the veterans in Ketchum's example who reported on a battle they could not have observed eventually developed subjectively real memories of the battle and believed they were telling the truth in the depositions.

Flashbulb Memories and Trauma Memories

Flashbulb memories refer to memories for details about a highly memorable, dramatic, and emotional event. The best example is John Kennedy's assassination. Everyone who is old enough can give a detailed account of precisely what they were doing when they first heard the news, who told them, what happened immediately afterwards, and how they felt. We all have great confidence in the veracity of such memories, which seem like photographs that preserve the scene forever.

Some researchers have hypothesized that there is a special memory mechanism that accounts for the fact, or supposed fact, that such memories are so enduring, vivid, and accurate (Brown and Kulik 1977). But research using the *Challenger* disaster shows that flashbulb memories are not as accurate as supposed. Neisser and Harsch (1992) gave 106 students a questionnaire the morning following the Challenger explosion and then two-and-one-half years later gave a new questionnaire to the 44 of the original students they could locate. Four months later they interviewed 40 of these. They assumed the original questionnaires, which were administered less than 24 hours after the event, were accurate and that any changes in the subsequent accounts would be the result of memory reconstruction.

The researchers found substantial errors in the later accounts. Only three subjects were accurate in all respects on the second questionnaire. Despite this, most of the subjects were highly confident in the accuracy of their memories and their reconstructed memories were completely resistant to correction. During the interview, the researchers attempted to jog the subjects' memories in various ways, and finally showed them the original questionnaires. But none of these procedures had any effect in retrieving the original memories. The subjects were completely surprised by their original reports and, as far as the researchers could tell, the original memories were completely gone.

Other researchers have conducted similar research on flashbulb memories using the *Challenger* disaster as well as other events, and the consensus now is that not only can flashbulb memories be inaccurate, there is no evidence for a special memory mechanism (Winograd and Neisser 1992). Whatever the relationship between affect and memory, there does not appear to be a special mechanism of storage that only comes into play during events that are highly emotional. There is no evidence that there is a qualitatively different memory mechanism for traumas than for other events.

Memory and Therapy

The practice of psychotherapy is flourishing, with more and more people offering services, basically talking, that are supposed to be healing and curative. Being a patient or client in psychotherapy is no longer shameful but may well be a badge of honor and an indicator of being squarely in the mainstream of American life.

There are two different views of the goals, methods, and expectations of psychotherapy. The first is that we can learn about the causes of a person's present problems through talking. The causes therefore have to be psychological and in the past. It is also necessary for the causes to be correctly identified through communication. This view assumes that the patient does not know what the causes are, so they must be unconscious or unrecognized forces. Through talking and identification of the causes, a cure is accomplished. This is the model of psychotherapy characteristic in claims of recovered memories.

The second view looks upon psychotherapy essentially as teaching and rehabilitation. It is more limited and less interested in deeply hidden causes of problems; it is instead focussed on what to do about the problems, whatever they may be. Actual changes in behavior are pursued to decrease the frequency of the symptoms and increase the frequency of adaptive behaviors. Again, this is accomplished through talking but the goal is not the understanding of hidden forces but learning a new skill.

The first view requires the therapist to interpret the data produced by the patient in talking about symptoms, relationships, history, life circumstances, beliefs, and feelings. The therapist supposedly brings together all the disparate material and offers an interpretation to make sense of it. The causal connections offered in the interpretation are crucial. If the proposed causal connections are incorrect, then the interpretation cannot cure and the entire venture of psychotherapy is an exercise in futility or the exercise of magic. Thus the validity of the interpretation is crucial. Reliability of the interpretation is also a concern but this is affected most by the level of the inferences leading to the interpretation. If words, gestures, facial expressions, and behaviors are the data for the deductions, these may possibly be more reliable than deducing from associations, dreams, or feelings to unconscious forces or processes. The danger is that the interpretation may be nothing more than the therapist's own assumptions, expectations, beliefs, values, or needs. Then the interpretation may become a powerful tool of persuasion and can even create something resembling that which it predicts or assumes. If this is the case and there is no historical truth in the interpretation, there can be no curative efficacy. Assume that an erroneous causal interpretation of childhood sexual abuse is made. Treatment through talking is given using the techniques described earlier. It cannot help, because the patient was not abused by his parents in the first place (Guze and Olin 1992). It can only harm.

The first kind of psychotherapy increases memory distortion. The process of verbally describing memories makes it even more difficult to distinguish between real and imagined events (Suengas and Johnson 1988). Bonanno (1990) notes that rather than uncovering *historical truth,* therapy results "in the production of an articulated narrative understanding or *narrative truth*" (p. 176). This narrative 'truth' is a product of the communication between the therapist and the patient. Therefore, the task of the therapist is not to help the patient to retrieve lost memories, but to help the patient revise the life story. This distinction between narrative and historical truth means that the theory and the therapy can never go beyond the level of metaphor.

According to this model, therapy involves the telling and retelling of life experiences (Lynn and Nash 1994). The therapist must sort through what the client says and feels, decide what is important, target relevant themes and concerns, and evaluate the nature of the problems. Therefore the therapist shapes the telling of the personal history by selectively reinforcing and validating the client's recollections. Memories can be shaped, combined with fantasies, distorted, and even totally created.

Research into the dependability of eye-witnesses indicates that the effect of being given misleading information is greater when the information is provided by an expert. Since the therapist is viewed as an expert, the client's recollections during therapy will be strongly affected by the questions the therapist asks, the interpretations given, and the reinforcement of the answers. When the therapist believes that a history of sexual abuse is found in one-fourth to one-half of all women, that half of these women do not remember it, and that this 'repressed' abuse is at the root of the client's problems, the risk of the client developing a false memory of abuse is great. This is especially true when abuse is discussed in every session or when the client is placed in a survivors' group.

The therapeutic techniques described in Chapter 5 increase the probability that the material 'remembered' in therapy is not true. The suggestibility of vulnerable clients and their desire to conform to what they believe the therapist expects and wants, the beliefs of the therapists about the reality and frequency of repressed abuse, the common use of unvalidated and questionable therapy techniques, and the conformity effect of a group combine to produce a massive learning experience for the client.

The second view of psychotherapy—teaching and rehabilitation, focussed on present problems—is much less likely to create false memories, attribute problems to erroneous causal schemes, or produce harm (Rettig 1993). There is a self-corrective mechanism built in so that if there is no change and no improvements are noted, another tack is taken until there is improvement.

Our First Memories: Infant Amnesia

Our very first memories have an almost magical quality about them. They are apparently the beginning of our conscious lives. Often the very first memory may be a common event, with nothing especially noteworthy, like sitting on the porch steps or eating cereal. Most early memories are visual, some in color, but the content varies widely. There seem to be three broad categories: trauma, transition, and trivia.

Almost all our first memories are located in the fourth year of life, between our third and fourth birthday. Infant amnesia refers to the fact that adults and older children do not usually remember incidents from their lives that happen prior to age three to four (Eisenberg 1985; Fivush and Hamond 1990; Howe and Courage 1993; Huyghe 1985; Loftus 1993; Nelson 1993; Nelson and Ross 1980; Pillemer and White 1989; Wetzler and Sweeney 1986). This inability to recall events from an early age is part of the normal process of growth and development and has nothing to do with dissociation, repression, or traumatic amnesia.

Some researchers have reported slightly younger estimates of how far back adults can remember. For example, Usher and Neisser (1993) found that some adults can recall the birth of a sibling or a hospitalization if these events occurred at age two. But these bits of memory may be the result of educated guesses about what was likely to have happened (Loftus et al. 1994). Even if we accept that some memories may be retrieved from age two, no study supports the ability to recover memories at or near birth.

Children also build 'script' memories during this period of life. Script memories are those we have for familiar, repeated events like eating dinner at home or going to the supermarket. Children need to understand what is going on and script memories are a way of organizing their experience. However, this causes children to have reasonably good general accounts of repeated events, such as dinner at home, but to have difficulty with giving an account of any specific dinner. The specific memory is lost as it is absorbed into the general script. Unique events, like going to the zoo, may be more memorable for a while, because they have not been repeated. But after a while, going to the zoo is not repeated and so it is forgotten. It is not adaptive to hold on to a memory that does not help in understanding what can happen or what the future may hold (Nelson 1981). Further research showed that, the more frequent the event, the more scriptlike was the child's memory of that event. Events experienced five or more times are formulated in general, present-tense terms and specific events are fused and confused (Nelson 1993).

Neisser (1993) notes several difficulties with studies where adults are asked about their earliest recollections and also how old they were at the time. These difficulties also, of course, refer to case studies and anecdotes where adults maintain they have memories from very early ages.

1. There is no way to know whether the subject got the age right.
2. There is no way to verify the accuracy of the memories.
3. The type of event reported is different for different individuals. Also, a lot of people's 'earliest memories' are not single events at all but are instead of such repeated events as playing in their backyard sandbox.
4. There is no control of 'rehearsal' (going over the events in one's mind). For example, lots of things that happen to children become oft-repeated family stories, while others are recorded in photographs.

The development of narrative accounts is markedly affected by talking with parents who play an active role in framing and guiding their children's formulation of what happened. This effect is strongest when parents simply talk with their children about events rather than question them (Nelson 1993). Without corroboration concerning the occurrence of the event and the age when it occurred and proof that the memory has not come from family stories or photographs, claims of memories from very young ages cannot be accepted.

These facts concerning infant amnesia are important since 'survivors' often claim to have recovered memories of abuse from a very early age, sometimes before the age of one. In the FMS Foundation survey project, 29 percent of the parents reported that the alleged abuse was said to have started below age two. Recovered memory proponents believe that such memories are accurate. For example, Terr (1994) unquestioningly accepts the account of a man who claims to have retrieved a memory of his mother attempting to drown him in a bathinet as an infant. Yapko (1994a; his survey is described in Chapter 5) reports that over half of the therapists he sampled believe in near-birth memories. The research evidence on infant amnesia contradicts these near-birth claims. The reality of infant amnesia means that the mind simply does not work that way. Any supposed memories of events before age four must be regarded very cautiously.

Forgetting

Much of what happens to us is simply forgotten. To forget an event does not mean that it is 'repressed' or 'dissociated' because it was so horrible; it can simply be forgotten because it wasn't thought about for years or wasn't that important in the first place. Even things that seem important at the time can later be forgotten. When they are reminded of an event, people's memories often return. Sometimes, however, people simply cannot recall an event, even when they have numerous cues and even when the event is one that they believed would 'certainly' be remembered (Bradburn et al. 1987). This passive process of forgetting is completely different from the hypothesized active process of repressing events that are too terrible to remember.

Gardner (1994) describes an experiment he did with himself in which he looked through his 1945 school yearbook from when he was 14 years old. His goal was to make a list of things that he could honestly say he would never have thought about again if he had not opened the book, but which, upon perusing the book, might result into his clearly remembering them. He elicited memories of a number of things he had not thought about in years.

One of us (H.W.) attempted the same experiment with her college and junior and senior high school year books. Whereas the yearbook photographs brought up no new memories of traumatic incidents, her memory returned for other completely forgotten events. A script fell out of the bookcase from a high school play that she had a major part in. Prior to this, she had not thought about this play in years and would not have remembered being in it even if asked. But as she read through the script, which contained her handwritten notes, her memories returned. She saw several photographs of herself in a pep band in college. She had not recalled being in a college pep band and, if asked, would have said that the last time she was in a band was in high school. But, with the photographs as cues, her memories of this band returned. Yet the memory of her membership in one high school club never returned, despite the club photograph with her in it.

Even events that we would think would be remembered can be forgotten in a relatively short period of time. Surprising though it may seem, research shows that people routinely fail to remember significant life events even a year after they occurred (Loftus 1993). Raphael et al. (1991) asked subjects to make monthly checklists of life events and then report retrospectively about these events at the end of a year. Only a fourth of the events appeared in both the monthly reports and the later retrospective report with many more events being reported monthly than retrospectively. These events included such major crises as job loss, illness, and injury. Although there were logical reasons for many of the discrepancies, the authors concluded that life-event checklists are not accurate for assessing the relationship between stressful life events and health. The period of time between the monthly reports and the later retrospective reports only ranged from one month to a year.

Research indicates that as many as 25 percent of victims of robbery, assault, or burglary in the previous year fail to recall the assault (Rettig 1993). Loftus (1993) describes a study with 590 persons known to have been in injury-producing motor vehicle accidents during the previous year, in which 14 percent did not remember the accident a year later. In another study, one-fourth of 1,500 people who had been discharged from a hospital did not remember the hospitalization a year later. Other researchers have compared a respondent's recall of important events with that of a significant other acting as a co-informant and have found frequent disagreements on items as significant as the birth or adoption of a child (Steele et al. 1980).

Once forgotten, an event can often be recalled when there are cues. Hudson and Fivush (1987) compared kindergarten children's immediate recall of a class field trip on the same day of the trip to their recall six weeks later, one year later, and six years later. Without cues, the event was forgotten by almost all of the children after one year, but with cues, 87 percent could recall details of the event even after six years.

Forgetting and Sexual Abuse

Some instances of sexual abuse may be forgotten—not 'repressed,' not 'dissociated,' not remembered only by an 'alter personality,' but simply forgotten.

> My guess is that nasty and unpleasant experiences can be forgotten too, if they occur only once and don't have obvious real-life consequences. . . . it's probably a mistake to suppose that every trauma—even every sexual trauma—hangs around in your head and causes trouble forever. . . . we cannot conclude that all such experiences are permanently damaging to everyone. Some may just be ignored, others forgotten. (Neisser 1993)

Sexual abuse is not invariably traumatic. Finkelhor (1990), reviewing the literature on the effects of sexual abuse states, "Almost every study of the impact of sexual abuse has found a substantial group of victims with little or no symptomatology" (p. 327). In fact, as is discussed in Chapter 2, many studies indicate that a portion of the subjects retrospectively assess their childhood sexual experiences with adults as neutral or positive.

This does not mean that we approve of adult-child sexual contact or believe it can ever be good. Sexual abuse of children is reprehensible and there are innumerable victims who bear significant and lasting scars. Nevertheless, some adults don't view their childhood abuse as traumatic and may not even define themselves as sexual abuse victims. Such people may have been too young to fully understand what was happening, especially if the abuse consisted only of fondling. For many others, the abuse may have been a disconcerting, unpleasant, but relatively unimportant event in the same category as countless other unpleasant but not highly traumatic childhood events (Spence 1993).

Given the number of things in our lives that are simply forgotten, it is not surprising that some abuse victims, for whom the abuse was not traumatic, will forget about the experience. Such people may well remember once reminded, but there is no need to postulate a mechanism of repression, dissociation, or traumatic amnesia. It is also unlikely that persons for whom the abuse *was* a highly emotional and traumatic experience will have no memories of it.

A recent newspaper article had the headline, 'Juror's Repressed Memory of Abuse Leads to Mistrial in Molestation Convictions' (Zack 1994). According to the article, the woman had answered 'no' to a question about abuse in a juror questionnaire. She was placed on the jury, but during the trial memories of childhood abuse returned. After the trial, in which the defendant was convicted, she contacted the judge who declared a mistrial. The article describes the abuse she remembered during the trial:

One incident occurred before she started school. She said the teenage son of friends took her into his bedroom, removed his pants and asked her to touch him orally. She said she didn't. . . . And when she was a teenager, the juror said, her father lay on top of her for about 40 seconds, making her uncomfortable. "I didn't like it," she said.

The woman interpreted what was simple forgetting as 'repression' and went into therapy to help her "let the pain and emotion surface so I can be healed." Such a response to being reminded of these childhood incidents is probably due to the way sexual abuse and repressed memories have been presented in the media.

Memory for Verified Traumatic Events

People who undergo severe trauma remember it. There is a large literature on the reactions of people to documented severe traumas, such as fires, airplane crashes, terrorist attacks, automobile accidents, hurricanes, and being held hostage. Such trauma victims show many symptoms, including feelings of unreality, detachment, numbing, disorientation, depersonalization, and flashbacks, but total amnesia for the entire event is not a common response (Eth and Pynoos 1985; Spiegel 1991; Wilson and Raphael 1993). The memories may be fragmented and impaired, but they are not usually completely obliterated.

Lenore Terr (1985, 1990) has treated and evaluated many traumatized children. Her best known research was with children from the Chowchilla school bus kidnapping who were buried for 17 to 18 hours until they escaped. All of these children had detailed memories of the experience, although some of the memories contained inaccuracies. Other cases she describes are similar.

In another study, Terr (1988) reports on 20 children under the age of 5 whose traumas were verified. The children were from 6 months to 4 years, 10 months old at the time of the traumas. The average interval between trauma and memory assessment was 4 years, 5 months, with a range of 5 months to 12 years between the time of the trauma and the time of the evaluation. Terr reports that age 28 to 36 months is the approximate cut-off point separating those children who can fully verbalize their past experiences from those who can only do so in part or not at all. All of the children past the age 36 months had memories. Although the children may have denied parts of the aftermath and the effect on them, they did not deny the event.

Terr (1991, 1994) hypothesizes that there are two types of trauma, which she calls Type I and Type II. This appears to be a distinctive theory of her own, and is unsupported in the research literature. According to Terr, Type I traumas, which occur when the child is subjected to a single, unanticipated traumatic event, include full, clear, detailed verbal memories, although there may be some errors and misperceptions. Type II traumas occur when there is long-standing or repeated exposure to traumatic external events. The responses to Type II traumas include denial, numbing, dissociation, repression, self-hypnosis, and rage.

Terr believes that repression of childhood abuse and other traumas occur and she uses the Type II trauma concept to account for it. But a careful review of Terr's case studies reveals no case descriptions where children of documented traumas are amnesic for the trauma unless they were under the age of infant amnesia. Their memories may be fragmented and incomplete but they are not totally gone.

Terr's finding that the children she studied did not forget the trauma unless they were under the age of infant amnesia is consistent with other studies of traumatized children. In discussing the effects on children who have witnessed acts of personal violence, including homicide, rape, or suicide, Pynoos and Eth (1985) state that such children "do not display traumatic amnesia" (p. 24).

Malmquist (1986) reports on 16 children between the ages of 5 and 10 who had seen a parent murdered. The details of the situations were often horrifying. All of the children met the

DSM-III-R criteria for post-traumatic stress disorder (PTSD) but not one 'repressed' the memory. Instead, the children had recurrent and intrusive thoughts of the murder along with a variety of other problems. All had vivid memories of the event.

Black et al. (1993) describe 46 cases involving 95 children where the father killed the mother. In 44 percent of these the murder was either visually witnessed by the child or the child had heard it taking place. There are no descriptions of any of the children developing amnesia for what they heard or saw.

Gordon and Wraith (1993) studied over 100 families affected by disasters including bushfire, massacre, hostage and plane crash disasters, as well as individual traumas involving murder, physical and sexual abuse, and transportation accidents. In their descriptions of the serious and complex responses of children and adolescents to these traumas, there are no accounts of anyone developing amnesia.

Macksoud et al. (1993) discuss the types of trauma children undergo in war, including witnessing the violent death of a parent or other close family member, terroristic attacks, kidnapping and life threat, and bombardment and shelling. They review the relevant literature and report on the short- and long-terms effects of such wartime experiences. In their lengthy discussion of the various effects, amnesia for the trauma is never mentioned. They observe that, although young children may appear mute and withdrawn, "The silence does not mean that the event is forgotten. Young children will often give full details of the traumatic event to a trusted person, at a later point in time" (p. 627). Older children are often troubled by intrusions of the traumatic memories. Since children traumatized in wartime include many who have undergone *repeated* traumas, the research on these children falsifies any claim that children will learn to dissociate repeated traumas in such a way that all memories for the traumas are gone.

There are many more studies on children exposed to traumas and disasters. We did not discover any where the children were described as developing amnesia.

Conclusions

Research on the nature of memory and forgetting does not support the assumption of the recovered memory therapists that some abuse is so traumatic that all memories for it will be removed from consciousness by an active filtering process of repression or dissociation until accurately retrieved years later. Memory is a process of reconstruction and is subject to errors and distortions. Many unpleasant childhood events, including some instances of sexual abuse, may be forgotten. Highly intrusive and traumatic events will be clearly and vividly remembered. The exception is when the traumatic events take place when the child is in the period of infant amnesia.

Chapter Seven
It Ain't Necessarily So

> *What I tell you three times is true.*
> Lewis Carroll, *The Hunting of the Snark*, Fit 1. *The Landing*

The song from the 1940s, 'It Ain't Necessarily So!', expresses a fundamental truth about memories. A memory may be clear, feel subjectively certain, not intentional dissembling or lying, and yet be partially or even completely false. In January 1987, President Ronald Reagan said that he had approved the plan for Israel to ship arms to Iran. He could not remember just when but he thought it was in August of 1985 and he had a clear recollection of giving approval. But by February 1987, he said that he had gone over his recollection several times with his advisor, Mr. Donald Regan. Now he specifically recalled that he was surprised to hear that Israel had shipped arms to Iran, and therefore he could not have given advance approval. Later in February, President Reagan explained his changing memory:

"In trying to recall the events that happened 18 months ago, I'm afraid that I let myself be influenced by others' recollections, not my own. . . . I have no personal notes or records to help my recollection on this matter. The only honest answer is to state that try as I might, I cannot recall anything. . . . the simple truth is, I don't remember, period" (Tower Commission Report 1987).

The president is correct. Misinformation from others can influence us to produce erroneous accounts of past events or false accounts of events that never happened. That we have memories of a past event does not mean that they are necessarily accurate. We may be very confident that our memories are true when they are not. In fact, it is likely that we are most confident and most certain about the errors in our memories (Weingardt et al. 1993).

When John Dean, President Nixon's counsel, testified before the 'Watergate' Committee of the Senate in June 1973, the mass of detail he remembered so impressed some that they called him 'the human tape recorder.' Dean had no notes or diary but he said he had kept a newspaper clipping file from the beginning and had pored over those stories to refresh his memory. When real tape recordings of the conversations and meetings were found, it turned out that Mr. Dean was entirely wrong about many of the conversations he said he remembered. He was right about the overall reality. There was a cover-up. Whether or not his use of the newspaper stories reinstated some memories or if he remembered some aspects but not others cannot be determined. But his detailed accounts show that it is not possible to assess the accuracy of memories from the amount or kind of detail produced (Neisser 1981). We may try very hard to produce accurate memories but still come up with large amounts of error.

Another problem in knowing whether memories are accurate or not is the reality that we live immersed in a sea of fiction. Movies, TV, books, newspapers, magazines inundate us with fictional claims, mistaken assertions, and dubious pronouncements which we may treat as reliable information. A startling example of this again involves President Reagan. In a CBS '60 Minutes' program he told a story to Navy personnel about an act of heroism by a pilot who went down with his plane. He attributed the event to an actual U.S. pilot. But no similar act of real heroism was ever found. Instead the President's tale was similar in every detail to a scene from a Dana Andrews movie from the 1940s. This illustrates the kinds of errors we may make in source monitoring (Johnson et al. 1993). (We discuss source monitoring errors in Chapter 6.)

Explanation-Based Learning

It does not take much to produce a full-fledged schema that may have no relationship to reality. The study of artificial intelligence has led to testing the idea of explanation-based learning (EBL) in humans. When we have fairly rich knowledge about a given domain even a single question or statement that provides an explanatory concept for the issue can result in a permanently learned and adopted explanatory scenario. When a statement or question provides a coherent causal structure, a single instance can produce a full-blown, comprehensive concept (Ahn et al. 1992). Most of us have considerable knowledge about our families and, when there may be some slight difficulty or a conflict arises, a single question from a therapist that seems to offer an explanation may produce a full-fledged scenario that can be highly erroneous. Even if it is a mistake, we are liable to defend it vigorously and maintain the truthfulness of the mistaken account (Loftus, Korf, and Schooler 1989). Three years after writing down where they were when the *Challenger* exploded and how they learned about it, the memories of college students had shifted and changed for 90 percent of them. When shown their own handwritten accounts, none of them changed their memories, but said they believed their present memory. Some said they were wrong the first time and knew their memories now were right (Neisser 1993).

Never In Doubt but Often In Error

The most surprising fact about human memory is that we can be so sure about our memories, never in doubt, but so often wrong. The problem is that my memories are mine. They come to me, some of them unbidden, and everything about them seems real, true, and I experience no doubt or question. I don't even think to ask how it is possible for the past somehow to be present in the 'now' moment. It is inside my head so the brain is involved somehow. The 100 billion neurons of the brain are part of it, but how? The chemical events in the individual neurons are implicated but how many neurons have to fire in what directions and through what connections in order to produce a given memory? A memory cannot be in an individual neuron so a number of neurons have to be related in some kind of pattern. Even so, it remains a mystery that the absent past can be in the material present.

The certainty I have about my memories can be a major factor in my life. This is what psychologists now call episodic memory, that is, a conscious awareness of earlier personal experience in a certain situation and at a certain time (Tulving 1993). We are capable of mental time travel for we can not only recall the past but we can also anticipate the future. This is a feat not possible for other kinds of memory.

Every married couple has had an experience of being at an event together, such as a family wedding, leaving, and getting into a fierce argument about what just happened. One says that Uncle Joe was drunk and offensive and the other says he was just being funny. Memories of a shared event, recent or far in the past, may be so disparate as to seem as if they cannot refer to the same event. We may know that there are differing perceptions or selective attention or variations in the meaning given, but we still argue and fight vehemently for the correctness of my memory and the incorrectness of yours. Much of personal, marital, and family conflict comes out of clashing and conflicting memories.

When Can Memory Be Distorted?

We are particularly vulnerable to the effect of misinformation and the development of a distorted memory when the passage of time allows any original memories to fade. The longer the intervening time, the more interference there can be, and thus any original memories are weaker (Zechmeister and Nyberg 1982). This means that any misinformation is less likely to be seen as discordant or discrepant and therefore becomes easier to accept and believe. The more subtle the misinformation, the more likely it is to be accepted (Loftus 1992). The weaker the original memory, the greater the effect (Loftus, Korf, and Schooler 1989). The more authoritative the source, the more likely that any misinformation will be accepted and incorporated into fabricated memories (Smith and Ellsworth 1987). There are also individual differences and some people are more readily influenced to produce erroneous memories than others (Lynn and Nash 1994). If misinformation is accepted, it appears to destroy any original information and make it impossible to recover (Ceci and Bruck 1993; Loftus 1992).

> Misleading information can turn a lie into memory's truth. It can cause people to believe that they saw things that never really existed, or that they saw things differently from the way things actually were. It can make people confident about these false memories and also, apparently, impair earlier recollections. Once adopted, the newly created memories can be believed as strongly as genuine memories. (Loftus 1992, p. 123)

The Prime Time Exposure

By the late 1980s we reached a point in the development of the child abuse system where there was an informal network of professionals from the justice system and the mental health professions who had a shared set of beliefs. There is no scientific evidence to support these beliefs but they are maintained in the face of disconfirming evidence. Remember the core ideas from Chapter 2: There are multitudinous internal events, psychodynamic in nature, that are powerful determinants of present behavior. They are not readily discernible but must be guessed. The past determines the present. Sexual abuse of children is a raging epidemic. Children must be believed at all costs. Men are bad and sexually abuse female children to socialize them. There are memories that are blocked or repressed but which can be uncovered. If a person has no memories of abuse, that doesn't mean it didn't happen.

Politicians have so manipulated the laws that the child abuse system now has no accountability, but enormous arbitrary power to invade the lives, liberties, and privacies of citizens. These next sections present three actual examples of how false memories are created in therapy, and illustrate what the sad consequences may be.

The Seduction Into Error: When Therapy Turns Into Terrorism

Zachary Bravos (1993) describes a case that illustrates how a mother and her daughter were taught to believe they had alter personalities and had been abused in satanic rituals.

> In January 1990 the Does were an intact, functioning family. They appeared to be the dream of average, middle-class America representing the fulfillment of traditional family values. The father was a college-educated and successful self-employed carpenter, the mother, a part-time cashier in her second marriage. The three children included an extremely intelligent seven-and-one-half-year-old daughter (IQ measured at 135–142), a four-year-old daughter of average intelligence, and the mother's 13-year-old son from her first marriage—a boy of average intelligence and with no behavior problems. The family lived in a pleasant upper-middle class suburb of Chicago and the children were all doing well in school. The mother was at home most of the time because they believed it was important for the children to have mother available during the day.

In January 1990, following the father's diagnosis of Attention Deficit Disorder (ADD), the mother was also diagnosed as probable ADD. The diagnosis was made by the family doctor, a self-described Christian general practitioner who also led a religious study group. Both the mother and father were members of this group. This diagnosis appears to have been a mistake and the physician had nothing to go on but his subjective impressions based on the behaviors in the study group. This diagnosis is a developmental disorder of children and should not be given to adults except when there is evidence of the disorder during childhood and the adult is in a residual phase. But this mistaken diagnosis began the process of the destruction of this family.

During the first four months after her diagnosis of ADD, the mother was medicated at various times with Prozac, Ritalin, and Norpramin. Dramatic behavior changes were noted during these four months including increasing nervousness, shortness of breath, inability to sleep, weight loss of 70 pounds, and starting to smoke cigarettes (previously this woman had been a complete non-smoker). Given these dramatic changes in behavior, the first thing that should have been checked is the medication and possible side effects.

At the end of four months, the mother was hospitalized after showing some preoccupation with suicide. The admission summary indicates significantly impaired ability to concentrate and impaired memory for recent events. She had also been experiencing paranoid feelings. She was discharged four days later with a diagnosis of Major Depression, Single Episode. The discharge diagnosis indicates that she had a great deal of anger directed at her father who had died approximately nine years before. She was described as having improved judgment and receded paranoid ideation. She was willing to see a psychologist for follow-up therapy and a psychiatrist who would administer anti-depressant medication.

Upon discharge, the mother began therapy with a licensed clinical social worker on a referral from her family doctor. In May 1990 she began work on *The Courage to Heal* workbook. She also received a book entitled *I Know I*

Am Hurting, described by her therapist as a book with themes of spirituality and child abuse.

By November 1990 the mother was hospitalized for her second psychiatric admission. The admission summary indicates that, over the prior seven months of therapy, the mother had uncovered tremendous amounts of grizzly details of her past. She was experiencing body memories and flashbacks. She described extreme emotional, physical, and sexual abuse by her maternal grandfather and his friend between the ages of two and five. She was described as extremely religious for the past two to three years. She believed the Lord had been helping her in a battle between good and evil.

During this psychiatric hospitalization, the mother was given a sodium amytal interview and was put in art therapy. This hospitalization lasted 65 days. Psychotic episodes are described in the medical record and by the end of her hospital stay, she had memories of satanic ritual abuse beginning the day she came home from the hospital after birth until age 13. The abusers now included her grandfather, his friend, and her maternal grandmother. Her memories centered around the killing of babies, cannibalism, and forced rape by "countless people." By the end of her hospitalization, the mother was beginning to suspect that her own mother was involved in the satanic activities and was contemplating divorce from her husband. Her discharge diagnosis on Axis 1 was Post-Traumatic Stress Disorder, Chronic with Depression and Satanic Cult Abuse. On Axis 2, she was diagnosed with Dissociative Disorder—Depersonalization.

Following discharge, she continued in therapy with the same clinical social worker. Her third psychiatric hospitalization occurred in October 1991. This was a two-day hospitalization and the mother left after one day at her request. She was now reporting memories of her own mother being involved in satanic abuse and her father being involved in Neo-Nazi activities, including snatching of Jews off the street and their subsequent murder and disposal in gas chambers and ovens, all in the Chicago area.

In December 1991 both daughters were hospitalized following an incident in which the mother was attempting an exorcism of demons. This hospitalization lasted 38 days. By the conclusion of the hospital stay, both children, but most especially the oldest, were reporting 'alter' personalities along with ritual sexual abuse by their maternal grandmother and mother. They also reported being 'triggered' by their grandmother and mother. Their father was described as being drugged during these episodes.

One week before the children's discharge, the mother was hospitalized for the fourth time. This was a 45-day hospitalization and was the first hospitalization that did not involve staff members who believed in recovered repressed memories and satanic ritual abuse. A psychological evaluation during this hospitalization indicated that the mother exhibited major psychopathology with acute emotional instability. Her thinking was described as affect-laden with faulty reasoning that was obvious in the interview. She was described as having an active delusional process with sufficient pathology to support a thought disorder showing a schizophrenic decompensation. Her test responses were described as bizarre with turmoil linked to active delusional processes exhibiting perverse aggression along with strong indications of sexual arousal towards children. The evaluation noted that sexual violation appeared to excite her and was linked to her psychotic processes.

A second evaluation obtained from an outside source indicated that the mother was a profoundly disturbed schizophrenic or schizo-affective woman who functioned reasonably well until approximately two years before, when she came under the influence of therapists who 'assisted her' in organizing her delusional thinking in the areas of sexual abuse and satanism. This outside consultation recommended that there be a careful review of any therapeutic input that was directly or indirectly reinforcing the mother's delusional preoccupations with satanism, cults, multiple personalities, and 'triggering concepts.' This report also noted that the previous therapy resulted in iatrogenic complications in the management of a severely impaired, thought-disordered, profoundly disturbed schizoaffective woman.

During this hospitalization, the mother described how she taught her oldest daughter to use hand signals in identifying internal 'parts.' She also described games she played with this daughter which gave her the information about the abuse by the maternal grandmother. The hospital concluded that the mother had trained her daughter unconsciously due to her need to justify her actions in cutting off her family. The hospital noted that there was great secondary gain and an excuse for everything that had gone wrong in mother's life if she could blame someone else. By the conclusion of this hospital stay, the mother had identified 13 persons as having abused her in the past, including ritual abuse by hospital staff alleged to have occurred during her second hospitalization.

Child Protective Services now became involved and filed a petition alleging that the mother had abused her children. She was allowed supervised visitation with her daughters with the visitations supervised by the father. Upon her hospital discharge the mother completely disagreed with her diagnosis. She was described as extremely angry and sarcastic and indicating that she had not been appropriately treated. She was further described as hysterical and extremely resistant to any further therapeutic intervention.

After her discharge, the mother continued the supervised visits with her children and was allowed to move back into the home after approximately one month. The children had also been discharged from their hospital stay with identical diagnoses of anxiety, depression, Post-Traumatic Stress Disorder, and Dissociative Disorder. The children continued in therapy with the same professionals who treated them during their hospital stay.

On May 17th 1992 the father was admitted for his first psychiatric hospitalization at the insistence of the mother. She demanded his hospitalization to determine the extent, if any, of his involvement in ritual cult activity. At the time of his admission, the father was beginning to express belief in the satanic cult involvement of his wife's family. The impressions on admission indicated recurrent Major Depression, Avoidant Personality Disorder with Passive-Aggressive features. During the course of his hospital stay, the father underwent hypnotherapy sessions and one sodium Amytal interview by hospital staff who believed in the reality of ritual abuse. But he became increasingly skeptical during his hospital stay and by the end of his stay rejected the concept of ritual abuse and felt manipulated by his therapist.

While in the hospital, the children continued to live with the mother and by the time the father was discharged on July 10th 1992 both children had developed stories of satanic ritual sexual abuse at the hands of their father. The oldest daughter, especially, began developing memories of satanic ritual abuse by her grandmother but now instead of her mother participating, she identified the participant as her father. Upon the father's discharge, his own therapist became the therapist for his oldest daughter and has continued to see this child.

Upon his hospital discharge, the father was identified as a sexual abuser of his children and orders were entered in Juvenile Court prohibiting contact by him or any of his family members with the children. The exact wording of the Order is "No family member other than the children's mother shall have contact with the children; the children are not to have contact with the other members." Child Protective Services was completely convinced of the reality of satanic ritual abuse and consulted with the mother's therapist and other satanic ritual abuse experts to formulate treatment plans.

During this period, the mother also consulted regularly with Chicago police officer Robert J. Simandl. Simandl is the 'cult cop' who claims to be an expert on satanic ritual abuse and who works with satanic cult 'survivors.'

Court-ordered visitation between the children and their father was eventually ordered beginning October 1992. But while the father began regular visitation with his youngest daughter, his oldest daughter has refused to see him. She expressed great fear of both her father and grandmother.

In January 1993, Dr. Underwager presented testimony challenging this entire process. The judge then ordered the family members to be seen by a court-appointed psychologist who indicated the children were at serious risk with their mother and that continued placement in her home was detrimental. The children therefore have remained in a third-party foster home pending resolution of the Juvenile Court proceedings. The court-appointed psychologist indicated to the Court that this family had been the victim of incompetent mental health services. The judge ruled there was no abuse, harshly criticized the child protection services and ordered there be only therapy aimed at bringing this family back together. The children are now with the father while the mother remains essentially nonfunctional. The father is instituting civil action against the hospitals, therapists, physicians, and social workers who fostered and implemented the treatments that destroyed this family.

How It Is Done

Here are excerpts from the testimony of the oldest daughter. The father's attorney, Zachary Bravos, is questioning her in a court hearing. In it she describes the influence of the mental health professionals and the techniques they use. The alleged therapeutic techniques which may produce false memories have been described in Chapters 4 and 5. We chose this testimony because the concepts of repression and blocked memories are also now being extended to children who have no memories of abuse.

Q: Janie, what would you like to see happen to your father?

A: I'd like to see him not being able to see me or Tamera and this should be like away from my family.

Q: Would you like to see him maybe in jail?

A: Yes.

Q: Do you think he should go to jail for a long time?

A: Just 'til he recognizes what he had done.

Q: You don't think he recognizes what he did?

A: No. . . . I just think he won't admit, sort of not remember.

Q: And when someone asked you about your

grandma, that makes you—your grandma, your mother's mother—that makes you scared too.

A: Yes.

Q: Even more than your dad or about the same?

A: Pretty much about the same.

Q: They both did—they both abused you?

A: Yes.

Q: And had they both did [sic] the same things to you?

A: Basically, yes. . . .

Q: These things that your father and that your grandmother did to you, did you always remember them?

A: Uh-uh (no).

Q: When did you first remember them?

A: Around Christmas time in 1990. . . .

Q: Did you get help in remembering these things in the hospital?

A: Yes.

Q: Who helped you to remember these things?

A: One of the nurses there, Susan. I don't remember what her last name was. And then Judy Martinez.

Q: How was it that they would help you to remember? . . .

A: Well, she just talked to me and started asking me questions and that's—we'd get into it.

Q: Get into what?

A: Get into talking about it. . . .

Q: Well, before you remembered these things, were you afraid of your father?

A: Not really.

Q: Janie, do you have parts inside you?

A: Yes. . . . They're like little people and—

Q: Do they have faces? Can you think that they each have like different faces?

A: Yes, I can think that.

Q: Do they talk to you?

A: Yes.

Q: Is that something like you can hear just inside your own head?

A: Yes. . . .

Q: Do they ever tell you about abuse?

A: Yes.

Q: Is there like—well, how many parts are there? . . .

A: Maybe between ten and fifteen, something like that.

Q: Do you sometimes find new parts?

A: Yes.

Q: When is the last time you found a part?

A: Probably last year when—maybe the fall, around then.

Q: Does that part have a name?

A: Not yet.

Q: What does that part do?

A: Holds in something, feelings about some people. Like that part helps in feelings about my dad.

Q: You say you have a part that has the feelings about your dad?

A: Yes.

Q: What are the feelings that that part has?

A: Angry, mad.

Q: Does that part talk to you?

A: Yes.

Q: What does that part tell you?

A: I don't know. It just tells me—not really how to feel, but how it feels and then I usually tell somebody else and—

Q: Well, you're going to have to help me a little bit with that.

A: I know.

Q: We'll talk about the part that has—holds your feelings about your dad. . . .

Q: Did you get these parts—did you find out about these parts in the hospital?

A: Yes.

Q: Was there somebody there to help you find out about these parts?

A: Yes.

Q: Who was that?

A: Susan.

Q: We didn't get into much about Judy Martinez. Who was she?

A: She was one of the therapists there.

Q: And what does she do?

A: She helped me about my feelings also. She— the only reason Judy Martinez was there, because Susan, she wasn't certified or something like that. Then Judy Martinez was her boss. . . .

Q: Do you like Judy Martinez?

A: Uh-uh (no).

Q: Why not?

A: She told me lies.

Q: Judy Martinez told you lies?

A: Yes.

Q: When did she tell you these lies?

A: At the hospital. She like—to be afraid of your mom. But I knew that I shouldn't be because she never did anything. . . .

Q: Was that something that she said just like one time or did she say that a lot to you?

A: She'd say that a lot.

Q: Did she ever tell you to be afraid of your dad?

A: Sometimes. But I already knew that, so—

Q: When was the first time that you remember being afraid of your dad?

A: It started a little bit in the hospital, but I only said it once in a while because—I was still questioning it and I didn't understand.

Q: You didn't believe it at first?

A: Yes.

Q: But since being in the hospital—since being out of the hospital, you have come to understand it better?

A: Yes.

Q: And you have come to believe it?

A: Yes.

Q: Who helped you to understand it?

A: I still, even though I wasn't in the hospital, but I'd still see Susan at a certain place.

Q: She'd help you to understand and to believe these things, the memories about your father?

A: Yes.

Q: Anybody other than Susan?

A: After Susan there was Dr. Freeman.

Q: Now, you still see Dr. Freeman?

A: Yes.

Q: Does Dr. Freeman help you to understand? Does he work with these parts that you have too?

A: Yes.

Q: What kind of things have you done with that?

A: He just does basically the same thing that— helps understand and then to find out ways to either not be afraid or to help it.

Q: When did you—Janie, when did you first start to really believe these memories about your dad and your grandma? Was it with Susan or was it with Dr. Freeman?

A: Really with Dr. Freeman.

Q: And what was it that you did with Dr. Freeman that you came to believe these?

A: Talked more and more about it. And then the more I talked the more I would believe. When the parts talked more I believed.

Q: The more the parts talked to you the more you believed.

A: Yes.

Q: Can you tell us the names of any of them?

A: There's Cuddles, there was Afraid and then Red. And Alone did I already mention? . . .

Q: And do they ever talk out of your mouth too?

A: Sometimes.

Q: How does that happen? Does it—does some-time one of these parts take you over or some-thing like that?

A: Yeah.

Q: How does that—tell me about how that works.

A: I don't know. Like—Susan, I don't know how she did it. But sometimes they just come out.

Q: You did that with Susan?

A: Yes.

Q: She was able to get these parts out?

A: Yes. . . .

Q: What happened to you? Where did you go?

A: Well, Susan made up a place, my safe place, and then wherever I felt the safest, that's where I would like go, somewhere in my head. . . .

Q: How about Dr. Freeman, can he do that?

A: Yes.

Q: How does he do it?

A: I don't know. He just like asks if I would let them come out. . . .

Q: When one of these parts comes out and you go to this safe place that you were telling us about,

A: Yes.

Q: —can you hear what's going on? Can you hear what your part is saying?

A: Sometimes, before I go to my safe place, Susan would say go to a certain room, like I couldn't hear, then sometimes I could.

Q: So sometimes when Susan sent you to the safe place, she'd send you to a place where you couldn't hear what your part was saying?

A: Yes. Sometimes she would. Depends on what they were going to talk about.

Q: How about Dr. Freeman, when he brings out your parts, can you hear what your parts are saying?

A: Same as Susan, depends on what they're going to say?

Q: Do you know what they're going to say?

A: Sometimes with Dr. Freeman he'd say, 'Could you handle here what we're going to talk about?' Then he'd say whatever, then—

Q: Let me ask you that. When you say he'll ask you, 'Can you handle hearing about,' then he'll actually tell you something?

A: Yes.

Q: Like what kinds of things?

A: Like the way he'd say it, he'd say, 'Can you handle hearing about some of the things that maybe your dad did at a certain time period or else your grandma did?'

Q: And at the time he asks you that, do you have any memory about it? Or does your part have to give a memory?

A: Depends on if the part had been talking to me, then I would know.

Q: But if the part hadn't been talking to you, then—

A: No.

Q: —you wouldn't know what the part was going to say.

A: No, not really.

Q: So if he asks you if you can handle—let's say you say, 'Can you handle talking about something that happened to your dad during this time period?' Sometimes you say, 'Yeah, I can handle that'?

A: Yes. Or else if I wasn't really sure, he'd say, 'Then I don't think you can,' just to be on the safe side.

Q: Then if you can't handle it, what happens?

A: Then I go to a place where I can't hear and then the parts would come up.

Q: And when you are in that safe place and your part is talking, you can't hear what that part is saying, is that what you are telling me?

A: Yes.

Q: When you are in that safe place, do you know what your body is doing?

A: Not really.

Q: Is it like falling asleep or something?

A: Yes.

Q: When you wake up, is it—how do you come back from that place? How does that happen?

A: I don't know. Sometimes he'd send another

part to get me or else he'd send that part back,
then I'd know.

Q: Is it like waking up from being asleep?

A: Yes. . . .

Q: Does he sometimes tell you things that you
didn't even know about until after he told you
that your part said it?

A: Once in a while.

Q: What kinds of things would he tell you that you
didn't even know about?

A: I don't know.

Q: Which were your dad and your grandma?

A: Yes.

Q: Bad things?

A: Yes.

Q: Did he tell you that you should believe those
things?

A: He said it was my choice if I would or not. I
would think it over and then say, 'Could this
like really have happened?' Then I would
question myself and then I'd tell Dr. Freeman
that I can't understand right now, but later
on—

Q: Later on you could understand it?

A: Yes.

Q: Then you can believe it fully with all of your
heart later on?

A: Yes.

Q: But sometimes you are told these things and at
first you don't believe them because it doesn't
make sense to you?

A: Yes.

Q: How do you come to believe it? How do you
make sure that it is true?

A: Sometimes I ask one of the parts to tell me that
is it really true, give me more details, I want to
hear it. . . .

Q: Do you remember playing the finger game?

A: Yes. With the gentleman and not with the
fingers.

Q: Yes. Who taught you that?

A: Susan.

Q: Was that a way that you could find out about your parts?

A: Sometimes.

Q: How did the finger game work?

A: I don't know. I raise one finger for yes, I would do it when my parts would, another finger for no, then if they weren't sure, then there was another finger for that.

Q: Would you raise like three fingers? But it wasn't really you raising your finger, it was the part.

A: Yes.

Q: Did you ever play the finger game with your mom too?

A: Sometimes. Because when I couldn't handle it I'd talk to my mom a little and it is hard for her to believe, so she'd ask also just to make sure. . . .

Q: She'd ask your parts with the finger game.

A: Yes.

Q: Then she would tell you whether or not you could believe it. Was it like a double check or something like that?

A: Yes.

Q: When she did that with you, did it usually check out to be true that you should believe it?

A: Yes.

Q: Now, your mom got memories too, she has parts too, doesn't she?

A: Yes.

Q: Do you ever talk to your mom's parts?

A: Sometimes I check with them to see if they—

Q: How would you check with one of your mom's parts?

A: I just ask her to ask them and then they would say.

Q: Can you give me an example? Can you remember anything about something where you had to ask your mom for her parts too?

A: When I first started believing about my dad,—

Q: Uh-huh.

A: —I asked her to ask her parts if they believe about what I was saying is true or not. . . .

Q: Well, can you remember any of the things that Dr. Freeman told you that your mom told him?

A: No.

Q: Was it stuff about your dad and grandma?

A: Yes. When I first started, was about my dad, she wasn't sure. At a certain point. And then she just asked him because she couldn't—

Q: Your mom would ask Dr. Freeman—

A: Yes.

Q: —about the things that your dad did to you?

A: Yes.

Q: And Dr. Freeman, what did he say?

A: Sometimes he'd say, 'We haven't talked about that much yet' or something.

Q: Dr. Freeman believes that your dad hurt you?

A: As far as I know, yes.

Q: Has he ever told you that?

A: Yes. When I was doubting myself a couple times.

Q: When was that?

A: Sometime later.

Q: You had been doubting sometimes if what you think you remember was really true?

A: Yes.

Q: But Dr. Freeman—what would he say?

A: He'd just say, 'Would you really have done all this for nothing?' and stuff.

Q: Did Dr. Freeman ever say that it is possible sometimes for people to remember things that didn't happen?

A: No.

Q: He never said that to you?

A: No.

Q: Janie, what's a trigger? Can you tell me what a trigger is? I know it is hard to explain. I tried to understand it too, so maybe you can help me a little bit.

A: Like something—I'll give you an example.

Q: Okay.

A: Maybe my dad, he'd do something and then he'd have something represent it or he'd have like a teddy bear or something like that, and then he'd make me act a certain way, then when he'd give me like that teddy bear, I'd act in that way again.

Q: Let's say—you just brought up a teddy bear. Did he give you a teddy bear?

A: Yes. While I was in the room he gave me one.

Q: Was that supposed to do something?

A: Yes.

Q: What was it supposed to do?

A: Make me scared, make me not talk anymore.

Q: How do you know that?

A: He planted it.

Q: He planted it?

A: Yes.

Q: Where? In your head?

A: Yes.

Q: How did he do that?

A: I think—before we stopped seeing him, he'd say—teddy bear of this color would say—tell you not to talk or not to do this, then he'd just keep on saying it so it would get in my head. Then when I'd see a teddy bear that color or something, I'd remember.

Q: Now, do you remember him telling you that with the teddy bear or is that something one of your parts told you?

A: One of my parts.

Q: Which part told you that?

A: That one was the one about the—the latest one.

Q: The latest one, it doesn't have a name yet.

A: Yes.

Q: So before that part told you you didn't remember your father planted that trigger, is that right?

A: Yes.

Q: Is that the way that triggers work, that you don't know about them?

A: Some ones I do, then sometimes I don't.

Q: Now, who else triggers you?

A: My grandma with some things.

Q: Janie, who taught you about triggers?

A: My parts that already know—with me, Judy Martinez did.

Q: And what did—she's the one who told you about how triggers work?

A: She would just tell me about them, and then my parts would say most of it. I don't know how.

Q: I don't know either because I can't see inside there.

A: I know. . . .

Examination By the Court:

Q: Janie, if I understood what you said, you first started remembering about the things that your father did in 1990. Is that what you said?

A: Something like that.

Q: December 1990. Now, were you about seven years old then when you started to remember? Is that about right?

A: Yes.

Q: If I understood what you said to Mr. Bravos, you had some parts for two and three years, is that right?

A: Yes.

Q: So you started to remember somewhere between two and three years ago, right?

A: (nodding positively)

Q: Now, when you were remembering, in your remembrances, do you know how old you were when these things happened?

A: No. . . .

The Court: Thank you, Janie, very much.

Adapted with permission from *Issues in Child Abuse Accusations* 5(4) (1993), 243–264.

A Private Investigator's Report

A father was accused by an adult daughter of sexual abuse during her childhood. There had been no memories or any suggestion of anything improper in the family until after the daughter had been in therapy for several months. The father received a letter from an attorney forbidding him to contact his daughter or their grandchildren and demanding the father pay for the daughter's therapy. When the father learned what she was accusing him of and who the therapist was, he sent a private investigator to play the role of a client with the therapist his daughter had been seeing. All of the sessions, in the last half of 1991, were taped.

> The environment was dimly lit with candles, even though it was mid-afternoon. The room was decorated with brass, coasters, bells, elephants, incense burners and a jade Buddha. Indian sitar music was playing softly and there was a heavy odor of incense. There was a small couch for the client and a chair for the therapist with a telephone and a tape recorder on a small table. There were no diplomas or licenses on the walls. The therapist was in her mid-thirties, with straight hair and no make-up, and was wearing gray slacks and a red pullover.
>
> The presenting complaint by the investigator-client was sleeplessness, fatigue, and a concern about possible alcohol abuse. In the initial session the therapist made two anti-male statements about the patriarchal system and the preferential treatment men get. When discussing the treatment she would provide, she described nontraditional therapy procedures and said that the client had to trust her regarding these techniques. The treatment procedures described were hypnosis, imaging, dream work, and body work. The therapist said that, although she did not know yet what her problems are, it was most likely a trauma in her life which she was repressing, though it was trying to emerge. This conclusion was based on the investigator-client's report that, when asked to recall her earliest memory, she said she heard a voice (a real voice, not a dream voice). The therapist instructed the investigator-

client not to drink any alcohol until the next appointment and recommended she attend a group therapy session and an AA group. At the AA group, for women only, at least four women described themselves as incest survivors who had broken all ties with their biological families, including siblings.

In the second session, after telling the therapist she had a terrible week, the investigator-client described conflict with her family over coming to therapy. She said her stepfather had criticized her for spending money inherited from her father on therapy and told her it was hurting her mother. She also said she had had a spell while sleeping when she awoke with a start, feeling someone was in the room, and she was terrified and numb.

The therapist said, "I have to tell you something because you are so upset and I sense you think you are losing your mind," although nothing was said by the investigator-client about losing her mind. "You are having body memories from a trauma which happened to you in your early childhood. You don't remember it now because your brain has blocked it out. The memory is too painful and horrible for you to deal with, so your brain has just locked it up but your body remembers and is trying to tell you. You are an incest victim!"

She then went to the bookcase and got the book, *The Courage to Heal*, and told the investigator-client to read it. She said she recommends it to all survivors even though it is hard to take. She also recommended the *Courage to Heal Workbook* and *Secret Survivors* by E. Sue Blume, from which she read the list of 40 symptoms of incest survivors, shaking her head as each one confirmed her diagnosis.

The investigator-client was instructed how to make herself feel safe at night by having a night light, putting pillows down her back, leaving the bedroom door open, and buying a stuffed animal to have in bed with her. She was told to treat herself as though a small child were with her and became frightened at night and it was her job to comfort her. Several times the concept of body memories was evoked and the investigator-client was told to treat the small child within.

In the third session, the investigator-client began by

saying that she was feeling angry and frustrated. She had been diagnosed as an incest victim two weeks earlier but she could not remember any events that would have caused that diagnosis. She reported that she had not had a drink for five weeks, she had spent the holiday with family, and she had had a sleep interruption but had been less frightened because of the night light. The therapist said she could only assume the diagnosis of incest victim from the "classic symptoms" which the investigator-client described. These "classic symptoms" were the body memories and the sleep interruption with fear. The investigator-client again said she was angry and frustrated because she had no memories of any such events. The therapist responded that "No visual memory is often the case."

The therapist told the investigator-client to continue reading *The Courage to Heal* even though it was very upsetting. She said it was a book for survivors and said one of the authors was a psychologist (this is not correct). She began to list the symptoms from *Secret Survivors* again and continued a monologue on them so that the investigator-client was not able to interject that everyone had some of these symptoms from time to time.

The investigator-client asked about treatment methods but the therapist would not be specific except to state that they use forms of memory retrieval. She also described hypnosis and self-hypnosis. She said, "Something is definitely coming to the surface. It is fear." She questioned the investigator-client about time periods in her life and men in her life. She ruled out the grandparents, stepfather, and brother as causing the fear, leaving only the father. She then asked about the father.

The investigator-client said she and her father were not affectionate and that he was a disciplinarian, that she wanted his approval, and that she feared him for his discipline. But, she added, this was not the same fear as in the dreams at night, which was a gasping, freezing, numbing feeling. The therapist asked if she feared death and if she felt small and shrinking. The investigator-client said yes to both. She was then given a breathing exercise which is essentially a trance inducing technique, and then the therapist told her that her body was ready to tell her what her fear was all about. "Your body memories are of your father coming in at night and touching you. They are consistent with my diagnosis!"

There followed a lengthy discussion of group therapy with several examples of women who had no visual memories of abuse but who had become convinced they were abused. "Try to stay in your body. As you do that we will work our way through this. You will think, 'I want to know what is going on. I am going to have a memory, so it's real to me.' Except, I have people who have memories of absolutely everything and say they think they made it up and are losing their minds and sometimes these are people who end up being hospitalized, maybe having reconstructive surgery, because it is so hard to believe."

In a final session the investigator-client told the therapist she did not believe she was an incest survivor and she did not relate to the books nor to the symptoms described in them. The therapist encouraged her to attend a meditation class conducted by the therapist's sister. She said that both she and her sister were former substance abusers and came from a severely dysfunctional family. She described her first spiritual experience as a result of meditation which followed her 12-step program.

A Report to the Court in a Civil Case

The following report by Dr. Lee Coleman concerns the suit between Susan Q. Smith and John V. Public. We, along with Dr. Lee Coleman, consulted in this case, which involved a civil lawsuit based on recovered memories. Dr. Coleman examined the Plaintiff and prepared this report to the court. The report documents the development of the memories of abuse.

In this case, a young woman, moderately depressed and unsure of her life goals, but in no way out of touch with reality or psychotic, eventually made allegations which were so bizarre that they might easily be thought to be the product of a major mental disorder. The case analysis demonstrates that the source of the woman's pseudomemories was not a disorder in the patient, but a 'disorder' in the therapist. We are reprinting this report in its entirety since it illustrates in detail how memories of childhood abuse can be created in therapy. Names and identifying information have been changed.

Judge John Q. Smith
Superior Court, All American County
Anywhere, U.S.A.

The following report concerns the suit between Susan Q. Smith and John V. Public. The opinions expressed are based on a study of the Amended List of Documents of the Plaintiff, dated April 6th 1992, Additional Documents (such as police records and Children's Services Records), Examination for Discovery transcripts of Mrs. Smith and Mr. Public, and my examination of Mrs. Smith on May 4, 1992, which lasted somewhat over three hours. I have also studied several videotapes pertinent to the case, enumerated below.

Based upon all this information, as well my prior professional experience, it is my opinion that the alleged 'memories' of Mrs. Smith, relating a variety of sexual and abusive acts perpetrated upon her by Mr. Public and others, are not memories at all. They are, instead, mental images which, however sincerely felt by her to be memories of past events, are nonetheless the result of a series of suggestions from both lay persons and professionals.

That Mrs. Smith has succumbed to these influences in no way implies that she suffers from any mental disorder. By her own account, she has had problems of low self-esteem, depression, and bulimia in her past. She has, however, never suffered and does not now suffer a mental disorder which would imply a loss of contact with reality. If the reliability of her claims are to be best evaluated by the Court, it should be understood that there is another way that a person may say things that may not be true, yet be entirely sincere.

Suggestibility is something we all share as part of our being human, with some persons obviously being more suggestible than others. In this case, Mrs. Smith has been involved with individuals and groups, over a period of years, the end result of which has been to promote a process of accepting the false idea that whatever mental image is conjured up, especially if part of 'therapy' is necessarily a valid retrieval of past experience, i.e. a 'memory.'

Let me now document the evidence which has led me to the above conclusions.

1. Mrs. Smith's suspicions about John Public and his daughter, Alice

From several sources, such as her deposition, my interview, and investigative interviews, it seems clear that Mrs. Smith suspected for several years that her cousin, John Public, was engaging in sexual behavior with his daughter Alice. When asked for examples which led to these suspicions, she mentioned alleged comments from him that "a child's hands" felt so good. She also mentioned that no other adults seemed to be concerned about such comments.

Seeing Mr. Public and Alice (approximately eight years old at the time) lying in bed together, in their underwear, reinforced her suspicion, as did the alleged comment from Mr. Public to Mr. Smith (not heard by Mrs. Smith), that his (Smith's) daughter would make him horny. Mrs. Smith also noted that, until age 18 months, her own daughter would cry if Mr. Public attempted to pick her up or get close to her, and Mrs. Smith noted to herself, "She's a smart child." (It should be noted that such behavior in infants of this age is perfectly normal.)

Mrs. Smith told me that she had informed family members on several occasions of her suspicions, but no one else apparently shared her opinions, or felt anything needed to be reported.

The 1986 video of a family Halloween party was the event that convinced Mrs. Smith she should report her suspicions. It is quite important that the Court view this video, in order to judge for itself whether the material could reasonably lead a person to believe something untoward was taking place. My own opinion is there was nothing happening that was unusual or abnormal. It was

Alice who first struck a somewhat playful and seductive pose, and such displays are hardly abnormal for a teenage girl. Police investigators likewise saw nothing untoward on this tape.

The question raised, then, is whether Mrs. Smith had for her own personal reasons, upon which I will not attempt to speculate, developed an obsession about Mr. Public and his daughter, one which was leading her (Smith) to overinterpret ordinary behaviors.

It is not surprising, then, that when the report was investigated by Children's Services, no evidence of abuse was uncovered. Mrs. Smith tells me, however, that she was not reassured, and only felt that she had fulfilled an obligation to report something.

2. Early Influences promoting in Mrs. Smith a belief that prior sexual abuse might have occurred but not be remembered

From numerous sources (deposition, my interview, journals, therapy records), it is clear that Mrs. Smith was strongly influenced by a statement she says Dr. Gwen Olson made to her regarding bulimia, a problem Mrs. Smith had suffered from to one degree or another since early adolescence.

Mrs. Smith states that Dr. Olson told her, sometime in early 1987 (the records indicate this was in December 1986), that "one hundred percent of my patients with bulimia have later found out that they were sexual abuse victims." Whether these words were actually spoken by Dr. Olson, or instead interpreted this way by Mrs. Smith, I of course do not know. But in either case, the words Mrs. Smith took away with her are extremely important, because the words "found out" would imply that a person could have been sexually abused, not be aware of it, and later recover such an awareness. I will later on be discussing the lack of evidence for, and major evidence against, any such phenomenon being genuine.

Mrs. Smith told me she was seriously affected by this, experiencing crying and feelings of fear. She began to wonder if she might have been sexually abused. When I asked her if she had ever before that time had such a question, she said that she "had no memories" of any such abuse. She had, in fact, told Children's Services shortly before, during the investigation of Alice, that John Public had "never before abused me . . . I was relying on my memory."

At this time, Mrs. Smith was being seen in psychotherapy, first by Edna Johnson, and then by Dr. Abraham, for what seem to have been feelings of anxiety and depression. Sexual abuse was apparently not an issue in this therapy. Instead, Mrs. Smith states that her self-esteem was low, and that she was "not functioning" well as a housewife, even though she felt good about her marriage. Both she and Dr. Abraham apparently felt she was "a bored housewife." She decided to start her own business, but this never happened because events leading to the current accusations against John Public intervened.

Mrs. Smith explains that she went to an Entrepreneurs' Training Camp in the Fall of 1987, was doing extremely well, but then "sabotaged myself" by performing poorly despite knowing correct answers on an examination. She felt, after the camp, that she needed to work on herself.

In addition, she saw an Oprah Winfrey program on the subject of child abuse. Mrs. Smith told me that she cried as she watched this program, "for me and not for them . . . I wondered at my feelings and where they were coming from."

Mrs. Smith confirms that it was shortly after seeing this program, with all of the above background in place, that she called the Women's Sexual Assault Center (WSAC) on September 3rd 1987.

After a telephone intake, she had a face-to-face contact with Joan Oliver, and told her that "I had concerns, feelings, but no memory of being sexually assaulted. . . . I thought it would be better to wait (for therapy) until I had a memory. They said OK, and put me on a waiting list."

The records of WSAC generally confirm this account which I received from Mrs. Smith on May 4th 1992. During the first telephone contact, Mrs. Smith related strong feelings of abuse as a child came up . . . She can't remember specific things . . . her GP told her most bulimics have been sexually abused as children . . .

A second telephone contact, September 16, include

occluded memories. Sister was abused by neighborhood man as a child. Susan gets very re-triggered by this and by shows about child abuse. Her doctor told her that close to 100 percent of bulimics have been sexually abused. This really brought up a lot of feelings and some images but not really a memory.

Yet another important event happened around Christmas 1987, before Mrs. Smith had entered the treatments (with Mary Brown and Veronica Erickson) where the mental images alleged to be 'memories' started. This was something I had not discovered from any written materials, and learned about for the first time from Mrs. Smith on May 4th 1992.

Mrs. Smith had a friend, Valerie White, who told her about her treatments for back problems. Biofeedback was used at the pain and stress clinic she attended, and Ms. White told Mrs. Smith that she had started to remember being abused. When I asked Mrs. Smith how she reacted to this, she said, "I felt . . . that if she was in therapy, remembering, maybe I should start as well. I had no memory, but if she was in therapy . . ."

To summarize, then, the suggestive influences to this point: Mrs. Smith is still not reassured that Alice is not being abused by John Public; Dr. Olson either says or Mrs. Smith believes she says that in her experience all bulimics are sexual abuse victims; finally, after she decides she shouldn't go into therapy "until she has a memory" of sexual abuse, a friend tells her "the remembering" can wait, and Mrs. Smith concludes she should give it a try.

It is my opinion, based on the above material, that Mrs. Smith was at this point being victimized by lay persons and professionals who were representing to her that sexual abuse might not be remembered, when in truth there is no evidence to support such a claim. While Mrs. Smith may have had her own personal problems and/or motivations for claiming abuse at the hands of Mr. Public (something I will not speculate upon) she was being profoundly influenced by unsound information. It is my opinion that this has persisted to this day.

3. Suggestive and Unprofessional Therapy Creates the 'Memories'

In March 1988, Mrs. Smith started seeing Mary Brown for individual psychotherapy, and also had interviews with Veronica Erickson, a student who was writing a thesis on 'Recovering Memories of Childhood Sexual Abuse.' On March 9, 1988, Ms. Erickson commented that Mrs. Smith had done

> a lot of great body work. Worked on her anger, hurt about being sexually abused. Has a few memories about it and wants more.

On March 28, the WSAC records show that the

> "memory recovery process" was getting into high gear: . . . had lots of memories come to her which she feels good about; 2 "rapes," 9 sodomies, and 2 oral sex (she has remembered both rapes and 1 sodomy and oral sex), 8 sodomies and 1 oral sex to go. Can't wait.

Further WSAC records of Ms. Erickson show just as clearly that she has lost all professional objectivity. Her April 5th 1988 note simply says "FUCK!", presumably her reaction to hearing Mrs. Smith verbalizing more and more outrageous claims about what Mr. Public did to her. The June 14th 1988 note gives an insight as to the position Ms. Erickson was taking with regard to whether Mrs. Smith's increasingly severe claims should be automatically assumed to be accurate:

> trying to remember a memory that was just beginning to flash . . . really scared that this memory is made up . . . I told her I believed her.

If there is any doubt about the stance being adopted by Ms. Erickson, i.e. that whatever Mrs. Smith 'recovers' from week to week is a reliable statement about past events, a reading of her Ph.D. thesis makes it abundantly clear that it was simply a 'given' for her and the selected sources she relies on, that the patient's claims must be taken at face value. She writes, for example:

> Validation, feeling believed, was seen as essential for incest survivors struggling to reconcile their memories.

Nowhere in the thesis is mention made of any concern that false claims may arise in therapy specifically aimed at such 'uncovering.' Next, she speaks of

> the ability of counselor . . . to facilitate the survivor's recall of the abuse . . . which of course assumes that abuse has taken place.

Just how broadly based is the source of these allegedly reliable 'memories' is indicated by her quoting the book, *The Courage to Heal,* which has been influential in promoting the very ideas at the center of this case:

> "Occluded" memories are vague flashbacks, triggered by touches, smells, sounds, body memories, bodily sensations as "warning signs." Some women just intuitively knew that they had been sexually abused and were struggling to trust their intuition.

It is also clear that the proper role for the therapist, according to Ms. Erickson, is not only to accept all images as 'memories,' but to actively encourage this process. She writes of her method which

> serves to continually promote an atmosphere in which the researcher is spontaneously both receptive and actively stimulating the recollection of the participant. . . . The participants and researcher . . . create the world within which this study is revealed."

Ms. Erickson says of 'Victoria' (pseudonym for Mrs. Smith),

> She thought about who might have abused her and when she said his name, she knew who the offender

was but she still had no memories as proof. (p. 56 of Erickson thesis)

Let me now turn to her other therapist, Mary Brown. Ms. Brown in her intake notes of March 1, 1988 refers to Mrs. Smith having

> flashbacks of childhood sexual abuse experiences, she believes by this same cousin.

Ms. Brown's treatment plan was to "assist Susan express and release the emotions associated with the sexual abuse experience." This is important, because it shows that Ms. Brown, from the beginning, assumed the truth of the allegations.

It wasn't too long after this, the night of March 12th/13th, that Mrs. Smith's calendar indicates she had a "nightmare" and her "first memories." When I asked Mrs. Smith about this, she said it was

> the nightmare which triggered the memory . . . In the nightmare, the neighbor had shot her husband in the chest. Her cleaning up his blood, I recalled John blotting up my blood after raping me.

There are, of course, no reputable data which would indicate that a patient or therapist can use dream material to reliably 'recover memories' of real events. Ms. Brown, however, seems to have utter confidence in the process, for she wrote to the police on August 3rd 1988:

> The treatment methods I use enable clients to express and release the very deepest feelings that may have been stifled . . . It is precisely because the emotional intensity of sexual abuse in childhood is greater than what most children can integrate that these experiences are quickly lost to memory. The ensuing, forgetting and denial are the mind's way of protecting the individual from total disruption of their cognitive functioning. This was particularly true of survivors of sexual abuse whose experiences occurred more than ten years ago. The reason for this is that there was not the social awareness nor the professional expertise for dealing with these problems at that time. Children

instinctively know when the adults around them are going to be able to help them. When they find themselves in situations where they may either be disbelieved . . . this forgetting and denial comes into play even more strongly. . . . Memories tend to return in fragments and to be unclear or non-specific in the beginning . . . the blocks in the way of memory are gradually removed. . . . This is precisely what occurred . . . with Susan Smith. It is my clinical judgment that Susan had reached a point in her healing process when the memories that were returning were completely reliable. . . . She was unprepared to report until she herself was certain and until she received validation from me that I was in agreement that the memories could be trusted . . .

That Ms. Brown was not only accepting all statements as real events, but actively encouraging them, is seen by the following passage from the same letter:

Susan herself questioned any inconsistency. . . . It took some education on my part for her to . . . understand the whole process of how it is that the recall process works . . .

Ms. Brown was even willing to assure the police that the other persons that Mrs. Smith was gradually naming as victims during that Spring and Summer of 1988 would also need 'help' in remembering.

It is highly likely that most or all of the children that Susan remembers . . . will be unable to remember these experiences. This does not mean they did not occur any more than Susan's former amnesia means that these events had not happened to her. One of these (youngsters) may be precipitated to remember and recapture the experiences through a process similar to what occurred for Susan.

There is, of course, absolutely no evidence that this whole process has anything to do with memory, or a recall of past events. The only professionals who advocate these ideas are those making up a small, fringe group who hold themselves out as 'specialists in treating sexual abuse,' but who (as this case shows) seem to assume that it is permissible to pass off wild theories, like the ones above, to both patients, families, and investigative agencies.

Most important, however, is that outsiders evaluate the possible impact of such ideas on persons like Mrs. Smith. The evidence is clear that she has raised doubts from time to time, but each time, these 'specialists' have told her that her mental images must represent real events. In this sense, I believe the professionals (Brown, Erickson, and others to be mentioned) are most responsible for creating the unreliable information in this case.

Not only do the ideas promoted by Brown and Erickson hold great potential to contaminate information coming from such counselling, but the techniques used with Mrs. Smith would likely heighten this possibility. Mrs. Smith described pounding pillows and being encouraged to express her anger in sessions with Ms. Erickson, and in individual and group sessions with Ms. Brown, she described exercises in which she was using hyperventilation or bending from the waist. The many group sessions she has attended, focussing on 'recovery from sexual abuse,' have a potentially profound influence on the participants.

In addition, Ms. Brown had a technique, which she called the 'denial game,' that was used when Mrs. Smith expressed caution about whether her mental images were reliable. This process had the intended effect of causing Mrs. Smith to once more *assume that whatever she could think of had actually happened.*

The police investigation was dropped for lack of evidence, for lack of corroboration from any of the many alleged victims named by Mrs. Smith, and because an outside consultant told the police that the impact of the therapy might be contaminating the information (see p. 160 of police investigation).

Mrs. Smith's statements to police include 'trying to see' alleged events, having

> a flash . . . (a) visual memory of a spirit part of me coming out of me via my mouth and sitting on a head

board. I now understand this to be dissociation. (p. 200 of police investigation)

The police, quite understandably, wondered whether this might be a sign of major mental disorder, like a psychosis. Instead, such statements reflect not that Mrs. Smith was suffering a major mental disorder, but simply that she was absorbing unsupported ideas from her therapists. I have studied the process by which some mental health professionals are passing these ideas to patients, via articles, speeches, and in therapy sessions. Many, if not most, patients, will accept these ideas as accepted scientific information, coming as they do from a professional therapist.

Just how much Mrs. Smith had come to believe in this process, already by April, 1988, is seen by her telling the police on April 20, 1988 that

These are not complete memories at this point but there are bits and pieces of which I would like to tell you now and when I have the complete memory back I will talk to you again. . . . I would like to add that I expect to have further recall of incidents as I have just begun to have recall in the last five weeks or so. (p. 206 of police records)

4. The Growth of the Allegations
The process described above will often lead to a virtual flood of allegations which grow and grow. Particularly if there are emotional rewards for producing more claims, the sky is the limit. In this case, it ultimately led to claims of ritual abuse, animal killings, gang rape, multiple personalities, etc. which Mrs. Smith now seems to disavow but which she at the time was claiming as legitimate memory. A brief review of these developments offers important perspective on the unreliable nature of this entire process.

Dr. Wagner saw Mrs. Smith from May 20, 1988 to January 27, 1989. He used a method Mrs. Smith describes as "regression," and which she now does not trust. She feels that some of the things she said as a result of these methods may not have happened.

For example, Dr. Wagner's notes of November 24, 1988 speak of "memory of John and 'Joe.' Tying her up—raping her. Two others came in, Evan and [unreadable]." Mrs. Smith says she doesn't recall saying this to Dr. Wagner, doesn't believe she said it to him, believes his records are incorrect, and believes she talked about "Sam."

Dr. Wagner, while nowhere in his records expressing any doubt about the reality of these statements, did mention at the outset (June 3rd 1988) that he thought Mrs. Smith was: "I suspect getting a lot of mileage out of sexual abuse. Attention and support from home she never got from mom and dad?"

When I questioned Mrs. Smith about other examples of statements drawn from the notes of the many therapists she saw in the coming months, I noted an interesting pattern. Whenever a statement in therapy records referred to events which she now says may not have happened, like seeing a boy with slits for eyes and no face, she says that she cannot recall saying any of this. She repeatedly said it was only her study of the therapy records which allows her to remember what she might have said in therapy.

However, when I asked her about a note from Morton Hunt's evaluation of January 15, 1991, she was quite clear that she did not say the following "Then had nightmare. Chose John. Just knew it was him (reviewed possible men)."

Such selective 'memory' merely reinforces my opinion that these multiple therapy contacts, of the nature described, make a mockery of the idea that claims growing out of the sessions, or growing out of the mental images of a patient between such sessions, are reliable.

The fact that Mrs. Smith was in much more therapy than I have yet summarized, only deepens the dilemmas. She was in group therapy with Ms. Summers, for 32 sessions, from March 21st 1989 to December 1st 1989, and Ms. Summers, who is another of those who specialize in "working mainly with women recovering from childhood sexual abuse," wrote in her records that "Susan's abuse was the most cruel and degrading I have encountered."

Once again, unquestioning acceptance seems to be the *sina qua non* of many of the therapists in this case. Sadly, such an attitude may be quite destructive to patients. A review of her journals, which I will highlight, shows that (as Dr. Wagner had indicated) Mrs. Smith was getting a lot of positive feedback from more and more 'memories.' A patient might feel good at the time of such feedback, but the encouragement of this process does not bode well for the long-term welfare of such patients.

May 24th 1988—"Another memory came back—arms tied, Sam passed a bowel movement into my mouth . . . I know there are things I can't even imagine yet that they did to me. I know I still have a lot of memories to go . . . I know I'll have the strength to handle them . . . I'm on my way to a happy successful life . . . I love my strength.

May 26th 1988—This morning at the Mom's Group . . . another memory came back. Sam lay on my face with his penis in my mouth, my nose blocked, suffocated by his belly then he urinated in my mouth . . . I called WSAC. The more I discover about what I've been through the more I wonder how I ever survived. . . . You're so strong Susan, so wonderful. You're capable of whatever you believe in. You're OK, Susan Smith. You're strong, you're a survivor, and a winner, you're going straight to the top, head of the class. You're OK, you're a winner I'm really truly beginning to like myself and I really like that—all these years I hated myself . . .

May 27th—I begin my workshop with my therapist. (Mary Brown)

May 28th— . . . we did rapid breathing . . . I went to my sexual abuse . . . my body was twitching and squirming just as if it were tied up by the hands . . . I started getting these vague recollections of this blond male being Warren and some occurrence happening. . . . I wasn't ready to look at it until I could intellectually figure out how this could be . . .

May 31st—Describes Dave meeting with Smith—He explained to him that these memories had been undisturbed for twenty years and had not been distorted . . . and that I was not making it up . . . I knew Dave was not ready to look at his abuse . . . at WSAC I went into denial mode . . . Veronica played the denial game with me just to show me that I was crazy to believe I was making this up.

June 14th 1988—Saw Veronica, talked about Yellowstone incident with Gretchen involved, how I was blocking everything because I had no proof John was in Yellowstone and the fact that Gretchen must have repressed and that she would probably deny remembering such an incident . . . so she had me 'hang' and it took a much longer time for the feelings to come, but they did, I cried, pound pillows, yelled, and got back more memories . . . so much doesn't make sense. Where is everyone else?

November 9th 1988—What I learned in therapy today: When I was abused it happened to my body. It happened to a part of me that I dissociated from. I have separated from and disowned the part of me that it happened to. . . . I am ashamed of my body . . . so I abuse it.

April 18th 1989—I love myself and that's something I couldn't have said a year ago. I've come a long way. . . . Signed Terrific Susan.

May ?, 1989— . . . I let my little girls talk . . . etc.

June 8th 1989—attended Conference on Child Sexual Abuse . . . I learned a lot . . . talked to Gretchen two weeks ago. More about her 'other personalities' . . . Memories, memories. Where are they? I want to remember all the mean sadistic things John did to me.

July 5th 1989—I know I am going to go on and achieve great things in my life . . . speak out against abuse of children, especially sexual abuse. I know I'm strong, a survivor, and a successeder [sic].

October 16th 1989—I got back memories of what

happened after John gave my body to the two 'tough men' in exchange for drugs.

October 29th 1989—I don't think this can happily, successfully end for me unless I have power over him.

November 29th 1989—Cousin Joe called and told me Warren had memories of being sexually assaulted by John. The memories are just beginning . . . I told Warren . . . I was really proud of him.

November 27th 1990— . . . I don't want any more memories!!! . . . I called WSAC this afternoon and bits of memories came up. One was John beside me, and about five men, in black robes, or gowns—full length with hoods on their heads. . . . These men had sword-like daggers in their hands . . . a memory of John slitting the throat of a cat with a knife . . . telling us that this is what would happen to us if we ever told about him.

December 16th 1990—I think I might have multiple personalities. It is something I've wondered about before, but believed you only developed multiples if you were severely abused before age 8. . . . My first day with Veronica there was this other part of me talking. She named herself Julie . . . it was really weird cause I knew what was happening . . . I'm going to get to the other side of this—new and improved. But in the mean time, I'm a nuttsy basketcase.

December 25th 1990—I started back in therapy mid-December, I could no longer contain the memories within me. . . . I want to write about and keep track of my memories. I've had a feeling for several months now that there might have been ritual abuse. When I started having flashes of white candles, lots of them, burning, I thought well, this is probably just an image I've seen on TV. . . . My 2nd day in therapy (3rd time I'd seen June) I had this memory—a faceless boy, . . . he had no nose and only slits for eyes. . . . They told us if we didn't behave, or if we

ever told they would burn our faces with an iron. . . .
They told the girls they use their genitals as eyes, then
when they grow older they'd have furry, hairy eyes
and everyone would laugh.

Toward the end of our meeting, I asked Mrs. Smith how
she distinguished between the many allegations which she
insists took place, and the many allegations which she made
but now says she cannot remember saying and isn't sure
they are real. The gist of her answer (the tape is of course
available) was that 'memories' which were like a 'videotape,' where a picture is complete, from start to finish, and
which occurred to her sometimes in therapy but often by
herself, are reliable. Brief images, or 'flashes,' which are
incomplete, and which were often in response to therapeutic techniques she now is critical of, like those of June
Schreiber and others, she distrusts.

I find this distinction, which I must assume to be
sincere on Mrs. Smith's part, to be utterly unreliable. First,
the therapy from the beginning has been manipulative,
even though I have no doubt that all the therapists were
sincere in wanting to help. They all, nonetheless, adopted
the position that 'the more memory the better.'

While this might be interpreted to mean that this is
standard practice in the therapeutic community, since so
many therapists in this case acted in this manner, it is
instead an artifact which resulted when Mrs. Smith sought
out or was referred to a selected group of therapists who
'specialize in recovery from sexual abuse.' Amongst this
group, whose work and education I have studied extensively, it is common practice to assume abuse occurs if anyone
claims it has, common practice to encourage as many
'memories' as possible, common practice to encourage
anger and 'empowerment,' and common practice to accept
all allegations, however unlikely, as being real.

All this is terribly unscientific, without general agreement from the mental health community, and in my view
highly destructive to many patients. Perhaps most important here, in the context of litigation, is the fact that these
techniques absolutely fly in the face of reliable fact-finding.

I cannot emphasize strongly enough how important it is

for the Court, in studying this case and deciding what is reliable and what is not, to understand that if common sense leads to one conclusion about where the truth lies, the use of psychiatric labels and esoteric explanations should not cause the Court to abandon what the facts otherwise seem to show.

Adapted with permission from *Issues in Child Abuse Accusations* 4(4) (1992), 169–176.

A Psychiatrist Loses Her License

On March 18, 1994th the Minnesota Board of Medical Practice ordered the suspension of the license of Dr. Diane Humenansky, a St. Paul psychiatrist accused of planting false memories of sexual abuse, and further ordered that she undergo a mental and physical medical evaluation. Dr. Gary Blackstone, who reviewed Dr. Humenansky's practice, said she had committed serious breaches of the physician-patient relationship. There were several complaints and five former patients have sued Dr. Humenansky charging that she improperly diagnosed them as having Multiple Personality Disorder and insisted that they recall being sexually abused in childhood. The former patients also claim that she forced them to watch sexually perverse films and misused powerful drugs under the guise of therapy. They also alleged that she controlled them through 'cult-like' procedures. Two of the women had accused Roman Catholic Bishop Gerald O'Keefe of sexually abusing them in their childhood. They later dropped the charges and one admitted the accusations were not true. Earlier, in 1992, the Board had also concluded that her treatment of patients was inappropriate but did not pursue an examination or suspend her license (Gustafson 1994).

These actions followed a series of TV programs by a local investigative reporter in which films of actual sessions of Dr. Humenansky were shown. The reporter also sent a young woman into sessions playing the role of client and filmed them.

The actions and behaviors of Dr. Humenansky are similar to those reported by the investigator-client above.

Conclusions

The unsupported and unscientific beliefs of mental health professionals lead them to use highly questionable techniques which are labelled psychotherapy. Error compounds error and individuals develop memories of childhood abuse which are probably false. As illustrated in the anecdotal material in Chapters 3 and 4, the effect of these inaccurate 'memories' is devastating to the individuals developing them and to their families.

Chapter Eight
Is There Repressed Memory?

I think our current regulations concerning 'truth in packaging' and 'protective product warnings' should be extended to the concept of repression. The use of the concept might be preceded by some such statement as, 'Warning. The concept of repression has not been validated with experimental research and its use may be hazardous to the accurate interpretation of clinical behavior.'

David S. Holmes (1990)

'Repression' has been used by the survivors' network to explain how people can have no memories of repeated and brutal sexual abuse but can later retrieve these memories in accurate detail. Recovered memory therapists believe that repression is a psychological defense that results in a person losing all memory for traumatic events. Repression is differentiated from dissociation and traumatic amnesia (which we discuss in Chapter 9) and some professionals, such as Terr (1994), believe that when retrieved, repressed events will contain much more detail than those that are dissociated.

According to recovered memory therapists, when abuse is repressed, although it disappears from consciousness, it still affects us in powerful ways. These terrible events from childhood influence our feelings and behavior and are responsible for our current problems. The multitudinous 'symptoms' of incest described in Chapter 5 are believed to result from such repressed abuse. In order to treat these symptoms, the client must be helped to remember the repressed abuse. Without memory retrieval, there can be no healing.

The type of repression needed to account for recovered memory claims would have to involve the banishment from consciousness of a series of traumatic and intrusive events that took place in different circumstances over a number of years. Ofshe and Watters (1993) term this 'robust repression.' Robust repression is much more than simple forgetting, which is a passive and ordinary process. It is not clear just how this robust repression is supposed to operate. If a person were raped innumerable times during childhood, the memories could be repressed serially, immediately following each event. Therefore, each rape would be like the first. Alternatively, all of the memories might suddenly be repressed at some later time after the abuse stopped.

The concept of repression itself is controversial and most experimental psychologists don't believe it exists. Can the human mind act in the way claimed? What is repression? How does it differ from dissociation and suppression?

Holmes (1990) describes three elements of repression as it generally used: "1. repression is the selective forgetting of materials that cause the individual pain; 2. repression is not under voluntary control; and 3. repressed material is not lost but instead is stored in the unconscious and can be returned to consciousness if the anxiety that is associated with the memory is removed" (p. 86). He notes that the fact that repression is not under voluntary control differentiates it from suppression and denial.

Repression is different from other concepts that are sometimes used interchangeably, such as forgetting, dissociation, splitting, traumatic or psychogenic amnesia, and suppression. The DSM-III-R (American Psychiatric Association 1987, Appendix C) defines the following terms (note: these are *not* diagnostic categories):

● *Repression:* A mechanism in which the person is unable to remember or to be cognitively aware of disturbing feelings, thoughts, or experiences.

● *Dissociation:* A mechanism in which the person sustains a temporary alteration in the integrative functions of consciousness or identity.

● *Suppression:* A mechanism in which the person intentionally avoids thinking about disturbing problems, desires, or experiences.

● *Denial:* A mechanism in which the person fails to acknowledge some aspect of external reality that would be apparent to others.

● *Splitting:* A mechanism in which the person views himself or herself or others as all good or all bad, failing to integrate the positive and the negative qualities of self and others into cohesive images; often the person alternatively idealizes and devalues the same person.

Of these terms, only dissociation is included in the glossary of technical terms in the DSM-IV (American Psychiatric Association 1994).

Repression is used in different ways by different researchers and theorists (Singer and Sincoff 1990). Vaillant (1990) notes the confusion and attempts to give clear definitions and differentiations between concepts. He says that "Unlike psychotic denial, repression prevents the identification of conflict-laden ideas rather than preventing recognition of external reality" (p. 261). His example:

> If a man were weeping in a cemetery but could not recall for whom he wept, this would be repression. If he denied the existence of his tears, that would represent psychotic denial. If he got the giggles or got drunk at the wake, that would be dissociation (neurotic denial). If he said he wept from happiness, that would be reaction formation. If he brushed aside his tears, said he would think about his father's death tomorrow, and indeed remembered to grieve the next day, that would be suppression. (pp. 261–62)

Repression must be differentiated from ordinary forgetting

(which we described in Chapter 6). If we don't think of an event for several years, even a traumatic event, such as being burned and hospitalized at age nine, but then are reminded of it, this doesn't mean that we repressed it. According to the repression concept, if we were asked if we had ever been badly burned or hospitalized, we would say "no" and, indeed, would have no memories even if we thought about it. The memories would not return unless they were uncovered through therapy or in some other specific way.

Freud

Repression is a key concept in Freud's psychodynamic theory. Freud relates that he first encountered stories of sexual abuse in several female patients but then determined that some of these had not actually been seduced but were imagining the events. He decided that these seduction accounts had come from his patients' fantasy lives and that what they were reporting was a confabulation of memories with unconscious fantasies (Wakefield 1992). The theory of repression developed out of Freud's attempt to deal with what he perceived as his patients' unacceptable impulses which led to the fantasies.

Freud believed that a considerable portion of human thought, communication, social behavior, or psychological symptomatology involves efforts to ward off from consciousness a variety of threatening cognitions or emotional reactions. Freud used 'repression' to refer to this process. Other terms used are 'suppression,' 'dissociation,' or 'inhibition,' and Freud sometimes used repression and suppression interchangeably (Erdelyi 1990; Singer 1990; Weinert and Perlmutter 1988).

Freud believed that nothing, once formed in mental life, could perish; everything is somehow preserved. Human frustrations and conflicts arise from memories that are not conscious. The person could be cured of ills by uncovering the unconscious strata of experience. Psychoanalysis was his method of reviving memories and thereby curing people.

For Freud, 'repression' referred to two phenomena. First, it was seen as the blocking of entry into consciousness of threatening or psychologically painful material (perceptual defense). Second, it was seen as the relegation into unconsciousness of material after it has been consciously recognized (mnemonic defense). In either case, repression was seen as an active filtering process.

Freud, however, also saw memories as remodelled and subjected to falsification. He didn't see them as complete inventions, but as false in the sense that events were shifted to different places or two people merged or one substituted for the other:

> In our effort at making an intelligible pattern of the sensory impressions that are offered to us, we fall into the strangest errors or even falsify the truth about the material before us . . . these falsifications of memory are tendentious, that is, they serve the purposes of repression and replacement of objectionable or disagreeable impressions. (Freud, quoted in Erdelyi 1990, p. 21)

Experimental Support For Repression

There is no empirical quantified evidence to support the theory of repression. The only 'evidence' comes from impressionistic case studies and anecdotal reports. Anecdotal case studies and clinical impressions are useful only during the early stages of scientific inquiry into certain theories or problem areas. They can be useful then to produce hypotheses or ideas about what might be going on which are then tested by more rigorous procedures. They cannot be used as confirming or disconfirming evidence in testing any particular concept. The reason is simply that they are isolated events with no comparative data to rule out alternative explanations. The goal of designing and running experiments is to structure events and observations so as to support one particular explanation and rule out others.

If a patient tells a physician he is having a runny nose, a cough, and a headache on the left side, he really does not want the physician to think about his grandmother who told him that goose grease rubbed on the chest and a flannel pad cures runny noses and coughs, because that's what cured Uncle Henry. The patient might be dead in a week from a fast-growing tumor in the left parietal lobe. What the patient wants is for the physician to run a series of tests ruling out alternatives like ague, flu, tumors, viral infections, tooth abscesses, and so forth, and produce a prescription for a specific antibiotic to knock out a sinus infection. Mental health professionals who rely on anecdotal case studies and clinical impressions, no matter what their credentials, are vulnerable to believing in goose grease and flannel pads.

> It is thus wrong to cite a testimonial or a case study as support for a particular theory or therapy. Those who do so mislead the public if they do not point out that such evidence is open to a wide range of alternative explanations, In short, the isolated demonstration of a phenomenon can be highly misleading. (Stanovich 1992, p. 56)

Over the years, there have been hundreds of studies testing the concept of repression (Hoch 1982; Holmes 1990, 1994; Hornstein 1992; Mackinnon and Dukes 1963). The search for corroborating evidence was wide-ranging. Concepts generating numerous experiments included word association, mental association, galvanic skin response, frustration, induced failure, interruption failure, degrees of stress, perceptual defense, subliminal perception, levels of awareness, and many others. None has produced unequivocal support for the idea of repression.

The response of Freud in 1934 was essentially the same response proponents of recovered memory make today. Freud wrote to Rosenzweig:

> I have examined your experimental studies for the verification of the psychoanalytic assertions with interest. I cannot put much value on these confirmations because the wealth of reliable observations on which these assertions rest make them independent of experimental verification. Still, it [experimental verification] can do no harm. (Mackinnon and Dukes 1963, p. 703)

Still today those who want to have claims of recovered memory believed put forth clinical observations and anecdotal evidence, as Freud did, as somehow superior to or independent of a more scientific, rigorous procedure. Briere (1993) makes repeated claims that what he and other proponents of recovered memories do is based on their clinical experience and judgment and ignores the research evidence. They have to do this because this is the only evidence they can produce. To ignore the overwhelming negative weight of the disconfirming research evidence and persist in relying upon flawed and unreliable evidence is the same as joining the Flat Earth Society and insisting that when people disappear over the horizon they fall off the edge of the Earth.

In 1974 Holmes published a review in which he concluded that there was no reliable evidence for repression. In 1990, he stated that he has not seen anything new in the literature to change this conclusion:

> [D]espite over sixty years of research involving numerous approaches by many thoughtful and clever investigators, at the present time there is no controlled laboratory evidence supporting the concept of repression. (p. 96) . . . We do not have another theory with which to overthrow repression, but despite numerous tests neither do we have data to support the theory, and therefore it might be appropriate to abandon the theory. (p. 98)

Bower (1990) discusses the concept of repression and recovery of forgotten memories and says that if repression is defined as forgetting it can be readily understood in terms of learning theory. Experimental psychologists define repression as 'motivated forgetting.' Bower analyzes motivated failures to remember in terms of learning theory but notes that psychoanalysts may resist this attempt to define the term in this way. Learning theory concepts include:

- *Motivated nonlearning.* People can control the initial registration of an event. Learning theorists have several plausible, mechanistic explanations of this including lack of attention, nonrehearsal, and so on. However, this has been difficult to test since there is a problem in specifying the conditions under which one of these mechanisms will come into operation.

- *Motivated overwriting of memories.* This is a form of retroactive interference. There is no research on this specifically.

- *Retrieval failures.* This is the largest contributor to forgetting. Bower is an associationist who sees the retrieval view of memory as one where some cues will fail whereas others will succeed in retrieving one and the same memory trace. Memories are dispositions that can be actualized in certain circumstances but not in others. They are like 'responses,' waiting for the right 'stimulus' to release them.

Bower (1990) is cautious about recovered memory therapy. He notes that although techniques, such as associations, can be successful in slowly retrieving lost memories, a problem is in ascertaining the accuracy of the memory that is retrieved. But veracity of the retrieved memories is necessary for the repression hypothesis and Bower concludes that the current evidence is that "depending on how repression is defined, it is either a well-known phenomenon (called 'conscious suppression') or an extremely weak, evanescent phenomenon in the laboratory" (p. 223). Although motivated suppression of the reporting of memories is commonplace, Bower agrees with Holmes regarding repression:

> On the other hand, obtaining reliable evidence for unconscious repression of memories in the laboratory has proved difficult despite years of conscientious experimentation by sympathetic investigators. . . . reliable evidence for unconscious repression, which is automatic with principal parts of it occurring outside awareness, is extremely meager, and its few apparent demonstrations are subject to alternative interpretations. (p. 223)

In conclusion, the construct of 'repression' cannot be said to be accepted in the scientific community, except among analytically-oriented therapists, who are basing their belief on anecdotal reports and clinical case studies. Hundreds of efforts to investigate repression experimentally have failed. But even if the Freudian concept were accepted, there is no confirmation of the type of repression necessary to support the recovered memory claims. There is nothing in the literature supporting the belief that repeated episodes of sexual abuse can be 'repressed' and inaccessible to memory, to be remembered only years later in bits and pieces. There is absolutely no support for the concept of robust repression as used in the recovered memory therapies.

Animal Experiments

An assumption basic to claims of recovered memories is that infancy and childhood are more important than any other developmental levels in determining adult patterns of behavior and adult experiences of fears and anxieties. This creates a problem. Infants and children are strikingly inferior to adults in many learning skills. How do we account for the fact that learned responses acquired so early in life have such an important role in adult life? In trying to answer this question, psychologists cannot experimentally induce traumas in children to see what happens. Fortunately, animals can be studied in learning experiments, and the results show few differences within mammalian species. We can learn something about people from rats, mice, and pigeons. We can also use electric shock and other aversive stimuli to create a true trauma for an animal. Again, literally hundreds of experiments have been done with animals, including experiments exposing them to traumatic events.

Campbell and Campbell (1982) have shown that learned fears acquired in infancy do not persist any longer nor show differences from learned fears acquired later in the life span of rats. When there is minimal re-instatement of a learned trauma response, it is remembered and persists indefinitely (Campbell and Jaynes 1966). Severe trauma during infancy has a long-lasting effect into adult hood and is not 'repressed.' Many experiments showing the induction of experimental neurosis by traumatizing a broad variety of animals demonstrate retention of the learning experience and do not support repression (Berelson and Steiner 1964).

Recovering Repressed Memories and Traditional Analytic Therapy

Traditional analytically-oriented therapists, who use the concept of repression, don't use it in the way it is used by the recovered memory therapists. The traditional analytic therapist is concerned with the patient's perceptions of reality, rather than the historical accuracy of the material uncovered in therapy. Although memories of abuse recovered in therapy may be psychically real for the patient, they cannot be considered to reflect actual events. It is simply a mistake to assume that childhood memories retrieved in therapy are historically truthful (Nash 1992; Wakefield 1992).

The analytical literature generally describes repression in terms of impulses, ideas, feelings, and experiences, rather than in terms of actual events. Although some writers speak of the repression of an isolated episode (Erdelyi 1990), there is nothing about repression of *repeated* distressing episodes. The case examples of repression in the literature demonstrate this.

Hedges (1994) provides an excellent and thorough analysis of the recovered memory assumptions and therapies from the viewpoint of traditional psychoanalysis. He observes that the notion presupposing massive forgetting of a traumatic experience and the later possibility of accurate video-camera-type recall is not a part of any existing psychoanalytic theory of memory. No known memory mechanisms support the belief that traumatic experiences resulting in total amnesia can later be lifted like a veil. There is no way that recovered memories, as they are now being promoted in the marketplace, public media, and court rooms, can be reliably counted on as objectively real or totally factual.

At the same time, Hedges believes such memories must be taken seriously in treatment. But rather than assuming that memories recovered in therapy reflect historical events, all memories should be understood as representations of the therapy experience and the relationship between the therapist and client—the transference and countertransference. For the analyst to consider memories recovered in therapy as literally and objectively true colludes with the resistance to transference analysis and runs the risk of (unethically) encouraging an acting out of memory that is recovered. This is what happens when abuse memories are recovered and parents are confronted, accused, or sued.

Therapists who assume that traumatic memories uncovered in therapy are literally true, and encourage their clients to take actions about these horrible memories, can harm their clients. The damage comes not only from any actions taken, but treatment is hampered through encouraging resistance to the transference which is necessary for healing in the psychoanalytic model. Hedges cautions therapists about the dangers to themselves when they accept such memories as true: "Escalating law suits, increasing disciplinary action by ethics committees and licensing boards, and skyrocketing costs of malpractice insurance make clear that the problem is real and that it is serious" (p. 29).

In summary, there is nothing in the literature on psychoanalysis or analytic therapy to support the assumptions and techniques of the recovered memory therapists. The bastardized versions of analytic therapy used by recovered memory therapists are not supported by traditional analysts.

Research on Repressed Abuse and Recovered Memories

There are a few studies on repressed abuse and validation of recovered memories. These are cited over and over by the recovered memory therapists as support for their claims. But these studies must be read carefully since there are serious problems about what they purport to demonstrate. The three articles most often referred to are by Herman and Schatzow (1987), Briere and Conte (1989, 1993), and Williams (1992, 1993). There are also a couple of other relevant articles along with a new book by Lenore Terr (1994).

Herman and Schatzow (1987)

Since we discussed Herman and Schatzow in detail in Chapter 2 their study will be described only briefly here. These authors report on their experience with a therapy group for incest survivors and maintain that three out of four of 53 women in the group were able to "validate their memories by obtaining corroborating evidence from other sources" (p. 1). But most of their sample was of women who had either full or partial recall of the abuse prior to therapy; only one-fourth (14) had severe memory deficits before entering the survivors' group. Therefore, only a minority of their sample addresses the issue of repressed memories. The report is also confusing with respect to what is included in the category of severe memory deficits.

The women with severe memory deficits were likely to report abuse that began early in childhood and ended before adolescence. Cases of violent or sadistic abuse were also most likely to be associated with "the resort to massive repression" (p. 5). These women recalled their abuse in a group environment that the authors describe as a "powerful stimulus for recovery of previously repressed traumatic memories" (p. 1). Therefore, the group influence is a significant issue. In addition to the powerful group pressure to recall memories of abuse, the average age of the 14 severe memory deficit women at the time they claimed the abuse began was 4.9 years. This means that around half were in the age period of birth to 4 or 5 where infant amnesia means they would likely have no independent memories.

Although this study is often cited as demonstrating corroboration of repressed abuse, it fails to do this. In discussing the claimed corroboration, no distinction is made between women who had always remembered the abuse and those who didn't recall it until entering therapy. There is no information concerning the corroboration of the recovered memories for the 14 women who had severe memory deficits prior to therapy.

In addition, the details of the corroboration are vague and depended upon the reports of the women in group therapy. Out of the four case examples the authors present to describe the verification process, in only two did the woman have complete amnesia for the abuse prior to therapy. For one of these, there was no corroboration of the abuse. For the other, the corroboration consisted of the woman's report in group therapy of discovering her brother's pornography collection and diary after he was killed in Vietnam. But there is no indication that anyone else saw the diary or verified what the woman said she found. Herman (Joseph DeRivera, personal communication, 1993) acknowledges that the diary was not seen by the group leaders.

Briere and Conte (1989, 1993)

Briere and Conte (1989, 1993) describe a sample of therapy clients with self-reported childhood sexual abuse histories and state that over half of their subjects reported some period before age 18 when they could not recall their first abuse experience. This is used as support for the repressed memory concept.

However, the reports of their study are confusing since in 1989 and 1993 their descriptions of the same study differ. In 1989 the authors say that they had 468 subjects; in 1993, the number was 450. In 1989 they say that 59.6 percent reported a period of being amnesiac for the abuse; in 1993, the figure was 59.3 percent. They only asked one question to investigate the lack of memory and they report different instructions to their subjects in 1989 and 1993:

> (1989) "During the period of time before the first forced sexual experienced [sic] happened and your eighteenth birthday was there ever a time when you could not remember the forced sexual experience?"

> (1993) "During the period of time between when the first forced sexual experience happened and your eighteenth birthday was there ever a time when you could not remember the forced sexual experience?"

The 1989 version of the subject instructions may well contain typographical errors and we assume the 1993 version is what was actually asked on the survey. But if not, the question would have been extremely confusing to the subjects.

But even assuming the 1993 version is correct, the phrase, 'could not remember' is vague and could mean many things besides amnesia or repression. It could be interpreted to mean just not thinking about the abuse for days or months, to mean forgetting about it until reminded somehow, or perhaps, to mean consciously determining not to think about it.

Briere and Conte conclude in their 1989 paper that "repression (partial or otherwise) appears to be a common phenomenon among clinical sexual abuse survivors" (p. 4). However, there is no definition of repression given nor is there any presentation of the presumed relationship between the answer to the question and amnesia, forgetting, or repression. There is no distinction made between ordinary forgetting and repression. The authors simply assume their single highly confusing question measures the postulated complex process of repression. They have apparently backed down from this now since in 1993, "repression" is changed to "amnesia for abuse" (p. 26) and the authors state, "Whether such amnesia is due to 'repression' or 'dissociation' is unclear" (p. 29).

At no point do Briere and Conte address the issue of the generalizability from their sample of patients recruited by therapists and the demand characteristics of being patients in a network of sex-abuse therapists. If their subjects' therapists believed that repression is common and that large numbers of women who have no memories of abuse are nevertheless abused, an indeterminate number of Briere and Conte's subjects may have answered 'yes' because they believed this had happened to them.

Briere and Conte assert that "some significant proportion" of psychotherapy clients who deny a history of sexual abuse have, nevertheless, been abused. Nowhere in their report, however, is there any information concerning verification of the claimed abuse. There is no corroboration presented for their subjects' claims. They simply accepted what the subjects reported. They assume that a client who recovers the memory under the guidance of a therapist is reporting an actual event. Briere and Conte therefore advise clinicians who have a reason to believe (in terms of the client's symptoms) that the client was abused to continue to suspect abuse, even in the absence of memories for abuse. In their 1993 paper (but not in 1989) they acknowledge the problem of the validity and accuracy of the subjects' reports.

Briere and Conte believe that their findings mean that control groups in studies of the effects of abuse are likely to contain subjects reporting no abuse who have, in fact, been abused. But they fail to recognize that abuse groups may contain subjects who have false memories and were not actually abused. They say that they "doubt that abuse confabulation is a major problem" (1993, p. 29).

This study cannot be advanced as establishing the reality of a process of repression of memories of sexual abuse.

Williams (1992, 1993)

In a longitudinal study, Williams (1992, 1993) reports on 129 women who were brought to the hospital emergency room for sexual abuse in childhood in 1973, 1974, or 1975. Information about the abuse was documented in the hospital records. The sexual abuse ranged from sexual intercourse (36 percent) to touching and fondling (33 percent) and the age at the time of the abuse ranged from infancy to twelve years.

The follow-up interviews took place when the women were approximately 17 years older and their ages at the time of the interviews ranged from 18 to 31. The women were asked several questions designed to elicit their responses about sexual victimization. Williams reports that 38 percent of the 129 women had "amnesia" for the abuse or chose not to report the abuse to the interviewers 17 years later. She claims that "qualitative analysis of these reports and non-reports suggests that the vast majority of the 38 percent were women who did not remember the abuse" (1992, p. 20). Williams interprets her results to support the contention that a large proportion of sexually abused women are amnesic for the abuse as adults.

There are several problems with this interpretation and conclusion. The subjects ranged from infancy to twelve years old at the time of the abuse. Therefore, an indeterminate number of the women were abused at such a young age that they would not be expected to remember any events that occurred during this time. As discussed in Chapter 6, events prior to age three, four, or sometimes even five are unlikely to be remembered because of childhood or infant amnesia. This is especially likely to be the case if the abuse consisted of fondling or touching, as occurred in 33 percent of the cases in Williams's study.

Williams addresses this criticism in her 1993 paper by dividing her sample into four age groups. She notes that the percentages reporting amnesia were 55 percent for those who were three and younger; 62 percent for those 4 to 6; 31 percent for those 7 to 10; and 26 percent for those aged 11 to 12. This suggests that infant amnesia was a factor for several but not for all of her subjects.

Another problem is the percentage for whom the abuse may not have been traumatic. As was discussed in Chapter 6, not all sexual abuse is experienced by the victim as highly distressing. A child who was only touched or fondled may not have remembered the abuse because it was not a noteworthy experience. Or the child may have been too young to realize she was being abused. For subjects who may simply forget abuse that was not particularly salient, a concept of traumatic amnesia or repression will not apply. Williams (1993) reports that there was a tendency for the women who did not recall the abuse to have been subjected to less force, which supports this possibility.

In addition, several subjects who failed to remember the event in the hospital records did recall other instances of childhood abuse. Since these subjects recalled some, but not all abuse incidents, the hypothesis of massive repression for abuse is not supported. When there are repeated similar incidents, they will merge together and it will become more difficult to remember a specific one. It is also possible that her sample contained some false allegations, although Williams minimizes the base rate of false reports and describes efforts to exclude women from the analysis who may not have really been abused.

The methods section does not give details about the questions that were asked and what subsequent probes were used if the woman failed to report the abuse. There is not sufficient information to evaluate her assertion that the "vast majority" of the women who failed to report the abuse were amnesic as opposed to simply choosing not to report the abuse to the interviewer. There is no information to support a claim that this study demonstrates repression, dissociation, or traumatic amnesia. But Williams's study, with its prospective design, represents an improvement over other research on this topic.

Femina, Yeager, and Lewis (1990)

Femina, Yeager, and Lewis (1990) conducted a follow-up study of 69 subjects who had been interviewed during young adulthood. On follow-up, 26 gave histories discrepant with those obtained from records and interviews conducted in adolescence. Eighteen denied or minimized abuse when it was in their records and 8 claimed abuse although there was none in the records. Clarification interviews were conducted with 11 of these subjects—8 who denied abuse although their records indicated abuse, and 3 who reported abuse when abuse was not in the records. The authors concluded from the interviews that all 11 had, in fact, been abused.

But none of the subjects who had originally denied abuse had forgotten or 'repressed' their childhood abuse. All acknowledged it in the second interview and gave reasons such as embarrassment, a wish to protect the parents, and a desire to forget for their previous denial or minimization. The differences between these results and those reported by Williams may well be in the type of questions asked in the interviews.

Loftus, Polonsky, and Fullilove (in press)

Loftus, Polonsky, and Fullilove (in press) studied 105 women in an outpatient treatment program for substance abuse. More than half of the women in their sample reported memories of childhood sexual abuse. Of these, 81 percent claimed to have remembered the sexual abuse for their whole lives while 19 percent reported that they had forgotten the abuse for a period of time but later regained the memory. Whether the abuse was remembered continually or forgotten for a period of time was not related to the violence of the abuse. The women who remembered the abuse their whole lives reported clearer and more detailed memories.

However, Loftus et al. did not explore what the subjects understood by 'forgot the abuse for a period of time.' The authors note that without this information it is difficult to interpret the meaning of the results. For example, conceivably a woman could classify her memory as 'forgotten then regained' if she spent a period of her life deliberately trying not to think about the abuse. Or, she might chose this category if she thought, 'I spent one nice summer in Europe where I didn't think about the abuse at all.' This study is one of those cited as support for the concept that traumatic abuse can be repressed and later remembered, although that is *not* the interpretation given by the authors.

Terr (1994)

Lenore Terr (1994) is a strong advocate of repression and dissociation of traumas and is often cited by the recovered memory advocates. Her recent book, *Unchained Memories: True Stories of Traumatic Memories, Lost and Found* (1994) is a Book-Of-The-Month Club selection. The book consists of seven detailed case studies designed to illustrate how memories can be repressed or dissociated and later retrieved.

Terr differentiates repression from simple forgetting and believes that repression is the main mechanism in the infamous Eileen Franklin case which is discussed in detail in two chapters in the book. Eileen Franklin's father was convicted of murder following the alleged recovery of Ms. Franklin's repressed memory of seeing her father murder her best friend.

Terr believes that repressed memories, once retrieved, are generally highly detailed and accurate, although there can be some minor mistakes in what is recalled. She sees repressed memories as different from those that are dissociated. In repression, the individual unconsciously and energetically defends against remembering. Dissociation results in the traumatic memories being set aside from normal consciousness during the event itself. Therefore, compared to the sharp and accurate details of retrieved repressed memories, those that are dissociated are likely to remain fuzzy, unclear, and filled with holes. Dissociated memories, according to Terr, rarely come back clear and complete.

Terr believes that traumatic memories operate differently from ordinary memories. As we discussed in Chapter 6, she claims that there are two types of trauma. Type I traumas, which occur when the child is subjected to a single, unanticipated traumatic event, include full, clear, detailed verbal memories, although there may be some mistakes. Type II traumas, which occur when there is long-standing or repeated exposure to trauma, result in dissociation or repression.

Terr maintains that, even when the memory is completely repressed, there will be signs that reflect the traumatic event. She believes that corroboration for the recovered memories comes from the person's symptoms and she illustrates this through writers, artists, and filmmakers, such as Stephen King, whom she says re-enact their trauma in their writings and art. Therefore, even when there is no external corroboration, the proof of the traumatic event comes from the person's feelings, behaviors, and actions.

Once repressed, Terr believes that even memories from early childhood and infancy can be retrieved through appropriate cues. In one of the cases in her book, a retrieved memory is of the man's mother trying to drown him in his bathinet. Terr herself reports having a memory of her grandmother putting hot tea in her mouth when she was 11 months old.

Although Terr's work is used to support the claim that recovered memories of repressed or dissociated trauma have been corroborated, neither this book nor her other writings accomplish this. The corroboration of the repressed memories in this book is simply not convincing. There are misleading elements in her account of the Eileen Franklin case and there is little or no independent corroboration in her other examples of recovered memories.

Harry MacLean, who has written a definitive analysis of the Eileen Franklin case in his book *Once Upon a Time* (1993), notes several major factual errors in Terr's two chapters on the Franklin case (MacLean 1994). For example, Terr says that

Eileen Franklin's memory returned when she happened to glance at her daughter who bore a startling resemblance to the child she saw her father murder. The fact that this was only one of five versions offered by Eileen Franklin of how the memory was recovered is not mentioned. MacLean describes several other equally egregious mistakes and concludes that Terr's account of this case resembles "a fable more than fact."

It is reasonable to assume that Terr's other accounts may well be no more factually accurate than her description of the Franklin case. In addition, other cases do not address repression of childhood traumatic events. One case essentially deals with a fugue state and another with a man's attempts to remember ordinary things about a brother who died when the man was four years old. The man had always remembered his brother's death. Another is of a false memory. The literary chapter is about an author, James Ellroy, and how his childhood experiences, including a seductive mother who was murdered, have influenced his writings. Although there is a lengthy discussion of the nature of his memories, there are no accounts of traumatic events that were repressed or dissociated but later retrieved.

Terr's theories that traumatic memories are processed differently from ordinary memories, that there are different mechanisms for repeated traumas compared to single instances of trauma, and that repressed memories, when retrieved, will be detailed and accurate, are not supported by scientific evidence. Her assertions about repression, amnesia, and trauma are not supported by her actual research with children who have undergone verified trauma. We were unable to discover a single case described by Terr in which a child over the age of three had total amnesia for a documented trauma.

Terr, however, apparently is not impressed by empirical research on repression. While testifying in the Akiki trial for the prosecution, this is what she said:

> **Q:** In terms of false memory, are there professional psychologists and psychiatrists who are debating the actuality of repressed memory, yes or no?

A: Yes.

Q: And among that debate is there some question about the scientific validity of the theory of repression, yes or no?

A: Yes. But I think that they are wrong. They are not clinicians, and they are not entitled to make that decision.

Q: Is it your position that only clinicians can make a decision concerning the scientific foundation of psychiatric or psychological principles?

A: Not all principles, but repression is a clinical principle, and I thought we were talking about repression.

Q: Is it your position that repression can only be addressed by clinicians and not by researchers?

A: The kind of researchers that are bringing this to question, sociology researchers, researchers who are doing cognitive psychology experiments, are not the ones who can make a value judgment on repression. It is the clinicians who can. (Lenore Terr, *California vs Akiki*, reported in the *FMS Foundation Newsletter*, December 1993, p. 5)

Claimed Corroboration of Abuse

The claimed corroboration in case study reports must be examined extremely carefully and not just accepted at face value. It can be difficult to get specific information about how abuse was verified. Rich (1990) notes that when he has asked for verification of self-reported childhood abuse, the 'confirmation' often consisted of sketchy hearsay information from other family members, apparently reported by the woman herself during therapy.

Young et al. (1991), report on 37 alleged satanic cult survivors. Although some of the survivors had memories of abuse, none had memories of the ritual satanic abuse until they entered therapy. Young et al. claim that there was corroboration of the alleged satanic ritual abuse for several of the patients. However, all of the alleged corroborative findings are completely nonspecific and cannot be said to provide verification. The 'corroboration' consisted of physical findings such as scars on the back, a distorted nipple, a 'satanic tattoo' on the scalp and a breast scar on one patient. But there is no information of detailed medical workups or photographs of these alleged physical markings. Other evidence of physical findings included three women with endometriosis diagnosed before age 16, one with pelvic inflammatory disease at age 15, and one whose school performance dropped from age 7 to 10 during the years she supposedly was in the cult until the family moved.

Briere (1990), in responding to criticisms about the validity of self-reports of childhood abuse, justifies accepting clients' reports in a study by Briere and Zaidi (1989) by noting that 1. the abuse rate was comparable to rates found in other studies; 2. aspects of the clients' victimization correlated with symptoms that made intuitive sense and that had been reported by other authors; and 3. the clinical experience of the authors suggested that the disclosures were accompanied by distress, shame, and fear of stigma, as opposed to enjoyment. None of these criteria meets acceptable standards for establishing the veracity of the reports. This is especially true when the reports of abuse come from supposed memories uncovered in therapy.

Briere (1992) believes that some adults are amnesic for some or all of their childhood abuse and claims that the problem of repressed memories in retrospective research is a "significant concern" because the abuse is therefore not reported (p. 197). But at the same time he admits there is no satisfactory way to ensure the validity of subjects' recollections. He acknowledges that the accuracy of sexual abuse reports cannot be assured in terms of ruling out either false positives or false negatives. Although he briefly mentions fantasies, delusions, or intentional misrepresentations for secondary gain as possible reasons for false positives, he shows no awareness of the danger of clients developing false accounts of abuse through therapy.

Falsification

Good scientific theories are not those that prove something by inductive reasoning. That may have been taught in high school but we now understand that a successful theory is not one that can explain everything that can possibly happen, because then it has no predictive power. Scientific theories must always be able to make predictions in such a way that they can be falsified—shown to be wrong. The U.S. Supreme Court adopted this principle of falsifiability as the determining factor for what is scientific in the *Daubert* decision in 1993 (*Daubert* is discussed in Chapter 11 below). Good candidates for theories are those that can be shown to be wrong, while bad theories are those that explain everything. Science advances by the process of producing hypotheses about how things work, finding a way to test them, and discarding those that don't work out. It keeps only those that are not proven wrong.

The all-encompassing theory that can explain everything after the fact has a powerful emotional appeal. To know that, no matter what happens, everything can be explained, can be tremendously satisfying. The world becomes a secure place because it is known and understood.

Falsification, however, means that the considerable support there may be for a theory is not nearly as crucial as one validated instance which contradicts the theory. Scientific research is not like the box score in a baseball game. You cannot simply add up hits or runs to see which one has the most. The quality of the research must always be examined. There are good, credible studies and bad, flawed studies. Only those that meet the minimum requirements for methodology should be attended to. Also, the number of times a theory has been supported is not the critical element. There can be a large number of supportive studies, but a single instance of credible falsification means that the theory ought to be discarded.

Science continuously challenges accepted beliefs and tests them to find out which are wrong. This is how there is progress. If everything is already explained, there is no progress. This is the position the recovered memory proponents are in. They explain away all contrary evidence and refuse to accept that any of their concepts have been falsified. When the three or four studies described above are held out as proof of repression and therefore supportive of the concept of recovered memories, only those who have no understanding of the principle of falsification can be persuaded. The weight of over 60 years of evidence failing to corroborate repression cannot be counter-balanced by three or four studies with highly suspect methodology when there is a consistent, repeatable negative pattern across decades and hundreds of experiments. Nevertheless, we welcome new research, much of which is already under way, though we would be surprised if any future research were to turn up any evidence of repression.

Conclusions

In contrast to the few dubious studies purporting to support the concepts of repressed abuse and the historical reality of memories uncovered in therapy there are the robust and repeated findings about the reconstructive nature of memory. The therapeutic techniques described in Chapter 5 greatly increase the probability that the material 'remembered' is not historically true. The suggestibility of vulnerable clients and their desire to conform to what they believe the therapist expects and wants, the repeated statements by therapists about the reality and frequency of repressed abuse, the common use of unvalidated and questionable therapy techniques, and the conformity effect of a group all combine to produce a massive persuasive impact upon the client. Before making any claim that research establishes repression as a dynamic internal objective entity, those who want to do so have a long ways to go to overcome the negative evidence that is already there. The best scientific conclusion is that repression has not been corroborated or upheld by any soundly-conducted research. It is time to stop fooling around with repression; when we do so, we are only fooling ourselves and other people.

Chapter Nine
Other Commonly Used Concepts

Junk science cuts across chemistry and pharmacology, medicine and engineering. It is a hodgepodge of biased data, spurious inference, and logical legerdemain, patched together by researchers whose enthusiasm for discovery and diagnosis far outstrips their skill. It is a catalog of every conceivable kind of error: data dredging, wishful thinking, truculent dogmatism, and, now and again, outright fraud.

Peter W. Huber (1991)

Following the scientific criticisms of repression, showing the weakness of the evidence for it, some recovered memory therapists have abandoned 'repression' and are now using other concepts to explain how memories of traumatic events can be completely banished from consciousness but later accurately recovered. This is an attempt to accommodate the disconfirming evidence rather than admit a mistake and abandon the claims of recovered memory.

'Dissociation' is now most often used to describe the process by which memories not known about before can somehow surface and be claimed to be true and accurate. One advocate of recovered memory therapy states: "[T]he issue of repression is a red herring because memory of trauma is primarily affected by the process of 'dissociation,' not repression" (Kristiansen 1994,

p. 13). Initially the proponents of recovered memory said it was repression. Now that they find it hard to deny that the evidence does not support repression, suddenly it is a red herring and 'dissociation' is in. But can dissociation account for the recovered memory claims?

Dissociation

There is no disagreement about dissociation comparable to that surrounding repression. No one denies that dissociation exists. Dissociation ranges from minor forms all of us are familiar with, such as becoming lost in a movie or book or 'spacing out' while driving, to daydreaming, to pathological forms such as amnesia, depersonalization, and fugue states. Dissociation can thus be conceptualized as lying on a continuum from normal forms to major forms which are disruptive and psychopathological (Bernstein and Putnam 1986).

Dissociation can occur during a traumatic incident. Trauma victims may report dissociative experiences while in the midst of a rape, accident, terrorist attack, or other ordeal. People may feel unreal or detached during the trauma or experience the trauma as though they were an observer watching it happen to somebody else. They may report being confused as to what is real opposed to what is imagined and the experience may seem like a dream. After the event, they may show some memory impairment or perceptual distortions (Spiegel 1991; Terr 1991).

Dissociation is defined by the DSM-IV (American Psychiatric Association 1994) as "a disruption in the usually integrated functions of consciousness, memory, identity, or perception of the environment. The disturbance may be sudden or gradual, transient or chronic" (p. 477). There are five dissociative disorders: dissociative amenesia, dissociative fugue, dissociative identity disorder (formerly multiple personality disorder), depersonalization disorder, and dissociative disorder not otherwise specified.

'Traumatic,' 'functional,' or 'psychogenic' amnesia are terms that differentiate this type of amnesia from amnesia resulting from brain injury or other organic cause. In the DSM-IV, this became 'dissociative' amnesia. The essential feature of dissociative amnesia is an inability to recall important personal information, usually of a traumatic or stressful nature, that is too extensive to be explained by normal forgetfulness. There are five types:

1. *Localized*, in which there is failure to recall events occurring during a circumscribed period of time, usually the first few hours following a profoundly disturbing event;
2. *Selective*, in which there is failure to recall some, but not all, of the events occurring during a circumscribed period of time;
3. *Generalized*, in which the failure encompasses the person's entire life;
4. *Continuous*, in which the person cannot recall events subsequent to a specific time up to and including the present; and
5. *Systematized*, in which there is a loss of memory for certain categories of information, such as all memories relating to one's family or to a particular person. (Systematized amnesia was not in the DSM-III-R).

According to the DSM-IV, dissociative amnesia generally presents as a retrospectively reported gap or series of gaps in memory for parts of the person's life history. These gaps are usually related to traumatic or extremely stressful events. The DSM-IV also notes that there has been an increase in the reports of dissociative amnesia that involve previously forgotten early childhood traumas but that this increase has been subject to very different interpretations.

The changes between the DSM-III-R and DSM-IV in the dissociative amnesia disorder reflect the attention given to recovered memory claims. A new type, *systematized* amnesia, is added. Whereas DSM-III-R states that dissociative amnesia "is rarely diagnosed under normal circumstances; it is more common in wartime and during natural disasters" (p. 274), according to DSM-IV the acute form that occurs during wartime and in natural disasters is *less* common. The main manifestation is now said to be a gap or *series of gaps* for aspects of the person's life history.

How are Dissociation and Traumatic Amnesia Used to Explain Lack of Memory for Childhood Abuse?

A person who undergoes repeated traumas is said to learn to use dissociation as a defense against the trauma. It is thought that there is a strong link between the development of dissociative symptoms and childhood trauma. Therefore, someone who has a pathological level or type of dissociation is believed likely to have a childhood history of trauma, particularly physical or sexual abuse (Saxe et al. 1993). Dissociation is involved in many psychiatric conditions and dissociative symptoms have been observed to be common in psychiatric patients as a whole (Bernstein and Putnam 1986). Since psychiatric patients also report disproportionately high abuse histories, this is seen as supporting the trauma-dissociation hypothesis.

Since dissociation is seen as a powerful and common defense against repeated childhood trauma, a repeatedly traumatized child is believed to learn to dissociate as a way of defending against unspeakable pain and terror. The argument is that because the child dissociates during the trauma, the trauma is lost from conscious awareness. If the trauma is sufficiently severe, the child may develop alter personalities.

This is the theory behind Terr's (1991; 1994) Type I and Type II traumas discussed previously. Remember that in Terr's own case examples there are no instances of children over the age of three who are completely amnesic for the event. Therefore the repeated trauma theory is used to explain why children with a documented trauma remember the trauma. Most of Terr's children experienced a single trauma. According to Terr's theory, if the children had been repeatedly traumatized, this would be Type II trauma and they would have learned to dissociate and therefore might not remember the trauma. However, some of Terr's cases do involve repeated trauma and, although the memories of these children may have been sparse and fragmented, there are none who had complete amnesia.

In using dissociation to account for recovered memory claims, it is assumed that the adult survivor does not recall her childhood sexual abuse because she dissociated the abuse so that it was not available to memory. Since she was in an altered state of consciousness when the abuse occurred, there is limited access to these memories during the ordinary state. Retrieval of the memories is therefore accomplished in adulthood by attempting to replicate the state in which the abuse occurred. This is done through altering the state of consciousness by techniques such as hypnosis or age regression.

A dissociated memory that is not available to consciousness is believed to be distinctly different from one that is simply forgotten. Spiegel (1991) gives an example of a rape victim who may have no conscious memory for the assault but yet shows signs of depression, stimulus sensitivity, and numbing of responsiveness, which indicates that traumatic memories are active. This is the reasoning behind the list of symptoms and signs of repressed or dissociated abuse we described in Chapter 5.

The idea that up to one quarter of the women in the United States have been abused but do not remember it because they dissociated the event has a major difficulty. If this were true, one would expect for the behaviors and symptoms of dissociation occurring in childhood to be observed in close to one quarter of young girls. Therefore dissociation should be a quite common diagnosis found in the literature on psychopathology in children. But recent review articles (Lahey and Kazdin, 1988, 1989, 1990) on childhood disorders do not even mention dissociative disorders. There are no data showing large numbers of children producing dissociative symptoms.

Furthermore, the connection between childhood trauma and dissociation has been questioned. Tillman, Nash, and Lerner (in press) critically examine the empirical literature and conclude there is not a simple linear relationship between trauma and dissociation. Instead, people who exhibit high dissociative symptoms also have greater psychological impairment in general. In addition, the research claiming a link between trauma and dissociation is plagued by conceptual and design problems. For example, it seldom controls for family

environment. Families where abuse occurs are more pathological than nonabusing families and subsequent psychological
problems, including dissociation, could be caused by the non-
specific effects of growing up in a dysfunctional family rather
than by the abuse itself. In addition, other events known to be
traumatic, such as Nazi concentration camps, do not lead to
widespread dissociation.

Loewenstein (1991) uses the concept of psychogenic amnesia to account for forgotten childhood abuse but broadens the
definition to include a *group* of events, which allows psychogenic amnesia to account for repeated instances of sexual abuse.
But there is no research supporting Loewenstein's conception
of psychogenic amnesia. There are no empirical data supporting
a concept of psychogenic amnesia for a category of events
stretching across several years at different times and under
different circumstances in differing environments. Literature
reviews on the consequences of sexual abuse (Beitchman et al.
1991, 1992; Cole and Putman 1992) do not include psychogenic amnesia as a sequel of sexual abuse.

Loewenstein does not explain just how the traumatic amnesia is supposed to work. Does the person completely dissociate
the event and develop traumatic amnesia immediately following
each event? If so, each new instance of abuse would be like the
very first time since the child would have no memories of the
previous incidents. Or, at some point after the abuse stops, does
the person suddenly and completely develop amnesia for all
memories of all of the abuse incidents which had previously
been remembered? Just how the dissociative process operates
to later produce amnesia is never satisfactorily explained by the
recovered memory proponents.

An important point about traumatic amnesia is that the
person is usually aware of having a memory gap. Although there
may be loss of memory for a specified time period, there is
memory for events before and after the gap. It is quite unlikely
that a person would have total amnesia for a series of events but
no awareness of these memory gaps until therapy is entered
years later.

The traditional case studies of psychogenic amnesia in the literature indicate that the person has undergone a severe life stress, such as violent physical abuse, torture, confinement in concentration camps, or combat. In such cases, the events should be able to be independently verified since without verification that an event has, in fact, occurred, one cannot talk about amnesia for the event. If traumatic or psychogenic amnesia is used to account for the fact that the memory of the abuse is buried within a conscious memory of a happy childhood, there must be verification of the abuse. But corroboration by parents, siblings, or others seldom occurs. And people experiencing documented trauma rarely develop amnesia for the trauma unless they were physically injured in rather specific brain traumas.

An interesting aspect of psychogenic amnesia is that it is not easy to tell when someone is faking it. Claims of amnesia show up frequently in a variety of legal situations, including criminal trials, disability and Social Security hearings, and personal injury suits in addition to recovered memory lawsuits. The consensus is that it is difficult to distinguish between real and simulated amnesia. There is no evidence that experts (psychologists and psychiatrists) can reliably distinguish between them (Brandt 1988; Wiggins and Brandt 1988).

It is not disputed that dissociation may serve as a defense against the painful affect of a highly traumatic event. Dissociation may result in memories being partial, incomplete, and fragmented. But this is very different from claiming that there is no conscious awareness and hence no memory whatsoever. Schumaker (1991) notes, "While one might argue that there are instances of 'pure' defensive dissociation (e.g., psychogenic amnesia) these tend to be rare and of short duration" (p. 126). It is highly unlikely that such a process would be going on with a quarter of the women in the United States, as has been surmised by Summit and others. There is nothing in the empirical research on dissociation to support Fredrickson's (1992) assertion that "Dissociation always occurs during abuse, because abuse is always traumatic" (p. 59).

With the exception of multiple personality disorder (discussed below), there is nothing in the literature on dissociation, including psychogenic or traumatic amnesia, that describes selective amnesia for a series of traumatic events which occur at different ages and at different times and places. Traumatic amnesia cannot be used to support the assumptions of the recovered memory therapists.

Post-Traumatic Stress Disorder

The diagnosis of Post-Traumatic Stress Disorder (PTSD) is often found when sexual abuse is alleged. In recovered memory cases, this diagnosis is sometimes used to explain the lack of memories for the event. However, whenever a diagnostic category from DSM-III or DSM-IV is used, the weakness of the DSM must be considered. In terms of the reliability and validity of the DSM, the field trials reported in the initial project raise very serious doubts. A careful analysis of the reported data shows the field trials to be meaningless. They are uncontrolled, nonrandom surveys by pairs of close colleagues attempting to diagnose nonrandomly selected patients and do little to provide a scientific basis for the DSM categories. In the adult diagnoses not a single major diagnostic category achieved the .70 kappa reliability the researchers themselves identified as minimally required. For children and adolescents 8 of 24 kappas reached .70 but four of those were for one patient only which is listed as 1.0 reliability (Kirk and Kutchins 1992). That a diagnostic category appears in the DSM is not a guarantee nor even strong support for the reliability or validity of the concept.

According to the DSM-IV, the PTSD diagnosis is given when a person develops characteristic symptoms following exposure to an extremely traumatic event which involves actual or threatened death or serious injury, or a threat to the physical integrity of self or others and the person's response involves intense fear, helplessness, or horror. The symptoms involve re-experiencing the traumatic event, avoidance of stimuli associated with the event or numbing of general responsiveness, and increased arousal.

But although the criteria for PTSD mention numbing and efforts to avoid thoughts or feelings along with psychogenic amnesia for an important *aspect* of the event, there is no mention of total amnesia for the *entire* event. Also, in order to diagnose PTSD, there must be a *known* stressful event. The diagnosis cannot be given on the basis of the symptoms alone without verification of the event.

Researchers, led by Bessel van der Kolk, have recently collected data that they believe justifies a new diagnosis, an elaborated and enlarged traumatic stress syndrome that they call DESNOS—disorders of extreme stress, not otherwise specified (Wylie 1993). This disorder reflects their experience in the field trials on PTSD. They report finding a range of symptoms in their patients that almost always showed up together, and were well-correlated with prolonged, severe childhood sexual abuse. The implications of this are that childhood sexual traumas may be responsible for many psychopathologies. Van der Kolk and his colleagues also state that 100 percent of patients testing high on the standard test for dissociative disorders reported having been sexually abused as children, compared with 7 percent whose scores were very low. But their proposed new disorder was not accepted for inclusion in DSM-IV and was not even allowed space in the appendix. At this point, any new formulation of a special syndrome resulting from sexual abuse is purely speculative.

Splitting

In 'splitting,' the child is said to 'split' into two different people. Terr (1994) describes splitting as a defense mechanism that allows the individual to see herself or others as all good or all bad and gives the example of Marilyn Van Derbur Atler, former Miss America, who claims to have been sexually abused by her father from age five until she left for college. Van Derbur Atler supposedly defended against this trauma by splitting into a 'day child' and a 'night child.' The day child was happy, loved her father, and did not think anything was amiss. But the night child, who was regularly abused, harbored all of the dirty secrets, unspeakable shame, and terror. Neither side knew about the other. The day child knew nothing of the sexual abuse—all of the abuse memories resided in the mind of the night child until Van Derbur Atler was 24 years old and her memories returned.

Terr maintains that this type of splitting into a day child and night child is a defense occasionally used by young children enduring repeated traumas. She says that some splitters may eventually develop multiple personality disorder. But there are no data to support the use of splitting in the way done by Terr. According to Appendix C of the DSM-III-R, splitting is defined as a mechanism in which the person views himself or herself or others as all good or all bad, failing to integrate the positive and the negative qualities of self and others into cohesive images; often the person alternatively idealizes and devalues the same person. There is no evidence for the use of this concept to support the claim that an individual can pass through childhood as two different selves that are completely unaware of one another.

(Terr also observes that Marilyn Van Derbur Atler had no history of blank spells as a child and showed no signs of a multiple personality or other dissociative disorder. Terr, however does describe a number of extremely pathological and highly disturbed behaviors in the former Miss America. She had a bout of paralysis at one point, lying immobile for several weeks. Several years later she had excruciating pains in her back, legs, chest, and skin and one time she woke up in horrible pain, feeling as if she had an ax embedded in her anus. This attack, which had no physical cause, lasted for several days. She often sobbed uncontrollably, was dysfunctional for long periods of time, had different types of psychotherapy, and was hospitalized. There is no mention of a physical basis for her unusual and multiple physical complaints.)

Multiple Personality Disorder (MPD)

Multiple personality disorder (MPD) is often given as a diagnosis in recovered memory cases, especially when the alleged abuse is violent and sadistic. The DSM-IV calls MPD 'Dissociative Identity Disorder' and defines it as the presence of two or more distinct identities or personality states. The disorder is believed to begin early in life and most people with this diagnosis are women. There is no reliability given for this specific diagnosis in DSM-III and DSM-IV research.

Many people believe that most individuals diagnosed with MPD were abused as children (Dunn 1992; Kluft 1987, 1991; Putnam et al. 1986). A 'protector' personality is said to emerge and take over for the child, who therefore escapes psychologically from the abuse (Spiegel 1991). The child, overwhelmed by trauma, learns to dissociate from the repeated abuse and MPD is therefore found in people with a history of severe physical or sexual abuse.

Support for this theory, however, is based only on clinical case reports and, in a recent review of the empirical literature on the long-term effects of child sexual abuse, Beitchman et al. (1991) conclude that as yet there is insufficient evidence to confirm a relationship between childhood sexual abuse and multiple personality disorder. Frankel (1993) reviewed the literature on MPD and notes that adults' accounts of childhood abuse are rarely corroborated. He believes that MPD patients' recollections of abuse are influenced by the recent enthusiasm for adult discovery of childhood abuse along with cues from therapy, both with and without hypnosis.

Even though it is found in the DSM-III-R and DSM-IV, MPD itself is controversial. Many clinicians and researchers believe that there is little empirical evidence supporting MPD and that it is heavily dependent upon cultural influences for both its emergence and its diagnosis (Aldridge-Morris 1989; Fahy 1988; Frankel 1993; Freeland et al. 1993; McHugh 1993; Merskey 1992; Piper, in press; Thigpen and Cleckley 1984). Even if it qualifies as a distinct psychiatric disorder, MPD is greatly overdiagnosed.

A few therapists are seeing most of the MPD cases, and the majority of them are in the United States. Most thinking about MPD has been through oral traditions of workshops and communication between therapists. Practitioners who are convinced of the reality of multiple personality belong to a professional subculture which favors hypnotherapeutic techniques, have an analytic orientation, and see their patients over very long periods of time (Aldridge-Morris 1989).

At the time of the publication of *The Three Faces of Eve* by Thigpen and Cleckley in 1957, MPD was considered an extremely rare disorder. However, the 1980s saw a marked increase in the number of reported cases and it has been estimated that over 6,000 cases were diagnosed during this period (Goff and Simms 1992). Although some clinicians working on dissociative disorder patients report 'inordinate numbers' of cases of MPD, others report none (Merskey 1992). Kluft, for example, in the mid-1980s was reported to have personally seen 171 cases (Aldridge-Morris 1989).

The nature of the cases has also changed. Goff and Simms compared 52 case histories of MPD patients published between 1800 and 1965 to 54 reports published in the 1980s. The mean number of personalities per individual patient in the recent cases was much greater (12 instead of 3), the age of onset was younger (11 instead of 20), there were fewer males (24 percent as against 44 percent), and there was a greater prevalence of reported childhood abuse in the histories (81 percent versus 29 percent).

After Thigpen and Cleckley (1957, 1984) described *The Three Faces of Eve*, thousands of people sought them out claiming to have MPD. They became extremely concerned over a so-called 'epidemic' of multiple personality cases and state that in the 30 years since Eve they have seen only one other case that they considered genuine MPD out of the thousands of patients they had seen. They conclude that, although there are degrees of dissociation, some serious, the diagnosis of multiple personality disorder should be reserved for those very few persons who are truly fragmented in an extreme manner.

Many psychologists doubt whether MPD exists at all except as a media or therapist-induced disorder. McHugh (1993) believes that MPD is created by therapists. He says it is an "iatrogenic behavioral syndrome, promoted by suggestion and maintained by clinical attention, social consequences, and group loyalties" (p. 2). Merskey (1992) observes that the widespread publicity for MPD makes it uncertain whether any case can now arise in the absence of suggestion or prior preparation. But when he reviewed the earlier literature he was unable to find a case in which MPD emerged spontaneously in the absence of shaping by physicians or preparation through the media.

Spanos and his colleagues (Spanos 1991; Spanos, Burgess, and Burgess, in press; Spanos, Weekes, and Bertrand 1985; Spanos, Weekes, Menary, and Bertrand 1986) note that relatively few patients show clear signs of multiple personality at the beginning of therapy. Instead, people learn to act out the role of the multiple personality patient, and the therapists play an important part in the generation and maintenance of this role. Since knowledge concerning the multiple personality role is widespread, some patients combine what they know about MPD with the information gleaned from therapy to enact the 'symptoms' of multiple personality. Spanos et al. found that subjects in role-playing experiments displayed the major signs of a multiple personality, including adopting a differently named identity, reporting amnesia, using the third person in self-reference, responding differently to psychological tests, and giving different accounts of childhood relationships and current relationships to others.

In experiments using a regression-to-past-lives technique, half of their subjects reported a past life. After the hypnosis was over, some subjects still believed they really did have a past life. In another study, they gave false information about what to expect in the past life to some of the subjects. These subjects incorporated the suggestions in their descriptions of past lives.

When child abuse suggestions were given to some subjects, the subjects reported severe abuse in their past lives.

They also investigated the role of the therapist in legitimizing patients' reports obtained under hypnosis. In one condition, subjects were told that past life experiences were interesting fantasies rather than real-life memories. Those in another condition were told that reincarnation was scientifically credible. Although subjects in the two conditions were equally likely to construct past life experiences, the imaginary creation group gave significantly less credibility to the identities than did the group that was told reincarnation was scientifically credible.

Spanos and his colleagues conclude that these experiences of having lived a past life are social creations that can be elicited easily from many normal people, and that they are determined by the understandings subjects develop about such experiences from the information they are given. They believe the same factors are operating in people who report encounters with UFO aliens, in those who uncover memories of ritual satanic abuse, and in those who develop symptoms of multiple personality disorder.

Weissberg (1993) describes the way alter personalities are often elicited by the MPD therapists—highly suggestive instructions, 8-hour interviews, refusal to allow breaks—and he notes that dissociative states that resemble MPD may be shaped into multiple personality states. Especially when hypnosis is used, there are significant problems with confabulation and pseudomemories. He reviews the famous case of Anna O, an early multiple personality treated by Josef Breuer (Sigmund Freud's mentor), and analyzes how Breuer's treatment was vulnerable to suggestion and iatrogenic amplification of her symptoms.

A case we were involved in illustrates how MPD can be developed, reinforced, and maintained by the therapist:

> Elisa claimed to have been sexually victimized by a neighbor when she was between 14 and 18 years of age. She maintained she repressed all memories of this abuse until her therapist questioned her about the possibility. She then

sued the neighbor, who denied the abuse. As part of the lawsuit, we evaluated Elisa and reviewed a large amount of documents, including therapy and hospital records.

Elisa came from a troubled and conflicted family and perceived her family as nonsupportive. After high school she worked as a secretary and attended community college part-time. She met her future husband when she was 18 and they were married two years later. Her life was complicated by rheumatoid arthritis which, although not life-threatening, was painful and difficult, and she was eventually hospitalized for depression. At the time we saw her she had had a total of five hospitalizations for emotional problems. The hospital records mention her anger and frustration over the chronic pain along with problems with her marriage and with her family, particularly her mother. But until three years ago she was employed and going to school part-time.

She began seeing Dr. Smith three years ago. Dr. Smith's case notes indicate that he questioned her a number of times about abuse and that she initially denied it. But he believed she had the symptoms of sexual abuse so he persisted in questioning her until she eventually agreed that her neighbor had 'touched' her.

Elisa didn't have many memories of this at first, but after a few months she had 'flashbacks,' and 'frightening things' came into her mind. She eventually recovered memories of her neighbor regularly grabbing her and kissing and fondling her when her parents were at work. The abuse went on for four years until shortly before she met her future husband but she claimed to have no memory of it until Dr. Smith began questioning her.

She saw Dr. Smith, who also managed her medications, for therapy three times a week. She was on a large number of mood-altering drugs. She became progressively more dysfunctional. At the time we saw her she was not only unable to work, her husband did the house cleaning, shopping, cooking, and laundry. She spent most days in bed, except when she was at therapy. Her inability to cope with these tasks was due to her emotional problems rather than her physical ones, which were currently under control.

Dr. Smith diagnosed her as multiple personality disorder and had this diagnosis confirmed by an MPD 'expert' in a nearby city. It was hard for Elisa to accept that she had MPD and she denied it until Dr. Smith told her "there was no doubt that I had multiple personalities." She now has seven different personalities and accepts that her MPD resulted from the abuse by her neighbor.

She reported that she screams, shouts and throws and breaks things when she is angry and said that she has one personality who is very violent. She believes that the multiple personalities are a coping mechanism for when she is in a difficult or stressful situation.

Dr. Smith's case notes indicates that the alters show up regularly in their therapy sessions. For example, she hallucinates monsters in the form of a man who is following her. She becomes frightened and hides and then 'Chrissy' comes out. She also reports hearing voices that say bad things about her. When this happens 'Judy' comes out and punishes her by cutting her arms and her legs. She says, 'I don't cut, Judy cuts.'

During our evaluation, Elisa was appropriate and co-operative. R.U. spoke to her for four hours and at no time did she display any sign of cognitive slippage, delusions or hallucinations, irrational behavior, or changing personalities. This was despite the stress of the evaluation. She also reported seeing the neighbor in a parking lot at lunch time, but no alters emerged to protect her from either R.U. or the neighbor.

Her psychological test results indicated significant exaggeration of problems. We interpreted this as a learned response to therapy and her hospitalizations rather than deliberate malingering. She has been told that she has severe psychological problems, including MPD, and has learned to play the role of a disturbed and dysfunctional MPD patient, especially when she is around people who expect this from her. After therapy three times a week, several hospitalizations, and constant talking about how the personalities help her cope and how the abuse has damaged her permanently, this has become her reality.

Body Memories

The concept of 'body memories' appears regularly in the recovered memory literature. The assumption is that, although there are no conscious memories, the body remembers and the client has physical symptoms that correspond to the childhood abuse. Body memories are thought to be especially likely to occur when the abuse happens before the age of two or so when the child can process verbal information. The survivor is said to be able to retrieve colors, hear sounds, experience smells, odors and taste sensations, and her body may react in pain reminiscent of the abuse and develop physical stigmata as the memory is retrieved.

Fredrickson (1992) provides a case history of body memories that illustrates the way recovered memory therapists use this concept:

> Jim was a survivor who had been sexually abused by his mother. He was rightfully very angry at his father for ignoring his distress signals and giving covert permission for the abuse. Whenever he talked about his anger at his father, however, he reported that his anus hurt. At first he passed this off as a random pain spasm, then thought of it as an idiosyncratic physical reaction to anger. When he began to work on dreams and imagery around the possibility of his father sexually abusing him, the pain intensified dramatically. His body was remembering the pain of his father's anal rapes. (p. 93)

Susan Smith (1993) has written an excellent critical analysis of the body memory concept which includes a survey of 38 counsellors specializing in sexual abuse recovery in Phoenix, Arizona. She found that these counsellors believed that body memories are emotional, kinesthetic, or chemical recordings stored at the cellular level and retrievable by returning to or recreating the chemical, emotional, or kinesthetic conditions under which the memory recordings are filed. Body memories occur when memories are repressed because the body has no intellectual defenses and therefore cannot 'screen out' memory imprints.

The body memory notion is bolstered by two theories which

have been adapted from traditional theories to weave an erroneous but superficially plausible argument: the 'traumatic memory' theory and the 'state dependent' learning or memory theory. According to the recovered memory therapists, it is possible to retrieve memories of early infancy and perhaps even of being in the womb. It is assumed that regression to the developmental stage for which no cognitive structure exists will produce 'memories' in the manner in which they were imprinted. For instance, survivors subscribing to this theory have reported feeling teething pain, losing the ability to read, losing motor control, loss of speech, and blurry vision, all characteristic of infancy.

The age at which sexual abuse allegedly occurred is pinpointed by physical symptoms or somatic sensations that generally correspond to developmental stages. For instance, if an adult becomes tongue-tied during a regression, trance or 'abreaction,' they are presumed to be on the infant level because an infant has very little control of the tongue. When clients in hypnosis or in a regressed state experience feelings of terror, rage, or being restrained, but cannot articulate the sources of these feelings, it is assumed that they are recovering 'memories' of infantile sexual abuse.

The body memory concept is loosely based on Freud's theory of repression and Piaget's theory of cognitive development in children which says that children function primarily through the senses until the age of six or seven. Since abstract thinking processes do not normally begin until the age of about seven or eight, traumatic memories for infancy and early childhood are supposedly imprinted as sensory memories that may have no cognitive support.

According to Smith, the concept of body memories presupposes that the body is capable of retaining memories and operates by an independent intelligence that attempts to communicate to the individual about the repressed abuse by literally manifesting signs, diseases, or stigmata. The body memory can be an actual physical representation of an event, such as 'handprints appearing around a survivors neck' or acute attacks of pain in the area that was purportedly abused. In *Michelle*

Remembers, the 1980 work about satanic abuse, several photographs of Michelle's arms and neck are shown. An asymmetrical rash on her neck was labelled a "body memory" of the "devil's tail" which had supposedly been wrapped around her neck to choke her. According to Dr. Lawrence Pazder, "the Devil" had literally manifested at a satanic ceremony, wrapped his fiery tail around Michelle's neck, and burned the imprint into her flesh (Smith and Pazder 1980).

The therapists in Smith's survey claimed that 59 percent of their clients experienced body memories, and 95 percent of the therapists said it was common for memories to surface via body memories. Several therapists claimed that 100 percent of their clients experienced body memories if they were 'working it through' or if they were sexual abuse survivors. Several therapists reported that their regular client load, or those without sexual abuse issues, did not experience body memories, that this symptom of repressed traumatic memories was unique to traumatic memories of sexual abuse.

Smith notes that the notion that body memories are specific to traumatic memories of sexual abuse is a curious assumption. If the body had the capability to record traumatic experiences, why would it not it would record all traumatic experiences? Body memories specifically deal with infantile sexual abuse. If the cognitive processes are not developed enough to recognize, understand, or remember sexual abuse, how would the body know the difference between a sexual trauma and any trauma? A trauma would simply be recorded as a trauma, if the theory had any validity at all. Smith observes that the fact that many therapists believed that body memories of preverbal trauma were only of a sexual nature demonstrated illogical biases and ideologies that have not been well-reasoned or thought out.

In the survey, therapists were asked to describe the concept of body memories, asked if the theory of body memories corresponded to the theory of cellular memories, asked how they knew that clients were experiencing body memories, and asked to explain how the body stores memories. Following are some of their verbatim replies (S. Smith 1993, pp. 226–27).

When asked to describe the concept of 'body memories':

Subject #1: Yes . . . When I first started working with someone and they were talking about their father and they dissociated in the middle of that and they were reacting like he was in the room right then and not only did their whole body shake, especially like, you could see goose bumps and the redness all up and down her legs, but you could also see like, a hand print across her throat. It's like even though she didn't really remember it consciously what was happening, her body registered what happened.

Subject #2: Let's see, what I believe is that memories can be stored in the tissues of the body, and ah, sometimes people will begin to have symptomology around their bodies before they have cognitive memories.

Most of the therapists gave similar scientifically illiterate descriptions of 'body memories.'

When asked if body memories corresponded to the theory of 'cellular memories':

Subject #3: Okay, to me cellular memories are similar to what I just described and often times there are actual data that comes up with it at the same time that people have often reported that maybe it didn't happen in this lifetime, that it happened in some other lifetime. Or that it did happen in this lifetime but they don't have a memory of it happening to them.

Subject #5: Yes, well I think whatever happens to us the body remembers in great detail and doesn't lose it.

Subject #17: Cellular memories in my understanding are that the very, within each cell there's a mitochondria that has the capacity for recording events.

The mitochondria theory was shared by the majority of therapists who unhesitatingly launched into similar explanations of 'cellular recordings.'

There is no scientific evidence supporting these assumptions. Smith believes that the recovered memory therapists use the body memory theory to manufacture traumatic memories of sexual abuse. She notes that when therapists teach clients to interpret a variety of physical symptoms as body memories of repressed abuse, "the notion of body memories becomes a means of indoctrination into survivor logic" (1993, p. 230). The logic may be absurd and flimsy but persuasive to clients who have had unresolved problems for many years and who are desperate to believe that once they recover the memories of abuse, they will overcome their problems.

Gardner takes a caustic view of body memories:

> Actually, I should be less mocking of these people and should appreciate that they may be on to something that can be a boon to medicine and should be a source of hope for people with Altzheimer's disease, brain tumors, and other degenerative diseases of the brain. These pockets of memory cells could be transplanted from the genital organs or anus to the brain, thereby restoring the individual to normal memory. Or, people might be able to be trained to use these cells as satellite brain replacements. Such brain cells in the genitals could conceivably contribute to a reduction in unwanted pregnancies (please excuse the pun) and sexually transmitted diseases (including AIDS). Furthermore, an individual might even be trained to think with his (her) anus. (1992b, p. 660)

Trauma Memory

The belief that trauma memory is different from other memories is central to the assumptions of the recovered memory therapists. Herman (1992) says that whereas normal memory is "the action of telling a story," traumatic memory is "wordless and static" (p. 175). Harvey (1993) maintains that traumatic memories are acquired in an altered state and are not stored in the same way as ordinary memories. She claims that because of this, the research on the memory of nontraumatized subjects has no relevance to what happens to memory when a child is abused.

Van der Kolk (1988a, 1988b; van der Kolk and van der Hart 1989) has developed a model of the biological changes associated with trauma along with the effect of this on later memory. He traces the physiological changes associated with trauma and how these biological shifts depend on the level of maturation of the central nervous system. He says that traumatized people appear to have an all-or-nothing response to emotional stimuli —they cannot modulate their responses, be they anxiety, anger, or intimacy. Therefore they react to stress with aggression and other inappropriate behaviors or they withdraw socially and emotionally.

The physiological changes resulting from trauma are supposed to account for most of the symptoms of PTSD, as well as fostering the development of later psychopathology. In addition, prior trauma is said to predispose adults to develop full-blown PTSD in response to later life stresses. Van der Kolk draws comparisons between animal studies demonstrating biochemical changes following inescapable shock and what has been discovered about the biochemistry of the human response to overwhelming trauma. These responses to stress are consistent across a wide variety of stressful events such as child abuse, rape, wars, and concentration camp experiences.

Van der Kolk believes that both the person's developmental level and the degree of physiological arousal will affect the way information is processed and memories are stored. He notes that research indicates that the hippocampus, which serves a mapping function for locating memories for experiences in space and time, does not fully mature until the third or fourth year of life. The taxon system, however, which serves memories relating to the quality (feel and sound) of things matures much earlier. Therefore, in the first few years of life, only the quality of events, but not their context, can be remembered.

Van der Kolk says that another way to look at this is in terms of the three modes of information processing: sensorimotor, pre-operational, and operational, which are related to central nervous system development. During periods of stress, people revert to earlier modes of representation. If the experience is terrifying, it overwhelms, which prevents the experience from being accommodated and assimilated. Therefore, the individual reverts to an earlier mode of representation—as horrific images, visceral sensations, or fight/flight/freeze reactions. In terms of the physiological model, stress disrupts the functioning of the hippocampus-based system and potentiates the taxon system.

Since the experience lacks localization in space and time and is encoded in sensorimotor form, it cannot be readily translated into the symbolic language necessary for linguistic retrieval. Such memories are therefore difficult to retrieve, although they can be retrieved by affective, auditory, or visual cues. This is analogous to the concept of state-dependent learning where information acquired in an aroused state is not available under normal conditions, but can be recovered when the altered state of consciousness is reintroduced.

Kandel and Kandel (1994) address the biological evidence for recovered memory claims, using repression rather than dissociation as the operative concept. They believe that biological research may support repressed memory and they cite animal studies suggesting that memory storage can be modulated and inhibited and that memory can later return. But they also acknowledge that there are no rigorous data to support the recovered repressed memory assumptions:

> Over the past 20 years neuroscientists have made considerable strides in understanding the workings of memory. Can science also explain the delayed recall of sexual trauma? The *rigorous* answer is no. There is, as yet, no proper understanding of what might happen in human brains when memories are repressed, or when they are recovered. (p. 36)

The difficulty with using these biological trauma memory concepts to support the recovered memory claims is that these concepts do not begin to explain how repeated, intrusive abuse, occurring in different circumstances and places and over a number of years, can be completely obliterated from memory and then retrieved, years later. Van der Kolk's explanations of how biological changes can explain PTSD symptomatology and contribute to later psychopathology does not need the assumption of some type of robust repression process during the trauma. And Van der Kolk does not distinguish between child abuse and other types of traumatic events in his model. The recovered memory therapists who want to use these concepts must also explain why people who have undergone documented traumas do remember their traumas.

Evaluating Trauma Memory

Can these assertions about biological events be used to account for and defend claims of recovered memories? In trying to answer that question, there are a number of factors to consider. Understanding the relationship between the brain and behavior can go two ways. One way is from the bottom up. It begins with the properties of the individual neurons and synapses and ends up with the behavior of the whole organism. The other is from the top down, beginning with the whole organism and ending up with the properties of the central nervous system.

The neurobiologists champion the bottom-up approach and this approach is what the claims about a special process or a separate memory system for trauma memory are based on. This is a reductionist stance and assumes that all mind events are brain events. It solves the mind-body problem by attending only to the body as if that were all there was. This is a dangerous position to take with the present discoveries in quantum physics, the epitome of a 'hard' science, producing some very puzzling, strange phenomena; it appears that there are no such things as 'things' until they are measured, a single photon can pass through two barriers simultaneously, particles that are millions of miles apart can affect each other instantaneously (*The Economist*, 1989). These findings from physics make any concepts that reduce everything to biology rather questionable.

The major barrier to using the biological bottom-up approach to claim support for recovered memories is that it cannot account for complex behavior. It is not at all clear what properties of the neurons are essential to collective behaviors. The inability of the neural approach to deal with complex, collective behaviors is shown in this passage from van der Kolk and Saporta 1993:

> The function of the septohippocampal system is to evaluate in which way incoming stimuli are important, and whether they are associated with reward, punishment, novelty, or nonreward. Thus, the hippocampus is thought to be the evaluative center involved in behavioral inhibition, obsessional thinking, inhibition of exploratory behavior, scanning, and construction of a spatial map (O'Keefe and Nadel 1978), and fulfills the crucial function of storing and categorizing information. When categorization is complete, the hippocampus disengages from active control of behavior. External stress increases corticosterone production, which decreases the firing rates of the hippocampus (Pfaff, Silva, and Weiss 1971). Lesions of the hippocampus lead to paralysis because of excessive susceptibility to interference from competing responses. (p. 28)

Because there is no way to account for collective neural behavior, van der Kolk must introduce a homunculus, the little man, or the ghost in the machine, that runs around somewhere in the hippocampus monitoring all the little computers and data banks to do the tasks van der Kolk says it does. The work of evaluating and categorizing stimuli and controlling behavior is what we normally ascribe to the perceptual apparatus of the individual, not to a marble-sized bundle of neurons. For all of the difficult and highly detailed descriptions of neurotransmitters, synapses, blocking, and so on, all that van der Kolk does is to reduce the person we are trying to deal with from a whole, visible, present individual we can talk to, to a microscopic ghost alive inside the hippocampus that we can only infer and guess about and cannot communicate with. Reductionist, brain-only models cannot account for the characteristic power human beings have of intending objects both cognitively and purposefully.

Somehow the story of George Bernard Shaw's response to Isadora Duncan seems to fit here. Ms. Duncan proposed to Shaw that he have a child by her. She enthusiastically described what a superb creature it would be, endowed with her body and

Shaw's mind. To which Shaw is alleged to have answered that the idea was an excellent one were it not for the unpleasant possibility that the child might turn out to have his body and her mind.

Another objection to the trauma memory concepts proposed by van der Kolk is the argument advanced by Meehl (1967) about the weakness in theory testing caused by the fact that everything in the brain is connected with everything else. There are several general state-variables, such as arousal, attention, or anxiety, which are affected by almost any kind of stimulus input. So people learning a list of words show an effect on performance if the faintest trace of essence of peppermint is infused into the air. There are very good reasons for expecting that any experimental manipulation would produce differences from a control group. The result is that what may look like a successful experiment can be only a very weak corroboration of any substantive theory. If this is not understood ". . . a zealous and clever investigator can slowly wend his way through a tenuous nomological network . . . *without ever once refuting or corroborating so much as a single strand of the network* (Meehl 1967, p. 114). The model of a biological base for trauma memory as proposed by van der Kolk, while he does acknowledge state variables and make claims about state-dependent learning, shows no awareness of the Bayesian inference considerations required by the fact that everything in the brain is connected to everything else.

Much of the information van der Kolk relies upon comes from learned helplessness research, where animals are exposed to stressors, often electrical shock, in situations where they can control or not control the experience of being stressed. This stressor paradigm is potent enough so that almost every neurotransmitter in some particular brain region, and some neurotransmitter in every brain region, is altered (Peterson, Maier, and Seligman 1993). But which is responsible for which? It is also evident that cognitive changes can be affected by learning about the stressor. These findings support the applicability of Meehl's (1967) argument to the concept of trauma memory.

Those researchers who have been involved from the beginning in the development of the learned helplessness studies conclude that child abuse is not an example of learned helplessness (Peterson, Maier, and Seligman 1993). This raises the question of the relevance of most of the actual data van der Kolk cites to what he is claiming about trauma memory.

These considerations suggest that considerable caution should be exercised in evaluating the claims of the trauma researchers that at least half of all emotionally disturbed patients are victims of child abuse (Wylie 1993). The effort to buttress claims of recovered memory by the idea that trauma memory is some sort of special process, that can account for a person who has no memories and then acquires them, has little or no support in the actual research and raises so many serious objections that it cannot be reasonably advanced.

Betrayal-Trauma Theory

Betrayal-Trauma theory (Freyd 1993) takes trauma memory theory one step further. This theory was formulated by Jennifer Freyd, the daughter of Pamela Freyd, the executive director of the FMS Foundation. It was presented at a scientific conference in which Dr. Freyd also made detailed personal accusations against her parents.

According to Freyd, Betrayal-Trauma theory asks: "if a child is abused and betrayed, what would we expect to happen to the *information* about that abuse and betrayal?" (p. 3). She states that the core issue in her theory is the concept of a betrayal of trust that produces conflict between external reality and a necessary system of social dependence. She does not consider that children do not have the cognitive capacity for the abstract concept of trust until well into the prepubertal stage. What can betrayal possibly mean to a four or five year old?

Also, Freyd must maintain that all abuse is traumatic in order to claim that the process she suggests is elicited. She cannot accept the scientific findings mentioned earlier that a large proportion of actually abused people later perceive the abuse to have been neutral or even pleasant. Her theory requires her to insist that all abuse is painful and horrible.

Freyd explains that in an evolutionary sense it would not be adaptive to have an animal spontaneously experience pain and then go to great lengths to get rid of the pain. It is more parsimonious to assume that pain exists to motivate changes in behavior. The immediate blocking of the pain would be adaptive only if the behavioral consequences of pain in a particular situation are maladaptive. For example, if a woman broke her leg, ordinarily the severe pain would keep her from walking; instead she would lie still until someone went for help. But if she were alone, she would be likely to spontaneously block the pain in order to hobble to safety.

According to Betrayal-Trauma theory, ordinarily, it is not to our survival advantage to go back to those who have betrayed (abused) us for further interaction. If, however, the betrayer is someone we depend upon, such as a parent, we need to ignore the betrayal. We therefore block out information about sexual abuse in order to preserve our attachments. Thus there is a survival advantage in traumatic amnesia and dissociation for sexual abuse.

Here, Freyd does not consider the evolutionary concept of reproductive capability which has replaced survival of the fittest as the operative principle of evolutionary adaptation (Littlefield and Rushton 1986). If evolutionary concepts of survival are going to be used by Freyd to support her theory, this concept of the opportunity for reproduction must be considered. We do not necessarily agree with these sociobiological concepts, but they do represent the current thinking among evolutionary scientists.

Buss (1990) discusses what evolutionary theory suggests as adaptive strategies and clearly warns that strategies that may be distasteful or repugnant because they are aggressive, impulsive, or wanton should not be labelled maladjustment. The earlier and more successfully an organism engages in reproductive behavior, the greater the advantage. Learning sexual behavior and having a longer time to reproduce the DNA is therefore adaptive. This leads to an opposite conclusion from Freyd's about the value of adaptable behavior and would logically lead to closer interaction with abusive parents rather than dissociation and loss of memory. That is, learning about sexual behavior from parents or engaging in sexual behavior with parents maximizes reproductive capability in an evolutionary sense (Zuravin 1988; Belsky, Steinberg, and Draper 1991; Buss 1987, 1990).

Freyd maintains that: "The cognitive mechanisms that underlie this blockage of information are modular dissociations between normally connected, or integrated, aspects of processing and memory. These cognitive dissociations lead to the more global phenomenology and symptomatology of clinical dissociation. The traumatic amnesia can be understood in terms of low-level failures of integration" (p. 15). Freyd then presents a complicated model with diagrams of boxes and arrows to illustrate how her theory works.

Freyd believes that people who don't agree with her theory are "dissociating from the realities of child abuse and psychological effects of child abuse" (p. 21). Yet despite this pejorative and judgmental plea, there is no empirical support for her theory that traumatic memories involving abuse by a parent or other care-giver are processed differently than are memories for other traumatic events.

Both van der Kolk's concept of traumatic memory and Freyd's concept of Betrayal-Trauma have to deal with the observations made of brain activities by using nuclear-magnetic-resonance imaging. When an individual is thinking or remembering, this process shows up in several areas of the brain simultaneously, not just one. Also, while there may be some constancy across people for some areas, brain activity varies from person to person and from episode to episode within the same person. What counts is the process within the brain rather than the gray matter itself (*The Economist* 1993). These findings, while they may not specifically falsify the claims about neural activity and a special system for trauma memories, certainly mean it is best to avoid hard and fast conclusions about localization of brain function and a simple reductionist view that there are only brain events.

Where Will the Recovered Memory Therapists Go Next?

The Therapists Don't Do It

The recovered memory therapists deny that they influence the memories of their clients. Instead, they depict themselves as noble pioneers who listen in shock to the horrible memories their clients spontaneously relate to them. Although they acknowledge the occasional bad therapist who encourages clients to develop false memories, they say that this is extremely rare. Fredrickson (1993) maintains that most therapists are only followers and that they only react to the accounts of abuse presented to them. Harvey (1993) claims to have seen only one or two patients whose memories came from the influence of a therapist. Wylie (1993) notes that many therapists assert that, far from encouraging abuse disclosures, they at first *disbelieved* the stories the clients were telling; instead they preferred to diagnose their clients as borderlines, hysterics, or schizophrenics rather than conclude that these people were in terrible shape because terrible things had been done to them.

These protestations run counter to the accounts of the retractors we have reported in Chapter 4. They are also contradicted by the writings and presentations of the recovered memory therapists themselves. As we showed in Chapter 5, recovered memory therapists routinely infer abuse from a wide range of common symptoms, question clients repeatedly about abuse, put them into survivors' groups even if they don't have memories of abuse, and use a variety of intrusive and highly suggestive techniques to 'uncover' the 'memories.'

The experience of the FMS Foundation with thousands of families who have reported memories only after therapy started also suggests that far more therapists do exactly what they say they do in their literature than simply follow the lead of patients. The claim that there are only a few bad apples in the barrel of recovered memory therapists is, we are afraid, hopelessly incredible.

Not All Was Forgotten

Mary Harvey (1993) illustrates another stance, which we expect to become more common in the future. In discussing the people she has seen at the Cambridge Hospital's Victims of Violence program, Harvey states that some people have always remembered clearly what has happened to them, others have no memory, while most fall in between these two extremes. Of course, a dilemma is that if a civil suit is contemplated, the claim must be that the memory was totally 'repressed' until recently; otherwise the statutes of limitations would preclude the lawsuit.

Recovered Memories as Symbols

Jennifer Freyd (1993) exemplifies the direction we expect the recovered memory therapists to take as they are increasingly confronted with the lack of scientific underpinnings for their theories. Freyd says it is a mistake to focus on the relationship between reported memories and external historical truth instead of internal emotional truth:

> The striking part of the psychological truth that gets overlooked in this debate is the *pain* that is expressed along with these memories. . . . In individual cases of reported trauma, we should never forget to ask about the *meaning* of that report to the person experiencing the memory, whether we do or do not have documentation of the trauma. Even if an adult claiming a particular type of abuse is proved to be in error about the historical facts, the emotional reactions may well be a sane reaction to a horrifying and confusing external world. An example of this would be a painful memory of being forced to eat one's own baby when in fact there was no external infant, but instead the psychological destruction of the survivor's own

childhood through more mundane but extremely damaging psychological abuse. In essence, she may have consumed parts of her very own soul in order to survive her ordeal through a process of dissociation. Her pain may be well captured by the metaphor of eating her infant, and it would seen overly simplistic and downright inhumane for the world to judge her memories as simply false. (p. 6–7)

Such a generous interpretation of 'truth' offers recovered memory therapists, who have uncritically accepted as historical fact whatever implausible stories their patients eventually tell, a convenient way to save face. In addition, the recovered-memories-as-symbols theory fits nicely into the climate of victimization that is prevalent today and supported by writers, such as John Bradshaw (1988), who maintain that all families are dysfunctional.

Similarly, the original allegation may be diluted:

Her father and I have been downgraded from child 'abusers' to 'negligent parents.' Mainly, it seems, we were negligent because, for one thing, her father was away at work a lot of the time (which is true). Another reason is that she remembers that I sometimes became angry. The third is . . . she did not feel 'safe.' Probing on my part revealed that this meant that she did not always feel 'safe' to disclose to her father and me all of her inner feelings. And that's it. She is now sure that she was not sexually abused. For this, I have not seen her or my grandchildren for more than four years and was not even spoken to for more than three. For this, I have received devastating, vitriolic letters. (*FMS Foundation Newsletter*, August/September 1993)

It is a giant leap from complaining about how an alcoholic father, an overly critical mother, or a nasty divorce made childhood difficult to accusing one's parents of rape and torture. Accused parents say that they could handle resentments about parenting shortcomings but being falsely accused of sexual abuse is an entirely different matter.

It should be clearly understood that, to date, the writings and presentations of recovered memory therapists, in the overwhelming majority of cases, fully endorse the literal allegations of abuse. They do not re-interpret them symbolically.

If, when confronted with massive disconfirming evidence as is now happening, recovered memory enthusiasts resort to claims of symbolic or mythical abuse, this eventually means the downfall of the child abuse system as it has developed up to now. We have lots of experience with what happens to a body of knowledge when it comes to be viewed as symbol or myth. The history of the theological movements in the Christian churches of the last century show that re-interpreting a historical truth-claim to accord it merely symbolic status is the final stage of acknowledged irrelevance.

The chief competitor to the Christian faith for the last three hundred years has been science. When Christian theologians who could not handle what looked like disconfirming evidence from science began to assert in the early part of this century that, after all, the Christian faith was symbolic, and theology became a process of demythologizing the historic truth-claims, the church died. In Europe, except for former communist countries, there is no longer a viable Christian church. In this country, the old-line denominations that diluted theology with demythologizing interpretations have diminished while those that maintain a historic truth-claim continue to grow. Hiding behind the dishonest façade of a claim of symbolic truth is the contemptible last refuge of fools and the beginning of conscious knavery. Jennifer Freyd's invoking this concept, and being given so much status and credit by the incest survivors' network for her courage and bravery in making this presentation, is the harbinger of the plunge into trivialization and the end of any respectability for the now so powerful child abuse system.

If the claims of recovered memories of childhood sexual abuse; satanic, ritualistic abuse; murder of babies; eating and drinking blood, feces, and urine; torture; orgies; and all manner of bizarre horrors are not factually *true*, why should anybody pay any attention? If the memories are symbols for what may be regrettable and unpleasant human experience but still within the range of normal frequency, they are not courageous but a whine for sympathy. If memories are symbolic and propel a person into the unproductive role of victim, anyone who cares about someone who has concocted such memories cannot and must not defend them, but should rather directly, openly, and forcefully expose them for the malignant untruths they are.

Conclusions

The recovered memory therapists began with repression as the construct accounting for the lack of memories for repeated, traumatic childhood sexual abuse. When this concept was criticized, they started using dissociation and traumatic amnesia. But skeptics noted that these concepts also failed to explain the recovered memory claims and observed that people who have undergone documented trauma remember the trauma.

Then they came up with the idea of different types of trauma. They said that, although single traumatic events will be remembered, repeated trauma will be dissociated. Now we are told that trauma with a parent as a perpetrator is processed differently than other types of trauma.

As the lack of empirical support for these theories becomes obvious, we expect that more recovered memory therapists will say that it doesn't matter if the memories are of real events—that the memories are symbolic for the psychological 'abuse' and emotional 'incest' the clients' dysfunctional parents perpetrated upon them.

Chapter Ten
Abusive Behaviors Alleged in Recovered Memory Claims

Some really bizarre things have been happening in this country. These strange happenings may be omens of one of the biggest secret conspiracies, or one of the biggest hoaxes, in recent history.

Jeffrey S. Victor (1993)

Recovered memory claims often involve allegations of highly deviant abuse, such as anal or vaginal rape of toddlers, violence, sadism, and even satanic ritual abuse. The abuse is frequently said to have began at a very young age, even at infancy. The accused are not just fathers, but mothers and other relatives are also accused, often of acting together. Such seemingly implausible claims are found in the books and articles by the recovered memory therapists where they are uncritically presented as actual events. Some examples:

- Steve believed his mother was sadistic and sexually abusive. One of his first memories to return was of her feeding him in his highchair. "I remember really liking what she was feeding me. I was making pleasure sounds and kicking my feet in anticipation of each bite. Then one bite was suddenly hideous. It was so awful-tasting I started to gag and vomit. Now I think she slipped a spoonful of calf feed into my mouth." (Fredrickson 1992, pp. 41–42)

• Colleen was only three when her grandmother began to fondle her genitals whenever she slept overnight with her. Sometimes she put things like pencils and bobby pins in Colleen's bottom and hurt her. (Fredrickson 1992, p. 58)

• (Allen, in a marathon treatment program for eating disorders, was asked if he had been abused. He denied it but the group confronted him saying he had the signs of an abuse victim. The staff told him that if he followed their program he would find the truth. He then uncovered memories about his father.) "I learned/recalled my father's abuse; from the time I was an infant (four to six months) until age six my father repeatedly sexually abused me: forcing me to suck on his penis until he had an orgasm in my mouth . . . and inflicting a great deal of pain on me by squeezing my testicles and by sticking his finger in my rectum, squeezing my throat, choking me, and threatening to kill me if I resisted or spoke a word." (Hunter 1990, p. 197)

• Vera was remembering being tied spreadeagled on a table with her grandfather looming over her, holding a knife in one hand and a live rat in another. . . . "He cuts the rope from around my neck and starts to shove the rat in my mouth. I am squirming, trying to get away, and he says, 'Do you want the rat or me?' Then he puts his penis in my mouth. I hold real still because I don't want him to push the rat down my throat." (Fredrickson 1992, pp. 113–14)

• Annette grew up in an upper-middle-class town in the Midwest. Her father held the same managerial job for over 30 years. Both her parents were community leaders, active in church affairs. Secretly they were involved with a group that performed ritualized abuse according to a satanic calendar. Town leaders, businesspeople, and church officials were all involved in this cult. From infancy, Annette was abused in rituals that included sexual abuse, torture, murder, pornography, and systematic brainwashing through drugs and electric shock: "I was what they called a 'breeder.' I was less than 12 years old.

They overpowered me and got me pregnant and then they took my babies. They killed them right in front of me." (Bass and Davis 1988, p. 417)

- The memory had just come for a woman in Ohio. She'd been involved in a Twelve Step ritual abuse group for about a year. She was six years old, maybe seven. She and some other neighborhood kids had been taken to the woods, again, for another ceremony. Shortly after arriving there, some chains were brought out. . . . They picked out David, one of Pam's school friends. David was seven too. As his legs were being chained to the trees, the other children were told that David had betrayed the cult. He had told one of the neighbors he had seen his mother have sex with a dog. The children were told to watch closely, because what was about to happen to David would happen to them if they ever talked about the cult. And, as the young child screamed in terror, his father approached him, and taking a knife, savagely cut his son's tongue out. The boy was then slowly skinned alive while the rest of the kids were forced to watch. (Ryder 1992, p. 213)

We have consulted on dozens of cases throughout the United States and in other countries where there have been bizarre and improbable accounts of murders, monsters, anal and vaginal penetration of preschoolers, sex with animals, animal and human sacrifice, feces and blood, and ritual abuse and torture. Other cases, not including satanic ritual abuse, have involved equally implausible allegations. Although the improbability of such behaviors should have made these accusations highly suspect, investigators and therapists found the stories believable enough to conclude that sexual abuse had taken place. There have been criminal prosecutions and civil lawsuits based on such claims.

The same thing is occurring in recovered memory cases. Implausible and uncorroborated claims are accepted as real. Are such highly deviant allegations typical of recovered memory accounts? How do these stories compare to verified abuse? This question has practical significance in evaluating the truthfulness of a sexual abuse allegation when the person accused denies the abuse and there is no corroborating evidence. If the alleged behaviors are extremely improbable and there is no corroborating evidence it is unlikely that the accusation is true.

Research on the Behavior of Child Sexual Abusers

There *is* information about the behavior of actual sexual abusers, although the studies vary as to the behaviors reported. This is not surprising since the studies differ in terms of the sample studied (community, college, clinical, prison, hospital, and so forth), whether victims or offenders are sampled, the method of obtaining the data (interviews, questionnaires, hospital records, etc.), the sex of the victim, the definition of terms, the specificity of the description of the behavior, whether the abuse is intrafamilial or extrafamilial, and the adequacy of the verification of the abusive acts.

The prison-based samples will under-represent offenses such as exhibitionism, since these may be considered misdemeanors and the offenders unlikely to be sentenced to prison. The community-based samples are likely to include more behaviors that are less serious. Samples that depend upon retrospective data are subject to the criticisms of all such studies concerning the unreliability of retrospective data and interview data (Bradburn et al. 1987; Brewin et al. 1993; Briere 1992; Halverson 1988; Raphael et al. 1991; Roy-Byrne et al. 1987). Despite this, the literature does give useful information about the type of abusive behavior engaged in by actual child molesters.

Tollison and Adams

Tollison and Adams (1979) describe the general behaviors engaged in by the pedophile:

> Pedophiliac behavior may involve caressing a child's body, manipulating a child's genitals, or inducing a child to manipulate an adult's genitals. Occasionally, the behaviors also include penile penetration (partial or complete—vaginal or anal), oral sex, and any practice utilizing the sexual parts or organs of a

child so as to bring the person in contact with the child's body in any sexual manner. Pedophiliac acts may be homosexual or heterosexual in nature and may include touching, caressing, masturbation, oral-genital contact, and intercourse, as well as pedophiliac exhibitionism, voyeurism, rape, sadism, and masochism . . . Physical violence to the child occurs in only 2 percent of instances. . . . (p. 326)

Tollison and Adams report that most pedophilia victims are girls, at a ratio of two to one, and that most heterosexual victims are between the ages of 6 and 12, peaking between the ages of 8 and 11. Homosexual pedophilia victims increase in numbers into puberty, the result being a statistical overlap with adult homosexuality victims, but the peak ages are between 12 and 15. They report that only a minority of heterosexual pedophiles engage in penetration and intravaginal coitus with their victims, and then mainly with the age group over 14 and with their permission. In male homosexual pedophilia, the most common contact is masturbation—done to rather than by, the boy—followed by fellatio.

The Kinsey Studies

The Kinsey report (Kinsey et al. 1953) gives information about the pre-adolescent sexual contacts with adult males in their sample of 4,441 females. This was a retrospective study which depended upon the recollections of incidents that occurred years earlier when the women were children. There is no way to substantiate the reports. Kinsey et al. defined an adult male as one who was at least 15 years old and at least five years older than the female and obtained data as to the incidence, frequency, and nature of the sexual contacts.

Kinsey et al. found that although 24 percent of their sample reported some type of sexual contact with an adult male, nearly two-thirds of these contacts were verbal approaches or genital exhibitionism. They report that in only one case was appreciable physical injury done to the child. Their sample reported the types of approaches and contacts seen in Table 1.

Another type of data involves information from the offender

TABLE 1 Nature of Sexual Contact
Preadolescent Females Reported with
Adult Males in the Kinsey Study

Nature of Contact	Percent
Approach only	9
Exhibition, male genitalia	52
Exhibition, female genitalia	1
Fondling, no genital contact	31
Manipulation of female genitalia	22
Manipulation of male genitalia	5
Oral contact, female genitalia	1
Oral contact, male genitalia	1
Coitus	3

From Kinsey et al. (1953), N = 1075

rather than the victim. In an early study, the Kinsey Institute (Gebhard et al. 1965) collected information on the sexual behavior of sex offenders during the offense. The sample consisted of 1,356 white males who had been convicted for one or more sex offenses, 888 white males who had never been convicted for a sex offense, but who had been convicted for some other misdemeanor or felony, and 477 white males who had never been convicted for anything beyond traffic violations.

Offenders were separately analyzed depending upon whether the offenses were heterosexual or homosexual, whether they were against adults, minors (age 12 to 16), or children (under 12), whether the sexual contact was accompanied by force or threat, and whether the victim was a daughter or stepdaughter. In the offenses against unrelated children, both heterosexual and homosexual, where no force was used, anal and vaginal penetration were very rare. In the great majority of cases with girls, the sexual behavior consisted of petting and fondling. Anal penetration did not occur. Mouth-genital contact occurred in about one-sixth of the cases. The ages ranged from 3 through 11; the average age was 8. In the cases with boys, the most common behavior was masturbation (45 percent) followed by fellatio (38 percent). Anal coitus only occurred in 4 percent of the cases. The average age of the boys was 10.

In the incestuous offenses, coitus was performed in 9 percent of the cases and attempted in another 9 percent. A large number (42 percent) used genital masturbation and mouth-genital contact (39 percent). The average girl was age 9 to 10; there was a definite tendency for the offenders to prefer their older daughters.

The men who used force with children constituted only a small percentage (6.6 percent) of the total offenses against children. When force was used, the percentages of coitus (23 percent) and attempted coitus (23 percent) were much higher than in the cases where no force was used. Only 3 percent of their victims were under 5 years of age and more than half were age 9 to 11. The group using force consisted entirely of heterosexual offenses.

The proportion of offenses in which coitus was reported became greater as the child became older. This held true among the nonaggression and aggression cases as well as among the father-daughter incest offenses.

Erickson, Walbek, and Seely

Erickson, Walbek, and Seely (1988) examined data from 229 verified and admitted child sex offenders from a locked prison-diversion treatment program that also provides presentence evaluations for courts in Minnesota. They corroborated self-report information during clinical evaluations by police records, family interviews, previous evaluations, and victim statements. When there were discrepancies, the offenders were confronted during clinical evaluations. This verification process is important since offenders often minimize the extent of their abusive behavior (Hindman 1988).

Erickson et al. (1988) reported that 70 percent of the victims were female, 26 percent were male, and only 4 percent of the offenders molested children of both sexes. Approximately one-fourth of the victims of both sexes were less than 6 years old, one-fourth were between 6 and 10, and half were between the ages of 11 and 13. The frequency of abusive behaviors is shown in Table 2.

Erickson et al. (1988) observe that vaginal and anal penetration were very rare in young children; penile rectal or vaginal contact for this age group usually consisted of touching the rectal or vaginal opening with the penis and rubbing the penis between the legs. Attempted insertion of offenders' fingers into victims' vaginas was fairly common, but insertion of fingers into their rectums was quite uncommon. It was very rare for the offender to insert objects into the rectum or the vagina. Descriptions of the pain of forcible anal penetration were graphic and when it occurred the victims had to be held forcibly and their cries muffled.

Bribery was more common than threat and incestuous sexual contacts were often repetitive, with gradual progression from touch to penetration. Although the wives of the incest offenders had a varying amount of knowledge about what was going on, none participated directly and none of the extrafamilial offenders had a female collaborator. Erickson et al. note that the severity of the offense in their sample is somewhere between a community-based sample and an incarcerated sample and mis-

TABLE 2 Frequency of Behaviors described in Cases of Child Molesting in the Erickson et al. Study

| | Percent | |
Nature of Contact	Males (N = 63)	Females (N = 166)
Vaginal contact	0.0	41.5
Anal contact	33.3	9.6
Offender oral	41.2	19.2
Victim oral	28.8	17.4
Offender fondle	42.8	54.2
Victim fondle	7.9	7.2
Other	7.9	9.6

From Erickson et al. (1988), N = 229

demeanor behaviors such as exhibitionism are clearly under-represented. There were no reports in their sample of elaborate sexual experiences involving urination and defecation, sadistic and bizarre assaults, people in costumes and robes, or ritual sacrifice, torture, and murder.

Kendall-Tackett and Simon

Kendall-Tackett and Simon (1987) studied 365 adults who entered a child abuse treatment program between 1984 and 1985. Data on the type of sexual molestation was available from 278 of the subjects. This sample differs from the Kinsey et al. (1953) study because it uses a clinical sample. It differs from the Erickson et al. (1988) study because the sample was of victims rather than offenders. The authors note that there is no way to substantiate the reports given by the respondents.

Kendall-Tackett and Simon (1987) report that the average age of both male and female victims at the onset of the abuse was 7.5 and that 97 percent of the perpetrators were men. The frequency of abusive behaviors is shown in Table 3.

The authors note that the percentage of intercourse is much higher than that reported in a study by Finkelhor (1979), who found 4 percent, similar to the 3 percent reported by Kinsey et

TABLE 3 Nature of Sexual Contact Reported with Adult Females in the Kendall-Tackett and Simon Study

Nature of Contact	Percent
Fondling from the waist up	64
Fondling from the waist down	92
Oral sex	48
Attempted intercourse	19
Simulated intercourse	10
Intercourse	44
Anal intercourse	9

From Kendall-Tackett & Simon (1987) N = 278

al., (1953). The reason for this difference is most likely that Kendall-Tackett and Simon used a clinical population whereas Finkelhor et al. and Kinsey et al. used community-based samples. Erickson et al. (1988), whose sample was verified and admitted offenders, reported a proportion (41.5 percent) similar to Kendall-Tackett and Simon.

There is no discussion of violent or bizarre abuse or satanic ritual abuse in the Kendall-Tackett and Simon (1987) study.

Other Studies and General Conclusions

Despite the variability in the different research studies, some generalizations can be made. Child sexual abusers are overwhelmingly male and most child victims of sexual abuse are girls. The average age of female victims is around ages 6 to 12; some studies report that male victims are somewhat older. Most victims know the offender. Most sexual behavior consists of fondling, exhibitionism, masturbation, and oral or genital contact. Anal and vaginal penetration of very young children is rare. Males are more likely to be victims of attempted or actual anal penetration than are females. Penetration becomes more likely with an older child. Vaginal penetration is more common in clinical samples compared to community samples. It is rare for an offender to have a partner who participates in the abuse or to molest children in groups.

Aggression and violence are not usually part of the behavior, although Lang and Langevin (1991) state that the literature suggests that at least one in five child victims are subjected to force or "gratuitous physical violence" as part of the abusive act. In incest, a grooming process is generally involved (Christiansen and Blake 1990; Erickson et al. 1988; Farber et al. 1984; Gebhard et al. 1965; Groth et al. 1978; Kendall-Tackett and Simon 1987, 1992; Kinsey et al. 1953; Mohr 1981; Peters 1976; Rimsza and Niggemann 1982; Swenson and Grimes 1958).

Erickson (1985) observes that vaginal and anal penetration are extremely rare in young children: "All but the most hardened of child sexual abusers tend to avoid anal intercourse with prepubertal children because it is painful and some strategy must be utilized to muffle the child's cries. It is impossible to accomplish without the use of lubricants or with any degree of impotence."

Sadistic, bizarre or homicidal forms of child sexual abuse can occur but are extremely rare. Gebhard et al. (1965) report that out of their total of 18,000 interviews, no man or woman reported being victimized as a child by a sadist. Langevin (1983) states that sadistic behaviors in general are very rare and Tollison and Adams (1979) report that coprophilia (sexual interest in feces) and urophilia (sexual interest in urine) are quite rare and generally associated with other deviant behaviors.

Dietz, Hazelwood, and Warren (1990) reported a sample of 30 sexually sadistic criminals that included 43 percent who victimized one or more children. Sexual sadists are sexually aroused by controlling, terrorizing, injuring, torturing, and sometimes murdering their victims. Dietz et al. report that most victims were strangers to the offenders. This is different from other forms of child sexual abuse where the offender is more likely to be related to or to know the victim. Dietz et al. observe that cases of criminal sexual sadism occur so infrequently in a given jurisdiction that it is difficult for researchers to observe enough cases to make statistically meaningful observations about them.

Difficulties With Some Research Samples

Researchers often observe that, despite their efforts, a nonabused group may include subjects who were actually abused. But the reverse is also true and false allegations may contaminate samples of abused subjects. When reading research reports, the criteria used for verifying samples as abused or nonabused must be carefully noted.

We suspect that some widely cited research on child sexual abuse is contaminated by false cases. This research will therefore give a misleading picture about the characteristics of child sexual abuse, including the type of abusive behaviors. An example of this is the report by Finkelhor and his colleagues (Finkelhor, Williams, and Burns 1988; Finkelhor, Williams,

Burns, and Kalinowski 1988) on 270 day-care cases. Finkelhor et al. report that 40 percent of the perpetrators were intelligent, educated, highly regarded women who had no histories of known deviant behavior. These women were accused of extremely deviant behaviors such as oral-genital penetration, urolagia and coprophagia, and ritualistic mass abuse.

There are serious difficulties with the Finkelhor et al. day-care study. Although the authors required the abuse to be "substantiated," their criterion of substantiation was simply that any one of the people assigned to investigate the report believed the abuse was real, despite whoever else may have thought it was false. Their sample includes an indeterminate number of cases which ended in dismissals or acquittals, or convictions that were later reversed. For example, the McMartin case in California and the Kelly Michaels case in New Jersey are included. No conclusions whatsoever can be drawn about the abusive behaviors alleged to have occurred in this study.

Another instance in which researchers have included likely false cases of abuse in their sample is found in the 1993 book, *Behind the Playground Walls,* by Waterman et al. The book describes an ambitious research project on the effects of alleged sexual abuse in two preschools compared to a control group of preschool children who had not been abused. One of the abused groups was said to have experienced ritualistic sexual abuse and these children were reported to have suffered much more distress than the nonritualistically abused children.

However, the ritualistic abuse group is comprised of subjects in preschool cases, mainly McMartin, where there were no convictions and where there is at the very least a serious question whether any child was actually abused. Therefore, the book is useless for describing anything other than the probable effects on children who become involved in these cases and may come to believe they were victims of ritualistic abuse (see Schultz and Wakefield 1993 for a more detailed examination of this book).

These studies then find their way into review articles where generalizations are made. For example, Kendall-Tackett, Williams, and Finkelhor (1993) reviewed and synthesized recent research on the impact of sexual abuse, including the characteristics of the abusive behavior, and included the above two studies in their review with no cautions or caveats. Their review was published in the *Psychological Bulletin*, a major APA journal. This contamination of the literature on sexual abuse with uncorroborated cases of improbable and bizarre abuse is a significant problem.

Our Study

We conducted a preliminary descriptive study to examine the kinds of behaviors alleged when the abuse allegations were most likely false. We looked at the behaviors alleged in two entirely different samples and compared the results to the types of behaviors engaged in by actual child molesters as is described above. We hypothesized that the behaviors alleged in these two samples would differ from those found in cases of actual child sexual abuse.

False Memory Syndrome Foundation Sample

Sample

This sample was taken from the questionnaire project from the False Memory Syndrome Foundation which we described in Chapter 3. In this project, lengthy questionnaires were sent to people whose adult children have accused them of childhood sexual abuse, following alleged recovery of long-lost memories. Subjects are people who responded to newspaper articles or other media presentations in several cities about the FMS Foundation. Questionnaires were sent to samples of callers who reported that their adult child had recently recovered a memory of repressed sexual abuse that the caller denies.[1]

---

[1] See Chapter 3 for a further description of the questionnaire project.

The sample of questionnaires used in the present study are 398 surveys that were mailed out at various times beginning in February, 1992 and were returned as of July 1993.[2] All of the families deny that the abuse happened. There has been no effort to make an independent determination of the veracity of the denial.

Procedure

As we described in Chapter 3, the questionnaires gathered a wide range of information. For the present study the portions of the questionnaire that were used were whether the accusing child was male or female, the age of the accusing child during the period of the alleged abuse, and whether the allegations were against mother, father, both mother and father, siblings, grandparents, or other (if 'other,' the respondent was asked to explain). Respondents were asked to describe the abuse allegations that had been made and were also asked specifically if the allegations included satanic cult or ritualistic abuse.

The open-ended question asking for the specific accusations was coded according to the abusive behaviors described. Three researchers and two assistants went through the cases and discussed the definitions and criteria until this question could be coded reliably.

Results

Of the adult children making the allegations, 93 percent were females. Table 4 indicates the age the accusing adult child maintains the abuse began. In 84 of the questionnaires the respondent did not know or respond or gave a nonspecific response such as 'very young' so the 314 cases with a specific response were used to calculate the percentages.

The abuse typically was said to have begun at a very young

---

[2] This sample is larger than the one used for the analysis in Chapter 3, because subsequent to the original analysis, a further sample of returned questionnaires was analyzed for this project.

TABLE 4 FMSF Questionnaire Sample: Age the Accusing Adult Child Claims Abuse Started N = 314

Age Range	N	
0 > age < 1	41	(13%)
1 > age < 2	51	(16%)
2 > age < 3	56	(18%)
3 > age < 4	50	(16%)
4 > age < 5	33	(11%)
5 > age < 6	30	(10%)
6 > age < 7	16	(5%)
7 > age < 8	7	(2%)
8 > age < 9	10	(3%)
9 > age < 10	4	(1%)
10 and above	16	(5%)

age. For 29 percent (92) of the cases, the alleged events began at under age 2. For 55 percent (169), the alleged events began from age 2 to 6. Only in 16 percent (53) did the alleged events first happen at age 6 or older. The median age for the age the accusing child claims the abuse began is between age 3 and 4.

Table 5 indicates the person accused.

Although fathers were usually the ones accused, mothers were often accused along with the fathers. In one third of the cases, a variety of other persons were accused, most often along

TABLE 5 FMSF Questionnaire Sample: Person Accused   N = 398

Person Accused	N	
Father only	244	(61%)
Mother only	6	(3%)
Both Mother and Father	113	(28%)
Siblings	50	(10%)
Grandparents	33	(15%)
Others	89	(22%)

with the parents. In a few cases, neither parent was accused and the accused was an uncle or other relative. But in most of the cases, others were accused along with the parents. This was especially likely in the cases where ritualistic cults were alleged.

Over half (203) of the respondents appeared to have little idea concerning just what it was they were alleged to have done and gave vague responses such as 'molesting,' 'sexual abuse,' or 'we have never been told.' But in the 195 cases where this information was known, the allegations included a very high proportion of extremely deviant and intrusive behaviors. Violence was alleged in 41 percent of the cases, rape in 44 percent, and witnesses to the abuse in 42 percent. There were 67 cases involving allegations of satanic ritual abuse, which is 34 percent of the cases where the respondents knew the nature of the allegations.

The percentages of behaviors alleged for the 195 cases are shown in Table 6.

Examples of the types of behaviors classified as highly deviant are:

1. Mother, father, and two babysitters forced her to sacrifice adults and children.
2. Incest by her father, two grandfathers, and one grandmother that included satanic rituals, murder, and child pornography.
3. Both grandmother and grandfather were involved in satanic rituals and sacrifices of animals and babies. Her father also abused her. Her siblings and mother were aware of this but have covered it up.
4. In addition to anal, oral, and vaginal intercourse, objects, such as knives, umbrellas, keys, and marbles, were inserted in her vagina.
5. Satanic ritualistic abuse by adults including mother, father, and maternal grandmother. Mother is the head cult priestess in the state. Her brother is the Anti-Christ. She was raped by Satan and had a child by Satan.
6. Satanic ritual abuse by her grandmother which was observed by her mother.
7. Mother put her on a table under a light and stuck things in her

TABLE 6   FMSF Questionnaire Sample:
Behaviors Alleged N = 398

Vague, Don't Know, Not answered, 'Sexual Abuse,' or 'Molesting'	203	(51%)
Mentioned Specific Behaviors	195	(49%)

Behaviors Alleged in the 195 Cases That
Mentioned Specific Behaviors

Fondling	50	(26%)
Masturbation and/or exposure	16	(8%)
Digital penetration	10	(5%)
Oral sex	104	(53%)
Vaginal penetration	40	(21%)
Anal penetration	31	(16%)
Rape	86	(44%)
Forced abortions by parent	8	(4%)
Violence involved	80	(41%)
Murder	16	(8%)
Witnesses or others involved	81	(42%)
Satanic ritual abuse	67	(34%)
Highly deviant behaviors	83	(43%)

genitals while her father held her down. Her father raped her and knocked her unconscious when she tried to stop him from raping her sister. Parents cut up animals and held the children's hands in the blood.

8. Father abused her from infancy while mother watched. Raped by older brother, uncles, and grandfather. Satanically abused by grandmother. Father and uncle were involved in pornography, murder, and prostitution.

9. Abused in satanic abuse where she was tied up, raped orally, rectally, and vaginally, and strangled until she lost consciousness.

10. Father, mother, and grandparents abused her in satanic rituals

while wearing hooded black robes. Forced to drink urine and blood. Raped by grandfather while grandmothers and mother watched. Hung by her heels. Abused with a hot poker, freezer, and washer wringer.

11. Group sex with father and stepmother and siblings. Beaten with bow and arrow and razors. Father attempted to drown her.

12. Murdered and dismembered young boys and buried the bodies in the State park.

13. Forced to have sex with a neighbor's dog and subsequently had a baby that was half dog.

14. Forced to have sex with her uncle and a dog. Head put in vice and when she screamed, a penis was put in her mouth. Raped by someone wearing a mask.

15. Beaten, raped, burned with cigarettes, thrown outside naked, given pills by her father and mother in an attempt to murder her.

16. Raped by father and uncle. Father performed an abortion on her in the coal bin with her two brothers helping.

17. Repeated episodes of rape, oral sex, beatings, hands tied to bed, torture with a coca cola bottle, and clothespins put on her breasts and clitoris.

18. Older sister held her down, blindfolded her, while father ejaculated into her mouth.

19. Father anally raped her and then rubbed her feces on her back. After he got her pregnant he performed a home abortion on her while laughing at her pain. Aunt, mother, and friend abused her. Father tried to drown her. The doctor, who reported that he found no abortion scars, was involved in a conspiracy to discredit her.

20. Mother tied her to the kitchen table, threatened her with a knife, and forced her to perform oral sex on her.

21. Father forced him to eat semen from a rusty pipe.

22. Father tied her, while naked, spread-eagled to an iron bed and placed a dead squirrel on her chest.

23. Raped by father, mother approved. Gang raped by older brother while younger brother watched and laughed. Molested by pastor. Raped by grandfather.

24. All family members were in a satanic cult. The mother was the high priestess. Was chosen as a 'breeder.' The cult engaged in murder and cannibalism.

25. Was forced to watch the murder of three women, including one cut up and put through a meat grinder at an uncle's meat market.

26. Satanic cult abuse including father, mother, and grandfather. Was taken to a ritual sacrifice by a lady in a green car. Was demon-possessed and exorcised. Father has multiple personalities.

27. Abused in a satanic cult that included mother and father, father's attorney, and the cantor of the synagogue.

28. Abused by mother, father, stepmother, siblings, and grandparents in a satanic cult. Mother was a breeder. She was forced to deliver and kill 12th child borne by mother. Babies were kidnapped and killed. Maternal grandmother was a witch. Weddings to Satan.

29. Abused by mother, father, and parents' friends. Forced to defecate on religious objects and smeared with excrement. Forced to simulate copulation with dead and dying babies and siblings. Forced to strap on a dildo and have intercourse with mother and female guests while men sat her on their penises. When she became pregnant by her father, she was forcibly aborted and the baby was stabbed to death.

30. Abused by mother, father, grandparents, brother, teacher, and father's business associates. Taken to witches' house where people in cages were eaten. Tortured by electric shock and thumbscrews, and made to walk on hot coals and glass. A man was shot and an old lady hanged.

31. Abused by mother, father, strangers, blind uncle, nursery school teacher, and others. Abuse included violent rape, rape with scissors, killing babies, worshipping Satan, eating ears and other organs, and being sold into child prostitution.

32. Abused by father, mother, grandparents, brother, and brother's friends. The abuse included torture, guns, knives, electrodes, carrots, chicken parts and water hoses in bath by mother, anal and vaginal rape and fish hooks in vagina by father. Raped by brother and his friends. Impregnated and forced to have four abortions. Placed in small boxes with dog feces and semen.

33. Satanic cult included parents and family friends who are also members of the KKK. Six adults molested 13 children. Killed cats and made them drink blood. Tied hands and legs and beat her and put crochet hooks in her vagina. Also abused grandchildren.

Divorce and Custody Archival Sample

Sample

The sample in this group was from 216 cases involving sexual abuse allegations during divorce and custody we had seen in our forensic practice from 1984 through 1991. The purpose of this archival research project was to examine the characteristics of these cases.

We analyzed 216 cases of sexual abuse allegations involving 325 children. We classified the cases into three groups—'abuse likely true,' 'no abuse probable,' and 'cannot determine'—on the basis of our judgment after reviewing the file. In the 'abuse likely true' group, in addition to our judgment, either the accused admitted the abuse or the justice system determined the abuse was real.

The 'no abuse likely' group was further subdivided according to the determination of the justice system. The group used for analysis here was the sample of 134 cases where we classified the group as 'no abuse probable' *and* where the justice system resulted in either no conviction in criminal court or a determination of no abuse in family court. Although in research in this area there is always the question of purity of groups, we believed this stringent criteria would result in a relatively pure group where the allegations were most likely to be false.

This sample is not random, since it came from cases where we were asked by attorneys to evaluate and consult on the case. We are therefore unlikely to see cases where the accused admits the abuse since such cases are apt to result in a guilty plea without the retention of experts. We are also less likely to see cases where the allegation is retracted or determined to be unfounded by child protection.

Procedure

H.W. reviewed the material available in the case files and recorded the information using forms developed by both of us. We examined variables such as the sex and age of the child, the origin and timing of the disclosure, the type of any reported physical evidence, the nature of the investigation, the type and quality of the evidence used by investigators, the personality characteristics and behavior of the parties involved, the nature of the allegations, and the characteristics of the interviews and of the child's statement. In addition, we rated the skill of the attorney who handled the case. The information was then entered into a computer for tabulation.

For this particular study, we looked at the sex and age of the child at the time the abuse was said to have occurred, who was accused, and the nature of the sexually abusive behaviors alleged.

Results

There were a total of 196 children involved in the 134 cases classified as no abuse probable. Of these 72 percent were girls and 28 percent were boys.

Table 7 indicates the age of the child at the time the abuse was alleged to have first occurred.

The abuse was said to have begun at a very young age, although not as young as in the FMS Foundation recovered memory sample. For 5 percent (10) of the cases, the alleged events began at under age 2. For 67 percent (131), the alleged events began from age 2 to 6. Only in 28 percent (55) did the alleged events first happen at age 6 or older. The median age for the age the abuse was said to have began is 4.6.

Most of the accused were the fathers or stepfathers of the children, although six women were also accused (5 mothers and 1 stepmother). There were also 2 grandparents and 4 boy-friends. Of the total accused, only 4 percent were females, which is consistent with what is known about actual sexual abuse, where the offenders are overwhelmingly male.

Table 8 indicates the types of behaviors alleged.

The allegations included a very high proportion of extreme-ly deviant and intrusive behaviors compared to cases of actual abuse. Violence was alleged in 22 percent of the cases, others involved or witnesses to the abuse in 11 percent, and highly deviant behaviors in 18 percent, including 5 cases of satanic

TABLE 7 Divorce and
Custody No Abuse Probable
Sample: Age the Abuse was
Alleged to Have Occurred
N = 196

Age Range	N	
0 > age < 2	10	(5%)
2 > age < 3	27	(14%)
3 > age < 4	39	(20%)
4 > age < 5	40	(20%)
5 > age < 6	25	(13%)
6 > age < 7	17	(9%)
7 > age < 8	9	(5%)
8 > age < 9	9	(5%)
9 > age < 10	4	(2%)
10 and above	16	(8%)

ritual abuse allegations. Although fondling was alleged in almost half of the cases, in only 18 percent was this all that was alleged.

Examples of the types of behaviors classified as highly deviant are:

1. The father brutally raped and beat the girl four nights in a row; the brother (on a separate occasion) put his entire fist up her vagina while wearing a mask and a Raggedy Ann costume.
2. The father put toys into the child's vagina.
3. The father put objects in the child's vagina, threatened to burn her on the stove, and engaged in sexual activities involving a dog.
4. The father pushed a shovel into the child's private parts.
5. The father pushed a spoon handle into the two girls' vaginas, put Q-tips down their noses and throats, hit and bit them, and defecated on them. The father wore the mother's blue nightgown, held the children upside down naked and made them walk on their hands while blindfolded outside in the back yard.
6. The children were orally and anally abused in a hot tub with several people while photographs were taken.
7. A knife was inserted into the child's genitals.

TABLE 8   Divorce and Custody No Abuse
Probable Sample: Abusive Behaviors Alleged
N = 119*

Behaviors Alleged	N	
Fondling only	22	(18%)
Fondling included	57	(48%)
Masturbation and/or exposure	7	(6%)
Made child touch adult's genitals	8	(7%)
Touched child's genitals with penis	4	(3%)
Digital penetration	34	(29%)
Oral sex, either to or by child	39	(33%)
(Oral sex to child)	29	(22%)
(Made child perform oral sex)	19	(16%)
Vaginal penetration	21	(18%)
Anal penetration	20	(17%)
Objects paced in vagina or anus	11	(9%)
Other people included	13	(11%)
Violence involved	26	(22%)
Satanic ritual abuse	5	(4%)
Highly deviant behaviors	23	(19%)

* In 15 of the total 134 cases in this category, the
behavior alleged was unknown so this analysis is only for
the 119 cases where the specific behavior alleged was
available.

8. The father made the child lick his genitals clean, knocked her off the bed, made her climb trees, and poked her with a stick that looked like a sword.

9. The father stuck marbles and sticks in the child's vagina, licked her pee pee and then cut it up and threw it away.

10. The father and his girlfriend were in a satanic ritualistic cult. One night the father and his girlfriend entered the children's house while the mother slept downstairs. The father had a knife and forced the children to drink his urine and to drink blood while the girlfriend defecated on the floor. Urine was then poured in their hair and they were forced to eat the feces. The father and girlfriend then left the house without awakening the mother.

11. The father defecated on the child.

12. Cats were involved in the sexual activities that included anal and vaginal penetration.
13. The child's penis was removed from his body, put in the father's mouth, and then superglued back on.
14. The child was abused in satanic rituals. The father took him through the woods to a Halloween dance with naked men. A robot bear ripped off the legs and arms of a man and all of the boys had to eat human flesh. Photographs were taken during this.
15. The father dug up dead bodies and dismembered them with a chain saw.
16. The father, wearing blue earrings, a pink dress, and a wig, scratched the child's pee pee while wearing pink press-on fingernails. The grandmother was in the house during this time. The abuse took place in the bathroom which had a secret passage.
17. The father called the children names and struck and laughed at them during the abuse. He put a dog collar and chain around one girl's neck and a wooden spoon up her crotch. A woman and the children's grandfather were involved in the abuse. One girl was forced to bite the other girl's crotch.
18. The child was anally raped by the father while the father's girlfriend held her down. Then, he urinated on her and they placed a lighted candle into her vagina.
19. Two children were subjected to an ritual orgy with five people, including the elderly grandparents. The children were urinated on during the abuse, and were forced to drink urine out of a baby bottle and to eat poopy sandwiches.
20. The father regularly subjected his two girls to ritual abuse. The children were tied to specially constructed 'chain boards' and then abused by the father and the father's girlfriend. The father kept extra chain boards at different locations. Photographs were taken. They attended a satanic church where the adults wore devil costumes and the children were forced to eat mouse stew during a satanic feast.
21. The mother took the child to satanic rituals involving several adults. During the abuse, the adults wore blue diapers into which they urinated. Photographs were taken.
22. The father pulled one child's hair, locked the children in the freezer, put guns to their heads, put his penis into their mouths, urinated on them, forced them to have sex with each other,

swung the boy by his penis, put a child's head in the toilet, gave the children drugs, put sticks up their anus, and threatened them with a gun. This was sometimes done with others present.

23. The father rubbed a magic pink lotion on the child and then hit her with a hammer and attacked her with pliers.

Differences between True and Bogus Abuse Allegations

There are substantial differences between both of our samples and the sexual behaviors reported by researchers in cases where the abuse is most likely true.

In both the divorce and custody and in the FMS Foundation samples, the abuse is said to have begun at a much younger age than is found in cases of actual abuse. Although some very young children are abused, most victims are not preschoolers. The literature indicates that the average age is between 6 and 12. But in the divorce and custody sample the median age the abuse was alleged to have begun was between 4 and 5 and only in 28 percent was it at age 6 and older. In the FMS Foundation sample, 29 percent claimed to have first been abused at under age 2 and only 16 percent said the abuse began at age 6 and older. The median age was between 3 and 4.

Given the information on infant amnesia, is it highly unlikely that actual events from such young ages would be accurately recalled. Adults and older children do not usually remember incidents from their lives that happen prior to age 3 or 4 (Eisenberg 1985; Fivush and Hamond 1990; Howe and Courage 1993; Loftus 1993; Nelson 1993; Nelson and Ross 1980; Pillemer and White 1989; Wetzler and Sweeney 1986). Although Usher and Neisser (1993) recently reported that some events can be remembered from age 2, there is no indication that people can remember from birth to 2, as was alleged in 29 percent of the FMS Foundation sample. This inability to recall events from an early age is a function of the normal process of growth and development. The phenomenon of infantile or childhood amnesia means that claims of remembering abuse that occurred at a very early age are suspect.

Whereas real abuse almost always takes place in secret with no witnesses or accomplices, both of these samples included a large proportion where others were alleged to have either witnessed or participated in the abuse. This was true for two-fifths of the FMS Foundation sample and one-tenth of the divorce and custody sample.

The behaviors alleged in both the divorce and custody sample and the FMS Foundation sample differ in substantial ways from what has been reported about the behavior of actual abusers. The behaviors described in both of these groups are much more unusual, intrusive, and deviant than has been found in cases of verified abuse. One in five cases in the divorce and custody sample and two in five in the FMS Foundation sample included such behaviors. Many of the purported behaviors are impossible or completely unbelievable and others have such low base rates that the probability of their actually occurring in a given instance becomes extremely small.

Allegations of satanic ritual abuse were found in 5 (4 percent) of the divorce and custody sample and in 67 (34 percent)[3] of the FMS Foundation sample. The large proportion of satanic ritual abuse allegations reflects the media attention to such allegations and has been seen in allegations in day care and other cases. Preliminary data from a survey by The American Bar Association indicated that approximately one fourth of local prosecutors have handled cases involving "ritualistic or satanic abuse" (Victor 1993a).

In only half of the FMS Foundation sample had the accused parents been given any details about what they were supposed to have done and the percentages were calculated only on the

---

[3] This is a higher percentage than has been reported elsewhere on this research (Wakefield and Underwager 1992a, 1992b). The reason is that in the present analysis, the percentages were calculated only on the 195 questionnaires where the respondents were able to give specific information about the nature of the allegations. If the percentage is calculated using the entire sample of 398 questionnaires, it is 17 percent.

half that reported specific information. It may be that the questionnaires where the response was too vague to code ('We've never been told just what we were supposed to have done,' 'You sexually abused me from ages 2 to 8,' 'You molested me.') include a high proportion of less deviant and extreme behaviors. But even if this were to prove to be the case, the proportions of highly improbable and bizarre allegations in this sample would still be much greater than has been reported in cases of actual abuse.

Satanic Ritual Abuse Allegations

Sue Blume's (1990) assertions about satanic ritual abuse (SRA) are typical of the recovered memory therapists' beliefs:

Ritual abuse—also called cult abuse and Satanic abuse—is a phenomenon whose pervasiveness is only now becoming clear to those who deal with child sexual abuse. The chilling stories told by unrelated victims around the country are virtually identical. The truths of this abuse are so shocking to society that the victimizers are protected by our disbelief.

Forced by groups of perpetrators to participate in all forms of violence as part of an indoctrination into various ideologies, the victims are often told they have a bond with the devil which may be enforced through 'marriage' or other 'bridal' ceremonies. The child's ability to connect with positive loving 'higher power' is often destroyed. Ceremonies may include sacrifice of animals, human torture, or cannibalism; victims have been forced to participate in the rape or murder of another child.

Mind control is accomplished through brainwashing; for instance, the victim is trained to believe that were she to reveal the truth of her experience she would have to commit suicide. This does not result in the internal self-protective 'splitting' described elsewhere in this book; rather she is literally robbed of her ability to remember, and forced to think and act in certain ways. She totally loses control.

Indicators of a history of ritual abuse include night terrors, extreme fear and guilt; images of blood, dead babies, circles of people (often in robes and hoods, with chanting or repeated phrases); fear of God; unexplained scars; extreme negative associations or blocking out of certain places. Survivors will fear death when they begin to remember, and have (justified) paranoia. They often suffer extreme disassociation [sic], self-injury, psychosis, multiple personality disorder, self-hate. They may become sadistic or murder.

Their flashbacks and memories may represent an unwanted truth, but a truth nonetheless. Believe them. Help them to see that they are good and that there is hope. Be careful, and go slowly. Be aware that they struggle with despair, and that suicide is a real risk at certain states of healing. And seek out the experts. (p. 60)

The evidence for satanic ritual abuse conspiracies comes from two main sources—the reports from survivors and their therapists of 'repressed' memories uncovered during therapy, and allegations involving young children, primarily in day-care cases, such as McMartin. These two different sources are used to bolster one another.

In cases involving young children, satanic ritual abuse is usually alleged to occur in a multi-perpetrator, multi-victim situation, such as the day-care setting. However, some children, in the divorce/custody battle of parents, produce descriptions of abuse said to be satanic and ritualistic. We have also been involved in cases where both parents were accused of ritual abuse with their own children.

Whether such allegations are true has been hotly debated in the professional community. There are some who believe there is a world-wide conspiracy of satan worshipers who sexually molest and torture untold numbers of children in bizarre and sadistic rituals (Blume 1990; Cozolino 1989; Fredrickson 1992; Friesen 1992; Ritual Abuse Task Force 1989; Ryder 1992; Shaffer and Cozolino 1992; Summit 1984, 1990). Similar allegations of satanic ritualistic abuse have surfaced in England, Holland, Australia, and New Zealand. Many of the recovered memory therapists and MPD experts believe in satanic cult abuse.

There are others, including us, who openly look upon belief in a world-wide satanic conspiracy as nonsense. The skeptics see the claims as resulting from collective hysteria or rumor panics, as similar to the UFO sightings, or as an example of urban legends that may be firmly believed but are false (for instance Balch and Gilliam 1991; Best 1991; Ellis 1992; Nathan 1991; Victor 1993a).

The skeptics point out that there have been no findings of physical evidence corroborating the claims of satanic cults, human sacrifice, orgies, or a widespread conspiracy. Despite hundreds of investigations by the F.B.I. and police, there is no independent evidence of ritual abuse, animal and human sacrifice, murder, and cannibalism of thousands of children by a conspiracy of apparently normal adults who are functional and organized enough to leave no trace of their activities (Hicks 1991; Lanning 1991, 1992; Putnam 1991b; Richardson, Best, and Bromley 1991; Underwager and Wakefield 1991; Victor 1993a; Wakefield and Underwager 1992a, 1992b, 1992c). In addition, contrary to the claims of the believers, historians do not find any evidence that satanic cults practicing a black mass, cannibalism, ritual murder, worship of Satan, and the sacrifice of children have ever existed (Noll 1989).

It is surely impossible for a conspiracy as complex, including as many people, and engaging in such extreme acts, to continue without someone talking about it. Groups that actually engage in secret rituals and commit murders and violence, such as the Mafia and the Ku Klux Klan, are known very quickly because there are corpses, and someone talks. In addition, conspiracy requires elaborate organization. Hicks (1991) comments about one instance of an alleged satanic cult:

> Further, in order to organize the events in which Smith participated, the Satanists must have shown skills of conference planning: obtaining snakes, making robes, arranging for members to give believable excuses to stay away from their jobs, ensuring no witnesses, arranging with cemeteries to exhume bodies, having effigies made, nabbing babies for sacrifice, efficiently cleaning up sacrificial messes, and so on. Yet no one could verify any of the details. (p. 144)

These arguments, however, do not deter those who believe

in the satanic cult conspiracy. Mayer (1991, pp. 261–62) lists
some of the arguments between the skeptics and the believers.
For example, in response to questions about the lack of remains
of supposedly murdered children, the believers reply that the
children were cremated or dissolved in acid or consumed in
cannibalistic rites. When confronted with the lack of any
forensic evidence, such as blood stains, the believers observe
that satanists are extremely careful. When told that the numbers of missing children killed according to the survivors'
accounts greatly exceeds the estimates of missing children, the
believers say that the cults keep breeders whose babies' births
were not recorded and that other babies were imported from
third-world countries.

The fact that patients all over the country are telling similar
tales of ritual abuse is seen as the most compelling evidence for
the reality of widespread satanic cults. This, of course, ignores
the fact that there is an extensive network of believing therapists who regularly interact with one another (Hicks 1991;
Mulhern 1991, 1992; Victor 1993a). This network extends
world-wide. In England, Christy and Walton (1990) note that
the allegations there can be traced to workshops and seminars
conducted by Americans claiming expertise in satanic ritualistic
abuse. Mulhern (1992) systematically analyzes 14 satanic cult/
ritual abuse training seminars held between 1987 and 1990 and
concludes that these seminars are focussed on converting the
participants to an uncritical belief in the realities of such cults
(see Chapter 5 for our discussion of Mulhern's research). When
therapists are in touch with one another, they are apt to ask
similar questions and therefore elicit similar stories in their
patients. Contributing to this is the widespread media attention
to satanic ritual abuse.

Unfortunately, many professionals and lay people believe in
the satanic cult myth. Bottoms, Shaver and Goodman (1991)
surveyed clinical psychologists and report that 93 percent of
those who had seen cases of ritual or religious abuse believed
the ritual abuse was true. Schutte (in press) conducted a mock
jury study in which the repressed memory scenarios were
identical except that one involved satanic ritual abuse while the

other only involved incest. The mean age of the mock jurors was 21.6. Although most (71.7 percent) verdicts were for the defendant in both versions, there were no significant differences in the number of plaintiff verdicts for the satanic ritual abuse case compared to the incest case. This is likely to reflect the fact that many media presentations have presented satanic ritual abuse as true. Schutte speculates that the wide dissemination of satanic ritual themes in books, movies, and television may have especially affected their young subjects.

There are disturbed people who abuse and murder children. The disturbance may sometimes include unusual religious ideas and an obsession with strange rituals. Some of these people may abuse a child in a bizarre and sadistic fashion. This may sometimes look like a satanic ritual, a possibility that becomes more probable given the current media attention and publicity. But there is no empirical evidence supporting the belief that there are widespread satanic cults which ritually abuse and torture children.

Conclusions

When therapists are unaware of the usual behavior of child molesters, or do not consider base rates, they may wrongly conclude that a highly unlikely allegation is true. The recovered memory therapists appear to be simply unaware of the typical behavior of actual sexual abusers. But this information is necessary in evaluating uncorroborated abuse claims. If the allegations do not fit what is known about verified abuse or if they include bizarre, improbable behaviors, they are most likely false. This is especially true when memory of the abuse was supposedly repressed and later recovered. The types of allegations found in many of the recovered memory cases simply are not plausible when compared to what we know about actual sexual abuse.

Chapter Eleven
When Memories are Real

> *You cannot play with the ani-*
> *mal in you without becoming*
> *wholly animal, play with false-*
> *hood without forfeiting your*
> *right to truth, play with cruelty*
> *without losing your sensitivity*
> *of mind. He who wants to keep*
> *his garden tidy doesn't reserve*
> *a plot for weeds.*
>
> Dag Hammarskjold

All mental health professionals know that sexual abuse is real and tragically common. Even if the lowest estimates of preva- lence and incidence are accepted as the most accurate, this still translates into thousands of children who are sexually abused each year. This means that large numbers of adults were sexually abused as children.

Most adults who were abused as children have always remembered the abuse, although they may never have talked about it. As we mentioned in Chapter 6, however, some sexually abusive experiences may be deliberately ignored, not thought about for years, or simply forgotten. When the child was not frightened or traumatized by the abuse, it may have been forgotten in the same way that countless other unpleasant childhood events were forgotten. With an appropriate cue, the person may remember the abuse. We believe that forgetting is unlikely to occur when the abuse was intrusive and highly distressing and traumatic—abuse in such cases will normally not be forgotten.

The following is a case of forgotten abuse that was later remembered:

> Cathy's parents were divorced when she was a preschooler and her father had custody of her and her older brother. Her father remarried when she was six and she lived with her brother, father, stepmother, and stepsister, Lisa, who was a year older than she was. When she was 16, Cathy began seeing a therapist for depression. Cathy felt her stepmother was overly critical and she was thinking of living with her biological mother and stepfather who were pressuring her to do so. The stepfather and mother, however, both had problems, and Cathy wasn't sure what she wanted to do. She felt trapped in the continuing conflicts between her biological parents as well as distressed by difficulties in her relationships with her family. Sexual abuse was not discussed in the therapy sessions.
>
> After she had been in therapy approximately a year, Cathy received a letter she had written to herself as part of a fifth-grade class assignment. The assignment had been for the children to write letters to themselves describing their current life and predicting what they would be doing in five years. They put the letters in envelopes and the teacher mailed them five years later. Cathy's letter said:
>
> *Dear Cathy,*
>
> *Hi, how's life? Right now I'm fine and busy and very happy. Fifth grade is nice and my teacher is nice too. . . . Maria is my best friend. She has been since kindergarten. I like her a lot, she's very nice. I don't want to get married, no kids, or car, I can use a bike. It would be more fun anyways. I hate boys this year. I got married to Tom Smith and had a kid and got divorced 5 months later. I like Prince.*

P.S. Today Lisa told our social worker that Daddy was sexually abusing us. I'm very scared.

Cathy was extremely upset by this letter as she had not thought about the abuse in years. A few days later she was hospitalized with significant distress, which was verified by an MMPI she took at this time. When she was discharged from the hospital she moved in with her mother where she continued therapy.

Although the letter stated that the teacher and social worker had been told about the abuse, no report had been made to child protection. With the support of her mother, Cathy filed a civil lawsuit against the school for failure to report as well as a lawsuit against her father.

This case had corroboration beyond the letter. As part of the lawsuit, the teacher and the social worker were deposed. Although the social worker had no records or recollection of the event, the teacher remembered that, following a *Good Touch Bad Touch* program, Cathy came into her room and told her that her father was touching her inappropriately. The teacher then talked to the social worker who spoke to the girls.

The abusive behavior was that Cathy's father took showers with Lisa and her, grabbed her buttocks when they wrestled and showered, walked around the house with no clothes on, and, when he kissed her good night, kissed her face, stroked her hair, sometimes stuck his tongue in her ear, and, on one occasion, tried to French kiss her.

Cathy's therapy was now focused on sexual abuse and she was eventually given the diagnosis of post-traumatic stress disorder because of the abuse, which was now interpreted as being the cause of all her problems. The medical records indicate that her adjustment became steadily worse. The civil suit was settled out of court.

What can be observed about this case? First, it is corroborated by the letter and the teacher's recollections in her formal deposition. Next, the abusive behaviors are not of highly intrusive, traumatic abuse. Cathy's father's behaviors were certainly inappropriate, but they can be understood as the types of events that, though troublesome and distressing at the time, could conceivably be put out of her mind and later forgotten. When the letter arrived, it gave Cathy a highly specific cue for recalling incidents that she had not thought about in five years. The abuse was not talked about in therapy until after she had received the letter she had written to herself.

The abuse was not the type of distressing and frightening event, such as a violent rape, needed for a concept of traumatic amnesia. Also, Cathy did not dissociate the abuse, rendering it unavailable to memory, since, after seeing the *Good Touch Bad Touch* program, she told her teacher about it.

Finally, the medical records suggest that the type of therapy received by Cathy after she had received the letter and remembered the abuse was not helpful to her. The abuse became the major focus of the therapy sessions and the medical records suggest that Cathy steadily became worse.

Partial Truth

Sometimes, there is childhood abuse that has always been remembered, but through therapy, new memories appear. An ambiguous or inappropriate but not clearly abusive situation can evolve into pseudomemories of sexual abuse. New people and new abuse can be added to memories for actual abuse. Lanning (1992), in his report of the F.B.I.'s investigations into ritual abuse allegations, concludes that, although there is no evidence for cults that engage in baby breeding, human sacrifice, and satanic conspiracies, "Some of what the victims allege may be true and accurate, some may be misperceived or distorted, some may be screened or symbolic, and some may be 'contaminated' or false" (p. 39).

Lynn Gondolf (1992), whose story we related in Chapter 4, also illustrates how false memories of abuse by her parents were added to memories of real abuse by an uncle:

When I entered therapy for my eating disorder we began to talk about the family dynamics. I told the therapist that, yes, I'd had some sexual abuse—that's the first thing he asked—by an uncle and that was well known in my family. My uncle is really sick. My family has known about it for years. It was not anything that I ever forgot. It was not any repressed memories.

But the therapist thought I wasn't showing enough emotion about the abuse by my uncle. However, I had all the feelings and pain of it but I had to live. I had to do day-to-day things. So, I didn't sit around and cry about it all the time. I think I dealt with it as well as anyone can. My family knew about most of it—it was no secret.

But once I got into therapy, the doctors said well, if your parents knew about the abuse they must have participated in it. And it wasn't just in the sense of they knew and let it happen. (My parents didn't know what happened at the actual time—they found out later.) Then they said things such as since you feel uncomfortable hugging your father, your father must have sexually abused you.

I was raised in a home that is sexually conservative . . . we were very conscious about appropriate sexual behavior and what my parents had led us to believe was appropriate and that there were certain things that were not. So if you had asked me if I felt uncomfortable hugging my dad, I would have said, 'Yeah, maybe, just like I do other people.'

I don't think there's anything my parents could have done differently that the therapists couldn't have interpreted as evidence that abuse happened. Once they're on that agenda, then anything you do can be twisted around to prove abuse. For example, the fact that I didn't like my mother washing my hair when I was eight or nine was seen as an indicator that my mother had done more than wash my hair in the bathtub. The fact that my parents moved a lot was also seen as a sign of abuse. The therapists believed this meant that my parents were afraid that people would find out about the abuse. The real truth is my parents never had enough money to pay the rent so they would get kicked out and move from house to house. That's the real truth.

But the fact that I wouldn't reveal the specifics was seen as a sign of my denial.

Eventually, after hearing all these interpretations, I began to believe that possibly my parents had been involved in something like this and even began to have almost visualizations of the incidents. I had been in the hospital only once. I had come in just with bulimia and some bleeding ulcers. And I did have serious eating disorders, no doubt about that. But I was also on eight different types of medications, psychiatric drugs that I'd never been on before. . . . Based on the fact that the therapist told me I'd suffered this traumatic sexual abuse, and I had from my uncle, that my father and his family had mental illness, that the MMPIs and different tests had showed this, I began to believe what he was saying.

The therapists twisted and distorted everything I thought I knew about my family and childhood. They told me that everything I knew for 20, 30, 40 years was wrong. These people that I loved, that I trusted, the values they had instilled in me as a child, were all garbage. I was taught that my family was really a bunch of satanic cult people who kill and eat babies and human flesh.

I began to believe the abuse by my parents was true. This was totally different than the situation with my uncle. When I said it about my father, the voice wasn't strong but there was a little voice inside there always doubted. But there was a lot of tears with it, too, and even today when I recall what I said or believed about what my dad might have done, it still hurts.

Civil Suits and the Statute of Limitations

If the adult survivor wants to sue her abuser years after the event, she will need to overcome the statute of limitations. Generally, the statutory time period begins to run when the event occurs. Having a statute of limitations protects people from having to defend themselves in court years later when memories have faded, witnesses have died, and evidence is lost. But the law recognizes that there are unusual circumstances, especially in medical malpractice. The usual example is that of a surgery patient who, years after the surgery, experiences pain and discovers that a sponge was left in his abdomen.

This principle has been generalized to that of 'repressed' sexual abuse. Several states have extended the statutory period of limitations in civil cases so that the statute of limitations does not begin until two or three years after the alleged abuse is remembered and/or after the claimant understands that the abuse caused injury (Bulkley and Horwitz 1994; Colaneri and Johnson 1992; Loftus 1993; Loftus and Rosenwald 1993; Slovenko 1993).

But if the abuse is always remembered, the statute of limitations is not extended and a civil suit is precluded. This may provide a powerful incentive for some people to claim repression for abuse they have always remembered. It is conceivable, in other words, that abuse may have occurred and the victim might lie about having forgotten it.

Although always remembered, the abuse may never have been discussed until the person entered therapy or was in some way motivated to talk about it. But if a lawsuit is seen as a possibility, the person *must* maintain that the abuse was completely repressed or dissociated. It must be claimed that the awareness of the abuse returned within the statutory period. We have no data on the frequency of such a scenario, but this possibility must be considered when there is a civil suit.

The following two examples are of corroborated and partially corroborated abuse where the veracity of the 'repression' is at issue:

- A man filed a civil suit against a priest on a recovered memory claim. The allegations were that the priest had abused the man several times a year. The abuse began with fondling when the man was 11 years old but then progressed to oral and then to anal sex. He was confused and troubled by this but accepted the priest's claim that they had a special relationship and were showing affection and love to each other. The abuse went on until the man left for college the fall after he graduated from high school. When he returned home for Christmas break three months later, the priest asked him to come for a visit, but the man refused.

Ten years later the man filed the civil suit. The priest admitted the abuse and fully corroborated the man's accounts. The man maintained that, although he recalled the abuse as it was occurring, by the time he returned home for Christmas, three months after the last episode of abuse, he had completely repressed all memories of the abuse. He said that the memories did not return until he was having difficulties in a relationship and was questioned about possible sexual abuse by his partner. He maintained that prior to this time, he had had no memories whatsoever of the abuse by the priest since he left for college. If he had always remembered the abuse, the statute of limitations would have precluded his lawsuit.

• A woman claimed to have been abused by a neighbor from the time she was 10 until she was 16. The alleged abuse began with fondling but then progressed to intercourse. She claimed to have no memories of the abuse until she was 27 and a friend, who knew what was happening, reminded her. The neighbor denied the earlier sexual activities but admitted having intercourse with her when she was 16. Such an act would not have been illegal in their state since 16 was the age of consent. After being reminded of the abuse by her friend, the woman sued her neighbor, claiming that she had no memories of the abuse, including the sexual intercourse, until talking to her friend. If she had always remembered the abuse, she could not have sued her neighbor because of the statute of limitations.

Can Mental Health Experts Tell Whether a Memory Is True or False?

Some memories are true, some are a mixture of fact and fantasy, and others are false. But mental health experts have no magic bullet enabling them to tell whether a given memory is true or is the product of imagination or fabrication. Nothing substitutes for external corroboration. In the absence of this, there is no way to reliably determine the historical truth of a claimed memory. Steele (1994) observes:

If a person says that something happened to him last night, or 20 years ago, he may be telling the truth, or lying, or mistaken. *Psychologists, psychiatrists, and other psychotherapists are no better able than you or I to determine which is the case.* Research has shown that therapists are actually rather poor at discriminating truth from falsehood. . . . However, there simply does not exist a body of technique which permits anybody to discern whether what someone says is the truth—beyond the well-known methods we may all adopt, such as trying to find independent corroboration, examining the story for plausibility and consistency, noticing whether related statements by the same person appear to be true, and so forth. (p. 40)

Despite these cautions, we nevertheless believe that psychologists can provide crucial information to the finder of fact in lawsuits involving memories of sexual abuse. Information about the nature of memory, the scientific status of the concepts used by the recovered memory therapists, the reliability and validity of techniques used, the nature of social influence and suggestibility, and the probabilities of the behaviors alleged are all necessary to evaluate such claims. Much of this information is not known or is seriously misunderstood by both lay people and uninformed professionals.

We know that real abuse can cause significant damage. We understand that real abuse may not be talked about until the victim is an adult. We know that real abuse that is not terribly distressing may be forgotten until the person is reminded in some way. There may be occasional instances of psychogenic amnesia for a single highly distressing incident, although this will be rare. But we are extremely skeptical of allegations involving satanic ritual abuse said to be remembered from infancy, and claims that repeated, traumatic abuse has been completely repressed only to be remembered years later.

Evaluating Claims of Recovered Memories for Civil Lawsuits

When a mental health professional becomes involved in a civil lawsuit involving recovered memories, it is necessary to get as much information as possible about the circumstances surrounding the disclosure and accusations. Daly and Pacifico (1991) suggest gathering the following information:

1. All medical, psychiatric, and school records of the person claiming abuse from childhood to the present.
2. Any information concerning relationships with peers, siblings and parents, or any childhood behavior problems of the person claiming abuse.
3. Any information concerning the sexual history of the person claiming abuse, including rapes, other childhood sexual abuse, abortions, etc.
4. The nature and origin of the disclosure, in as much detail and specificity as possible.
5. Information about any current problems or stresses in the life of the person claiming abuse.
6. The nature of any current therapy, e.g. whether techniques such as hypnosis and survivors' groups were used, the training and background of the therapist, and whether he or she specializes in treating MPD or 'recovered' abuse.
7. Any books, television shows, or workshops about sexual abuse or rape to which the person claiming abuse may have been exposed.
8. Any exposure to recovered memory cases though a highly publicized case in the media or through friends who may have reported that this happened to them.
9. The work history of the person claiming abuse, including any problems with supervisors or co-workers, especially any allegations of sexual harassment.
10. The psychological characteristics and social and family history of the accused adult(s), including any drug or alcohol use, sexual history, family relationships, and job history.
11. Any criminal record or prior behaviors in the accused adult which would support or undermine the credibility of the allegations.
12. A detailed description of the behaviors alleged to have occurred.
13. Possible ways by which the person making the accusation might benefit from or receive reinforcement from making the accusation (e.g. a civil lawsuit, an explanation for why life has not gone well, the expression of anger for perceived childhood injustices,

power over a dominant parent, attention, acceptance, new friends [in survivor group], etc.).

Some professionals have proposed ways of evaluating claims of alleged sexual abuse based on recently recovered memories. This is a new area, lacking in empirical research, so all such suggestions are based primarily on existing knowledge about such areas as memory, social influence, suggestibility, conformity, the psychotherapy process, hypnosis, and the characteristics and behavior of actual sexual abusers.

Gardner (1992a, 1992b)

Although Gardner believes that some accusations of recently recovered memories are true, he observes that others are false. He offers guidelines in terms of characteristics of cases that suggest they are false.

False accusations are often characterized by a strong need to bring the abuse to the attention of the public along with the belief that all of one's psychological problems come from the abuse. Gardner sees the women who make false allegations based on recovered memories as very angry, hostile, and sometimes paranoid. He believes that all will have demonstrated some type of psychopathology in earlier parts of their lives.

Gardner is harshly critical of the therapists who participate in the 'uncovering' of false memories of childhood abuse and sees them as incompetent and dangerous. He observes that they show no awareness of well-known facts and concepts in psychology, such as the nature of memory. Therefore, an indication that an allegation is likely false is the involvement of an inadequately trained or incompetent therapist who specializes in uncovering repressed abuse and who finds abuse in the majority of his or her patients.

An important guideline for Gardner for ascertaining the truth or falsity of an allegation of recently remembered abuse is the length of time over which the alleged abuse took place—the longer the period of abuse, the less the likelihood of its being repressed. Repression at age six or seven of events that occurred over a two- or three-year period is more credible than the repression of events that took place from ages two to 18. The age at which the abuse is said to have stopped is another factor. Although one may forget events that took place when one was about five, it is less credible that memory experiences taking place during the teen years have been completely obliterated. Gardner adds that an accusation is more likely to be false if the individual showed no observable symptoms of the abuse during the time the abuse supposedly took place.

Memories uncovered with the use of hypnosis run the risk of being false, especially since individuals who are good candidates for hypnotherapy are more suggestible. Another hallmark of a false accusation is the inclusion in the allegations of preposterous and even impossible events. Also, the failure to see the alleged perpetrator and get his input reflects the therapist's overdetermined bias and therefore strongly suggests a false accusation. An important indicator of a false accusation for Gardner is when the accuser cuts off contact with those who don't believe the accusation and surrounds herself only with 'enablers,' such as support groups, therapists, survivor groups, and friends and relatives who support and encourage the accusations.

Rogers (1994, in press)
Rogers discusses clinical assessment methods for evaluating claims of traumatic memories and describes factors hypothesized to be associated with valid or invalid complaints. Her focus is on civil litigation and in her 1992 paper she describes several actual cases to illustrate her observations. She notes that, despite the lack of empirical data, there are some commonsense clues and observations that can be helpful.

In evaluating a case for litigation, an important consideration is whether the claimant is a *bona fide* patient or is in treatment for reasons other than pain or dysfunction. Rogers describes a case in which the individual entered therapy at the time her financial resources were depleted and decided on a lawsuit soon afterwards. The woman's psychological testing suggested malingering and the cousin she recovered abuse memories about was the only person in her extended family who was comparatively well off.

The claim is more likely to be true when the testing and presenting symptoms are consistent with the claim. Although no single pattern of symptoms is uniquely attributable to sexual abuse, the claim is less likely to be true when the symptoms and test results appear inconsistent, feigned, and exaggerated.

Abuse is more likely to be true if the abuse memories have always been present as opposed to surfacing during therapy. Rogers, however, believes that there may be legitimate cases in which memories return in therapy after being shoved aside for years. In those examples she has seen that appeared to be valid, the therapist did not use intrusive techniques such as hypnosis, body work, emotional regression, repeated probing, or directed reading about abuse, and the individual was not placed in group treatment until the abuse had already been fully detailed and documented. Also, the knowledge and training of the therapist is important. If the therapist is aware of the possibility of therapeutic influence and has guarded against it, has focussed on broader issues other than a purely sexual abuse focus, has used validated techniques and kept adequate records, and conducted a careful history of the patient, the recovered memory is more likely to be credible.

When the memory is suddenly recalled, the specifics of the situation which 'triggered' the recall are important. In a memory of a real event, the trigger is apt to be specific and reminiscent of the environment at the time the abuse was occurring. In real cases, the individual can discriminate the source of this recall from potential suggestive influences such as fantasies, dreams, and input from others. Rogers also believes that individuals who are fantasy-prone personalities or 'Grade 5' (highly hypnotizable) are more likely to be suggestible.

Memories that are inconsistent with verifiable abuse, such as memories from infancy, past lives, space abductions, and satanic ritual abuse are unlikely to be of real events. If there are significant changes in the core accounts of the memory over time, the changes may be the result of current influences and the credibility of the recall is less.

False or exaggerated claims are much more likely to portray the alleged perpetrator as a totally bad person who used force and engaged in sadistic activities. True claims show more balance and ambivalence.

Descriptions of the abuse incidents in false claims may be much more sparse and lacking in details compared to other memories during the same time period. However, some claimants evidence extremely detailed, highly elaborated accounts —accounts that are far more detailed than other events purported to have occurred during the same or earlier time periods. These detailed accounts characteristically lack any contextual embedding or information about related events— other things that happen before, during, or after the key events in question. These individuals seemed to have been more deeply involved in survivors' groups and recovery programs, and to have done extensive reading as well as journal-writing, with its attendant introspective processing.

Rogers stresses that there are no proven indicators that discriminate historically accurate from false memories, indicators that meet the rules of evidence in court. Her observations come from limited laboratory experience, field study evidence, and her experience and therefore should be used cautiously and conservatively.

Wakefield and Underwager (1992)

In an article that appeared in *Behavioral Science and the Law* in 1992, we discussed several criteria for assessing the probability or improbability of an allegation of recently remembered abuse. This article, written two years before *Return of the Furies*, was one of the earliest to attempt to deal with recovered memory claims. The criteria were therefore provisional. But they made sense to us and we viewed them as an attempt to formulate hypotheses. We will repeat them here.

We recommend assessing the allegations in terms of what is known about the behavior of actual child sexual abusers. In the absence of corroborating evidence, when the allegations are of deviant and low-probability behaviors, the memory is unlikely to represent a real event. It is even more unlikely if the person accused is psychologically normal or if the accusations include the mother.

If the memory is for abuse that occurred at a very young age, such as abuse during infancy or under age three or four, the phenomenon of childhood or infantile amnesia makes it unlikely that the memory is of a real event. In addition, this is much younger than the average age of documented sexual abuse victims.

If the abuse has only recently been 'remembered,' it is less likely to be true than if it has always been remembered but the person is only now disclosing. It is especially unlikely to be true if the accusations only emerge following reading *The Courage to Heal*, hypnosis, survivors' group participation, or dream analysis. In such cases, the recovered memories are likely to be products of therapy.

Although psychopathology in some individuals may well make them more susceptible to this influence, since many of the adult children in the questionnaire project had no history of significant problems prior to the recovered memories, the absence of serious problems does not mean that the recovered memory is necessarily real.

If there are allegations of a series of abusive incidents across time in different places and situations, the recovered memory is less likely to be true than if it is for a single highly traumatic incident for which the person may have developed psychogenic amnesia. Although it is rare, an individual can develop amnesia for a highly traumatic event.

Any claims that the individual must have been abused because of problems in her life must be viewed cautiously. The existence of eating disorders, sexual dysfunction, anxiety, depression, or low self-esteem cannot be used to support the probability of abuse since these can all be caused by a variety of factors. Beitchman et al. (1992) concluded that as yet there is insufficient evidence to confirm a relationship between childhood sexual abuse and borderline or multiple personality disorder. Pope and Hudson (1992) reviewed studies on bulimia and sexual abuse and report that these studies did not find that bulimic patients show a higher prevalence of childhood sexual abuse than do control groups.

When the disclosures progress across time to ever more intrusive, abusive, and highly improbable behaviors, the growth and embellishment of the story is likely to represent suggestions and reinforcement in therapy. Allegations of ritual abuse by intergenerational satanic cults are highly unlikely to be true.

Corroborating evidence, such as a childhood diary with unambiguous entries or pornographic photographs, obviously makes the allegations more likely to be true. Ambiguous evidence, however, such as a childhood story or drawings now reinterpreted in light of the believed-in abuse, cannot legitimately be taken as proof that the abuse actually occurred.

Daubert v. Merrell Dow Pharmaceuticals

A recent United States Supreme Court decision should be highly relevant to repressed memory cases in court. The unanimous U.S. Supreme Court decision in *Daubert v. Merrell Dow Pharmaceuticals* (U.S. Supreme Court 1992–93 term, No. 92–102) in June 1993 dramatically changes the criteria by which scientific testimony will be admitted as evidence in court. The ruling states that the major criterion of the scientific status of a theory is its falsifiability, refutability, or testability. This, in effect, replaces the *Frye* test (*Frye v. United States,* 293 F. 1013) with the Popperian principle of falsification as the determinant of scientific knowledge. Although the decision is limited to federal court, it will be applicable wherever federal rules of evidence apply.

Blackmun, who wrote the opinion, identified four factors that the court should consider in determining whether an expert's opinion is valid under rule 702:

1. Whether the expert's theory or technique has been or can be tested or falsified;

2. Whether the theory or technique has been subjected to peer review or publication;
3. What the known or potential rate of error is for any test or scientific technique that has been employed;
4. Whether the technique is generally accepted in the scientific community.

Therefore, although general acceptance in the scientific community (the *Frye* test) is one consideration, the lack of such by itself does not preclude the proposed testimony. This will make admissible new scientific evidence that was excluded under *Frye*.

At the same time, if properly understood and followed, this ruling is likely to render inadmissible testimony based on such concepts and theories as used by the recovered memory proponents. Any claim that childhood sexual abuse has been 'repressed' should be able to be challenged under *Daubert*. Here is an example of the second sense of the criterion of falsifiability. As discussed in Chapter 8, repression, a Freudian theoretical concept, has not been supported and, arguably, has been falsified. Although proponents of recovered repressed memories offer the three studies that were critically evaluated in Chapter 8 to support a claim of repression (Briere and Conte 1989; Herman and Schatzow 1987; Williams 1992, 1993), none of these really assess repression nor do any of them provide any credible scientific evidence.

Faced with the massive weight of over 60 years of research that fails to corroborate the concept of repression, we believe a reasonable judge would rule that testimony based upon the concept is not scientific and cannot be relevant or helpful to the finder of fact. Therefore, it is not admissible. This would make it impossible for civil suits seeking monetary damages based upon a claim of recovered repressed memories to be pursued. The other concepts used by the recovered memory proponents should meet the same fate.

Daubert could conceivably result in repeal of laws that have been passed in the states that have changed the statute of limitations to permit actions based on claims of recovered repressed memory whenever they are remembered. Criminal convictions based upon evidence or testimony that derives from a claim of a recovered repressed memory could be reversed and remanded for a new trial or dismissed. (See Underwager and Wakefield 1993 and Stewart 1993 for discussions of the *Daubert* decision.)

Conclusions

There are many survivors of childhood sexual abuse. The abuse may have always been remembered but never talked about. Sometimes, actual abuse may be forgotten in the way that other unpleasant, but not highly traumatic, events from childhood are forgotten. When the person is reminded somehow, the abuse is remembered. In such cases, attempts to postulate concepts of repression, dissociation, or traumatic amnesia are both unnecessary and in error. Although often a false memory appears to be have absolutely no basis in truth, in other cases there was an ambiguous event that was the kernel of truth out of which pseudomemories were developed. There also may have been real abuse by a different person.

Especially when there is a civil lawsuit, mental health professionals and the legal system must attempt to sort out the truth and falsity of an allegation. The hypotheses and suggestions by ourselves, Martha Rogers, and Richard Gardner are provisional since there is little research as yet on the criteria differentiating real from false allegations of childhood abuse. Each case must be evaluated on its own merits. We should be suspicious of cases involving low base rate, implausible, bizarre abuse and of allegations that traumatic, intrusive, repeated events are completely banished from memory, only to be retrieved by a sexual abuse specialist years later.

Many professionals and attorneys now discourage lawsuits based on uncorroborated accounts. When cases go to court and when decisions that affect people lives are made, legal and mental health professionals must be extremely cautious. In the absence of corroboration, there is no foolproof way to know what actually happened.

Chapter Twelve
Good and Bad Therapists: How to Tell the Difference

I swear by Apollo Physician and Asclepius, and Health, and Panacea, and all the gods and goddesses, that according to my ability and judgment I will keep this oath and this stipulation. . . . I will use whatever treatment that, according to my ability and judgment, I consider benefi-cial to my patients, and abstain from whatever is deleterious and mischievous. I will give no deadly medicine to anyone when asked, nor suggest any such counsel. . . . With purity and holiness I will pass my life and practice my art.

Hippocrates, Oath, Excerpt

Unfortunately, nonsense like this can have a profound effect on other people's lives, and it is expensive nonsense.
Robyn Dawes (1994)

There are good therapists and there are bad therapists. All mental health professionals have a short list of those therapists to whom they would send their spouse, their children, or their parents. Those on the list are likely to be therapists who share the theoretical orientation of the mental health professional. They are apt to be smart, warm and empathic, and visible in the mental health community. These are the qualities valued by mental health professionals.

But even this personally-recommended short list may not include good therapists. The kicker is that the theoretical position of the recommending mental health professional can produce bad therapists if that standard or measure is itself flawed. For example, recovered memory therapists are probably going to think other recovered memory therapists are good therapists. They are also likely to think that therapists who don't believe in repressed memories are not good therapists. So personal recommendations from other mental health professionals, even when liked and respected, can turn out to be unreliable. We believe recovered memory therapy is harmful and that the therapists who do it are mistaken and foolish. We would not have any recovered memory therapists on our short list.

The consumer of services has the right to find out as much as possible about any service being considered for purchase. The yellow pages or word-of-mouth endorsements are not sufficient. Potential clients should make careful and thorough inquiries about any therapist and feel free to ask them questions.

The Mental Health Professions

For practical purposes there are three mental health professional groups—psychiatry, psychology, and social work. In the social hierarchy, psychiatry is on the top, then psychology, and at the bottom, social work. This is reflected in the fees charged, with psychiatry the most expensive and social work the cheapest. In addition to the major three groups, there are a variety of 'counsellors,' marriage and family therapists, and unlicensed people who call themselves 'psychotherapists.'

Neither psychiatry nor social work are scientific disciplines. Psychiatry is an art or craft, not a science. The method of learning to be a psychiatrist is by serving an apprenticeship, called a residency. After getting an M.D. from a medical school, the newly coined physician goes into a three-year residency program in the same manner as does a surgeon or obstetrician. From the first day on the floor, the new psychiatric resident is responsible for the treatment of patients, under the supervision of a staff psychiatrist who is expected to show the beginner what to do. There is little formal class work but there will be weekly case conferences and grand rounds. There is no training in advanced statistics, research design and methods, philosophy of science, or related basic issues of human behavior. The method of training is essentially the apprenticeship method of the craft unions.

Generally it is easier to get into a medical school program than into a clinical psychology program. In Minnesota about one out of three applicants to medical school is accepted while doctoral programs in psychology accept fewer than one out of six. The undergraduate grade point average of psychologists is significantly higher than that of medical students (Ernsberger 1980).

The methods of treatment available are drugs, electroconvulsive therapy, the hospital itself, called milieu treatment, usually some sort of group, and often occupational therapy. This is usually making small craft objects like wallets, copper enamel ash trays, or costume jewelry. The nursing staff operates under the instructions of the physicians. Often locked wards and physical restraints are available if the physician orders it. If a psychiatrist sees outpatients, it is most often for medication review.

Psychiatry has also moved to solidify its position within medicine by emphasizing organic factors and biological concepts. Hospitals and drugs and their administration have become the main treatment activity of psychiatrists so that training for psychotherapy has been sharply reduced in psychiatric training programs (Strupp and Binder 1992). Also insurance companies have begun stopping payment for traditional psychoanalysis of four to five sessions per week for several years; they may limit payment to short-term psychotherapy of eight to twelve sessions, if they pay for psychotherapy at all.

Social work as a profession has grown more rapidly recently than either psychiatry or psychology. There are far more persons trained as social workers and now vending psychotherapy services than there are either psychologists or psychiatrists (Goleman 1985). They are mostly in hospitals or governmental units but increasing numbers are entering private practice. The high-prestige activity remains individual psychotherapy and most mental health professionals think of individual psychotherapy as the core of the profession and the most rewarding work. It is the defining activity.

But it is also the case that social workers have the least amount of training and the least exposure to scientific methodology and training. Social work training programs generally comprise two years of post-graduate work. A considerable portion of the two years is spent in practicum training programs rather than academic classes. The goal of the training is to provide knowledge and understanding of the relationship between individuals and the broader society.

The practice of social work is intended to be in the interface between the individual and society. In social work curricula there is no training in diagnosis, assessment, developmental psychology, memory, or methods and practices of science. Feld (1994) reports that materials selected by social work professors for their classes are based on personal experience rather than scientific research. Required readings are weighted toward less scientific content rather than more. If a master's thesis is required, it is not required to be a demonstration of ability to do scientific research. There is a serious question whether graduate social work education equips persons to do the tasks they endeavor to do. The evidence available suggests that it does not (Steen and Rzepnicki 1984).

Psychology is the only mental health profession that is also a scientific discipline (McFall 1991). The model of the clinical psychologist is to be first a scientist and then to apply the science to human behavior. This is called the Boulder model because the idea was formally expressed at a conference in Boulder, Colorado, in 1946 (Garfield 1982). The Boulder model guided training for clinical psychology until fairly recently and remains the official concept (O'Sullivan and Quevillon 1992).

The position taken by the American Psychological Association in 1990 in testimony in front of the 'Physician Payment Review Commission' is that in areas in which both psychologists and physicians provide services to patients, psychologists "actually have much more training in those areas" (Welch 1990). In a comparison of various graduate training programs, Ph.D.s in clinical psychology produced close to one standard deviation higher scores on intelligence testing as entering freshman than did those who graduated with Ph.D.s in the natural sciences (Wolfle 1955).

However, free-standing professional schools of psychology, not affiliated with a university but granting a Psy.D. degree, have proliferated. Psy.D. degrees are supposed to be like law degrees or medical degrees permitting a person to practice a profession but are also regarded as less rigorous and requiring much less training in science and scientific methods. Current training programs appear to leave much to be desired as producers of trained scientists since there is a deficit in science training (Howell 1992; Matarazzo 1993). As Robyn Dawes notes:

> The scientific training of clinical psychologists has—I'm afraid —gone to hell. Fewer and fewer (now somewhere between 13 percent and 18 percent) are being trained at the top 200 graduate institutions, while more and more (almost 40 percent) are being graduated from professional schools. (The former figure was close to 40 percent in 1970 and the latter was 0.) (Dawes 1992, p. 217)

While the quality of training is no necessary guarantee of competence, there is some relationship. The shift in the training of psychologists has resulted in large numbers of people being graduated with degrees which are supposed to mean that they have comprehensive knowledge of the science of psychology when, in reality, they have only a trivial and peripheral knowledge of the science of psychology (Hayes 1989).

In summary, the situation with psychotherapy today is that while there are large numbers of people advertising themselves as psychotherapists and selling psychotherapy, there is no profession that can claim to be adequately training the people who are doing it to do it.

Licensing

Psychologists are now licensed at the doctoral level throughout the United States and Canada. Psychiatrists are also licensed as physicians. Social workers are licensed in most jurisdictions in the United States. Professional licensing boards are created by politicians for the avowed purpose of protecting the public by regulating areas of professional practice, reviewing credentials, setting standards for practice, and disciplining professionals who violate codes of conduct (Simon 1993). This might seem like a most advantageous development for both the public and the mental health professions. The implication is that the public is safeguarded from incompetent practitioners.

But this simply is not the case. Licensing practices are confused enough so that substantial evidence suggests that, instead of protecting the public, they may actually serve to institutionalize a lack of public accountability (Koocher 1979). The implied promise that the public will be protected by revocation of the licenses of incompetent practitioners is the most deceitful impression given the public. Incompetence is not in itself considered unethical by licensing boards. The professions are notorious for doing an inadequate job of policing themselves. Once some credentials are granted, they cannot be revoked (Koocher 1979). Licensing laws cannot measure nor assess competence (Menne 1981). As of yet, the basic problem is that there is no agreement on what to measure in order to assess competence (Loveland 1985). The one thing that licensing laws do effectively is to divide up the economic pie.

Professional Associations

Membership in professional associations is not of much use as a guide to selecting a competent and effective psychotherapist. Pronouncements or positions taken by professional associations must be viewed cautiously and examined for any bias before being accepted as authoritative. On the whole, it is most accurate to consider professional associations essentially as trade or craft guilds. From medieval times to now, craft guilds have functioned to define an economic area as the proper province of a group claiming some special expertise. Ostensibly, guilds claim to protect the public's interest. In reality, that goes only as far as it serves the interests of the guild to do so. In any crunch, the aims and goals of the guild to protect the economic interests of the members of the guild will determine guild actions taken, not the interest of the consumer.

For the most part, guilds have understood that maintaining at least adequate performance and avoiding noticeable exploitation of the consumer is also in their interest. It keeps the implicit agreement with the consumer intact and the guild members continue to benefit from whatever domain has been carved out for them by the politicians. So for several hundred years consumers have been able to assume that one guild carpenter has roughly the same knowledge as another. There is a body of common, practical, and real knowledge that is shared. There may be individual skill levels, but they will not be so disparate as to create much trouble. This is true of plumbers, electricians, accountants, neurosurgeons, airline pilots, or chemical engineers. *This cannot be said or assumed about mental health professionals* (Meehl 1989).

Not only is there no scientific body of knowledge undergirding psychiatry and social work, but what should inform these professions—the science of psychology—is not being effectively taught even to psychologists. The American Psychological Association, in effect, has abandoned responsibility for assuring that the practice of psychology is based on the science of psychology. This is the basic cause of the schism that occurred in psychology in 1988, when psychologists deeply concerned about the integrity of the science of psychology split off from the American Psychological Association and formed the American Psychological Society. This drastic action was a protest against the dominance of the APA by the nonscientific concerns of some practitioners. Founders of the APS believed that there was no other way to preserve and strengthen the science of psychology. The reason for the schism is powerfully and clearly set forth in the letter of resignation from the APA sent to the Council of Representatives of the APA by Robyn Dawes (Dawes 1989):

I am resigning my membership in the American Psychological Association as of midnight tonight, August 16th, 1988. I will therefore no longer be a member of the Council of Representatives. A brief statement of reasons is attached.

I am not happy to resign. I am aware of the efforts of many members of the American Psychological Association (APA) to provide service to the public. Psychotherapy does work, although the reasons for its success are not yet clearly understood . . .

What the APA has failed to do—and in my view *failed miserably*—is to assure that the professional practice of psychology is based on available scientific knowledge. Instead, something termed 'clinical judgment' predominates as a rationale for practice; it is based on 'experience'—despite all the well-documented and researched flaws of making experience-based inference in the absence of a sound theoretical base . . .

Rather than insist on the application of research findings to practice, the APA has concentrated its efforts on improving the power, status, and income of practitioners . . .

The major thrust of APA policy has been to convince the American public that its practicing members have a special expertise and power that *simply doesn't exist* . . . And the willingness of psychologists, without facing APA sanctions, to hypothesize in court settings child abuse in the absence of physical evidence—but on the basis of interviews, unvalidated tests, and tests that have been shown to be invalid—is appalling. It is one thing to push for professional status and income based on true expertise. Doing so in the absence of evidence for such expertise —or in the face of evidence that it does not exist—is socially fraudulent.

Once again, the inappropriate exaggeration of the status and power of the group of practitioners within APA can create serious social harm. (p. 14–16)

Unfortunately the schism and the warnings and criticisms of the APS, now numbering over 16,000 members committed to the science of psychology, has not led to any changes. The economic concerns and unscientific views of the practitioners continue to dominate the APA.

Hundreds of parents and family members have written or

called the APA and complained about the actions of psychologists in leading people to fabricate false recovered memories of childhood abuse. The APA formed a task force to study the issue of recovered memories. Strangely, the documents provided to the members of the task force make it clear that the reason for the formation of the task force was the complaints of practitioners about the families and their criticism of the practitioners (Elizabeth Loftus, personal communication, March 19th, 1994), not the other way around. This may explain why the task force is composed of three practitioners who firmly and dogmatically believe in the recovery of repressed memories, two research psychologists who question it, and a third research psychologist who tries to stay in the middle. The composition of the group makes it clear that it is unlikely to accomplish anything of substance.

The influence of practitioners and the bias of the APA is evident in several actions of the APA Ethics Committee of which we are aware. It appears that the decisions made by the committee are often in the direction of protecting its members who accept the current politically correct beliefs while punishing those who do not. Two examples:

- In 1986, a psychologist who holds the views of radical feminism concerning child sexual abuse was the expert witness for a woman who claimed her husband had sexually abused their young daughter. The psychologist wrote in a report and then testified under oath that in an interview with the child and father together, the child said to the father. "Yes! You did those things, Daddy!" This was used to inculpate the father. The interview was videotaped. On the evening after she testified, after months of trying to get access to the videotape, and being forced to pay $3,000 for the privilege of seeing it, the father, his lawyer, the psychologist and the mother's lawyer, and Dr. Underwager viewed the videotape of the interview at the psychologist's office. What the psychologist had testified the child had said was not there.

    The next day, Dr. Underwager testified to that effect in the trial. In spite of this flagrant contradiction, the judge ruled there had been abuse and denied the father contact with the child. After the trial, the father made a formal complaint to the American Psychological Association's Ethics Committee. He sent copies of the psychologist's report, the testimony with the false statement, and Dr. Underwager's testimony that the child did not say what had been reported, and said that a copy of the videotape was available through the court. The Ethics Committee, after several months, ruled there was insufficient evidence of any violation of the ethical code by the psychologist. The father's complaint against the psychologist was dismissed.

• In that same year, a psychologist wrote a short article criticizing the use of anatomical dolls in assessing accusations of child sexual abuse. The article was published in a small local magazine for attorneys. Two other psychologists made a complaint to the American Psychological Association's Ethics Committee charging that the article was not balanced because it was critical of the dolls and did not cite literature by those who believe the dolls are useful. The Ethics Committee formally reprimanded the psychologist for lack of balance in his article. When he appealed the committee's decision, they appointed a review panel who asked a leading proponent of the dolls to criticize his article. Naturally, the reprimand was upheld.

In spite of knowing about many instances of complaints made by lay people that we believe involve legitimate questions about a practitioner's actions, we are not aware of one of these that has been upheld by the APA Ethics Committee. Similar experiences have been reported by accused parents and others making complaints to the state psychological association ethics committees and to the various state boards. The information we have about the APA Ethics Committee and several state ethics committees suggests that they protect the guild, the practitioner, and essentially thumb their noses at the public and the ethical requirement not to harm individuals or diminish their rights. At the same time, they may unjustly punish psychologists who have opinions contrary to the establishment on controversial issues such as homosexuality, religious cults, and child abuse.

An article in a recent *Practitioner*, the official publication of the APA Practice Directorate (Herndon 1994), deplores what the author maintains is the one-sided, biased publicity given to claims of recovered repressed memories in suggesting that they may be false. The false memory syndrome is described as the implantation of memories of early sexual abuse during psychotherapy. The FMS Foundation is described as a resource and advocate for individuals who consider themselves victims of the syndrome. The FMS Foundation is said to be "contributing to the overgeneralized attack on therapy." The APA's Public Affairs Office is said to have "briefed dozens of reporters and producers in an attempt to balance the issue." Finally, the article asks for input from members on this issue:

> The APA Practice Directorate has identified a matter related to false and repressed memories where it is seeking member input. The directorate's legal and regulatory affairs department would like to know about any instances where psychologists are denied reimbursement in cases involving the care of individuals with recovered memories.
>
> "This issue requires a tremendous collaborative effort on the part of the mental health community," says Dr. Newman. "Nothing less than the integrity of the mental health professions and the trust inherent in the client relationship is at stake." (p. 15)

The APA Practice Directorate could have identified the issue of the devastation of thousands of people or the weak and questionable scientific evidence for claims of recovered repressed memories. It could have asked for input about the validity and reliability of various therapeutic techniques used in recovered memory therapy. It could have asked about the scientific quality of the few studies said to support the concept of repressed memories. What they do ask about is whether or not the practitioner is getting paid! How does that come even close to affecting the integrity of the mental health professions and the trust in the client relationship?

Another official APA publication, *Psychology of Women*, contains an editorial (Quina 1994) harshly critical of the FMS

Foundation and asserting: "it is time to be feminists and look deeper into the contexts." What are the contexts that Quina thinks should be looked into? She complains about the media coverage of claims of recovered memories, makes personal *ad hominem* defamatory attacks on members of the FMSF Advisory Board and the director of the FMS Foundation, and asserts that there are strong threads of antifeminism and sexism in the opposition questioning the validity of recovered repressed memories. Both of these recent publications are part of a pattern of behavior strongly suggesting the bias of the APA as an organization. It can no longer be relied upon to represent the science of psychology fairly and objectively.

Experience

Can we pick out a good therapist by looking at experience? After all, we all learn from experience and we look for experienced mechanics, teachers, political leaders, even lovers. Benjamin Franklin is often quoted as saying 'Experience is the best teacher.' He really did not say that. What he actually said was that "Experience is a dear [expensive] teacher and fools will learn from no other" (Franklin 1973, p. 31). Remember, physicians had several hundred years of experience in curing people of all manner of illnesses by draining blood out of them. They could make the cut in the vein very precisely and measure the amount of blood reliably and stop the bleeding when they felt they had enough of the poison drawn out. They had the wrong theory and they killed people but they did it with lots of experience.

The research evidence is clear and unavoidable. There is no relationship between years of clinical experience and competence as a therapist (Brehmer 1980; Dawes 1989b; 1994; Faust 1989; Garb 1989). Professional training does not increase the effectiveness of therapist (Berman and Norton 1985; Campbell 1994). The only way experience contributes to effectiveness as a therapist is through learning and using the methods that are shown to make a difference (Dawes 1989b).

Does Psychotherapy Work?

Yes, it does. The evidence shows that psychotherapy is effective. It makes a significant and practical difference. People get better. For a time it appeared that psychotherapy did not make any real differences but the research is more sophisticated now, and it is clear that there is a real benefit from competent therapy using the methods that are known to be effective. Lipsey and Wilson (1993) report on 302 meta-analyses of therapy outcome studies using effect sizes to assess the impact of psychotherapy. Their refined sample of 156 meta-analyses includes 9,400 individual treatment effectiveness studies and more than 1,000,000 individual subjects. Beginning with the pioneer meta-analysis of Smith and Glass (1977) showing a positive effect of psychotherapy, hundreds of meta-analyses have been carried out in different treatment research areas. Lipsey and Wilson (1993) report that only six show negative effects while the rest show effects that are both positive and significant. They conclude that "well-developed psychological, educational, and behavioral treatments generally have meaningful positive effects on the intended outcome variables" (p. 1,199).

It is not yet quite clear, however, just what factors or variables are the effective ones. At the same time, there is a frequent finding that behavioral, learning theory-based psychotherapy is the best and produces the largest benefit (Casey and Berman 1985; Kazdin 1986; Lipsey and Wilson 1993; Stiles, Shapiro, and Elliot 1986; Tuma 1989; Weisz et al. 1987).

Weisz, Weis, and Donenberg (1992) report a further meta-analysis in which they distinguish studies that are located in a clinic population. Their finding is that in the real world where therapy is actually delivered, the outcomes are more grim than expected. Weisz and Weis (1993) report on research that can be interpreted to suggest that therapy as dispensed in the real world can actually be harmful to children. A likely cause is that nonbehavioral play therapy that does not involve the parents is most often used with children.

The most frequent therapy approaches among practitioners are the psychodynamic, psychoanalytically-oriented talking therapies that emphasize insight and expression of feelings. Such approaches are *not* the most helpful. A meta-analysis of short-term psychodynamic psychotherapy outcomes showed little improvement over no treatment at all and large inferiority to other treatment methods. The psychodynamic therapy treatment was particularly less effective than cognitive-behavioral therapy (Svartberg and Stiles 1991).

In addition, Campbell (1994) points out that to be effective therapy must address the problems *between* the client and significant others. He therefore recommends a family therapy approach as the most likely to succeed. If family therapy is not feasible, the therapist must recognize that any client is more than an isolated individual and, whenever possible, help people who are important to the client to support and assist the client.

Despite the fact that we don't have full knowledge about what variables are associated with good outcomes, we have to make choices now with incomplete information. The current state of scientifically reliable and valid information about psychotherapy indicates that positive benefits are most likely with a behavioral, learning-theory-based treatment approach that focusses on the client's everyday relationships. The therapist should be a scientifically alert and responsible clinician who co-operates with the client to establish and work towards clear and achievable goals. Any other choice maximizes the possibility of being not helped or even of being harmed.

The good news is that effective and appropriate psychotherapy can be helpful. The bad news is that you may not get it without effort.

The Practitioner and Scientific Research

The distressing, almost inexplicable, fact is that scientific clinical research has little or no impact on the practitioner (Campbell 1994; Dawes 1994; Stricker 1992). This fact should be electrifying to a profession which for close to 50 years has tried to convince the American public and itself that mental health professionals integrate the advancing scientific knowledge into what is actually done to assist troubled persons. Instead, scientific research is largely ignored by clinicians. The modal number of publications of clinical psychologists is 0. Practitioners read few journal articles and fewer books. The average frequency of citation for articles published in the 57 leading mental health journals is .92 and the modal frequency is .10 (Matson et al. 1989). With a citation frequency of less than one, almost all the journal articles published simply disappear in the mass of literature. But the publish-or-perish goal has been met and nobody really appears to care too much about whether published research makes any difference. It is the rare researcher and the rare article that has any impact on the real world (Millman et al. 1990).

Most mental health professionals don't seek out continuing education and where CE credits are required they can take workshops for CE credit that have no component of research data but instead are rehearsals of established models of psychotherapy (Steen and Rzepnicki 1984). The dominant model of therapy is still the psychodynamic, analytical, insight-oriented, feeling-expressive talking therapy. When scientists believe there is a scientific consensus, many will refuse to accept any research challenging the perceived consensus (West 1992), so this mistaken concept of therapy may appear to be the scientific consensus when it is not.

Blind adherence to outdated or superseded models is one of the principal causes for scientists to resist scientific advances and new research (Barber 1961). When therapists believe in unscientific concepts, such as astrology, their bias affects their perception of scientific research so that they ignore disconfirming information contradicting their belief and attend to supportive material (Dawes 1994; Goodstein and Brazis 1970). Treatment decisions are not made on the basis of research; instead most therapists choose treatment goals and methods on the basis of their intuitive appeal (Campbell 1994).

When many psychotherapists reach a conclusion about a person, not only do they ignore anything that questions or contradicts their conclusion, they actively fabricate and conjure up false statements or erroneous observations to support their conclusion (Arkes and Harkness 1980). When given information by a patient, therapists attend only to that which supports the conclusion they have already reached (Strohmer et al. 1990). The jaundiced view of humanity held by mental health professionals is shown in the much greater awareness of and the greater attention given to research demonstrating problems than research showing good performance (Christensen-Szalanski and Beach 1984).

The frightening fact about conclusions reached by therapists with respect to patients is that they are made within 30 seconds to two or three minutes of the first contact (Gauron and Dickinson 1969; Meehl 1959; Weber et al. 1993). Once the conclusion is reached, mental health professionals are often impervious to any new information and persist in the label assigned very early in the process on the basis of minimal information, usually an idiosyncratic single cue (Rosenhan 1973).

These facts lead to the conclusion that people are often not helped, and may well be harmed, by the inept application of the treatments intended to heal them (Strupp 1980). It is a strange phenomenon. The mental health professions put a great deal of effort and energy into making differential diagnoses and striving to increase the reliability of the process of diagnosis. This is supposed to allow for increased specificity of the treatment and therefore more effective treatment. The sad reality is that while there may be differential diagnosis, in the real world and as a practical matter, there is no differential treatment readily available. Even after a diagnosis is made, for the most part everybody gets the same treatment, the talking cure that doesn't help.

When the Therapist's Needs Take Over

Campbell (1994) observes how therapy can deteriorate into a damaging experience for the client when the therapist's needs take precedence over those of the client. Clients who fail to respond enthusiastically to therapy are blamed and criticized and a failure to go along with the therapist's agenda is termed 'resistance.'

Such therapists may be responding to their own needs for power and adulation rather than to the needs of their clients. A variation of this is the 'bait-and-switch' tactic in which a client comes to therapy with a specific problem looking for a straightforward solution. But the therapist then tells the client that there are other, more complicated problems that must be addressed. Campbell believes that when therapists resort to such tactics they disregard their obligation to design a treatment procedure to genuinely help their clients. Instead, they are defining the client problems so that their preferred techniques appear helpful and they can do the kind of therapy they want to do.

This approach is seen in recovered memory therapy when a broad range of presenting problems are identified as indicative of sexual abuse, even when sexual abuse memories are denied. If sexual abuse is acknowledged, it is apt to become the focus of therapy while little attention is given to the presenting problem. If the therapist is convinced that repressed abuse is at the core of the client's difficulties, the course of therapy may be devoted to uncovering these memories while specific treatment for the eating disorder, depression, anxiety, or headaches that brought the client to therapy is ignored. The first-person accounts we reproduce in Chapter 4 give descriptions of this.

Muddleheaded and Simpleminded

At an academic banquet Alfred North Whitehead was asked to comment on the philosophy of Bertrand Russell who was also present at the banquet. They had collaborated years earlier to produce the great book, *Principia Mathematica*. Whitehead praised Russell but allegedly concluded "but he is, I fear somewhat simpleminded." Russell's jocular rejoinder admitted this descriptor but went on to characterize Whitehead as "muddleheaded." Meehl (1973) considers this dimension, simpleminded/muddleheaded, to be a potent and pervasive factor in the disagreements in psychology. Simplemindedness can be understood as the stance that "Everything that can be said about a person is reducible to . . . statements about behavior or behavior dispositions . . . the muddleheaded thesis [is]: Since clinical psychology deals with the human person—that person being an inner entity not equatable with his overt behavior—the usual questions about the behavioral implications of personological statements and the usual 'academic, scientific' demands for behavioral evidence, are inappropriate in this field" (p. ix–x). The basic problem of the muddleheaded is their weak standards for what counts as evidence. This means that muddleheadedness is a terminal disease. You cannot persuade the muddleheaded that he is thinking sloppily because part of muddleheadedness is not knowing that one is thinking sloppily (Meehl 1986).

Those clinicians and therapists who vend their services without regard to the scientific research and perpetuate a potentially harmful therapy are the muddleheaded. Unfortunately, there is no relationship with smarts or training since some very bright and well-trained people adopt the muddleheaded position and practice therapy accordingly, believing that what counts is their brilliant clinical insight rather than hard data from a more rigorous scientific approach.

- However, although it may not be unethical to practice in the absence of knowledge, it is unethical to practice in the face of knowledge. We all must labor with the absence of affirmative data, but there is no excuse for ignoring contradictory data. An insistence on relying on overlearned, favored, but invalid approaches is not justifiable. (Stricker 1992, p. 546)

- What is objected to . . . is the persistence in approaches (whether diagnostic or therapeutic) despite clear *negative* evidence against their validity or efficacy . . . To say . . . I don't care if the research evidence on the Minnesota Tennis Ball in Bushel Basket Projective Test shows it doesn't predict anything. I'm not in a laboratory, I'm in a clinic and so I'll use it anyway. This latter is not only intellectually disreputable, it is unethical. (Meehl 1986, p. 5)

Another basic fact about the experience of psychotherapy is that you cannot trust what therapists tell you about what they do in therapy. There are alarming discrepancies between therapists' accounts of what takes place in an interview or therapy session and what is demonstrated in video- or audiotapes of the same sessions (Campbell 1994; DeLipsey and James 1988; Mulhern 1991; Underwager and Wakefield 1990). Even when therapists gain experience, the accuracy of their recall does not improve (Campbell 1994).

Recovered Memory Therapy is Unethical

For us the scientific tradition of clinical psychology is best exemplified in our contacts with Paul Meehl and what we have learned from him about the science of psychology and the clinical practice of that science. Recently, in an invited address at the American Psychological Society Convention, June 1992, Meehl (1993) said:

> My teachers at Minnesota (psychologists Hathaway, Paterson, Heron, Skinner, statistician Treloar, philosophers Castell and Feigl) differed widely as to both method and substance. But they shared what Bertrand Russell called the dominant passion of the true scientist—the passion not to be fooled and not to fool anyone else. Only Feigl was a positivist, but all of them persistently asked the two searching questions of positivism: 'What do you mean? How do you know?' If we clinicians lose that passion and forget those questions, we are little more than be-doctored, well-paid soothsayers. I see disturbing signs that this is happening and I predict that if we do not clean up our clinical act and provide our students with role models of scientific thinking, outsiders will do it for us. (pp. 728–29)

In an earlier article on clinical psychology, Meehl (1960) wrote:

> If there is anything that justifies our existence . . . it is that we think scientifically about human behavior and that we come from a long tradition, going way back to the very origins of experimen-

tal psychology in the study of human error, of being critical of ourselves as cognizing organisms and of applying quantitative methods to the outcomes of our cognitive activity. If this methodological commitment is not strong enough to compete with the commitments clinicians have to particular diagnostic instruments, the unique contribution of our discipline will have been lost. (p. 26–27)

The scientific clinical psychology tradition of quantification also shows up in Meehl's (1954) description of the clinician's requirement for validation:

The honest clinician cannot avoid the question 'Am I doing better than I could do by flipping pennies?' (p. 136).

The tradition of scientific clinical psychology requires an exercise of critical acumen and compassionate skepticism in examining the claims of recovered memory of childhood abuse and the putative therapeutic techniques which elicit the claims while purporting to be treatment. This is the only way clinical psychology can claim to be scientific. Scientific clinical psychology is the only legitimate form of clinical psychology. Can anybody seriously assert that the alternative of an unscientific clinical psychology is acceptable and proper?

The time has come . . . to declare unequivocally that there is only one legitimate form of clinical psychology: grounded in science, practiced by scientists, and held accountable to the rigorous standards of scientific evidence. Anything less is pseudoscience. It is time to declare publicly that much of what goes on under the banner of clinical psychology today simply is not scientifically valid, appropriate, or acceptable. When Section III members encounter invalid practices in clinical psychology, they should 'blow the whistle,' announce that 'the emperor is not wearing any clothes,' and insist on discriminating between scientific and pseudoscientific practices. (McFall 1991, p. 79)

The ethical practice of scientific clinical psychology requires that all theories, concepts, methodologies, and techniques be firmly grounded in science. The clinician must know the current status of the science and be able to provide an acceptable scientific rationale for all opinions, views, and acts. Anything else is a violation of the central ethic of the profession (Singer 1980; Stricker 1992; Sechrest 1992).

McFall (1991) proposes that psychological services should not be administered to the public until they have satisfied four minimal criteria:

1. The exact nature of the service must be described clearly.
2. The claimed benefits of the service must be stated explicitly.
3. These claimed benefits must be validated scientifically.
4. Possible negative side effects that might outweigh any benefit must be ruled out empirically.

The gap between what is bogus and what is genuine scientific psychology is seldom addressed, much less exposed and acted upon. Sechrest (1992) laments the lack of courage psychologists show in their failure to identify pseudoscience both inside and outside the profession. If there is no action taken to check the drift of clinical psychology into unscientific, invalid, and unreliable beliefs and practices, we will soon find ourselves competing only with the witch doctors for the federal dollars in a national health program. This does not mean that we must be able to claim full and complete knowledge in order to act but rather that we can show we do not act in the face of negative evidence or invalidating, disconfirming data (Meehl 1986).

Recovered memory therapy does not meet the minimal criteria noted above. In addition, serious harm is inflicted on individuals and families when there are false allegations. The person who is led by unscientific and unsupported concepts and techniques to produce pseudomemories of abuse is damaged.

The only answer given by proponents of recovered memories to the question 'How do you know?' is the presentation of anecdotes, case studies, and personal, subjective feeling. It is wrong to cite a testimonial or case study as support for a particular theory or therapy. Those who do so mislead the public if they don't point out that such evidence is open to a wide range of alternative explanations and can be highly misleading (Stanovich 1992). To the best of our knowledge no proponent of claims of recovered memories even attempts to answer the question whether or not they do better than chance. We know of no scientific quantified data supporting any of the techniques passed off as therapeutic and healing.

Recovered memory therapy as it is practiced is unethical and constitutes malpractice.

Effective Therapy for Adult Victims of Sexual Abuse

Since there is evidence demonstrating that cognitive-behavioral therapy is the most effective, people who are truly victims of sexual abuse should be treated using those methods. Without going into great detail, cognitive-behavioral treatment of a person who has been sexually abused during childhood would first mean a careful assessment using valid and reliable measurements. This assessment should include evaluation of the strengths of the person as well as any problems. The strengths of the person will provide the tools used in working on the problems. Next should come behavioral assessment of the current functioning level and targeting of any problem behaviors. If there are no problem areas, therapy is not needed. Sometimes, a client may need only one or two sessions that are primarily educational in nature. When the assessment is complete, decisions may be made about individual, family, or group therapy. The client may be referred to a physician for consultation regarding medication.

Well-defined treatment goals are negotiated with the client. The goals should be specific behaviors and may include a gradual step-by-step description of several levels of behavior to reach final behavioral goals. At the beginning, the goals should emphasize movement toward adequate functioning and coping with current life circumstances. Only when the client has reached a level of satisfactory coping with immediate concerns about self-maintenance, should therapy address broader goals.

However, significant family members may need to become involved from the beginning.

Problems involving the client and significant others must be addressed and often marriage therapy or family therapy will be included as part of the treatment. Problems with the marriage or with sexual dysfunction cannot be adequately treated without involving the partner. When important family members cannot attend therapy sessions, conflicts and difficulties concerning these people should be addressed in the individual sessions. Suggestions can be made as to what the client can do to make things work better.

Treatment methods should emphasize active, authoritative and responsible behaviors by the therapist. Cognitive-behavioral therapists take responsibility for what they do since it is their task to design the contingencies and the behavioral assignments. There is minimal attention to the feelings of the client since the main interest is in changing behavior and maladaptive thinking. The behavioral therapist knows that changes in feelings are much more likely to be generated following changes in behavior rather than the other way around. Clients can understand this when it is explained to them.

In cognitive-behavioral therapy it is assumed that the person's cognitions are in some fashion in error. Therefore, an important part of therapy is challenging the beliefs of the client. Re-attribution of causal relationships held by the clients may be a first step. The therapist should have credible scientific data to support any causal chains taught to the patient.

Challenging the beliefs of clients leads to improvement (Jones et al. 1993; Silberschatz and Curtis 1993). This finding is not limited to cognitive-behavioral therapy. In a thorough analysis of a five-year-long psychoanalytic therapy, the finding was that the therapist challenging the patient's point of view correlated .43 with the improvement of the patient (Spence, Dahl, and Jones 1993). The clearest model for this is Albert Ellis's 'Rational-Emotive Therapy,' now termed Rational Emotive Behavior Therapy (Ellis 1963).

Active homework assignments are given with the express purpose of acquiring new behavioral skills. In marriage and family therapy sessions, homework assignments are also given. There is little or no encouragement to express anger or to experience catharsis of any emotion. Instead, the goal is to learn effective interpersonal skills that increase the effectiveness of the client in reaching more goals. Instead of the expression of anger, a cognitive-behavioral therapist teaches assertiveness and competent communication and conflict-resolution skills.

What about confrontation sessions with the perpetrator? We have sometimes arranged such sessions when the survivor had never talked to her father or mother about the childhood abuse by the father and wanted to do so. The confrontation session is only arranged after careful exploration with the client as to what goals she wants to accomplish and after careful preparation as to just what is to take place in the session. We generally ask for as many immediate family members as possible to be present and arrange for other therapists be involved. One of the additional therapists is given the assignment of looking out for the welfare of the accused father. The goal of the session is to expose the family secret in a way that promotes healing, not only for the adult survivor, but also for the family and all its members. We allow as much time as necessary—the sessions typically last two to three hours.

When carefully planned in this way, we have found that the confrontation sessions result in closure and healing, not only for the adult survivor, but for the perpetrator. The father has always admitted the behavior during the session and has been relieved that it was finally talked about. None of these cases, however, involved recovered memory claims—the survivor had in every case remembered the abuse but never talked about it.

Some of the recovered memory therapists argue that it is a therapeutic necessity to believe the patient even if the memories are not real. They claim that it has therapeutic benefit and helps clients when the therapist believes their story. There are no quantified data to support this claim and the idea is wrong and foolish. It rests upon the assumption that error can be beneficial. We believe that error can never, in the long run, contribute to healing nor to a better life. Science can be about lots of things but one thing it is not about is encouraging error.

Anyone familiar with the history of medicine can see that it is not enough to be a compassionate, empathic, warm, even bright person, who wants to help people who are hurting. This is the error that led to medical practices like insulin shock therapy, prefrontal lobotomies, curing schizophrenia by pulling all the teeth, or, until fairly recently, putting premature babies in an oxygen enriched environment which blinded them. Most recently, breast mastectomies and heart bypass surgery have been shown to be ineffective and unnecessary for many.

The competent psychologist can discriminate between explanations that have some credibility and truth and support for accuracy and myths or dogmas that don't (Meehl 1959; 1960). Making an accurate determination of claims of recovered memory involves a probability assessment from what is seen on the outside at present and an inferred unobservable inner state including complex internal dynamics enduring over long periods of time and then back to an unobserved and largely uncorroborated outside event. The less that is known about any of the multitudinous entities, intervening variables, the many layers of interactions, and the antecedent probability of all postulated phenomena, the greater the likelihood of errors.

Questions for Choosing a Therapist

Remember, you are the consumer. You pay the bill. You have the right to make the most informed choice of therapist that you can. This means that you essentially interview therapists before choosing one. Don't ask friends or relatives for recommendations. What may have worked for them may not work for you. And if this one doesn't work, you have a potential problem with the friend or relative.

The most rational choice for a therapist to maximize the likelihood of benefit from psychotherapy is a behaviorally-oriented, learning theory-based approach. The therapist should be knowledgeable about the scientific research on psychotherapy and use it to inform actual practice. He or she should recognize the importance of your family and other significant others and enlist their input and support in making the changes you want—both in your own behaviors and in the behaviors of those around you.

Ask directly about what therapeutic approach the individual therapist takes. Don't accept a description of 'eclectic.' This is supposed to mean therapy that takes from all schools and uses what works. The difficulty is that it leaves the door open for choices emphasizing the favored model of psychoanalytically-oriented practices. Ask about the techniques and procedures described throughout this book, practices that have no support and may do actual harm.

Start with psychologists who have a Ph.D. Then, if needs be and there is some utility to having medication available, question some psychiatrists. Because of their more limited training and lack of any scientific training, we advise caution and careful assessment of any social workers whom you may talk with.

Be cautious of anyone without a license. Some practitioners call themselves 'psychotherapists,' but there is no such thing as a licensed psychotherapist. People using this designation can be anything from a high school graduate to an unlicensed Ph.D. If a psychologist is in the supervisory period necessary after completing graduate school before licensing is possible, inquire about supervision. In some states social workers may not be licensed, but psychologists are licensed in all states. Marriage and family counsellors are licensed in some states.

It may well be that you must pay for an introductory session in order to have enough time to get complete answers to these questions. But, given the commitment and the potential effect on your life, it is a wise investment. A therapist who is unwilling to answer your questions should be avoided.

Here are some possible questions to ask:

1. What kind of therapy do you believe you provide?
2. What professional journals do you subscribe to?

3. What is your understanding of the research evidence on the outcomes of psychotherapy for adults/children?
4. What is the most recent article you have read in a professional journal? Did it have any research findings?
5. What is the most recent book dealing with psychotherapy that you have read? Did it report on research?
6. Tell me the best book or article to read to find out more about what you do in psychotherapy?
7. How smart do you think you are in comparison to other psychotherapists?
8. How many hours a week do you spend doing actual therapy? (We have always defined a full week of psychotherapy as 24–26 hours' direct service. Any more than that and the therapist begins to burn out and lose individual focus.)
9. How many sessions are there in the average treatment you provide? (It is best if the average is somewhere between 16 and 20 sessions.)
10. What diagnostic tests do you use? What is the validity and reliability of those tests? Do any of them have any limitations or qualifications that you are ethically bound to tell me about?
11. What is your understanding of the ethical responsibilities you have toward patients?
12. Do you videotape or audiotape your sessions? (This should not be done without your written permission.)
13. If I want to, do you permit me to record the sessions? If not, why not?
14. Do you make yourself available for telephone calls? If so, what expectations do you have for phone calls?
15. Do you give any homework assignments for patients to do?
16. What kind of records or documentation of treatment do you keep?
17. Do you do any follow-up on treatment?
18. Have you done any clinical research or published any articles or books?
19. Do you have any consulting relationship or supervisory relationship with another therapist? If so, tell me about it.
20. What is your understanding of the relationship between scientific research and the practice of psychotherapy?
21. Do you have a Ph.D. or Psy.D.? Tell me what the difference is.

We suggest you agree to enter therapy only with a therapist

who takes the fundamental position on the relationship between science and therapy that we have outlined above. Also it is best to have a therapist who remains current with the scientific research and both reads and understands the professional literature. This choice will produce the greatest chance of finding a mental health professional who will be an effective therapist.

Questions for Firing a Therapist

For those who may be involved with a therapist and want some idea of the effectiveness of the treatment, here are some suggested questions to consider. 'Yes' answers to more than a few questions indicate that you need to talk to your therapist about your treatment and, if the questions cannot be satisfactorily resolved, consider terminating therapy with this therapist. Most of these are questions are adapted from Campbell 1994:

1. Does your therapist show preoccupation with your insight into the causes of problems and neglect or ignore any specific courses of action that may make things better?
2. Do you spend a lot of time in therapy describing and exploring minute details of your fantasies, feelings, and thoughts?
3. Do you feel more worried, discouraged, and depressed now than when you started therapy?
4. Does your therapist assume that when you understand your problems, they are cured?
5. If you felt you were done with therapy, has your therapist repeatedly persuaded you that you need to continue?
6. Do you spend almost all your time talking about your childhood and the terrible things that happened to you then and ignore your present experience?
7. Does your therapist spend a lot of time dealing with your shortcomings, weaknesses, and problems rather than supporting and affirming your strengths and capacities?
8. Does your therapist see himself as intellectually superior to you and most other people?
9. Does your therapist spend a lot of time explaining to you how you supposedly feel about him?

10. Does your therapist tell you things about yourself that just don't seem right or feel just bizarre?

11. Do you feel like a fly on a pin sometimes and the therapist is just curious to see what you will do?

12. If there is a difference of opinion, does your therapist insist he is right?

13. Does your therapist frequently accuse you of sabotaging the therapy or resisting the true understanding of your problems?

14. Does your therapist seem to assume that he is a charismatic figure?

15. Does your therapist talk a lot about other people in your life but refuse to see them with you even if they are available?

16. Does your therapist see other people in your life as malevolent and their motivations as evil and then criticize them severely?

17. Does your therapist suggest or require you to postpone any important decisions in your life until you get his permission or approval?

18. Do you feel at times that you are being pulled apart between the therapist and other people in your life?

19. Does your therapist insist that you cannot discuss your therapy with anyone else in your family?

20. Has your therapist become a good friend and are your sessions spent mostly in friendly conversation?

21. Does your therapist seem to think he is uniquely important in your life so that you cannot get what he gives you anyplace else?

22. Do you spend a lot of time and energy dealing with poorly-defined goals or concepts like growth, self-concept, existential quests, personal fulfillment?

23. Do you spend a lot of time talking about and interpreting dreams?

24. Are you encouraged to ventilate your anger and therefore pound pillows, scream, or use bataca bats in sessions?

25. Does your therapist talk a lot about his wishes or feelings?

26. Does your therapist assume or expect you to adopt his values and beliefs?

27. Does your therapist seem very concerned about your feelings and less concerned about what influences your feelings?

28. Has your therapist subjected you to any kind of physical stress, ordeal, or pain?

29. Does your therapist assume your relationship with him will solve all your problems?

30. Does your therapist expect you to understand and value all of his feelings?
31. Does your therapist tell you there are feelings in your body and try to find out where some feeling or emotion is located in your body?
32. Does your therapist tell you what diagnosis he assigns to you and then predict your future course on the basis of that diagnosis?
33. Does the therapist give you his diagnosis and you feel vaguely accused and put down?
34. Does your therapist change the diagnosis given to you when your insurance limits run out so that you can get continued coverage?
35. Is your therapist unaware of who is in your family and how they may affect you?
36. Is your therapist unresponsive to your suggestion of including other people in your therapy?
37. Does a great deal of your therapy seem to focus on issues that are trivial or obscure?
38. Does your therapist convey the belief that he is in a unique position to really know the truth about you?
39. Does your therapist depend upon sympathetic platitudes such as 'trust yourself,' 'be kind to yourself,' or 'take care of your inner child'?
40. Does your therapist insist that something must have happened to you in your past, even if you don't remember it?

Conclusions

The difficulties in identifying an effective and competent therapist make it less surprising that people are in danger of finding themselves in recovered memory therapy. The recovered memory therapists exhibit many of the shortcomings therapists are vulnerable to, be they psychiatrists, psychologists, social workers, or unlicensed 'counsellors.' Such therapists don't use the empirical research about memory, learning theory, or therapy outcomes. Their assumptions and techniques are unproven and unsupported. They have mistaken notions about the cause of people's problems and their own needs may supersede those of their clients. It is our position that this therapy is unethical and amounts to malpractice. Unfortunately, as of yet, the professional organizations and licensing boards don't appear to be taking strong and effective action to stop such ill-conceived and misguided treatment. The therapy for which there is scientific support demonstrating effectiveness is behavioral and learning-theory-based. This is the kind of therapist we recommend.

Chapter Thirteen
Reply to the Furies

> *The union of male and female is the seed-bed, so to speak, from which the city must grow. . . . Since, then, a person's home ought to be the beginning or elementary constituent of the city, and every beginning serves some end of its own, and every part serves the integrity of the whole of which it is a part, it follows clearly enough that domestic peace serves civic peace, that is, that the ordered agreement of command and obedience among those who live together in a household serves the ordered agreement of command and obedience among citizens.*
>
> Augustine, *The City of God*,
> 15, 16; 19, 13

How men and women get along together is the single most important dimension in human life. What a woman and a man are to each other determines the rest of life. We can no longer take either male or female for granted. We cannot ignore the absolute need of each for the other if the fullness of humanity is to be maintained and lived. The ancient Greeks understood this. Their solution to women and men needing each other worked to produce the world we know today. The solution was a mutuality, respect, and co-operation while acknowledging the distinctive life and character of each. This is the end of the Aeschylus trilogy and the resolution of the conflict between Orestes and the Furies. Added to this is the child, the shared burden of providing for children, and the agreement with the Furies that they protect children.

How men and women get along together is the basis of every culture. The quality and shape of the woman-and-man relationship determines every other relationship. We can only do to other people what we learn to do in the most basic relationship of man and woman. Our most intimate relationship sets the outer limits in one direction—unity and wholeness. This, we believe, is the aim and goal of all humanity. In the other direction, it is the opposite of intimacy that defines the content of hatred. We can only know how to hate because we already know how to love. Love has to come first because if hate came first, we would never get out of it. There would never be any attraction to move us across space and time to approach another person and offer interest and friendship.

A free democracy with personally responsible citizens develops only within the relationship of mutuality and co-operation between women and men. History shows that it is natural to live in slavery or tyranny. It has taken us over 2,000 years to reach a point in history where free democracy is at least available to everyone. Across that time there has been a steady parallel between the growth of freedom and democracy and the growth of mutuality and respect between men and women. However, even as freedom is not the natural state of humanity, so mutuality and co-operation are not the natural state of the relationship between men and women. Men and women both seek to dominate and control each other. This proclivity is what continually needs to be overcome and can only be overcome by reason and freedom undergirded by love and intimacy.

Love and intimacy is necessary for freedom and reason to grow. Love keeps us all willing to seek a mutual and co-operative behavioral pattern toward each other. Knowing that I love and I am loved is the only basis for me to choose voluntarily to consider the wants and needs, strengths and capacities, weaknesses and failings of another person and remain committed to finding ways to respect, cooperate, and be together in mutuality.

Apart from love and intimacy there is no reason for me to expect anything of another person other than dominance, control, and exploitation. For this reason as societies moved away from hunting-and-gathering tribes toward more settled agriculture, warfare and enslavement of captives increased. Economic factors supported the early spread of slavery, as economic considerations have been used to support opposition and resistance to mutuality between men and women. The economic value of the productivity of women has been the basic reason for resisting the full mutuality between men and women that freedom and reason require. So long as men controlled the economic output of women, they were in a more advantageous position.

Sexuality, as a part of intimacy, mutuality, and unity is also a necessary condition for freedom and reason to prevail and be nurtured. Here, too, love and mutuality must be the basis for sexual behavior and not aggression or power. Learning mutuality and co-operative behaviors in our intimate relationships lets us extend those behaviors to others as we find the rewards and reinforcements there, too, to be greater. Every sexual act, whether by men or women, that is aggressive, violent, or based on power is an act against freedom and democracy, against reason and intimacy.

Together with the free exercise of reason that originated contemporary scientific knowledge and skills, democracy has generated a better life. Science has accumulated knowledge that contributes to the ability to have a better life for more and more persons. There is no way that humanity could ever turn back from the knowledge of the world that science has produced. That entire effort shows there is one indivisible nature. So there can be only one set of regularities, laws, that govern the one nature. It is not possible to go backwards. There is a linear progression and, in spite of all the criticisms that can be made, the progress of western civilization is toward a better world.

Opening the door to intimacy and love and seeking a greater fulfillment of sharing and caring for each other is possible. There are some who may question the place of intimacy, love, and sex between same-sex partners. At this point in history, we can agree that if mistakes are to be made, it is far better to make them on the side of loving rather than hating. What is possible for a woman and a man in loving and caring for each other may be possible for same-sex partners or it may not. If it is not, it still is least troublesome and most rewarding to intend it and to reach the highest possible level of mutuality and love.

From the time of ancient Athens until now, we have managed gradually to reach a resolution of the political and economic questions confronting us. Free democracy and free markets are the accepted reality world wide. For this reason our leaders can talk of a new world and a new world order. But the moment it began to look as if a new order was possible, ancient rivalries and ancient tribal enmities erupted once again. The break-up of the Soviet Union, the wars between tribal groups, the conflicts of fundamentalist Moslems, ethnic cleansing, and the inability of the other nations of the world to stop these conflicts are not just happenstance or some sort of natural rush to fill a vacuum. These are the opening rounds in the resistance to the next step in the fulfillment of the Athenian model—the mutuality, co-operativeness, and love between woman and man extended to the broader society. The movement is toward a world of peace and stability. Never before has a peaceful world been as possible as it is now. This is the next step in filling out the aim and promise of western civilization.

Concurrent with the resistance toward change to greater mutuality and co-operation, the current attack on reason and freedom emerges as hostility toward the ability of reasonable and free people to move toward a more peaceful and harmonious world. Part of that movement is the choice of our nation to reduce the frequency of child abuse, including child sexual abuse. This choice is the first time in the history of the world that the care and nurturance of children has been placed squarely in the middle of a society's agenda. Unfortunately, as often occurs, in the rush to make social changes a path is chosen in the absence of factual knowledge that turns out to be a mistake. This is what has taken place in the system we have established to respond to child abuse and to decrease the savagery visited on children. The Furies have returned with their lust for vengeance, impulsivity, irrationality, and enmity toward men. We have chosen a path of punishment, aggression, irrationality, and flight from reason. The consequence is that we may have harmed more people than we have helped.

The swift emergence of claims of recovered repressed memories is the logical extension of the errors and foolishness chosen at the beginning of the rush to social change. It shows the effect of turning away from freedom and reason toward vengeance and vitriol, the return of the Furies. At every step along the progression of the child abuse system to claims of recovered memories, it has become more clear that the system dealing with child abuse is based on nonscientific, irrational, and foolish dogmas. The engine driving this development has been the radical feminist rhetoric and the readiness to substitute emotion for reason.

The progression to claims of recovered memories also demonstrates that it is not enough to tinker with the system, to spend more money and get more people doing the same foolishness. Bureaucratic solutions of task forces, study groups, commissions, improving lines of communication, more forms or different forms to fill out will not do. The entire system must be scrapped and a new start made.

The basic problem with the system is that it is an attack upon the family as an institution. The enmity toward a mutual and co-operative relationship between women and men is clearly expressed in the radical feminist rhetoric. The hostility toward men and the rejection of the patriarchal society, that is, western civilization that began in Athens, leads to the antisexuality, the linkage of sex and aggression so as to eliminate love from human life, the abandonment of scientific reason for subjective emotion in the mental health professions, and the intrusion of the state into the life of the family. This, along with the destruction of families when there is a claim of a recovered repressed memory, makes family life very dangerous.

The mental health professions have been enlisted in the system dealing with child abuse as principal players. Poorly and nonscientifically trained mental health professionals have generated conspiracy theories, paranoia, and an inability to escape muddleheadedness. They supplied the dogmas, catch phrases, speculations, and unfounded, amplified statistics and labelled it all science. They eagerly described the overblown epidemic of abuse and the horror of bad touching. The media seized upon the sensationalism of the exaggerated consciousness-raising rhetoric and the questionable advocacy numbers. Politicians thought they had an opportunity to look good at no cost. The initial laws were passed with no appropriations to pay for them.

The outcomes are finally clear in the recovered memory claims. The cost to all of us is much greater than anybody ever thought. Billions of dollars are spent to carry on the destruction of children and families. The amount of damage done to individuals, families, adults, children, and the nation is impossible to assess. The damage to our ability to live together in mutuality and co-operation is widespread and pervasive. The system manufactures victims and creates a world filled with monsters, monstrous acts, and indescribable dangers. Civility, courtesy, kindness, and generosity disappear under the weight of fear, anxiety, hatred, and rage.

It should be apparent now that this policy and the system set up intended to reduce abuse of children has not worked. It should be possible to give another idea a try. The proponents of recovered memory therapy and the bureaucrats of the child abuse system should now admit their mistakes. If nothing else, they must admit that the phenomena they claim happen, the behaviors they say require their services, and the assertions they have made about science, are, at best, low-frequency behaviors. In the worst case, they are self-serving fabrications. They must admit that credible and more careful research has begun to come out. It all points in the direction of disconfirming the shibboleths of the child abuse system and pointing to the folly of what has been wrought. They must admit that the evidence for a more realistic, less overblown, and much more cautious approach gets stronger every day. They should give our nation a chance to correct the excesses.

They should also say they are sorry to those persons whose lives they have needlessly destroyed.

The mental health professions should take responsibility for their own behavior. This means to admit their mistakes and stop doing and saying things that cannot be supported. The only hope for the science of psychology is to blow the whistle on any practice, any technique, any method that cannot be shown to have validity, reliability, and to produce demonstrable benefit.

Radical feminists should abandon their policy of encouraging rage, at least temporarily. It does not serve their interests but is counterproductive as has become clear in recovered memory therapy. If there is truly any regard for children, radical feminists should co-operate in an effective effort to assist children and decrease the frequency of abuse and exploitation.

If we really want to reduce child abuse, we should strengthen families and increase the reinforcement for mutuality and co-operativeness between men and women. Children are not abused in close, intimate, loving families. When there is a mutuality and love between a woman and a man it is less likely that they, or one of them, will abuse a child.

To pursue this shift, politicians must carefully examine the opportunities in a democracy for government to support families and family life. It is not enough to talk about preserving family values. What does not work, and what injures and wounds families, must be stopped. Politicians need to be courageous enough to admit error and reverse some laws. The laws that extend statutes of limitations to accommodate repressed memories should be repealed. What may encourage women and men to be mutual and intimate should be pursued.

What is the alternative? Men could complain about being blamed for everything. They could relax and let women take care of them. They could become aggressive, hostile, punitive, and even violent. They could go off in the woods and prance about in Iron John male-bonding ceremonies. They could try separatism and build an all-male society. None of these responses are rational. Intensifying the conflict and initiating gender warfare is not a reasonable response.

Women could complain bitterly, and often rightly, about male insensitivity, dominance, and harassment and remind men of their dark side. They could drop into depression and despair.

They could become aggressive and punitive. Women, also, could try to build an all-female refuge. None of these responses are rational or effective.

The response we propose is that men and women offer each other the invitation of Isaiah, "Come now, let us reason together." It is reason that has formed our civilization and offers the basis for our political structures, our economic systems, and our scientific ventures. It is reason to which men and women should now turn to solve the tensions that have arisen between them.

At the beginning of Western civilization the conflict between men and women was settled by reason, balance, and fairness. This is still the best response to the Furies. An illustration may lie in the oft-repeated assertion that men are more violent than women and that domestic violence is almost exclusively men battering women. But the facts include several studies suggesting that women are as violent, if not more violent than men, that they inflict more serious damage, and that more men than women are victimized by their intimates. Domestic violence is not a women's issue; it is a human issue. To permit radical feminists to claim exclusive ownership of this tragic reality is to perpetuate the divisiveness in our society and make any improvements more difficult. Recognizing the essential humanness of domestic violence can lead to more immediate co-operation and heightened awareness of the full extent of our society's recourse to violence.

The main difficulty in reasoned discourse is the impact of political correctness and the readiness on the part of many to refuse to consider some assertions and to simply rule them out. But here, too, reason may prevail. An example is the shift that has occurred in dealing with child sexual abuse allegations. As the research has accumulated, more and more clarity has emerged and consensus has shifted toward a greater acceptance of factual information in areas such as suggestibility of children, interview methodology, and the desire for greater accuracy and reliability. The interest in factual data should be nourished. If nothing else, everybody can agree that increased accuracy of decision-making at all levels is good for everybody. Here is a potential starting point for co-operation and mutuality. Let us agree that accuracy is our common goal. Then we can work together to jointly produce more accurate choices.

Neither men nor women have to abandon virtue, autonomy, identity, or self.

Let us carry the burden together!

References

Abel, G. G., Lawry, S. S., Karlstrom, E., Osborn, C. A., and Gillespie, C. E. 1994. Screening Tests for Pedophilia. *Criminal Justice and Behavior* 21, 115–131.

Adorno, T., Frenkel-Brunswick, E., Levinson, D., and Sanford, R. N. 1950. *The Authoritarian Personality.* New York: Harper.

Aeschylus (Trans. R. Lattimore) 1953. In *The Libation Bearers.* Chicago: University of Chicago Press.

Aguilera-Hellweg, M. 1994. The Lost Daughter. *Esquire* (March), pp. 76–87.

Ahn, W., Brewer, W. F., and Mooney, R. J. 1992. Schema Acquisitions From a Single Example. *Journal of Experimental Psychology: Learning, Memory, and Cognition* 18, 391–412.

Aldridge-Morris, R. 1989. *Multiple Personality: An Exercise in Deception.* Hove: Erlbaum.

Altemeier, W., O'Connor, S., Vietze, P., Sandler, H., and Sherrod, K. 1984. Prediction of Child Abuse: A Prospective Study of Feasibility. *Child Abuse and Neglect* 8, 393–400.

American Bar Association. 1984. *The Judicial Response to Lawyer Misconduct.* Chicago: American Bar Association.

American Psychiatric Association. 1987. *Diagnostic and Statistical Manual of Mental Disorders—Revised (DSM-III-R).* Washington, DC: Author.

American Psychiatric Association. 1994. *Diagnostic and Statistical Manual of Mental Disorders—Fourth Edition (DSM-IV).* Washington, DC: Author.

APS Observer. 1993. Letter to the editor signed by several people. *APS Observer* (March), p. 23.

Arkes, H. R. 1989. Principles in Judgment/Decision Making Research Pertinent to Legal Proceedings. *Behavioral Sciences and the Law* 7, 429–456.

Arkes, H. R., and Harkness, A. R. 1980. Effects of Making a Diagnosis on Subsequent Recognition of Symptoms. *Journal of Experimental Psychology: Human Learning and Memory* 6, 568–575.

Armbrister, T. 1993. When Parents Become Victims. *Reader's Digest* (April), pp. 101–06.

Armbrister, T. 1994. Justice Gone Crazy. *Reader's Digest* (January), pp. 33–40.

Armstrong, L. 1978. *Kiss Daddy Goodnight.* New York: Pocket Books.

Aronson, E. 1988. *The Social Animal: Fifth Edition.* New York: Freeman.

Bakan, D. 1966. *The Duality of Human Existence.* Chicago: Rand McNally.

Bakan, D. 1971. *Slaughter of the Innocents.* San Francisco: Jossey-Bass.

Balch, R. W., and Gilliam, M. 1991. Devil Worship in Western Montana: A Case Study in Rumor Construction. In J. T. Richardson, J. Best, and D. G. Bromley (eds.), *The Satanism Scare* (pp. 249–262). New York: Aldine.

Barber, B. 1961. Resistance by Scientists to Scientific Discovery. *Science* 134, 596–602.

Barden, R. C. 1994. *Testimony of R. Christopher Barden, Ph.D., J.D., LP Regarding 'Recovered Memory' Statutes.* March 1994. Draft of testimony to be presented to the Minnesota Legislature. Also, presentation made to the Minnesota chapter of the False Memory Syndrome Foundation, St. Paul, Minnesota, March 19th 1994.

Barrett, W. 1958. *Irrational Man.* Garden City, NY: Doubleday.

Barstow, D. 1993. A Critical Examination of the 'False Memory Syndrome.' *Family Violence and Sexual Assault Bulletin* 9(4), 21–23.

Bass, E., and Davis, L. 1988. *The Courage to Heal.* New York: Harper and Row.

Beitchman, J. H., Zucker, K. J., Hood, J. E., daCosta, G. A., and Akman, D. 1991. A Review of the Short-Term Effects of Child Sexual Abuse. *Child Abuse and Neglect* 15, 537–556.

Beitchman, J. H., Zucker, K. J., Hood, J. E., daCosta, G. A., Akman, D., and Cassavia, E. 1992. A Review of the Long-Term Effects of Child Sexual Abuse. *Child Abuse and Neglect* 16, 101–118.

Belsky, J., Steinberg, L., and Draper, P. 1991. Childhood Experience, Interpersonal Development, and Reproductive Strategy: An Evolutionary Theory of Socialization. *Child Development* 62, 647–670.

Berelson, B., and Steiner, G. A. 1964. *Human Behavior: An Inventory of Scientific Findings.* New York: Harcourt, Brace.

Berliner, L., and Conte, J. R. 1993. Sexual Abuse Evaluations: Conceptual and Empirical Obstacles. *Child Abuse and Neglect* 17, 111–125.

Berman, J. S., and Norton, N. C. 1985. Does Professional Training Make a Therapist More Effective? *Psychological Bulletin* 98, 401–07.

Bernard, F. 1981. Pedophilia: Psychological Consequences for the Child. In L. L. Constantine and F. M. Martinson (eds.), *Children and Sex: New Findings, New Perspectives* (pp. 247–253). Boston: Little, Brown.

Bernstein, E. M., and Putnam, F. W. 1986. Development, Reliability, and Validity of a Dissociation Scale. *Journal of Nervous and Mental Disease* 174, 727–735.

Besharov, D. J. 1992. Beware of Unintended Consequences: Too Many Questions Remain Unanswered. *Public Welfare* (Spring), pp. 18–19.

Best, J. 1988. Missing Children, Misleading Statistics. *The Public Interest* 92, 84–92.

Best, J. 1989. Dark Figures and Child Victims: Statistical Claims About Missing Children. In J. Best (eds.), *Images of Issues: Typifying Contemporary Social Problems* (pp. 21–37). New York: Aldine.

Best, J. 1991. Endangered Children in Antisatanist Rhetoric. In J. T. Richardson, J. Best, and D. G. Bromley (eds.), *The Satanism Scare* (pp. 95–106). New York: Aldine.

Best, R. 1983. *We've All Got Scars: What Boys and Girls Learn in Elementary School.* Bloomington, In: Indiana University Press.

Black, D., Kaplan, T., and Hendriks, J. H. 1993. Father Kills Mother: Effects on the Children in the United Kingdom. In J. P. Wilson and B. Raphael (ed.), *International Handbook of Traumatic Stress Syndromes* (pp. 551–59). New York: Plenum.

Blume, E. S. 1990. *Secret Survivors: Uncovering Incest and its Aftereffects in Women.* New York: Wiley.

Boardman, J., Griffin, J., and Murray, O. (eds.) 1986. *The Oxford History of the Classical World.* New York: Oxford University Press.

Bonanno, G. A. 1990. Remembering and Psychotherapy. *Psychotherapy* 27(2), 175–186.

Bottoms, B. L., Shaver, P. R., and Goodman, G. S. 1991. *Profile of Ritualistic and Religion-Based Allegations Reported to Clinical Psychologists in the United States.* Paper presented at the 99th Annual Meeting of the American Psychological Association, San Francisco.

Bower, G. H. 1990. Awareness, the Unconscious, and Repression: An Experimental Psychologist's Perspective. In J. L. Singer (ed.), *Repression and Dissociation* (pp. 209–231). Chicago: University of Chicago Press.

Bradburn, N. M., Rips, L. J., and Shevell, S. K. 1987. Answering

Autobiographical Questions: The Impact of Memory and Inference on Surveys. *Science* 236, 157–161.

Bradshaw, J. 1988. *Healing the Shame That Binds You.* Deerfield Beach, Fl: Health Communications.

Brandt, J. 1988. Malingered Amnesia. In R. Rogers (ed.), *Clinical Assessment of Malingering and Deception* (pp. 65–83). New York: Guilford Press.

Brannigan, M. 1989. The Accused: Child-Abuse Charges Ensnare Some Parents in Baseless Proceedings. *The Wall Street Journal* (August 23rd), 1A, 12A.

Bravos, Z. 1993. Iatrogenically Induced Multiple Personality Disorder and Ritual Abuse Memories in a 10-Year-Old Child. *Issues in Child Abuse Accusations* 5, 243–264.

Brehmer, B. 1980. In One Word: Not From Experience. *Acta Psychologica* 45, 223–241.

Brewin, C. R., Andrews, B., and Gotlib, I. H. 1993. Psychopathology and Early Experience: A Reappraisal of Retrospective Reports. *Psychological Bulletin* 113, 82–98.

Briere, J. 1989. *Therapy For Adults Molested as Children.* New York: Springer.

Briere, J. 1990. Letter to the Editor. *American Journal of Psychiatry* 147, 1389–1390.

Briere, J. 1992. Methodological Issues in the Study of Sexual Abuse Effects. *Journal of Consulting and Clinical Psychology* 60, 196–203.

Briere, J. 1993. *Debate With Elizabeth Loftus.* Presented at the 101st Annual Convention of the American Psychological Association, Toronto, Ontario.

Briere, J., and Conte, J. 1989. *Amnesia in Adults Molested as Children: Testing Theories of Repression.* Paper Presented at the 97th Annual Convention of the American Psychological Association, New Orleans.

Briere, J., and Conte, J. 1993. Self-Reported Amnesia for Abuse in Adults Molested as Children. *Journal of Traumatic Stress* 6(1), 21–31.

Briere, J., and Zaidi, L. Y. 1989. Sexual Abuse Histories and Sequelae in Female Psychiatric Emergency Room Patients. *American Journal of Psychiatry* 146, 1602–06.

Brigham, J. C. 1988. Is Witness Confidence Helpful in Judging Eyewitness Accuracy? In M. M. Gruneberg, P. E. Morris, and R. N. Sykes (eds.), *Practical Aspects of Memory: Current Research and Issues (Vol. 1: Memory in Everyday Life)*, pp. 77–82. Chichester: Wiley.

Brody, J. 1993. Women's Anger Study. *Star Tribune* (Minneapolis, December 5th), p. 3E.

Brown, R., and Kulik, J. 1977. Flashbulb Memories. *Cognition* 5, 73–99.

Brownmiller, S. 1975. *Against Our Will.* New York: Simon and Schuster.

Bulkley, J. A., and Horwitz, M. J. 1994. Adults Sexually Abused as Children: Legal Actions and Issues. *Behavioral Sciences and the Law* 12, 65–87.

Bunge, N. 1993. Child Abuse and Creativity: A New Look at Sherwood Anderson's Breakdown. *Journal of Psychohistory* 20, 413–426.

Buss, D. M. 1987. Evolutionary Hypotheses and Behavioral Genetic Methods: Hopes for a Union of Two Disparate Disciplines. *Behavioral and Brain Sciences* 10(1), 20.

Buss, D. M. 1990. Toward a Biologically Informed Psychology of Personality. *Journal of Personality* 58(1), 1–16.

Butler, S. 1986. Thinking About Prevention Education. In M. Nelson and K. Clark (eds.), *The Educator's Guide to Preventing Child Sexual Abuse*, pp. 6–14. Santa Cruz: Network Publications.

Caldwell, R. A., Bogat, G. A., and Davidson, W. S. 1988. The Assessment of Child Abuse Potential and Prevention of Child Abuse and Neglect: A Policy Analysis. *American Journal of Community Psychology* 16, 609–624.

Campbell, B. A., and Campbell, E. R. 1982. Retention and Extinction of Learned Fear in Infant and Adult Rats. *Journal of Comparative and Physiological Psychology* 55, 1–8.

Campbell, B. A., and Jaynes, J. 1966. Reinstatement. *Psychological Review* 73, 478–480.

Campbell, T. W. 1992. Diagnosing Incest: The Problem of False Positives and Their Consequences. *Issues in Child Abuse Accusations* 4, 161–68.

Campbell, T. W. 1994. *Beware the Talking Cure.* Boca Raton: Upton.

Cantwell, H. B. 1988. Child Sexual Abuse: Very Young Perpetrators. *Child Abuse and Neglect* 12, 579–584.

Cardena, E. and Spiegel, D. 1991. Suggestibility, Absorption, and Dissociation. In J. F. Schumaker (ed.), *Human Suggestibility*, pp. 93–107. New York: Routledge.

Carlson, M. 1994. Full of Grace. *Time* (March 14th), p. 37.

Carroll, G., Annin, P., Fleming, C., Barrett, T., and Liu, M. 1993. Children of the Cult. *Newsweek* (May 17th), pp. 48–50.

Casey, R. J., and Berman, J. S. 1985. The Outcome of Psychotherapy With Children. *Psychological Bulletin* 98, 388–400.

Casson, L. 1987. Once Upon a Time There Were No Lawyers. *Smithsonian* (October) 18(7), pp. 122–131.

Celano, M. P. 1992. A Developmental Model of Victims' Internal Attributions of Responsibility for Sexual Abuse. *Journal of Interpersonal Violence* 7, 57–69.

Ceci, S. J., and Bruck, M. 1993. The Suggestibility of the Child Witness: A Historical Review and Synthesis. *Psychological Bulletin* 113, 403–439.

Champion, D. J. 1988. Child Sexual Abusers and Sentencing Severity. *Federal Probation* (March), pp. 53–57.

Champion, D. J. 1991. *On Increasing the Penalties for Child Sexual Abuse: Some Recent Trends in State Court Sentencing Severity.* Long Beach: Department of Criminal Justice, California State University.

Christensen-Szalanski, J. J. J., and Beach, L. R. 1984. The Citation Bias: Fad and Fashion in the Judgment and Decision Literature. *American Psychologist* 39, 75–78.

Christiansen, J. R., and Blake, R. H. 1990. The Grooming Process in Father-Daughter Incest. In A. L. Horton, B. L. Johnson, L. M. Roundy, and D. Williams (eds.), *The Incest Perpetrator: The Family Member No One Wants To Treat*, pp. 88–98. Newbury Park: Sage.

Christy, M., and Walton, A. 1990. Satan: We Reveal Three Experts Behind the Gory Tales. *Daily Star* (London, September 20th).

Chu, J. A. 1992. The Critical Issues Task Force Report: The Role of Hypnosis and Amytal Interviews in the Recovery of Traumatic Memories. *ISSMP and D News* (June), pp. 6–8.

Clark, L. M. G. 1986. Boys Will Be Boys: Beyond the Badgley Report. *Canadian Journal of Women and the Law* 2 (March), 135–149.

Clark, W. H. 1958. *The Psychology of Religion.* New York: Macmillan.

Clute, S. 1993. Adult Survivor Litigation as an Integral Part of the Therapeutic Process. *Journal of Child Sexual Abuse* 2(1), 121–27.

Colaneri, J. K., and Johnson, D. R. 1992. Coverage For Parents' Sexual Abuse. *For the Defense* (March), pp. 2–5.

Cole, P. M., and Putnam, F. W. 1992. Effect of Incest on Self and

Social Functioning: A Developmental Psychopathology Perspective. *Journal of Consulting and Clinical Psychology* 61, 174–184.

Coleman, L. 1992. Creating 'Memories' of Sexual Abuse. *Issues in Child Abuse Accusations* 4, 169–176.

Conte, J. R. 1982. Sexual Abuse of Children: Enduring Issues For Social Work. *Journal of Social Work and Human Sexuality* 1(1,2), 1–19.

Cote, I. 1993. False Memory Syndrome: Assessment of Adults Reporting Childhood Sexual Abuse. *Western State University Law Review* 20, 427–433.

Coulborn-Faller, K. 1991. Polyincestuous Families. *Journal of Interpersonal Violence* 6, 310–322.

Courtois, C. A. 1992. The Memory Retrieval Process in Incest Survivor Therapy. *Journal of Child Sexual Abuse* 1(1), 15–31.

Coxe, A. C. 1957. *The Ante-Nicene Fathers, Vol. V.* Grand Rapids: Eerdmans.

Cozolino, L. J. 1989. The Ritual Abuse of Children: Implications for Clinical Practice and Research. *Journal of Sex Research* 26(1), 131–38.

Crichton, M. 1994. *Disclosure.* New York: Knopf.

Crnich, J. E., and Crnich, K. A. 1992. *Shifting the Burden of Truth: Suing Child Sexual Abusers: A Legal Guide For Survivors and Their Supporters.* Lake Oswego: Recollex.

Crocker, J. 1981. Judgment of Covariation by Social Perceivers. *Psychological Bulletin* 90, 272–292.

Cronbach, L. J. 1992. Beyond the Two Disciplines of Scientific Psychology. *American Psychologist* 30, 116–127.

Curtiss, A. 1992. Some on Ritual Abuse Task Force say Satanists are Poisoning Them. *Los Angeles Times* (December 1st), pp. B1, B8.

Daly, L. W., and Pacifico, J. F. 1991. Opening the Doors to the Past: Decade Delayed Disclosure of Memories of Years Gone By. *The Champion* (December), pp. 42–47.

Darwin, C. 1936. *The Origin of Species and the Descent of Man.* New York: Modern Library.

Daugherty, L. B. 1986. What Happens to Victims of Child Sexual Abuse? In M. Nelson and K. Clark (eds.), *The Educator's Guide to Preventing Child Sexual Abuse.* Santa Cruz: Network Publications.

David, S. J. 1992. *Tools of the Trade.* Seminar presented in Victoria, B. C. Canada, February 23rd.

Dawes, R. M. 1988. *Rational Choice in an Uncertain World*. San Diego: Harcourt Brace.

Dawes, R. M. 1989a. Letter of Resignation. *American Psychological Society Observer* 2(1), 14–15.

Dawes, R. M. 1989b. Experience and Validity of Clinical Judgment: The Illusory Correlation. *Behavioral Sciences and the Law* 7, 457–467.

Dawes, R. M. 1992. Why Believe That for Which There is No Good Evidence? *Issues in Child Abuse Accusations* 4, 214–18.

Dawes, R. M. 1994. *House of Cards: Psychiatry and Psychotherapy Built on Myth*. New York: The Free Press.

Dawes, R. M., Faust, D., and Meehl, P. E. 1989. Clinical Versus Actuarial Judgment. *Science* 243, 1668–1674.

DeLipsey, J. M., and James, S. K. 1988. Videotaping the Sexually Abused Child: The Texas Experience, 1983–1987. In S. M. Sgroi (ed.), *Vulnerable Populations: Evaluation and Treatment of Sexually Abused Children and Adult Survivors: Vol. 1*, pp. 229–264. Lexington: Lexington Books.

Dewey, J. 1939. *Freedom and Culture*. New York: Capricorn.

Dietz, P. E., Hazelwood, R. R., and Warren, J. 1990. The Sexually Sadistic Criminal and his Offenses. *Bulletin of the American Psychiatry and the Law* 18, 163–178.

Dolan, Y. M. 1991. *Resolving Sexual Abuse*. New York: Norton.

Duchschere, K. 1992. Their Love Was Illegal. *Star Tribune* (Minneapolis, December 18th), pp. 1A, 9A.

Dunn, G. E. 1992. Multiple Personality Disorder: A New Challenge for Psychology. *Professional Psychology: Research and Practice* 23, 18–23.

Economist. 1989. The Queerness of Quanta. January 7th, pp. 71–74.

Economist. 1993. Looking at Inner Landscapes. July 3rd, pp. 79–80.

Edwards, R. D. 1993. Our First 150 Years: The Pursuit of Reason. *The Economist* (September 4th), pp. 23–25.

Edwards, D., and Potter. J. 1993. Language and Causation: A Discursive Action Model of Description and Attribution. *Psychological Review* 100, 23–41.

Einhorn, H. J., and Hogarth, R. M. 1978. Confidence in Judgment: Persistence of the Illusion of Validity. *Psychological Review* 85, 395–416.

Eisenberg, A. R. 1985. Learning to Describe Past Experiences in Conversation. *Discourse Processes* 8, 177–204.

Ellis, A. 1963. *Reason and Emotion in Psychotherapy*. New York: Lyle Stuart.

Ellis, B. 1992. Satanic Ritual Abuse and Legend Ostension. *Journal of Psychology and Theology* 20, 274–77.

Enns, C. Z. 1992. Toward Integrating Feminist Psychotherapy and Feminist Philosophy. *Professional Psychology: Research and Practice* 23, 453–466.

Erdelyi, M. H. 1990. Repression, Reconstruction, and Defense: History and Integration of the Psychoanalytic and Experimental Frameworks. In J. L. Singer (ed.), *Repression and Dissociation*, pp. 1–31. Chicago: University of Chicago Press.

Erickson, W. D. 1985. Unpublished manuscript.

Erickson, W. D., Walbek, N. H., and Seely, R. K. 1988. Behavior Patterns of Child Molesters. *Archives of Sexual Behavior* 17(1), 77–86.

Ernsberger, D. 1980. Psychiatrist, Psychologist: What's the Difference? *IPT Newsletter* 16 (January).

Eth, S., and Pynoos, R. S. (ed.) 1985. *Post-Traumatic Stress Disorder in Children*. Washington, DC: American Psychiatric Press.

Euripides (Trans. William Arrowsmith) 1959. *The Bacchae*. Chicago: University of Chicago Press.

Ewing, C. P. 1992. Suing Your Perpetrator: Response to a Survivor's Story. *Journal of Child Sexual Abuse* 1(2), 129–132.

Fahy, T. A. 1988. The Diagnosis of Multiple Personality Disorder: A Critical Review. *British Journal of Psychiatry* 153, 597–606.

Fairbairn, W. R. D. 1943. The Repression and Return of Bad Objects. In *Psychoanalytic Studies of the Personality*. London: Tavistock/Routledge, 1990.

Farber, E. D., Showers, J., Johnson, C. F., Joseph, J. A., and Oshins, L. 1984. The Sexual Abuse of Children: A Comparison of Male and Female Victims. *Journal of Clinical and Child Psychology* 13(2), 294–97.

Faust, D. 1989. Data Integration in Legal Evaluations: Can Clinicians Deliver on Their Premises? *Behavioral Sciences and the Law* 7, 469–483.

Feld, A. 1994. *MSW Education: Where is the Content on Memory?* Paper presented at the 40th Annual Program Meeting of the Council on Social Work Education, Atlanta.

Femina, D. D., Yeager, C. A. and Lewis, D. O. 1990. Child Abuse: Adolescent Records vs. Adult Recall. *Child Abuse and Neglect* 14, 227–231.

Festinger, L., Riecken, H. W., and Schachter, S. 1956. *When Prophecy Fails*. Minneapolis: University of Minnesota Press.

Finkelhor, D. 1979. *Sexually Victimized Children*. New York: The Free Press.

Finkelhor, D. 1984. *Child Sexual Abuse: New Theory and Research*. New York: Free Press.

Finkelhor, D. 1986. *A Sourcebook on Child Sexual Abuse*. Beverly Hills: Sage.

Finkelhor, D. 1990. Early and Long-Term Effects of Child Sexual Abuse: An Update. *Professional Psychology: Research and Practice* 21, 325–330.

Finkelhor, D., Williams, L. M., and Burns, N. 1988. *Nursery Crimes*. Newbury Park: Sage.

Finkelhor, D., Williams, L. M., Burns, N, and Kalinowski, M. 1988. *Sexual Abuse in Day Care: A National Study*. Family Research Laboratory. University of New Hampshire.

Fivush, R., and Hamond, N. R. 1990. Autobiographical Memory Across the Preschool Years: Toward Reconceptualizing Childhood Amnesia. In R. Fivush and J. A. Hudson (eds.), *Knowing and Remembering in Young Children*, pp. 223–248. New York: Cambridge University Press.

Fleischhauer-Hardt, F., and McBride, W. 1975. *Show Me! A Picture Book of Sex for Children and Their Parents*. New York: St. Martins Press.

FMS Foundation Newsletter. 1992–1994. False Memory Syndrome Foundation, 3401 Market Street, Suite 130, Philadelphia, Pa 19104–3315.

Frankel, F. H. 1993. Adult Reconstruction of Childhood Events in the Multiple Personality Literature. *American Journal of Psychiatry* 150, 954–58.

Franklin, B. 1973. *Poor Richard's Almanac*. New York: McKay.

Fredrickson, R. 1992. *Repressed Memories: A Journal to Recovery From Sexual Abuse*. New York: Simon and Schuster.

Fredrickson, R. 1993a. Affidavit of Renée Fredrickson dated 16th July 1993.

Fredrickson, R. 1993b. Presentation at the 'Memories of Abuse' Conference, Minneapolis, Minnesota, June 24th–25th.

Freeland, A., Manchanda, R., Chiu, S., Sharma, V., and Merskey, H. 1993. Four Cases of Supposed Multiple Personality Disorder: Evidence of Unjustified Diagnoses. *Canadian Journal of Psychiatry* 38, 245–247.

Freyd, J. J. 1993. *Theoretical and Personal Perspectives on the Delayed Memory Debate.* Center for Mental Health at Foote Hospital's Conference on Controversies Around Recovered Memories of Incest and Ritualistic Abuse. Ann Arbor, Michigan, August 7th.

Freyd, P., Roth, Z., Wakefield, H., and Underwager, R. 1993. *Results of the FMSF Family Survey.* Paper presented at the conference on 'Memory and Reality,' False Memory Syndrome Foundation, Valley Forge, Pa, April 16th–18th.

Friedrich, W. N., Grambsch, P., Broughton, D., Kuiper, J., and Beilke, R. L. 1991. Normative Sexual Behavior in Children. *Pediatrics* 88, 456–464.

Friesen, J. G. 1992. Ego-Dystonic or Ego Alien: Alternate Personality or Evil Spirit? *Journal of Psychology and Theology* 20, 197–200.

Funder, D. C. 1987. Errors and Mistakes: Evaluating the Accuracy of Social Judgment. *Psychological Bulletin* 101, 75–90.

Futrelle, D. 1993. Suffer the Children. *In These Times* (August 9th), pp. 14–17.

Gambrill, E. 1990. *Critical Thinking in Clinical Practice.* San Francisco: Jossey-Bass.

Ganaway, G. K. 1991. *Alternative Hypotheses Regarding Satanic Ritual Abuse Memories.* Paper presented at the 99th Annual Convention of American Psychological Association, San Francisco, August 19th.

Ganaway, G. K. 1993. *Dissociative Disorders: Trauma vs. Conflict and Deficit.* Paper presented at the conference on 'Memory and Reality,' False Memory Syndrome Foundation, Valley Forge, Pa, April 17th.

Garb, H. N. 1989. Clinical Judgment, Clinical Training, and Professional Experience. *Psychological Bulletin* 105, 387–396.

Gardner, R. A. 1992a. Belated Realization of Child Sex Abuse by an Adult. *Issues in Child Abuse Accusations* 4, 177–195.

Gardner, R. A. 1992b. *True and False Accusations of Child Sex Abuse.* Creskill, NJ: Creative Therapeutics.

Gardner, R. A. 1994. Comments on Linda Meyer Williams Study. *FMS Foundation Newsletter* (January), pp. 2–4.

Garfield, S. L. 1982. The Emergence of the Scientist-Practitioner Model: Background and Rationale. *The Clinical Psychologist* 36(1) (fall), pp. 4–11.

Gauron, E. F., and Dickinson, J. K. 1969. The Influence of Seeing the Patient First on Diagnostic Decision Making in Psychiatry. *American Journal of Psychiatry* 126(2), 85–91.

Gavigan, M. 1992. False Memories of Sexual Abuse: A Personal Account. *Issues in Child Abuse Accusations* 4, 246–47.

Gebhard, P. H., Gagnon, J. H., Pomeroy, W. B., and Christenson, C. V. 1965. *Sex Offenders.* New York: Harper and Row.

Geiselman, R. E. and Fisher, R. P. 1989. The Cognitive Interview Technique for Victims and Witnesses of Crime. In D. C. Raskin (ed.), *Psychological Methods in Criminal Investigation and Evidence,* pp. 191–217. New York: Springer.

Gilbert, N. 1991. The Phantom Epidemic of Sexual Assault. *The Public Interest* 103, 54–65.

Gleitman, H. 1993. *Some Reflections on Memory.* Paper presented at the conference on 'Memory and Reality,' False Memory Syndrome Foundation, Valley Forge, Pa, April 18th.

Goff, D. C., and Simms, C. A. 1993. Has Multiple Personality Disorder Remained Consistent Over Time? *The Journal of Nervous and Mental Disease* 181, 595–600.

Goldstein, E., and Farmer, K. 1993. *True Stories of False Memories.* Boca Raton: SIRS Books.

Goleman, D. 1985. Social Workers Vault Into a Leading Role in Psychotherapy. *New York Times* (April 30th), pp. C1, C9.

Goleman, D. 1993. Studies Reveal Suggestibility of Very Young as Witnesses. *New York Times* (June 11th), pp. A1, A23.

Gondolf, L. P. 1992. Traumatic Therapy. *Issues in Child Abuse Accusations* 4, 239–245.

Goodman, G. S., and Hahn, A. 1987. Evaluating Eyewitness Testimony. In I. B. Weiner and A. K. Hess (eds.), *Handbook of Forensic Psychology,* pp. 258–292. New York: Wiley.

Goodstein, L. D., and Brazis, K. L. 1970. Psychology of Scientist: XXX. Credibility of Psychologists: An Empirical study. *Psychological Reports* 27, 835–38.

Gordon, R., and Wraith, R. 1993. Responses of Children and Adolescents to Disaster. In J. P. Wilson, J. P. and B. Raphael (eds.), *International Handbook of Traumatic Stress Syndromes,* pp. 561–575. New York: Plenum.

Gould, C., and Cozolino, L. 1992. Ritual Abuse, Multiplicity, and Mind Control. *Journal of Psychology and Theology* 20, 194–96.

Grand, S., Alpert, J. L., Safer, J. M., and Milden, R. 1991. *Incest and Amnesia—How Do We Know What Really Happened?* Symposium presented at the 99th Annual Convention of the American Psychological Association, San Francisco, August 17th.

Gravitz, M. A. 1994. Are the Right People Being Trained to Use Hypnosis? *American Journal of Clinical Hypnosis* 36, 179–182.

Greeley, A. 1994. Truth Won Out For Cardinal Bernardin. *Star Tribune* (Minneapolis March 11th) p. 17A.

Gross, J. 1994. Suit Asks, Does 'Memory Therapy' Heal or Harm? *New York Times* (April 8th), pp. A1, B9.

Groth, N., Burgess, A., Birnbaum, H., and Gary, T. 1978. A Study of the Child Molester: Myths and Realities. *LAE Journal of the American Justice Association* 41(1), 17–22.

Gundersen, B. H., Melas, P. S., and Skar, J. E. 1981. Sexual Behavior of Preschool Children: Teachers' Observations. In L. L. Constantine and F. M. Martinson (eds.), *Children and Sex: New Findings, New Perspectives*, pp. 45–61. Boston: Little, Brown.

Gustafson, P. 1994. Psychiatrist Sues After Order to Have Exams. *Star Tribune* (Minneapolis March 18th), pp. 1B, 4B.

Guze, S. B., and Olin, S. T. 1992. Psychotherapy: Psychotherapy and the Medical Model. In S. B. Guze (ed.), *Why Psychiatry is a Branch of Medicine*, pp. 68–83. New York: Oxford University Press.

Halverson, C. F. 1988. Remembering Your Parents: Reflections on the Retrospective Method. *Journal of Personality* 56, 435–443.

Hartman, C. R., and Burgess, A. W. 1988. Information Processing of Trauma: Case Application of a Model. *Journal of Interpersonal Violence* 3, 443–457.

Harvey, M. 1993. *Traumatic Memory: Research and Practice.* Paper presented at the 'Memories of Abuse' Conference, Minneapolis, June.

Haugaard, J. J., and Tilly, C. 1988. Characteristics Predicting Children's Responses to Sexual Encounters With Other Children. *Child Abuse and Neglect* 12, 209–218.

Hayes, S. C. 1989. An Interview With Lee Sechrest: The Courage to Say 'We Do Not Know How.' *APS Observer* 2(4), 8–10.

Hedges, L. E. 1994. Taking Recovered Memories Seriously. *Issues in Child Abuse Accusations* 6, 1–32.

Helfer, R. E. 1991. Child Abuse and Neglect: Assessment, Treatment, and Prevention, October 21st, 2007. *Child Abuse and Neglect* 15(Sup. 1), 5–15.

Herman, J. L., 1981. *Father-Daughter Incest.* Cambridge, Ma: Harvard University Press.

Herman, J. L. 1992. *Trauma and Recovery.* New York: Harper Collins.

Herman, J. L., and Schatzow, E. 1987. Recovery and Verification of

Memories of Childhood Sexual Trauma. *Psychoanalytic Psychology* 4(1), 1–14.

Herndon, P. L. 1994. False and Repressed Memories Gain Media Spotlight: APA Seeks Balance in Coverage. *Practitioner* 7(1) (February), pp. 2, 15.

Hicks, R. D. 1991. *In Pursuit of Satan.* Buffalo: Prometheus.

Hindman, J. 1988. Research Disputes Assumptions About Child Molesters. *National District Attorneys Association Bulletin* 7(4), pp. 1, 3.

Hoch, E. L. 1982. Perspective on Experimental Contributions to Clinical Research. In P. C. Kendall and J. N. Butcher (eds.), *Handbook of Research Methods in Clinical Psychology*, pp. 13–57. New York: Wiley.

Hofstadter, R. 1967. *The Paranoid Style in American Politics and Other Essays.* New York: Vintage.

Hollingsworth, J. 1986. *Unspeakable Acts.* New York: Congdon and Weed.

Holmes, D. S. 1974. Investigations of Repression: Differential Recall of Material Experimentally or Naturally Associated with Ego Threat. *Psychological Bulletin* 81, 632–653.

Holmes, D. S. 1990. The Evidence for Repression: An Examination of Sixty Years of Research. In J. L. Singer (ed.), *Repression and Dissociation*, pp. 85–102. Chicago: University of Chicago Press.

Holmes, D. S. 1994. Is There Evidence for Repression? Doubtful. *Harvard Mental Health Letter* 10(12), 4–6.

Horner, T. M. and Guyer, M. J. 1991a. Prediction, Prevention, and Clinical Expertise in Child Custody Cases in Which Allegations of Child Sexual Abuse Have Been Made: I. Predictable Rates of Diagnostic Error in Relation to Various Clinical Decision Making Strategies. *Family Law Quarterly* 25, 217–252.

Horner, T. M. and Guyer, M. J. 1991b. Prediction, Prevention, and Clinical Expertise in Child Custody Cases in Which Allegations of Child Sexual Abuse Have Been Made: II. Prevalence Rates of Child Sexual Abuse and the Precision of 'Tests' Constructed to Diagnose it. *Family Law Quarterly* 25, 381–409.

Horner, T. M. 1992. *Expertise in Regard to Determinations of Child Sexual Abuse.* Unpublished manuscript.

Hornstein, G. A. 1992. The Return of the Repressed: Psychology's Problematic Relations with Psychoanalysis, 1909–1960. *American Psychologist* 47, 254–263.

Horwich, P. 1982. *Probability and Evidence*. Cambridge, Ma: Cambridge University Press.

Howe, M. L., and Courage, M. L. 1993. On Resolving the Enigma of Infantile Amnesia. *Psychological Bulletin* 113, 305–326.

Howell, W. 1992. Field's Science Deficit Will Have Dire Results. *APA Monitor*, 23(12) (December), 21.

Howson, C., and Urbach, P. 1993. *Scientific Reasoning: The Bayesian Approach*. Second edition. Chicago: Open Court.

Huber, P. W. 1991. *Galileo's Revenge: Junk Science in the Courtroom*. New York: Basic Books.

Hudson, J. A., and Fivush, R. 1987. As Time Goes By: Sixth Graders Remember a Kindergarten Experience. *Emory Cognition Project, Report #13*, Emory University, Department of Psychology, Atlanta.

Huff, R. C., Rattner, A., and Sagarin, E. 1986. Guilty Until Proved Innocent: Wrongful Conviction and Public Policy. *Crime and Delinquency* 32, 518–544.

Hughes, R. 1993. *Culture of Complaint: The Fraying of America*. New York: Oxford University Press.

Hunter, M. 1990. *Abused Boys: The Neglected Victims of Sexual Abuse*. New York: Ballantine.

Huyghe, P. 1985. Voices, Glances, Flashbacks: Our First Memories. *Psychology Today* (September), pp. 48–52.

James, K., and MacKinnon, L. 1990. The 'Incestuous Family' Revisited: A Critical Analysis of Family Therapy Myths. *Journal of Marital and Family Therapy* 16(1), 71–88.

Jenkins, P. 1993. Believe the Children? Child Abuse and the American Legal System. *Chronicles: A Magazine of American Culture* (January), pp. 20–23.

Johnson, T. C. 1988. Child Perpetrators—Children Who Molest Other Children: Preliminary Findings. *Child Abuse and Neglect* 12, 219–229.

Johnson, T. C. 1989. Female Child Perpetrators: Children who Molest Other Children. *Child Abuse and Neglect* 13, 571–585.

Johnson, M. K., Hashtroudi, S., and Lindsay, D. S. 1993. Source Monitoring. *Psychological Bulletin* 114, 3–28.

Jones, E. E., Ghannam, J., Nigg, J. T., and Dyer, J. F. P. 1993. A Paradigm for Single-Cases Research: The Time Series Study of a Long-Term Psychotherapy for Depression. *Journal of Consulting and Clinical Psychology* 61, 381–394.

Kahneman, D., and Tversky, A. 1979. Prospect Theory: An Analysis of Decision Under Risk. *Econometrica* 47, 263–291.

Kandel, M., and Kandel, E. 1994. Flights of Memory. *Discover* (May), pp. 32–38.

Kazdin, A. E. 1986. Comparative Outcome Studies of Psychotherapy: Methodological Issues and Strategies. *Journal of Consulting and Clinical Psychology* 54, 95–105.

Kendall-Tackett, K. A., and Simon, A. F. 1987. Perpetrators and Their Acts: Data From 365 Adults Molested as Children. *Child Abuse and Neglect* 11, 237–245.

Kendall-Tackett, K. A., and Simon, A. F. 1992. A Comparison of the Abuse Experiences of Male and Female Adults Molested as Children. *Journal of Family Violence* 7, 57–62.

Kendall-Tackett, K. A., Williams, L. M., and Finkelhor, D. 1993. Impact of Sexual Abuse on Children: A Review and Synthesis of Recent Empirical Studies. *Psychological Bulletin* 113, 164–180.

Ketchum, R. M. 1991. Memory as History. *American Heritage* (November), pp. 142–48.

Kilpatrick, A. 1992. *Long-Range Effects of Child and Adolescent Sexual Experiences*. Hillsdale, NJ: Erlbaum.

Kincaid, J. R. 1992. *Child Loving*. New York: Routledge.

Kinsey, A. C., Pomeroy, W. B., Martin, C. E., and Gebhard, P. H. 1953. *Sexual Behavior in the Human Female*. Philadelphia: Saunders.

Kirk, S. A., and Kutchins, H. 1992. *The Selling of DSM: The Rhetoric of Science in Psychology*. New York: Aldine.

Kluft, R. P. 1987. The Parental Fitness of Mothers with Multiple Personality Disorder: A Preliminary Study. *Child Abuse and Neglect* 11, 273–280.

Kluft, R. P. 1991. Multiple Personality Disorder. In A. Tassman and S. M. Goldfinger (eds.), *Review of Psychiatry*, pp. 161–188. Washington, DC: American Psychiatric Press.

Koocher, G. P. 1979. Credentialing in Psychology: Close Encounters With Competence? *American Psychologist* 34, 696–702.

Kotelchuck, M. 1982. Child Abuse and Neglect: Prediction and Misclassification. In R. H. Starr, Jr. (ed.), *Child Abuse Prediction: Policy Implications*, pp. 67–104. Cambridge, Ma: Ballinger.

Kristiansen, C. M. 1994. Bearing Witness to the Patriarchal Revictimization of Survivors. *SWAP Newsletter* 20(2), 7–16.

Krivacska, J. J. 1990. *Designing Child Sexual Abuse Prevention Programs: Current Approaches and a Proposal for the Prevention,*

Reduction, and Identification of Sexual Misuse. Springfield, Il: Thomas.

Krivacska, J. J. 1991. Sexual Abuse Prevention Programs: Can They Cause False Allegations? *Issues in Child Abuse Accusations* 3, 1–6.

Krivacska, J. J. 1992. Child Sexual Abuse Prevention Programs: The Prevention of Childhood Sexuality? *Journal of Child Sexual Abuse* 1(4), 83–112.

Krivacska, J. J. 1993. Antisexualism in Child Sexual Abuse Prevention Programs—Good Touch, Bad Touch . . . Don't Touch? *Issues in Child Abuse Accusations* 5, 78–82.

Lachnit, C. 1991. Children Who Molest Children a Growing Trend. *Orange County Register* (October 26th), pp. B1, B5.

Lahey, B. B., and Kazdin, A. E. 1988. *Advances in Clinical Child Psychology, Vol. 11*. New York: Plenum.

Lahey, B. B., and Kazdin, A. E. 1989. *Advances in Clinical Child Psychology, Vol. 12*. New York: Plenum.

Lahey, B. B., and Kazdin, A. E. 1990. *Advances in Clinical Child Psychology, Vol. 13*. New York: Plenum.

Lang, R. A., and Langevin, R. 1991. Parent-Child Relations in Offenders Who Commit Violent Sexual Crimes Against Children. *Behavioral Sciences and the Law* 9, 61–71.

Langevin, R. 1983. *Sexual Strands: Understanding and Treating Sexual Anomalies in Men*. Hillsdale, NJ: Erlbaum.

Langfeldt, T. 1981. Sexual Development in Children. In M. Cook and K. Howells (eds.), *Adult Sexual Interest in Children*, pp. 99–120. New York: Academic Press.

Lanning, K. V. 1991. Ritual Abuse: A Law Enforcement View or Perspective. *Child Abuse and Neglect* 15, 171–73.

Lanning, K. V. 1992. *Investigator's Guide to Allegations of "Ritual" Child Abuse*. Quantico, Va: National Center for the Analysis of Violent Crime.

Lepore, S. J. 1991. Child Witness: Cognitive and Social Factors Related to Memory and Testimony. *Issues in Child Abuse Accusations* 3, 65–89.

Letwin, S. R. 1991. Law and the Unreasonable Woman. *National Review* (November 18th), pp. 34–36.

Levine, M. 1994. *How the Origins of Child Protective Service Laws in the Police Power and Parens Patriae Power of the State are Reflected in the Job Experiences of Child Protective Service Workers and Mandated Reporters*. Paper presented at the Biennial Meeting of the American Psychology-Law Society, Santa Fe, March 12th.

Li, C. K., West, D. J., and Woodhouse, T. P. 1993. *Children's Sexual Encounters With Adults.* Buffalo: Prometheus.

Lindsay, D. S., and Read, J. D. (in press). Psychotherapy and Memories of Childhood Sexual Abuse: A Cognitive Perspective. In M. Zaragosa, J. R. Graham, G. C. N. Hall, R. Hirschman, and Y. S. Ben-Porath (eds.), *Memory and Testimony in the Child Witness.* Newbury Park: Sage.

Linton, M. 1979. I Remember it Well. *Psychology Today* (July). pp. 45–52

Lipsey, M. W., and Wilson, D. B. 1993. The Efficacy of Psychological, Educational, and Behavioral Treatment: Confirmation From Meta-Analysis. *American Psychologist* 48, 1181–1209.

Littlefield, C. H., and Rushton, J. P. 1986. When a Child Dies: The Sociobiology of Bereavement. *Journal of Personality and Social Psychology* 51, 797–802.

Loewenstein, R. J. 1991. Psychogenic Amnesia and Psychogenic Fugue: A Comprehensive Review. In A. Tassman and S. M. Goldfinger (ed.), *Review of Psychiatry*, pp. 189–221. Washington, DC: American Psychiatric Press.

Loftus, E. F. 1992. When a Lie Becomes Memory's Truth: Memory Distortion After Exposure to Misinformation. *Current Directions in Psychological Science* 1(4), 121–23.

Loftus, E. F. 1993. The Reality of Repressed Memories. *American Psychologist* 48, 518–535.

Loftus, E. F., Garry, M., Brown, S. W., and Rader, M. 1994. Near-Natal Memories, Past-Life Memories, and Other Memory Myths. *American Journal of Clinical Hypnosis* 36, 176–79.

Loftus, E. F., and Ketcham, K. 1991. *Witness for the Defense.* New York: St. Martin's Press.

Loftus, E. F., Korf, N. L., and Schooler, J. W. 1989. Misguided Memories: Sincere Distortions of Reality. In J. C. Yuille (ed.), *Credibility Assessment*, pp. 155–174. Dordrecht: Kluwer.

Loftus, E. F., Polonsky, S. and Fullilove, M. T. (in press). Memories of Childhood Sexual Abuse: Remembering and Repressing. *Psychology of Women Quarterly.*

Loftus, E. F., and Rosenwald, L. A. 1993. Buried Memories, Shattered Lives. *ABA Journal* (November), pp. 70–73.

Logg, C. 1990. Trend of Younger Sexual Offenders on Increase. *Bellingham Herald* (July 11th), pp. A1, A2.

Loveland, E. H. 1985. Measurement of Competence: Some Definitional Issues. *Professional Practice of Psychology* 6(1), 129–143.

Lundberg-Love, P. 1989. *Research and Treatment Issues Concerning Adult Incest Survivors.* Paper presented as part of a symposium titled 'Treating Incest Victims and Offenders: Applying Recent Research' at the 97th Annual Meeting of the American Psychological Association, New Orleans, August.

Lundberg-Love, P. J. (undated). *Treatment of Adult Survivors of Incest.* Unpublished manuscript.

Lynn, S. J., and Nash, M. R. 1994. Truth in Memory: Ramifications for Psychotherapy and Hypnotherapy. *American Journal of Clinical Hypnosis* 36, 194–208.

Mackay, C. 1932 [1841]. *Extraordinary Popular Delusions and the Madness of Crowds.* New York: Farrar, Straus, and Giroux.

Mackinnon, D. W., and Dukes, W. F. 1963. Repression. In L. Postman (ed.), *Psychology in the Making: Histories of Selected Research Problems*, pp. 662–744. New York: Knopf.

Macksoud, M. S., Dyregrov, A., and Raundalen, M. 1993. Traumatic War Experiences and Their Effects on Children. In J. P. Wilson and B. Raphael (eds.), *International Handbook of Traumatic Stress Syndromes*, pp. 625–633. New York: Plenum.

MacLean, H. N. 1993. *Once Upon a Time: The True Story of a Memory, a Murder, and a Trial.* New York: Harper Collins.

MacLean, H. N. 1994. Analysis of Lenore Terr's Account of the Eileen Franklin Trial. *Issues in Child Abuse Accusations* 6(2).

Mallia, M. 1993. Adult Survivor Litigation as an Integral part of the Therapeutic Process: A Reply. *Journal of Child Sexual Abuse* 2(1), 129–130.

Malmquist, C. P. 1986. Children Who Witness Parental Murder: Posttraumatic Aspects. *Journal of the American Academy of Child Psychiatry* 25, 320–25.

Maltz, W. 1990. Adults Survivors of Incest: How to Help Them Overcome the Trauma. *Medical Aspects of Human Sexuality* (December), pp. 42–47.

Manross, M. 1992. Mandatory Sentencing. *Issues in Child Accusations* 4, 17–20.

Manshel, L. 1990. *Nap Time.* New York: Morrow.

Martinson, F. M. 1981. Eroticism in Infancy and Childhood. In L. L. Constantine and F. M. Martinson (eds.), *Children and Sex: New Findings, New Perspectives*, pp. 23–35). Boston: Little, Brown.

Marty, M. E. 1964. *Varieties of Unbelief.* New York: Holt, Rinehart, and Winston.

Mason, M. 1993. Presentation at the 'Memories of Abuse' conference, Minneapolis, Minnesota, June 24th and 25th.

Masters, W. H., and Johnson, V. E. 1970a. *Human Sexual Inadequacy.* Boston: Little Brown.

Masters, W. H., and Johnson, V. E. 1970b. *The Pleasure Bond.* Boston: Little Brown.

Matarazzo, J. 1993. Without Science Base, There Won't be Much to Practice in 15–20 years. *The National Psychologist* (July-August), p. 16.

Matson, J. L., Gouvier, W. D., and Manikam, R. 1989. Publication Counts and Scholastic Productivity: Comment on Howard, Cole, and Maxwell. *American Psychologist* 44, 737–39.

Mayer, R. S. 1991. *Satan's Children: Case Studies in Multiple Personality.* New York: Putnam.

McFall, R. M. 1991. Manifesto for a Science of Clinical Psychology. *Clinical Psychologist* 44(6), 75–88. In *Clinical Psychology Review* 11(6).

McGovern, C. 1994. Summoning Demons in the Mind. *Alberta Report* (February 14th), p. 31.

McHugh, P. R. 1993. Multiple Personality Disorder. *Harvard Mental Health Letter* 10(3), 1–2.

McHugh, P. R. 1994. Psychotherapy Awry. *American Scholar* (winter), pp. 17–30.

McHugh, P. R. (undated). *History and the Pitfalls of Practice.* Unpublished Manuscript.

McMullen, J. G. 1992. The Inherent Limitations of After-the-Fact Statutes Dealing with the Emotional and Sexual Maltreatment of Children. *Drake Law Review* 41, 483–510.

Meehl, P. E. 1954. *Clinical Versus Statistical Prediction: A Theoretical Analysis and a Review of the Evidence.* Minneapolis: University of Minnesota Press.

Meehl, P. E. 1959. Some Ruminations on the Validation of Clinical Procedures. *Canadian Journal of Psychology* 13, 102–128.

Meehl, P. E. 1960. The Cognitive Activity of the Clinician. *American Psychologist* 15, 19–27.

Meehl, P. E. 1967. Theory-Testing in Psychology and Physics: A Methodological Paradox. *Philosophy of Science* 34, 103–115.

Meehl, P. E. 1973. *Psychodiagnosis: Selected Papers.* Minneapolis: University of Minnesota Press.

Meehl, P. E. 1986. Psychology: Does Our Heterogeneous Subject Matter Have Any Unity? *Minnesota Psychologist* (summer), pp. 3–9

Meehl, P. E. 1989. Law and the Fireside Inductions (with Postscript): Some Reflections of a Clinical Psychologist. *Behavioral Sciences and the Law* 7, 521–550.

Meehl, P. E. 1993. Philosophy of Science: Help or Hindrance? *Psychological Reports* 72, 707–733.

Meiselman, K. C. 1978. *Incest: A Psychological Study of Causes and Effects with Treatment Recommendations.* San Francisco: Jossey-Bass.

Meiselman, K. C. 1990. *Resolving the Trauma of Incest.* San Francisco: Jossey-Bass.

Melton, G. B. 1993. *Expert Opinions: Not for Cosmic Understanding.* Paper presented at the 101st Annual Convention of the American Psychological Association, Toronto, August.

Menne, J. W. 1981. Competency Based Assessment and the Profession of Psychology. *Professional Practice of Psychology* 2(1), 17–28.

Merskey, H. 1992. The Manufacture of Personalities: The Production of Multiple Personality Disorder. *British Journal of Psychiatry* 160, 327–340.

Metcalfe, M., Oppenheimer, R., Dignon, A., and Palmer, R. L. 1990. Childhood Sexual Experiences Reported by Male Psychiatric Patients. *Psychological Medicine* 20, 923–29.

Miller, A. 1981. *Prisoners of Childhood.* New York: Basic Books.

Miller, A. 1983. *For Your Own Good.* New York: Farrar, Straus, and Giroux.

Miller, A. 1984. *Thou Shalt Not be Aware.* New York: Farrar, Straus, and Giroux.

Miller, D. 1994. *Critical Rationalism: A Defence and Restatement.* Chicago: Open Court.

Millman, J., Samet, S., Shaw, J., and Braden, M. 1990. The Dissemination of Psychological Research. Comment on Kupffersmid. *American Psychologist* 45, 668–69.

Millon, T. 1981. Disorders of Personality: DSM-III: Axis II. New York: Wiley.

Milner, J. S., Gold, R. G., Ayoub, C., and Jacewitz, M. M. 1984. Predictive Validity of the Child Abuse Potential Inventory. *Journal of Consulting and Clinical Psychology* 52, 879–884.

Mohr, J. W. 1981. Age Structures in Pedophilia. In M. Cook and K.

Howells (eds.), *Adult Sexual Interest in Children*, pp. 42–64. New York: Academic Press.

Money, J. 1991a. *Epidemic Antisexuality: From Onanism to Satanism.* Paper presented at the 10th World Congress of Sexology, Amsterdam, June.

Money, J. 1991b. Sexology and/or Sexosophy, the Split Between Sexual Researchers and Reformers in History and Practice. *SIECUS Report* (February-March), 1–4.

Mosher, D. L. 1991. Ideological Presuppositions: Rhetoric in Sexual Science, Sexual Politics, and Sexual Morality. *Journal of Psychology and Human Sexuality* 4(4), 7–29.

Mould, D. E. 1984. *The Politics of Victimization.* Unpublished manuscript.

Mulhern, S. 1991. Satanism and Psychotherapy: A Rumor in Search of an Inquisition. In J. T. Richardson, J. Best, and D. G. Bromley (eds.), *The Satanism Scare*, pp. 145–172. New York: Aldine.

Mulhern, S. A. 1992. Ritual Abuse: Defining a Syndrome versus Defending a Belief. *Journal of Psychology and Theology* 20, 230–32.

Myers, J. E. B. 1993. Expert Testimony Describing Psychological Syndromes. *Pacific Law Journal* 24, 1449–1464.

Nash, M. R. 1992. *Retrieval of Childhood Memories in Psychotherapy: Clinical Utility and Historical Veridicality Are Not the Same Thing.* Paper presented at the Centennial Meeting of the American Psychological Association, Washington DC, August.

Nathan, D. 1991. Satanism and Child Molestation: Constructing the Ritual Abuse Scare. In J. T. Richardson, J. Best, and D. G. Bromley (eds.), *The Satanism Scare*, pp. 75–94). New York: Aldine.

Nathan, D. 1992. Cry Incest. *Playboy* (October), pp. 84–86, 162, 164.

NCAC (National Coalition Against Censorship. 1993. *The Sex Panic: Women, Censorship and 'Pornography.'* New York: National Coalition Against Censorship.

NCPCA (National Center for the Prosecution of Child Abuse). *Update.* 1991–1993. Alexandria, Va: American Prosecutors Research Institute. Newsletter published several times a year.

Neisser, U. 1981. John Dean's Memory: A Case Study. *Cognition* 9, 1–22.

Neisser, U. 1993. *Memory with a Grain of Salt.* Paper Presented on the Conference on 'Memory and Reality', False Memory Syndrome Foundation, Valley Forge, Pa, April 16th.

Neisser, U., and Harsch, N. 1992. Phantom Flashbulbs: False Recollections of Hearing the News about Challenger. In E. Winograd and U. Neisser (eds.), *Affect and Memory in Recall: Studies of Flashbulb Memories*, pp. 9–31. New York: Cambridge University Press.

Nelson, B. J. 1984. *Making an Issue of Child Abuse: Political Agenda Setting for Social Problems*. Chicago: The University of Chicago Press.

Nelson, J. A. 1982. The Impact of Incest: Factors in Self-Evaluation. In L. L. Constantine and F. M. Martinson (eds.), *Children and Sex: New findings, New Perspectives*, pp. 247–253. Boston: Little, Brown.

Nelson, J. B. 1978. *Embodiment*. Minneapolis: Augsburg.

Nelson, K. 1981. Social Cognition in a Script Framework. In J. Flavell and L. Ross (eds.), *Social Cognition and Development*, pp. 97–118. Cambridge: Cambridge University Press.

Nelson, K. 1993. The Psychological and Social Origins of Autobiographical Memory. *Psychological Science* 4(1), 7–14.

Nelson, K., and Ross, G. 1980. The Generalities and Specifics of Long-Term Memory in Infants and Young Children. *New Directions for Child Development* 10, 87–100.

Nohlgren, S. 1991. Making a Case to Punish Incest. *St. Petersburg Times* (April 28th), pp. 1B, 5B.

Noll, R. 1989. Satanism, UFO Abductions, Historians and Clinicians: Those Who do not Remember the Past. . . . (Letter to the Editor). *Dissociation* 2(1), 251–54.

Oates, W. E. 1973. *The Psychology of Religion*. Waco, Texas: Word Books.

Ofshe, R. J. 1992. Inadvertent Hypnosis During Interrogation: False Confession Due to Dissociative State; Mis-identified Multiple Personality and the Satanic Cult Hypothesis. *International Journal of Clinical and Experimental Hypnosis* 40(3), 125–156.

Ofshe, R., and Watters, E. 1993. Making Monsters—Psychotherapy's New Error: Repressed Memory, Multiple Personality, and Satanic Abuse. *Society* 30(3), 4–16.

O'Gorman, T. 1991. Defense Strategies in Child Sexual Abuse Accusations Cases. *Queensland Law Society Journal* (June), pp. 195–207.

Okami, P. 1989. *Retrospective Self-Reports of 'Positive' Childhood and Adolescent Sexual Contacts with Old Persons*. Paper presented at the annual meeting of the Society for the Scientific Study of Sex, Toronto, Ontario, November 9th–12th.

Okami, P. 1990. Sociopolitical Biases in the Contemporary Scientific Literature on Adult Human Sexual Behavior with Children and Adolescents. In J. Feierman (ed.), *Pedophilia: Biosocial Dimensions*, pp. 91–121. New York: Springer.

Okami, P. 1992. Child Perpetrators of Sexual Abuse: The Emergence of a Problematic Deviant Category. *Journal of Sex Research* 29, 109–130.

O'Keefe, J., and Nadel, L. 1978. *The Hippocampus as a Cognitive Map*. Oxford: Clarendon.

Orne, M. T., Soskis, D. A., Dinges, D. F., Orne, E. C., and Tonry, M. H. 1985. *Hypnotically Refreshed Testimony: Enhanced Memory or Tampering With Evidence?* Washington, DC: U.S. Dept. of Justice, National Institute of Justice.

O'Sullivan, J. J., and Quevillon, R. P. 1992. 40 Years Later. Is the Boulder Model Still Alive? *American Psychologist* 47, 67–70.

Paradise, J. E. 1989. Predictive Accuracy and the Diagnosis of Sexual Abuse: A Big Issue About a Little Tissue. *Child Abuse and Neglect* 13, 169–176.

Patterson, O. 1991. *Freedom: Vol. 1. Freedom in the Making of Western Culture*. New York: Basic Books.

Paxton, C. 1991. A Bridge to Healing: Responding to Disclosures of Childhood Sexual Abuse. *Health Values* 15(5), 49–56.

Penelope. 1992. Suing my Perpetrator: A Survivor's Story. *Journal of Child Sexual Abuse* 1(2), 119–124.

Peters, J. 1976. Children who are Victims of Sexual Assault and the Psychology of Offenders. *American Journal of Psychotherapy* 30(3), 398–421.

Peterson, C., Maier, S. F., and Seligman, M. E. P. 1993. *Learned Helplessness*. New York: Oxford University Press.

Pezdek, K. 1992. Letter to the Editor, *APS Observer*, p. 37.

Pfaff, D. W., Silva, M. T., and Weiss, J. M. 1971. Telemetered Recording of Hormone Effects on Hippocampal Neurons. *Science* 172, 394–395.

Pillemer, D. B., and White, S. H. 1989. Childhood Events Recalled by Children and Adults. *Advances in Child Development* 21, 298–340.

Piper, A. 1994. Amytal Interviews and 'Recovered Memories' of Sexual Abuse: A Note. *Issues in Child Abuse Accusations* 6, 39–40.

Piper, A. (in press). A Skeptical Look at Multiple Personality Disorder. In Cohen, L. (Ed.), *Multiple Personality Disorder: Critical Issues and Controversies*. Northvale, NJ: Jason Aronson.

Pope, H. G., and Hudson, J. I. 1992. Is Childhood Sexual Abuse a Risk Factor for Bulimia Nervosa? *American Journal of Psychiatry* 149, 45–463.

Powell, G. E. and Chalkley, A. J. 1981. The Effects of Paedophile Attention on the Child. In B. Taylor (ed.), *Perspectives on Paedophilia*, pp. 59–75. London: Batsford.

Putnam, F. W. 1991a. Dissociative Phenomena. In A. Tassman and S. M. Goldfinger (eds.), *Review of Psychiatry*, pp. 145–160. Washington, DC: American Psychiatric Press.

Putnam, F. W. 1991b. The Satanic Ritual Abuse Controversy. *Child Abuse and Neglect* 15, 175–79.

Putnam, F. W., Guroff, J. J., Silberman, E. K., Barban, L., and Post, R. M. 1986. The Clinical Phenomenology of Multiple Personality Disorder: Review of 100 Recent Cases. *Journal of Clinical Psychiatry* 47(6), 285–293.

Pynoos, R. S., and Eth, S. 1985. Children Traumatized by Witnessing Acts of Personal Violence: Homicide, Rape, or Suicide Behavior. In S. Eth and R. S. Pynoos (eds.), *Post-Traumatic Stress Disorder in Children*, pp. 17–43. Washington, DC: American Psychiatric Press.

Quina, K. 1994. Editorial. *Psychology of Women* 21(1), 12–13.

Rabinowitz, D. 1990. From the Mouths of Babes to a Jail Cell. *Harper's* (May), pp. 52–63.

Raphael, K. G., Cloitre, M., and Dohrenwend, B. P. 1991. Problems of Recall and Misclassification With Checklist Methods of Measuring Stressful Life Events. *Health Psychology* 10, 62–74.

Realmuto, G., Jensen, J., and Wescoe, S. 1990. Specificity and Sensitivity of Sexually Anatomically Correct Dolls in Substantiating Abuse: A Pilot Study. *Journal of the American Academy of Child Adolescent Psychiatry* 29, 743–46.

Rettig, S. 1993. Can Relating the Past Disclose the Future? *Journal of Mind and Behavior* 14(2), 133–144.

Rich, C. L. 1990. Accuracy of Adults' Reports of Abuse in Childhood. *American Journal of Psychiatry* 147, 1389.

Richardson, J. T., Best, J., and Bromley, D. G. (eds.). 1991. *The Satanism Scare*. New York: Aldine.

Rimsza, M., and Niggemann, E. 1982. Medical Evaluation of Sexually abused Children: A Review of 311 Cases. *Pediatrics* 69, 8–13.

Ritual Abuse Task Force. 1989. *Ritual Abuse: Report of the Ritual Abuse Task Force*. Los Angeles County Commission for Women.

Roan, S. 1990. Experts See Adult Effects of Molestation. *Los Angeles Times* (August 7th), pp. E1, E11, E12.

Roberts, P. C. 1993. Mounting Abuses Make Mockery of Law and Order. *Star Tribune* (Minneapolis, September 5th), p. 29A.

Roberts, Y. 1988. It Can Happen Here. *New Statesman and Society* (July 1st), pp. 19–20.

Rogers, M. 1992. Evaluating Adult Litigants Who Allege Injuries From Child Sexual Abuse: Clinical Assessment Methods for Traumatic Memories. *Issues in Child Abuse Accusations* 4, 221–238.

Rogers, M. (in press). Factors to Consider in Assessing Complaints by Adult Litigants of Childhood Sexual Abuse. *Behavioral Sciences and the Law*.

Roiphe, K. 1993. Lorena Bobbitt Exposed the Raw Hostility Between the Sexes. *Star Tribune* (Minneapolis, December 12th), p. 29A.

Rokeach, M. 1960. *The Open and Closed Mind.* New York: Basic Books.

Rosenfeld, A., Bailey, R., Siegal, B., and Bailey, G. 1986. Determining Incestuous Contact Between Parent and Child: Frequency of Children Touching Parents' Genitals in a Nonclinical Population. *Journal of the American Academy of Child Psychiatry* 25, 481–84.

Rosenfeld, A., Siegel, B., and Bailey, R. 1987. Familial Bathing Patterns: Implications for Cases of Alleged Molestation and for Pediatric Practice. *Pediatrics* 79, 224–29.

Rosenhan, D. L. 1973. On Being Sane in Insane Places. *Science* 179, 250–58.

Roy-Byrne, P., Geraci, M., and Uhde, T. W. 1987. Life Events Obtained Via Interview: The Effect of Time of Recall on Data Obtained in Controls and Patients with Panic Disorder. *Journal of Affective Disorders* 12, 57–62.

Rubin, D. C. 1985. The Subtle Deceiver: Recalling our Past. *Psychology Today* (September), pp. 39–46.

Rush, R. 1980. *The Best Kept Secret: Sexual Abuse of Children.* New York. McGraw Hill.

Russell, D. E. 1986. *The Secret Trauma: Incest in the Lives of Girls and Women.* New York: Basic Books.

Rutter, M. 1971. Normal Psychosexual Development. *Journal of Child Psychology and Psychiatry* 11, 259–283.

Ryckman, L. L. 1992. Mother Lands in Jail for Breast-Feeding. *The Wanatchee World* (February 5th), p. 11.

Ryder, D. 1992. *Breaking the Circle of Satanic Ritual Abuse.* Minneapolis: Comp Care.

Salten, M. G. 1984. Statues of Limitations in Civil Incest Suits: Preserving the Victim's Remedy. *Harvard Women's Law Journal* 7(1), 189–220.

Salter, S. 1993. Recalling Abuse in the Mind's Eye. *San Francisco Examiner* (April 4th–9th). Special series.

Sandfort, T. 1982. *The Sexual Aspect of Paedophile Relations.* Amsterdam: Pan/Spartacus.

Sandfort, T. 1987. *Boys and Men: A Study of Sexually Expressed Friendships.* Elmhurst, NY: Global Academic.

Sandfort, T. 1993. The Sexual Experiences of Children. *Paidika* 3(1), 21–32.

Saxe, G. N., van der Kolk, B. A., Berkowitz, R., Chinman, G., Hall, K., Lieberg, G., and Schwartz, J. 1993. Dissociative Disorders in Psychiatric Inpatients. *American Journal of Psychiatry* 150, 1037–1042.

Schultz, L., and Wakefield, H. 1993. Review of J. Waterman, R. J. Kelly, K. Oliveri, and J. McCord, Behind the Playground Walls (1993). *Issues in Child Abuse Accusations* 5, 203–05.

Schumaker, J. F. 1991. The Adaptive Value of Suggestibility and Dissociation. In Schumaker, J. F. (ed.), *Human Suggestibility,* pp. 108–131. New York: Routledge.

Schutte, J. W. (in press). Repressed Memory Lawsuits: Potential Verdict Predictors. *Issues in Child Abuse Accusations.*

Sechrest, L. 1992. The Past Future of Clinical Psychology: A Reflection on Woodworth (1937). *Journal of Consulting and Clinical Psychology* 60, 18–23.

Shaffer, R. E., and Cozolino, L. J. 1992. Adults Who Report Childhood Ritualistic Abuse. *Journal of Psychology and Theology* 20, 188–193.

Shore, M. F. 1993. Social Policy: The Wheels of Change (Editorial). *American Journal of Orthopsychiatry* 63(4), 498.

Sifford, D. 1992. When Tales of Sex Abuse Aren't True. *The Philadelphia Inquirer* (January 5th), pp. 1–I, 8–I.

Silberschatz, G., and Curtis, J. T. 1993. Measuring the Therapist's Impact on the Patient's Therapeutic Progress. *Journal of Consulting and Clinical Psychology* 61, 403–411.

Simon, N. 1993. Licensure Issues for the Nineties. *The Independent Practitioner* (Spring), 13(2), 70–73.

Singer, J. L. 1980. The Scientific Basis of Psychotherapeutic Practice:

A Question of Values and Ethics. *Psychotherapy: Theory, Research, and Practice* 17, 372–383.

Singer, J. L. 1990. Preface. In J. L. Singer (ed.) *Repression and Dissociation*, pp. xi–xxi. Chicago: University of Chicago Press.

Singer, J. L., and Sincoff, J. B. 1990. Summary Chapter: Beyond Repression and the Defenses. In J. L. Singer (ed.), *Repression and Dissociation: Implications for Personality Theory, Psychopathology and Health*, pp. 471–496. Chicago: University of Chicago Press.

Slovenko, R. 1993. The 'Revival of Memory' of Childhood Sexual Abuse: Is the Tolling of the Statue of Limitations Justified? *The Journal of Psychiatry and Law* (Spring), 7–34.

Smith, B., and Ellsworth, P. 1987. The Social Psychology of Eyewitness Accuracy: Misleading Questions and Communicator Expertise. *Journal of Applied Psychology* 72, 294–300.

Smith, J. 1991. Aftermath of a False Allegation. *Issues in Child Abuse Accusations* 3, 203.

Smith, M., and Pazder, L. 1980. *Michelle Remembers*. New York: Congdon & Lattes.

Smith, M. L., and Glass, G. V. 1977. Meta-Analysis of Psychotherapy Outcome Studies. *American Psychologist* 32, 752–760.

Smith, P. 1993. *Feminist Jurisprudence*. New York, Oxford University Press.

Smith, S. E. 1993. Body Memories: And Other Pseudo-Scientific Notions of 'Survivor Psychology.' *Issues in Child Abuse Accusations* 5, 220–234.

Smith, T. W. 1992. Hostility and Health: Current Status of a Psychosomatic Hypothesis. *Health Psychology* 11, 139–150.

Smith, V., Kassin, S., and Ellsworth, P., 1989. Eyewitness Accuracy and Confidence: Within Versus Between-Subjects Correlations. *Journal of Applied Psychology* 74, 356–59.

Solomon, J. C. 1992. Child Sexual Abuse by Family Members: A Radical Feminist Perspective. *Sex Roles* 27 (9/10), 473–485.

Spanos, N. P. 1991. *Hypnosis, Suggestion, and Creation of False Memories and Secondary Personalities*. Paper presented at the 99th Annual Convention of the American Psychological Association, San Francisco, August.

Spanos, N. P., Burgess, C. A., and Burgess, M. F. (in press). Past Life Identities, UFO Abductions and Satanic Ritual Abuse: The Social Construction of Memories. *International Journal of Experimental and Clinical Hypnosis*.

Spanos, N. P., Cross, P. A., Dickson, K., and DuBreuil, S. C. 1993. Close Encounters: An Examination of UFO Experiences. *Journal of Abnormal Psychology* 102, 624–632.

Spanos, N. P., Quigley, C. A., Gwynn, M. I., Glatt, R. L., and Perlini, A. H. 1991. Hypnotic Interrogation, Pretrial Preparation, and Witness Testimony During Direct and Cross Examination. *Law and Human Behavior* 15, 639–653.

Spanos, N. P., Weekes, J. R., and Bertrand, L. D. 1985. Multiple Personality: A Social Psychological Perspective. *Journal of Abnormal Psychology* 94, 362–376.

Spanos, N. P., Menary, E., Gabora, N. J., DuBreuil, S. C., and Dewhirst, B. 1991. Secondary Identity Enactments During Hypnotic Past-Life Regression: A Sociocognitive Perspective. *Journal of Personality and Social Psychology* 61, 308–320.

Spanos, N. P., Weekes, J. R., Menary, E., and Bertrand, L. D. 1986. Hypnotic Interview and Age Regression Procedures in the Elicitation of Multiple Personality Symptoms: A Simulation Study. *Psychiatry* 49, 298–311.

Spence, D. P. 1993. *Narrative Truth and Putative Child Abuse.* Address given at the 101st Annual Convention of the American Psychological Association, Toronto, Ontario, August.

Spence, D. P., Dahl, H., and Jones, E. E. 1993. Impact of Interpretation on Associative Freedom. *Journal of Consulting and Clinical Psychology* 61, 395–402.

Spiegel, D. 1991. Dissociation and Trauma (1991). In A. Tassman and S. M. Goldfinger (eds.), *Review of Psychiatry*, pp. 261–275. Washington, DC: American Psychiatric Press.

Stanovich, K. E. 1992. *How to Think Straight About Psychology (3rd Ed.).* New York: Harper Collins.

Starr, R. H. 1979. Child Abuse. *American Psychologist* 34, 872–78.

Star Tribune. 1993. There Just Isn't a Question That Hillary Can't Answer About Health Care Reform. Minneapolis, October 2nd, p. 7A.

Steele, D. R. 1994. Partial Recall. *Liberty* 7(3) (March), 37–47.

Steele, G. P., Henderson, S., and Duncan-Jones, P. 1980. The Reliability of Reporting Adverse Experiences. *Psychological Medicine* 10, 301–06.

Steen, T., and Rzepnicki, T. 1984. Decision Making in Child Welfare Services (Chapter 3). *Judgment and Decision Making.* Boston: Kluwer.

Stewart, D. O. 1993. Decision Creates Uncertain Future for Admissibility of Expert Testimony. *ABA Journal* (November), pp. 48–51.

Stiles, W. B., Shapiro, D. A., and Elliott, R. 1986. Are All Psychotherapies Equivalent? *American Psychologist* 41, 165–180.

Stricker, G. 1992. The Relationship of Research to Clinical Practice. *American Psychologist* 47, 543–49.

Strohmer, D. C., Shivy, V. A., and Chiodo, A. L. 1990. Information Processing Strategies in Counselor Hypothesis Testing: The Role of Selective Memory and Expectancy. *Journal of Counseling Psychology* 37, 465–472.

Strommen, M. P., Brekke, M. L., Underwager, R. C., and Johnson, A. L. 1972. *A Study of Generations*. Minneapolis: Augsburg.

Strupp, H. H. 1980. Psychotherapy: Assessing Methods. *Science* 207, 590.

Strupp, H. H., and Binder, J. L. 1992. Current Developments in Psychotherapy. *The Independent Practitioner* 12(3), 119–124.

Suengas, A. G., and Johnson, M. K. 1988. Qualitative Effects of Rehearsal of Memories for Perceived and Imagined Events. *Journal of Experimental Psychology: General* 117, 377–389.

Summit, R. 1984. Statement given at the National Symposium on Child Molestation, UCLA Medical Center, Los Angeles, October 1st–4th.

Summit, R. 1986. *Ideas: Out of the Mouth of Babes*. CBC. Radio Toronto.

Summit, R. 1990. *Reaching the Unreachable*. Presentation at the Midwest Conference on Child Abuse and Neglect, Madison, Wisconsin, October 29th–November 1st.

Summit, R. 1993. *McMartin Children Vindicated*. Presentation at a conference sponsored by The National Children's Advocacy Center, 106 Lincoln Street, Huntsville, AL 35801.

Sutton-Smith, B., and Abrams, D. M. 1978. Psychosexual Material in the Stories Told by Children: The Fucker. *Archives of Sexual Behavior* 7, 521–543.

Svartberg, M., and Stiles, T. C. 1991. Comparative Effects of Short-Term Psychodynamic Psychotherapy: A Meta-Analysis. *Journal of Consulting and Clinical Psychology* 59, 704–714.

Swenson, W. M., and Grimes, B. P. 1958. Characteristics of Sex Offenders Admitted to a Minnesota state hospital for Pre-Sentence Psychiatric Investigation. *Psychiatric Quarterly*, Part 1, 110–123.

Szasz, T. S. 1984. *The Therapeutic State—Psychiatry in the Mirror of Current Events.* Buffalo: Prometheus.

Tavris, C. 1993. Beware the Incest-Survivor Machine. *New York Times* (January 3rd), pp. 1, 16.

Terr, L. C. 1985. Children Traumatized in Small Groups. In S. Eth and R. S. Pynoos (eds.) *Post-Traumatic Stress Disorder in Children,* pp. 45–70. Washington, DC: American Psychiatric Press.

Terr, L. C. 1988. What Happens to Early Memories of Trauma? A Study of Twenty Children Under Age Five at the Time of Documented Traumatic Events. *Journal of the American Academy of Child and Adolescent Psychiatry* 27(1), 96–104.

Terr, L. C. 1990. *Too Scared to Cry.* New York: Harper and Row.

Terr, L. C. 1991. Childhood Traumas: An Outline and Overview. *American Journal of Psychiatry* 148, 10–20.

Terr, L. C. 1994. *Unchained Memories: True Stories of Traumatic Memories, Lost and Found.* New York: Harper Collins.

Thigpen, C. H., and Cleckley, H. M. 1957. *The Three Faces of Eve.* New York: McGraw Hill.

Thigpen, C. H., & Cleckley, H. M. 1984. On the Incidence of Multiple Personality Disorder. *International Journal of Clinical and Experimental Hypnosis* 32, 63–66.

Thompson, J. E. 1992. Your Child Sex Offender Client is Going to be Sentenced: Ready or Not? *Issues in Child Accusations* 4, 21–23.

Thompson, J. E. 1993. Healing is an Unenforceable Order. *Journal of Child Sexual Abuse* 2(1), 131–33.

Thompson, T. L. 1989. Boy, 10, Faces Rape Charges in South Bay. *San Francisco Chronicle* (September 15th), p. A4.

Tillman, J. G., Nash, M. R., and Lerner, P. M. (in press). Does Trauma Cause Dissociative Pathology? In S. J. Lynn (ed.), *Dissociation: Clinical, Theoretical and Research Perspectives.* Washington, DC: American Psychological Association.

Tollison, C. D., and Adams, H. E. 1979. *Sexual Disorders: Treatment, Theory, and Research.* New York: Gardner.

Tower Commission Report. 1987. *President's Special Review Board: John Tower, Chairman.* New York: Bantam.

Tsai, M., Feldman-Summers, S. and Edgar, M. 1979. Childhood Molestation: Variables Related to Differential Impacts on Psychosexual Functioning in Adult Women. *Journal of Abnormal Psychology* 88, 407–417.

Tuchman, B. 1984. *The March of Folly.* New York: Knopf.

Tulving, E. 1983. *Elements of Episodic Memory.* New York: Oxford University Press.

Tulving, E. 1993. What is Episodic Memory? *Current Directions in Psychological Science* 2(3) (June), 67–70.

Tuma, J. M. 1989. Mental Health Services for Children: The State of the Art. *American Psychologist* 44, 188–199.

Turk, D. C., and Salovey, P. 1985. Cognitive Structures, Cognitive Processes, and Cognitive-Behavior Modification: II. Judgments and Inferences of the Clinician. *Cognitive Therapy and Research* 9(1), 19–33.

Tyler, T. R. 1990. *Why People Obey the Law.* New Haven: Yale University Press.

Underwager, R. 1984. Love and Sexuality. *IPT Newsletter.* Institute for Psychological Therapies, Minneapolis, Minnesota, Fall.

Underwager, R., and Wakefield, H. 1989. Prosecution and Child Sexual Abuse. *Issues in Child Abuse Accusations* 1(3), 28–38.

Underwager, R., and Wakefield, H. 1990. *The Real World of Child Interrogations.* Springfield, Il: Thomas.

Underwager, R., and Wakefield, H. 1991. Cur Allii, Prae Aliis? (Why some and not others?). *Issues In Child Abuse Accusations* 3, 178–193.

Underwager, R., and Wakefield, H. 1992. False Confessions and Police Deception. *American Journal of Forensic Psychology* 10(3), 49–66.

Underwager, R., and Wakefield, H. 1993a. Antisexuality and Child Sexual Abuse. *Issues in Child Abuse Accusations* 5, 72–77.

Underwager, R., and Wakefield, H. 1993b. A Paradigm Shift for Expert Witnesses. *Issues in Child Abuse Accusations* 5, 156–167.

U.S. Department of Justice. 1981. *Sourcebook of Criminal Justice Statistics — 1981.* Washington, DC: Bureau of Justice Statistics.

U.S. Department of Justice. 1989. *Sourcebook of Criminal Justice Statistics — 1989.* Washington, DC: Bureau of Justice Statistics.

U.S. Department of Justice. 1992. *Sourcebook of Criminal Justice Statistics — 1992.* Washington, DC: Bureau of Justice Statistics.

Usher, J. A., and Neisser, U. 1993. Childhood Amnesia and the Beginnings of Memory for Four Early Life Events. *Journal of Experimental Psychology: General* 122(2), 155–165.

Vaillant, G. E. 1990. Repression in College Men Followed for Half a Century. In J. L. Singer (ed.), *Repression and Dissociation: Implications for Personality Theory, Psychopathology and Health,* pp. 250–273. Chicago: University of Chicago Press.

Van der Kolk, B. A. 1988a. The Biological Response to Psychic Trauma. In F. M. Ochberg (ed.), *Post-Traumatic Therapy and Victims of Violence,* pp. 25–38. New York: Brunner/Mazel.

Van der Kolk, B. A. 1988b. The Trauma Spectrum: The Interaction of Biological and Social Events in the Genesis of the Trauma Response. *Journal of Traumatic Stress* 1, 273–289.

Van der Kolk, B. A., and Saporta, J. 1993. Biological Response to Psychic Trauma. In J. P. Wilson and B. Raphael (eds.), *International Handbook of Traumatic Stress Syndromes,* pp. 25–33. New York: Plenum.

Van der Kolk, B. A., and van der Hart, O. 1989. Pierre Janet and the Breakdown of Adaptation in Psychological Trauma. *American Journal of Psychiatry* 146, 1530–1540.

Vander Mey, B. J. 1988. The Sexual Victimization of Male Children: A Review of Previous Research. *Child Abuse and Neglect* 12, 61–72.

Vernon, M. D. 1970. *Perception Through Experience.* New York: Barnes and Noble.

Victor, J. S. 1993a. *Satanic Panic: The Creation of a Contemporary Legend.* Chicago: Open Court.

Victor, J. S. 1993b. Sexual Attitudes in the Contemporary Legend about Satanic Cults. *Issues in Child Abuse Accusations* 5, 83–87.

Wakefield, H. 1984. Sexuality and Intimacy. *IPT Newsletter* (Fall). Institute for Psychological Therapies, Minneapolis.

Wakefield, H., and Underwager, R. 1979. Intimacy and Sexuality. *IPT Newsletter* (December). Institute for Psychological Therapies, Minneapolis.

Wakefield, H., and Underwager, R. 1988. *Accusations of Child Sexual Abuse.* Springfield, Il: Thomas.

Wakefield, H., and Underwager, R. 1992a. Assessing Credibility of Children's Testimony in Ritual Abuse Allegations. *Issues in Child Abuse Accusations* 4, 32–44.

Wakefield, H., and Underwager, R. 1992b. Recovered Memories of Alleged Sexual Abuse: Lawsuits Against Parents. *Behavioral Sciences and the Law* 10, 483–507.

Wakefield, H., and Underwager, R. 1992c. Uncovering Memories of Alleged Sexual Abuse: The Therapists Who Do It. *Issues in Child Abuse Accusations* 4, 197–213.

Wakefield, J. 1992. Recovered Memories of Alleged Sexual Abuse: Memory as Production and as Reproduction. *Issues in Child Abuse Accusations* 4 (June 20th), 219–220.

Walker, L. E. 1992. When an Incest Survivor Sues Her Father: A Commentary. *Journal of Child Sexual Abuse* 1(2), 125–27.

Waterman, J., Kelly, R. J., Oliveri, K., and McCord, J. 1993. *Behind the Playground Walls.* New York: Guilford.

Weber, E. U., Bockenholt, U., Hilton, D. J. and Wallace, B. 1993. Determinants of Diagnostic Hypothesis Generation: Effects of Information, Base Rates, and Experience. *Journal of Experimental Psychology: Learning, Memory, and Cognition* 19, 1151–1164.

Weinert, F. E., and Perlmutter, M. 1988. *Memory Development: Universal Changes and Individual Differences.* Hillsdale: Erlbaum.

Weingardt, K. R., Toland, H. K., and Loftus, E. F. 1993. *Reports of Suggested Memories: Do People Truly Believe Them?* Manuscript submitted for publication.

Weissberg, M. 1993. Multiple Personality Disorder and Iatrogenesis: The Cautionary Tale of Anna O. *International Journal of Clinical and Experimental Hypnosis* 41(1), 15–32.

Weisz, J. R., and Weiss, B. 1993. *Effects of Psychotherapy With Children and Adolescents.* Newbury Park: Sage.

Weisz, J. R., Weiss, B., Alicke, M. D., and Klotz, M. L. 1987. Effectiveness of Psychotherapy with Children and Adolescents: A Meta-Analysis for Clinicians. *Journal of Consulting and Clinical Psychology* 55, 542–49.

Weisz, J. R., Weiss, B., and Donenberg, G. R. 1992. The Lab Versus the Clinic. *American Psychologist* 47, 1578–1585.

Welch, B. L. 1990. Letter to Colleagues. American Psychological Association. October 30th.

Wenatchee World. 1991. Indecency Alleged. June 12th. Wenatchee, Washington, p. 13.

Wernick, R. 1994. Don't Look Now—But All Those Plotters Might be Hiding Under Your Bed. *Smithsonian* (March), pp. 108–124.

West, R. 1992. Assessment of Evidence Versus Consensus or Prejudice. *Journal of Epidemiology and Community Health* 46(4), 321–22.

Wetzler, S. E., and Sweeney, J. A. 1986. Childhood Amnesia: An Empirical Demonstration. In D. C. Rubin (ed.), *Autobiographical Memory*, pp. 191–201. New York: Cambridge University Press.

Whalen, J. 1991. Florida Abuse Registry Loses in Federal Court. *Issues in Child Abuse Accusations* 3, 228–231.

Wiggins, E. C., and Brandt, J. 1988. The Detection of Simulated Amnesia. *Law and Human Behavior* 12, 57–78.

Wilkinson, S. 1989. The Impact of Feminist Research: Issues of Legitimacy. *Philosophical Psychology* 2, 261–69.

Williams, L. M. 1992. Adult Memories of Childhood Abuse: Preliminary Findings From a Longitudinal Study. *APCAC Advisor* (Summer), pp. 19–21.

Williams, L. M. 1993. *Recall of Childhood Trauma: A Prospective Study of Women's Memories of Child Sexual Abuse.* Paper presented at the Annual Meeting of the American Society of Criminology, Phoenix, October.

Wilson, J. P., and Raphael, B. 1993. *International Handbook of Traumatic Stress Syndromes.* New York: Plenum.

Winograd, E., and Neisser, U. (eds.) 1992. *Affect and Memory in Recall: Studies of Flashbulb Memories.* New York: Cambridge University Press.

Wolfle, D. 1955. Comparisons Between Psychologists and Other Professional Groups. *American Psychologist*, 213–237.

Wylie, M. S. 1993. The Shadow of a Doubt. *Networker* (September-October), pp. 18–29, 70, 73.

Yapko, M. D. 1994a. Suggestibility and Repressed Memories of Abuse: A Survey of Psychotherapists' Beliefs. *American Journal of Clinical Hypnosis* 36, 163–171.

Yapko, M. D. 1994b. Response to Comments. *American Journal of Clinical Hypnosis* 36, 185–87.

Yorokuglu, A., and Kemph, R. 1966. Children Not Severely Damaged by Incest with a Parent. *Journal of the American Academy of Child Psychiatry* 5, 111–124.

Young, W. C., Sachs, R. G., Braun, B. G., and Watkins, R. T. 1991. Patients Reporting Ritual Abuse in Childhood: A Clinical Syndrome. Report of 37 Cases. *Child Abuse and Neglect* 15, 181–89.

Zack, M. 1994. Juror's Repressed Memory of Abuse Leads to Mistrial in Molestation Convictions. *Star Tribune* (Minneapolis, March 29th), pp. 1A, 15A.

Zechmeister, E. B., and Nyberg, S. E. 1982. *Human Memory.* Monterey: Brooks/Cole.

Zeitlin, H. 1987. Investigation of the Sexually Abused Child. *The Lancet* (October 10th), pp. 842–45.

Zuravin, S. J. 1988. Fertility Patterns: Their Relationship to Child Physical Abuse and Child Neglect. *Journal of Marriage and the Family* 50, 983–993.

Index